THE DIARY OF
SAMUEL PEPYS

THE DIARY
OF
SAMUEL PEPYS

A new and complete
transcription edited by

ROBERT LATHAM
AND
WILLIAM MATTHEWS

VOLUME XI · INDEX

Compiled by
ROBERT LATHAM

HarperCollins*Publishers*

Published in 1995 by
HarperCollins College Division
An imprint of HarperCollins*Publishers* Ltd, UK
77-85 Fulham Palace Road
Hammersmith
London W6 8JB

First published in 1971 by Bell & Hyman Limited

British Library Cataloguing in Publication Data
A catalogue record for this book is available from the British Library

ISBN 0 00 499031 5

Printed and bound by Scotprint Ltd, Musselburgh, Scotland

CONTENTS

PUBLISHER'S NOTE

The publication of Volumes X (the *Companion*) and XI *(the Index)* marks the completion of the eleven-volume edition edited by the late Robert Latham and the late Professor William Matthews.

Professor Matthews' main work as Joint Editor was the transcription of the original manuscript of the *Diary* in the Pepys Library at Magdalene College, Cambridge. He had arrived at the end of this immense task shortly before his death in 1975 but sadly did not live to see the completion of publication.

Mr Latham had borne the responsibility alone for the *Companion* and *Index* volumes. He started work on the eleven-volume edition in 1950. Since that time he held academic posts in England, the USA and Canada, and from 1972 until 1982 was Fellow and Pepys Librarian at Magdalene College, Cambridge. Throughout these years he spent an enormous amount of time on the research required for this edition and the publishers are deeply grateful to him for the scholarly dedication and skill he brought to this massive undertaking. Mr Latham died in January 1995.

PREFACE

In this volume an index is provided to the text of the diary, the principal footnotes and the editorial introduction. It does not cover the *Companion* (volume X) which is designed to be in most respects self-indexing.

References to everyday or recurrent events, such as attendance at the office or at church, are not indexed if Pepys makes no more than a passing mention of them. Other omissions are indicated in the head-notes to the entries, and in this preface under *Places*.

An attempt has been made to avoid excessive use of that bane of indexes – the unbroken run of numerals. In avoiding that extreme I may have been guilty of using more words than is usual in an index. This has often been necessary for the sake of clarity. It has also been due to an attempt to catch something of the diary's flavour – hence the use of Pepys's own phrases where briefer ones could easily have been substituted. Here and there, as in the entry on the diary itself, it is hoped there are passages which will not only serve the reader who is looking for references but may also give pleasure to the reader who wants to browse.

Persons

Where the diary is the only authority for the spelling of a surname it appears in that form. In other cases it is spelt in the form used, or used most often, by its owner (if that is known), or in the standard books of reference, with Pepys's spelling (if substantially different) added in brackets. Occasionally, as with Will Hewer, all Pepys's variants are recorded.

Brief identifications are added in many cases, and are always given – if the information is available – in those cases where no identification is given either in the footnotes to the text or in the *Companion*.

The longer entries are divided into sections and sub-sections arranged in logical rather than alphabetical order. Thus the section 'misc[ellaneous]' may come last, and that on 'public affairs' may precede that on 'private life'. Within the sections and sub-sections the order in which the references are given is usually that of the diary, though occasionally a thematic order has seemed preferable. 'Social' is a subject-category borrowed from Dr de Beer's index to Evelyn – a model to all indexers. Pepys's sociability gives the category a special value, but it should be added that its use is limited to those occasions about which he reports nothing beyond the social encounter itself. If he has at those points a statement about any other subject, the reference is omitted from 'social' and entered under another heading such as 'news from' or 'business with'. Where he records, as he so often does, what was eaten or drunk on those occasions the reference is repeated in the entries 'Food' and 'Drink'.

The treatment of Pepys and his wife has called for special measures. A small number of references to Pepys has been gathered under his name, covering events before the diary period. For the rest it has been taken for granted that the diarist is himself the subject of his diary. References to him are therefore distributed throughout the index. Some entries (e.g. 'Clerk of the Acts') are devoted exclusively to him; others such as 'Dress' include references to him which are signalled by a prefatory '(P)'; while certain large subjects have two distinct entries – e.g. 'Tangier' and 'Tangier (P)'. A list of the principal entries relating directly to Pepys is given below at page xiii.

A different policy has suggested itself for his wife. She is indexed for the most part under her name, but other references to her (marked 'EP') are entered elsewhere, principally under the subjects to which cross-references are given in the headnote to her entry.

It is probable that the index, like the diary itself, is unfair to Elizabeth. There are many occasions when Pepys takes his wife's presence for granted and does not accord her a mention.

Places
London and Westminster are treated similarly to Pepys, since – almost as much as Pepys himself – they may be assumed to be omnipresent in the text. Streets, buildings and other places within the two cities are indexed under their names except for those grouped as taverns or theatres. The entries 'London' and 'Westminster' are confined to listing events and corporate affairs.

No attempt is made to include passing references to well-known streets such as the Strand.

Subjects
Many subjects are dealt with under group headings rather than individually. Animals for instance are mostly impounded in a single entry. Similarly with other topics – books, naval stores, pictures, plays, sermons and so on. The longer lists of items are usually arranged alphabetically; the shorter ones in the order of their appearance in the diary. In the case of certain subjects (books, prices, plays, ships, taverns) some editorial information (specified in the headnotes) has been added.

Extensive use has been made of subject-entries in order to make accessible the mass of information which the diary contains, even though in many instances this involves the repetition of material to be found elsewhere in the index under other entries. 'Parliament' and 'Privy Council' for instance carry many of the references given in 'Navy' and 'Navy Board'.

Format

The form of reference to volume- and page-numbers, different from that used elsewhere in this edition, has been chosen as the most convenient for note-taking.

Asterisks and daggers are occasionally added to the references to convey editorial information. Their meaning is explained in the head-notes.

The sub-heading 'also' is used for minor but substantive references, and is distinct from 'alluded to' which introduces passing mentions only.

The tilde (∼) indicates material tangential to the main subject of the entry – in the case of persons, often a servant or relative.

PRINCIPAL INDEX ENTRIES CONCERNING PEPYS

ACKNOWLEDGEMENTS

My wife Linnet has shared in the making of this Index. I laid down the ground plan, but she involved herself in every process of its construction. She read aloud the entire text of the diary while I took notes – discussing with me, as we went along, exactly what words might best introduce the successive groups of references, and thus converting what might have been a chore into a paper-game. At later stages she undertook innumerable investigations into detail, and checked from the text every reference in the typescript.

My thanks are also due to David and Susan Yaxley who, once the ground plan had been established, read the whole of the diary text and compiled index slips in draft which I found useful as a basis for my own slip-notes.

Various scholars have contributed to parts of the Index. There are several subjects which it would have been impossible to index adequately without the information which only experts can provide. The entry 'Health', for instance, is at some points organised around diagnoses made by Dr C. E. Newman. Similarly Professor W. A. Armstrong helped with 'Theatre', Professor Kerry Downes with 'Whitehall Palace', Professor A. Rupert Hall with 'Science', Dr Richard Luckett with 'Music' and Mr J. L. Nevinson with 'Dress'. The entry 'Prices' is based on a study made by Hugh Walton. I thank them all.

My publisher's editor, Mary Butler, and her assistant Elizabeth Brooke-Smith, have been a tower of strength in the preparation of the book for the press, and have been quick to lighten my task in every way they could.

Once again I express my warmest thanks to Mary Coleman who has typed the manuscript and (with her colleague Aude Fitzsimons) has undertaken much of the checking. I cannot believe that there are many as fortunate as I in having secretarial help of such quality.

Robert Latham

'A man may think a place is missing, when it is only put in another place.'

PEPYS, 8 JUNE 1663 (on Newman's *A Concordance to the Holy Scriptures*)

INDEX

ABBOT, George, Archbishop of Canterbury 1611–33: his hospital and tomb at Guildford, 9/273 & n. 3

ABEBURY: *see* Avebury

ABERGAVENNY, Lady: *see* Nevill

ABINGDON, Berks: custard fair, 9/227 & n. 2; P visits Christ's Hospital, 9/227–8 & n.; MSS at, ib. & nn.

ABLESON, Capt. [James], naval officer: killed in action, 6/122

ABRAHALL, [Thomas], ship's chandler: gift to EP, 4/415

ABRAHAM, [John], bo'sun: acquitted of murder, 4/76 & n. 3

ACTON, Mdx: 7/240

ACWORTH, [Elizabeth], wife of William: her good looks, 1/147; 2/13; 4/20; rock, 4/20; balsam, 4/64; P tries to 'begin acquaintance' with, 4/241; refrains from making advances to, 5/155; illness, 9/484–5

ACWORTH, [William], storekeeper, Woolwich: at The Hague, 1/147; his pretty house, 2/13; incompetent accountant, 3/136; consulted about masts, 4/50; reports malpractices, 4/241; 5/181 & n. 1; his malpractices, 5/130 & n. 2, 156, 181; 9/123–4 & n.; case against, 9/145, 258, 281, 291, 382 & n. 3; consulted on history of naval administration, 9/484; social: 4/20; 5/306; his Dutch clerk, 6/216–17

ADAMS, Henry, of Axe Yard: marriage, 1/190; social: 1/21, 77, 287; 2/228; alluded to: 1/270

ADAMS, Ald. Sir Thomas, Bt; Lord Mayor 1645–6: M.P. London 1654–5, 1656–8: death, 9/136 & n. 2; kidney stone shown to P, ib.

ADDIS, [?John], navy victualler: gives fish dinner, 1/287; gift to P, 3/28

ADMIRAL, the LORD HIGH: *see* James, Duke of York

ADMIRALTY [*see also* Coventry, W.; James, Duke of York; Justice, administration of; Wren, M.]: COMMISSION OF: report of commission of 1618, 4/96 & n. 4; rumoured proposal to create (1668), 9/278, 279; P's career in (1673–9) vol. i, pp. xxxvi–viii

PREMISES: moved from Derby House to Whitehall, 1/174 & n. 4, 229; P does business, 1/87, 89, 90, 174, 226–7; writes letters, 1/176; and diary, 1/204; Navy Board meets, 1/229, 241

ADMIRALTY AND NAVY, COMMISSIONERS of the, Feb.–April 1660: replace Treasurers at War, 1/82; to reduce fleet, 1/102–3 & n.

AFONSO VI, King of Portugal 1656–83 [*see also* Luisa Maria, Queen-Mother and Regent]: simple-minded, 2/197; 3/91; deposed, 8/578 & n. 3; alluded to: 3/252

AFRICAN (Guinea) HOUSE, [Old] Broad St: P visits, 4/395, 437; 5/48, 52, 66, 124; 7/323

AGAR, [Thomas], Chancery clerk: 2/222; 6/79

AGRICULTURE: P's observations on harvest, 4/220; and calf-rearing, 6/179; fall in rents, 7/355; 8/84, 158 & n. 1, 199; 9/1, 44; cultivation of tobacco, 8/442 & n. 2; flax, 9/496; failure of gentry to export corn, 9/1

AILESBURY, Earl of: *see* Bruce

AIX-LA-CHAPELLE, TREATY OF (1668): alluded to: 9/281–2

ALBEMARLE, Duke and Duchess of: *see* Monck

[ALBRICI], Vicenzo (Vincentio), composer: 8/56 & n. 6, 64–5

ALCOCK, Harry, P's cousin: goes to Ireland, 1/260; asks for place, 3/119; 9/208; social: 3/132

ALCOCK, [Stephen], of Rochester, Kent: social: 2/68 & n. 1, 70, 72; 3/31

ALCOCK, Tom, P's schoolfellow at Huntingdon: 1/87, 90

ALDEBURGH (Alborough, Albrough) Bay, Suff.: Sandwich's fleet in, 6/35; also, 7/142, 143

ALDERSGATE: regicides' corpses displayed on, 1/269–70

ALDERSGATE ST [*see also* Taverns etc.: Red Lion]: new Prize Office, 8/16; new Excise Office, 9/265; fire, 8/316, 320–1; alluded to: 2/58; 9/391

ALDGATE (Allgate): city watch at, 7/240; hackney-stand, 7/283; alluded to: 3/66; 7/181; 8/465; 9/470

ALDGATE ST [Aldersgate St in text: ed. error]: 9/148, 520

ALDRIDGE, Capt. ——, servant to Berkeley of Stratton: 8/255

ALDRIGE, ——: Sings, 9/320

ALDWORTH, [Richard], Auditor of the Revenue in the Exchequer: 9/561

ALEHOUSES: *see* Taverns etc.

ALEXANDER the Great: alluded to in sermon, 5/97

ALEXANDER VII, Pope 1655–67: quarrels with Louis XIV, 3/253 & n. 3; 4/24 & n. 1, 26, 63; 5/42, 60; 6/156 & n. 1; death rumoured, 6/257, 259; dies, 8/336; building works, 8/26 & n. 1; alluded to: 4/224; ~ book on Rome under, 4/425 & n. 3

ALEXIS I, Tsar of Russia 1645–79: his palace etc., 5/272 & n. 4

ALEYN (Allen), Ald. Sir Thomas, Lord Mayor 1659–60: as judge at trial of regicides, 1/263; as magistrate, 2/73; 3/43–4; house in Bread St, 4/181; alluded to: 1/71, 92, 143, 168

ALGIERS (Argier, Argiers) [often 'the Turks']: condition of slaves, 2/33–4 & n.; government, 4/386; fleet ordered to, 2/46, 79; Sandwich's naval action at, 2/184 & n. 2, 189; storm, 3/21 & n. 2; Lawson's action, March 1662, 3/79 & n. 2; treaty with, Apr. 1662, 3/89 & n. 1, 97, 121–2 & n., 263, 271; plague, 4/340 & n. 2; dispute about right of search, 4/369–70 & nn.; squadron sent against, Jan. 1664, 4/369, 370, 415 & n. 1; Lawson's action, Apr. 1664, 5/141 & n. 4; peace concluded, Oct. 1664, 5/332 & n. 3; fear of privateers, 5/41–2 & n.; grievances against Tangier, 9/272 & n. 1; privateers less active, 9/274; breaks peace, 9/427–8 & n.; Sir T. Allin makes peace, Feb. 1669, 9/473 & nn. 1, 4; renewed hostilities, 9/492, 516

ALICANTE, Spain: Sandwich ill at, 2/153, 163, 167

ALINGTON, Lady, Juliana, wife of the 3rd Baron: said to be 'a great man's mistress', 8/117

ALINGTON, William, 3rd Baron Alington of Killard (d. 1685): buys governorship of Tangier, 8/117 & n. 1, 127

ALLBON, Dr ——, a debtor in Eagle Court: Deb Willet lodges with, 9/364–5, 366

ALLEN: *see* Allin, Sir T.

ALLEN, Maj. [Edward], of the Victualling Office: 4/16

ALLEN, Capt. [John], Clerk of the Ropeyard, Chatham: good musician, 2/71; reports sharp practice by Batten, 3/155, 157; at muster, 4/228; sells his place, 4/429; 5/1; warns P of (false) accusation of bribery, 9/90, 91; social: 2/68, 77, 125, 126, 175; 9/495, 497, 500; ~ his wife, 4/228–9; 9/90, 495; unmarried daughter, 2/68, 69, 78; 4/227

ALLEN, Rebecca, daughter of Capt. John: *see* Jowles

ALLEN, Sir Thomas, M.P. Middlesex: 3/296

ALLEN, Dr [Thomas], physician (d. 1684): defends Galenical against chemical medicine, 4/361–2 & n.; on explosive power of gold fulminate, 4/378 & n. 4; social: 7/87

ALLESTRY, [James], bookseller: P buys from, 8/521 & n. 2

ALLGATE: *see* Aldgate

ALL HALLOWS, Barking, church of (Barking church): King's arms set up, 1/113; funeral, 3/233; T. Fuller preaches, 5/292; in Fire, 7/275, 276

ALLIN (Allen), Sir Thomas, kted 1665, cr. bt 1673, naval commander:
PERSONAL: Coventry's high opinion, 4/170, 196; love of money, 6/314 & n. 2; portrait by Lely, 7/102 & n. 3
CHRON. SERIES: accused of cowardice (1650), 8/161 & n. 4; transferred from *Dover* to *Plymouth*, 1/224; to sail to Constantinople, 1/250; on *Foresight* 3/153; on *Resolution*, 4/101; to be admiral in Downs, 4/171; concludes peace with Algiers, Oct. 1664, 5/332

& n. 3; his ships aground off Gibraltar, 6/8 & n. 3, 12; attacks Dutch fleet off Cadiz, 6/13–14 & n., 19; returns to Portland, 6/62 & n. 4; made Rear-Admiral, 6/147; on *Royal James*, 6/287; dispute about pay, 7/93–4 & n.; and about chaplain's groats, 7/97 & n. 1; neglected by Albemarle, 7/178; captures Dutch merchantman, 7/249, 255; complains of Rupert's misgovernment of fleet, 7/332; presses men for winter voyage, 7/355; elected Elder Brother, Trinity House, 7/382; ill, ib.; to be 'land-admiral' at Plymouth, 8/149; engagement with La Roche, 9/96–7 & n.; low reputation in Mediterranean, 9/137; Tangier voyage, 9/272, 274, 427–8 & n.; victuals sent to, 9/382; concludes peace with Algiers Feb. 1669, 9/473 & n. 1; returns, 9/508, 510 & n. 3; to be sent back, 9/513 & n. 2; discusses policy towards Algiers, 9/516; said to be P's enemy, 9/529

SOCIAL: 4/4, 53, 340; 8/140; 9/544, 563
MISC.: house, 4/405; coach, 8/479
ALLUDED TO: 9/276

ALPS, the: 9/206

ALSOP, [Josias], Rector of St Clement Eastcheap 1660–6: preaches, 2/219

ALSOP, [Timothy], brewer to the King: anecdote by, 4/156; court gossip from, 5/56–61 & nn.; victualling contract, 5/196, 199, 204, 210; illness and death, 5/217–18, 221, 223, 224; social: 5/195

AMEIXIAL, battle of: 4/198 & n. 2, 202–3, 215 & n. 1, 220

AMERICA: see New England, New Netherland

AMSTERDAM: city gives yacht to Charles II, 1/222 & n. 1; plague in, 4/340 & n. 2, 358; 5/142; quarantine on ships from, 4/399 & n. 2; comet reported, 5/134 & n. 1; bank, 7/252 & n. 4; burgomaster, 8/68; propose cession, 8/108

ANABAPTISTS [see also Fanatics]: dismissed from fleet, 1/101, 109 & n. 2; elected to Parliament for London, 2/57 & n. 1 [error]

ANDERSON, Charles, physician, P's contemporary at Magdalene: 1/149–

50; 2/103; ~ his brother, 1/90

ANDREW(S), John, steward to Lord Crew: transactions with P, 1/4, 32, 43, 64, 95; alluded to: 1/313

ANDREWS, John, timber-merchant, Bow: pessimistic about public affairs, 8/377; musical: 6/324–5; 7/422; social: 7/421; 8/483

ANDREWS, ——, wife of the foregoing: expecting child, 6/325; social: 7/421–2; 8/483

ANDREWS, Matt, coachman to Lord Crew: social, 1/18

ANDREWS, [Thomas], merchant, of St Olave's parish: contract for Tangier victualling, 5/223, 226, 236, 263; 6/37, 85, 86, 139, 193, 337; discusses Tangier business with P/Povey, 6/38, 97–8, 105, 130, 185, 201(2); gifts to P, 6/57, 202, 251, 337; accounts, 6/201, 202; in country during Plague, 6/185; P's regard, 6/201–4 passim; to resign victualling to Gauden, 6/203–4, 226–7, 251; receives sacrament, 6/210; also, 8/205; musical: sings, 5/120, 194, 199, 209, 217, 226, 325, 332, 337, 342, 349; 6/24, 27, 32, 39, 44, 55, 73, 80, 88, 98, 125, 131, 219; social: 6/62, 86, 210; 7/413; 8/64, 377; 9/220, 404; ~ his wife [Hester], 5/342; 9/220, 404; his son, 9/404

ANGEL, [Edward], actor: 9/85 & n. 5

ANGIER, John, sen., tailor, P's cousin, of Cambridge: drinks King's health, 1/67; EP visits, 2/180; asks for place, 4/363–4, 409; bankrupt, 4/439; social: 1/69; 2/89; 3/217, 218; alluded to: 2/136; 4/409; ~ his wife, 2/89; 4/430

ANGIER, John, jun.: asks for place, 4/178, 363; to be sent to sea, 4/409; a rogue, 4/439; death, 5/291

ANGIER, Percival, P's cousin, of London: at East India House, 4/384 & n. 4; burial, 6/16; social: 4/364

ANGLESEY, Earl of: see Annesley

ANIMALS [For domestic animals and household pets, see Household etc.; and under names of owners. Horses are principally indexed under Travel (road). See also Entertainments; Games etc.]:
GENERAL: menagerie at Tower, ?1/15 & n. 2; 3/76 & n. 2; noises made by

animals in Rochester, 8/313; P's dislike of cruelty to, 9/154, 203; theories of generation, 2/105 & n. 4, 160
PARTICULAR: baboon [?chimpanzee; gorilla]: from Guinea, 2/160 & n. 3; bears: in Baltic, 4/413; boars: in Baltic, 4/413; bulls: 2/209 & n. 2; 7/245–6; cat(s): P/EP's, 1/325; 8/553; experiments on, 6/95–6; survives Fire, 7/277; colt: allegedly mistaken for sturgeon, 8/232–3 & n.; cows and calves: 3/221 & n. 2; 6/179; deer: in Baltic, 4/413; hunting terms, 8/475; dogs: P tempted to steal, 2/149; kill child, 3/205; P chased/frightened by, 4/131; 7/26; experiments on, 5/151; 6/57, 84; 7/370–1 & n., 373, 389; 9/263 & n. 1; guard dogs, 7/133 & n. 1; sheepdog, 8/339; elephant: hunting of in Siam, 7/251; foxes: hunting of in Baltic, 4/413; frogs: 2/105; horses: manège, 4/120; kidney stones, 4/146; staggers, 8/390; Royal Mews, 5/70–1; performing, 9/297, 301; kitten: experiment on, 6/64; lions: ?1/15 & n. 2; monkeys: performing, 2/166; 4/298; snakes: story of, 3/22 & n. 2; sow, Hamburg: alluded to, 9/420; toad: in drink, 7/290; whale: skeletal remains of, 1/150 & n. 2; fished off Greenland, 4/125; wolves: in Baltic, 4/413
ANJOU, Duc d': *see* Philippe
ANNE of Austria, wife of Louis XIII of France (d. 1666): Bristol's intrigues with, against Mazarin, 4/212 & n. 1
ANNE (b. Hyde), Duchess of York (d. 1671):
PERSONAL: plain, 2/80; proud and extravagant, 3/64; 8/286–7; 9/38; dress, 6/172; portraits by Lely, 3/112–13 & n.; 7/82 & n. 1; her 'silly devotions', 9/164
CHRON. SERIES: birthplace, 6/198 & n. 1; to visit Portsmouth, 4/24; jealous of Monmouth, 4/138; Western progress, 4/321; ill, 4/436, 439; 5/4; to visit Harwich, 6/104; effect of Clarendon's fall on, 8/424, 506; 9/11, 153; reconciled to Coventry, 9/336, 342; receives French ambassador, 9/284; favours French alliance, 9/536;

friendly with Lady Castlemaine, 9/417
MARRIAGE AND FAMILY: marriage, 2/40–1 & n.; also, 1/275, 315, 319, 320; 2/1; 7/261, 354; birth of son, Duke of Cambridge, 1/260–1, 273; his death, 2/95; death of daughter Princess Mary, 3/75; of son, James, Duke of Cambridge, 4/229; about to lie in, 6/19; birth of son, Charles, Duke of Kendal, 7/201 & n. 2; of son, Edgar, Duke of Cambridge, 8/436 & n. 2; death of grandmother, 2/213; and of mother, 8/570; jealousy, 3/248; dalliance with husband, 4/4; love affairs, 6/302 & n. 1; 7/8, 323; said to have poisoned Lady Denham, 8/8; and (with children) to have pox, 9/154–5 & n.; domineers over husband, 9/342
HOUSEHOLD: maids of honour, 6/41
SOCIAL: at theatre, 2/80, 164; 7/347; 8/167; gives play at court, 7/325; attends Feast at Inner Temple, 2/155; at Durdans, 3/184; Whitehall chapel, 3/42; 9/163–4; Somerset House, 3/191; 5/300; ball at Whitehall, 3/300–1; 7/372; dines in public, 4/407; 8/161; at court lottery, 5/214; in state at Whitehall, 8/33; plays cards on Sunday, 8/70; at Hinchingbrooke's wedding, 9/51; at Deptford party, 9/468–9
ALLUDED TO: 9/344, 407
ANNESLEY (Anslow), Arthur, cr. Earl of Anglesey 1661, politician and Treasurer of the Navy:
CHARACTER: 5/336; 8/301, 327
CHRON. SERIES: appointed to Privy Council, 1/171; opposes motion in Commons to reward Sandwich, 1/178; chairs Council's Admiralty Committee, 5/319; 6/45; at Fishery Committee, 5/336; at Privy Council/Council committees, 8/278, 291; pessimistic about war, 8/288, 291; (untrue) rumour of appointment to Treasury commission, 8/367; manager of conference between Houses, 8/551 & n. 4, 561; rumoured dismissal from Council, 8/571, 596, 600; views on issues in Skinner v. E. India Company, 9/196 & nn.
AS TREASURER OF THE NAVY: appoint-

ment, 8/295 & n. 3, 297, 301, 322; attends Board, 8/327; 9/39, 196; anxious to learn from P, 8/334; his allowance, 8/334–5 & n., 378; proposals for paying-off fleet, 8/397, 456, 567, 571; active in sale of prize ships, 8/484; rumoured dismissal, 9/10; promises reforms, ib.; annoys Duke of York, 9/253, 256, 310; criticises P, 9/244, 295, 306 & n. 1, 308; 'suspended and discharged', 9/340–1 & n., 346 & n. 3, 357; resists order, 9/341, 342–3, 344–5, 416; petitions King, 9/351, 362 & n. 1; Board's complaints of, 9/428; unspecified business, 8/462; also, 9/42, 67 & n. 3
POLITICAL NEWS FROM: 8/375, 555, 561, 565; 9/8–9, 25, 323
ALLUDED TO: 1/66; 9/145, 209
ANNIS, [Robert], workman, Woolwich yard: to be tried for embezzlement, 3/137 & n. 2
ANSLEY (Annesley), Capt. [Abraham]: appointed Master-Attendant, Deptford, 9/441 & n. 1
ANSLOW: see Annesley
ANTIGUA, Leeward Is.: captured by French, 8/38 & n. 1
ANTRIM, Earl of: see Macdonell
ANTWERP: 9/396
APPLEYARD, ——, of Huntingdon: 9/224
APPRENTICES: riots/demonstrations, 1/39 & n. 1, 54; 5/99–100 & n., 101; 9/129–30 & n., 132, 133, 152 & n. 2; church attendance, 3/194; in good seats at theatre, 9/2; affray in Moorfields between Weavers and Butchers, 5/222–3 & n.; hard life of apprentice fisher-boy, 6/241–2
APSLEY, Sir Allen, M.P. Thetford, Norf.: reports news of battle of Ameixial, 4/215 & n. 1; drunken speech in Parliament, 7/416; establishment as Master-Falconer reduced, 8/394–5 & n.; alluded to: 7/73
APSLEY, Sir Anthony [recte Sir Allen]: 7/73
APSLEY (Appesley), Col. [John]: accused of forgery, 3/43–4
ARCHANGEL: hemp from, 4/175, 394; map of river, 4/390

ARCHER, Betty, sister of Mary: admired by P as undergraduate, 2/220
ARCHER, Mary, of Bourn, Cambs., later wife of Clement Sankey: at theatre, 2/220 & n. 4, 226; her portion, 2/220; alluded to: 2/225; ~ her uncle's house, 2/220
ARCHES, Court of: see Justice, administration of
ARCHITECTURE, P's taste in [asterisks denote the occasions when he makes a descriptive comment]: admires Audley End House, 1/69–70*; 8/467–8*; disappointed with alterations at Hinchingbrooke, 3/220*; with Old Wanstead House, 6/102* & n. 4; and Wilton, 9/230*; admires Gauden's house at Clapham, 4/244*; Wricklemarsh, 6/94* & n. 3; Swakeleys, 6/215*; Dagnams, 6/159; Clarendon House, 7/32* & n. 2, 42*; Sir P. Warwick's new house, 7/64*; Bridewell, 8/6; Belasyse's new house, 9/202; and Goring House, 9/276
ARGIER(S): see Algiers
ARITHMETIC: see Science and mathematics
ARMADA, Spanish [see also Navy, Royal]: 3/187; alluded to: 8/293
ARMIGER, [William], relation of P: in pre-coronation procession, 2/82; attempts to court EP, 2/208; lodges with Tom P, 3/6; 4/183; social: 1/54, 88; 2/43, 53, 60; ~ his son, 5/71
ARMORER, ——, [? the following]: claims to have enjoyed favours of Duchess of York, 4/138
ARMOURER, [?Sir Nicholas], Equerry of the Great Horse to the King: in drunken frolic, 8/446–7 & n.
ARMY [For P's service in, see Mountagu, E., 1st Earl of Sandwich. See also Commonwealth; Militia; Tangier]:
CHRON. SERIES: Lifeguards routed in Venner's rising, 2/10; troops sent to Portugal, 3/48, 63; their conduct in campaign, 4/215 & nn.; Guards quell riots by seamen, 7/416; 8/28; by apprentices, 9/129, 130, 132; blow up houses in Fire, 7/269; regiments raised against invasion threats, 7/395; 8/265; troops moved to Portsmouth and

Sheerness, 8/98; deployed against Dutch raids, 8/276; conduct in Medway crisis, 8/308, 309; numbers reduced by disbandment, 8/476; 9/32; soldiers man ship, 8/147, 153; Lifeguards stop tobacco-growing, 8/442
CEREMONIES: Lifeguards escort Russian envoy, 3/267–8; Horseguards at Whitehall and Somerset House, 5/56
FINANCES [see also Fox, Sir S.]: Guards paid from excise, 8/572, 576; 9/197; Albemarle gives precedence to payment of, 8/591
OFFICERS: attempts to dismiss Catholic officers, 7/354, 378 & n. 2
QUARTERS: at inn, 6/245
REGIMENTS: alleged corruption and cowardice of Lifeguards, 4/377; Admiral's regiment, 8/334 & n. 5
REVIEWS: in Hyde Park, 4/216; 9/308, 557
STANDING ARMY: parliament's distrust, 3/15; 8/324, 352–3, 355; and city's, 8/260; fear of Duke of York raising new army in north, 6/277 & n. 2, 302; 7/395; and of King's intention to rule by, 7/307; 8/332 & n. 1, 366 & n. 3; 9/32; King's denial, 8/360–1
ARRAN, Earl of: see Butler, Lord R.
ARTHUR, [?Robert], of Ashtead, Surrey: 4/245
ARTILLERY GROUND, Spitalfields: 9/528
ARUNDEL HOUSE, Strand: gardens and gallery, 2/110; sculptures, ib. & n. 2; Royal Society /its council meets, 8/7, 11, 17, 242–3, 528, 540–1, 553–4; 9/113, 263, 334, 379; alluded to: 9/353
ARUNDEL STAIRS: 2/110
ARUNDELL, ——, organist: 4/283
ARZILL: see Azila
ASCENSION DAY: beating the parish boundaries, 2/106 & n. 1; 9/179 & n. 2; parish dinner, 9/179; Navy Board holiday, 4/162
ASCUE: see Ayscue
ASHBURNHAM, John, Groom of the Bedchamber to the King: part in Charles I's escape from Hampton Court (1647), 6/316–17 & nn.; said to have sold viscountcy (1646), 8/126 & n. 1; anger at shortages in King's

household, 8/417–18; also, 7/383; 8/419
ASHBURNHAM, William, Cofferer of the King's Household: business concerning money for Household, 7/92, 133, 134; 8/112, 193, 198; 9/269, 280, 306; P's regard, 7/383, 407; court news from, 7/384, 385; congratulates P on parliamentary speech, 9/105; admires P's shorthand, 9/269; house, 7/160; 8/198–9 & n.; social: 6/300; 7/160, 335, 406; 9/280, 320
[ASHBY, Capt. Arthur], naval officer: killed in action, 7/231 & n. 4
ASHE, Simeon, Presbyterian minister (d. 1662): sermons mimicked, 1/280
ASHFIELD, [Sutton], of Brampton: 8/220; ~ his wife [Lucy], 8/117
ASHLEY, Lord: see Cooper, A. A.
ASHMOLE, Elias, savant (d. 1692): P sings with, 1/274 & n. 1; his views on generation, 2/105 & n. 4
ASHTEAD (Asted), Surrey: P's boyhood memories, 3/152 & n. 1; P and Creed lodge at, 4/245 & n. 3; visit church (St Giles), 4/247
ASH WEDNESDAY: Exchequer open, 8/73
ASHWELL, Mary, companion to EP: CHRON. SERIES: engaged, 3/298; 4/14, 16, 19, 21, 32, 40, 49, 72; at Chelsea school, 4/45 & n. 2, 59; pleases P, 4/74, 79, 81, 88, 90; EP jealous, 4/122, 165, 180; accused of stealing, 4/171; neglected, 4/175; visits Brampton with EP, 4/183, 184, 205; quarrels with EP, 4/210, 262, 274, 276; dismissed, 4/278, 279–80, 287; to resume teaching, 4/280; informs P about Sandwich's liaison, 4/392; revisits Seething Lane, 5/18; also, 4/84, 96, 97, 107, 128, 155, 162, 285; 5/10
MUSICAL: plays harpsichord, 4/75; virginals, 4/79, 87, 93, 99, 103, 120; P buys music for, 4/76; P teaches, 4/122
SOCIAL: accompanies EP on visits etc., 4/73, 74, 82, 99, 108, 141, 142, 149, 154; visits parents, 4/83, 173, 284; dances, 4/106, 109, 141, 179; plays cards well, 4/107; entertains P and EP with recitations, 4/112
ALLUDED TO: 4/92, 113, 118, 133, 150
~ her uncle, 5/10

ASHWELL, Samuel: 1/272

ASHWELL, Mr ——, of the Exchequer: daughter proposed as EP's companion, 4/16, 21, 32(2); musical: 1/5; social: 1/33, 272; 2/31, 227; alluded to: 4/83, 173, 274, 278 ~ his wife, 4/32, 83; sister, 3/286

ASIA: stories (unspecified) of travels in, 5/34

ASKEW, Askue: see Ayscue

ASSHETON, family of: at Great Lever Hall, Lancs., 3/254

ASTED: see Ashtead

ASTROLOGY: see Popular beliefs etc.

ASTRONOMY: see Royal Society; Science etc.; Scientific and Mathematical Instruments

ATHENS: proposers of new laws in [error], 9/60 & n. 2

ATKINS, Col. [Samuel], merchant: news from, 7/348; supplies coal to Tangier, 7/381 & n. 3; 9/249; house, 9/345; also, 6/46; 7/44

ATKINSON, [Thomas], goldsmith: 1/7

AUBIGNY, Lord d': see Stuart, L.

AUCTIONS (by inch of candle): of ships, 1/284 & n. 2; and naval stores, 2/45, 69; bidding described, 3/185–6

AUDLEY, [Hugh], scrivener, Fleet St: death and estate, 3/264 & n. 2; biography, 4/22 & n. 5; alluded to: 8/497

AUDLEY END HOUSE, Essex: described, 1/69–70 & nn.; 8/467–8 & nn.; pictures, 1/70; 8/467 & n. 4; garden, 8/468; King and Duke of York visit, 7/68, 71; 9/325; King buys, 7/68 & n. 2; alluded to: 8/470

AUSTIN (Augustine) FRIARS, Old Broad St: 5/282–3; alluded to: 7/44

AUSTIN, Godfrey, scrivener, King St, Westminster: 1/34

AUSTRIA: see Empire, Holy Roman; Germany

AVEBURY (Abebury): P visits, 9/240 & n. 2

AXE YARD, Westminster: P takes up residence in, vol. i, p. xxiii; 1/1 & n. 2; pays rent, 1/87, 88; returns after Dutch voyage, 1/179, 182; expenditure, 1/213; sells lease, 1/213,

218, 219, 235, 244, 245, 247; removes papers, 1/248; ~ coronation bonfires in, 2/87

AXTEL, Col. Daniel, regicide: executed, 1/268 & n. 1, 269

AYLESBURY, Anne, Lady Aylesbury, widow of Sir Thomas: Duke of York in mourning for, 2/213 & n. 1

AYLESFORD, Kent: P visits Sir J. Banks's house, 9/495–6 & n.; and Kit's Coty House, 9/496–7 & n.

AYLETT, Capt. [John], naval officer: dismissed for cowardice, 7/174 & n. 1

AYNSWORTH, [Elizabeth], prostitute: at Reindeer, Bishop's Stortford, 8/466, 467; 9/209; expelled from Cambridge, 8/466 & n. 1; bawdy song, ib. & n. 3; to move to London, 9/210

AYRES: see Eyres

AYSCUE (Ascue, Askew, Askue), Sir George, naval commander: opposes sending convoy to Turkey, 6/10 & n. 4, 11; serves under Sandwich, 6/147; refuses share of prize-goods, 6/260–1; taken prisoner by Dutch 7/153, 169; 8/426; portrait by Lely, 7/102 & n. 3; also, 2/173, 185; 5/27, 149, 186, 288, 317; 6/241

AZILA (Arzill), N. Africa: offered to England, 8/347–8 & n.

BABER, Sir John, royal physician, Covent Garden: 7/14, 71–2

BACKWELL, Ald. Edward, goldsmith-banker, Lombard St:

CHARACTER: industry, 4/396; pride, 9/517

BUSINESS WITH P: Tangier: 5/339; 6/274; 9/152, 249; unwilling to lend money, 6/85, 109; provides money/credit for garrison, 8/528(2); 9/253, 315, 316, 328, 415; Navy Board: informs P about marine insurance, 4/394, 395; and difficulties with Navy Treasury, 7/214–15 & n.; refuses further credit, 7/330–1; private: changes foreign money, 1/183; sells plate etc. to, 1/322, 323, 324; 2/4; 5/47; P deposits cash with, 2/76; 5/269 & n. 1; accounts, 7/34

BUSINESS WITH SANDWICH: sells plate, 1/185, 192; loan, 2/120, 122; changes

Portuguese money, 3/102, 103, 114, 115

BUSINESS WITH GOVERNMENT: in Flanders, 6/149–50 & n., 155, 163, 165, 171, 322–3; creditors create difficulties, 6/149–50, 151, 165; is confident of King's backing, 7/215 & n. 2; survives run on banks in Medway crisis, 8/263, 528–9; pays Swedish envoys at Breda, 8/528

HIS NEWS/OPINIONS: on new coinage, 4/396; prospects of war, 5/134; announces Peace of Breda on Exchange, 8/328

PRIVATE AFFAIRS ETC.: new buildings in Lombard St, 4/214 & n. 3; 9/517 & n. 1; buys estate near Brampton, 9/185 & n. 2; new house in London, 9/517 & n. 1; health, 8/557

SOCIAL: 2/119; 3/200; 9/21, 400, 560

BACKWELL, [Mary], wife of Edward: P's admiration, 3/94, 114; 9/21, 185 & n. 2, 400; at St Olave's, 9/508, 514, 555; pride, 9/517; ∼ her mother, 9/508, 514

BACON, Capt. [Philemon], naval officer: killed in action, 7/148, 154

BADILEY (Boddily, Bodilaw), Capt. [William], Master-Attendant, Deptford: sale of stores, 2/45; 4/319; narrowly escapes death, 3/173

BAGG, Frank: 2/193–4

BAGSHOT, Berks.: King hunts at, 8/444; 9/302

BAGWELL, [William], ship's carpenter, Deptford: welcomes P's visits, 4/233–4; 5/351; asks for place, 4/266; 5/163, 302; on *Providence*, 7/176; returns to fleet, 7/189, 282; master-carpenter of *Rupert*, 8/39 & n. 1, 95; ∼ his father, 6/189; mother, 6/201; 9/469

BAGWELL, ——, wife of William: her good looks, 4/222; P plans to seduce, 4/222, 266; visits, 4/233–4; finds her virtuous, 4/234; and modest, 5/163; asks P for place for husband, 5/65–6, 163; P kisses, 5/287; she grows affectionate, 5/301–2; he caresses, 5/313; she visits him, 5/316, 339; her resistance collapses in alehouse, 5/322; amorous encounters with: at her house, 5/350–1; 6/40, 162, 189,

201, 253, 294; 7/166, 284, 285; 8/39, 95; 9/221; Navy Office, 6/186; 7/351, 380; tavern, 6/20; assignations frustrated, 9/25, 217; P's valentine, 6/35, 226, 294; asks for promotion for husband, 6/39–40; P strains a finger, 6/40; she returns from Portsmouth, 7/96; has sore face, 7/191; returns from Harwich, 9/12, 25; also, 6/158; 7/96, 210, 339; 8/99; ∼ servant dies of plague, 7/166

BAILEY, [Francis], shipbuilder: *see* Baylie

BAINES, [Jeremy], P's schoolfellow at St Paul's: 'a great nonconformist', 5/37 & n. 4

BAKER (Barker), Capt. [Richard], Excise Commissioner: 1/14–15 & n.

BAKER, [Roger], purser: dispute with commander, 9/505 & n. 1

BALDOCK (Baldwick), Herts.: P overnight at, 2/148–9; visits church, 2/148 & n. 1; and fair, 2/183 & n. 6; increase of Quakers, 2/149 & n. 1; also, 4/314; 8/475

BALES: *see* Bayles

BALL, Capt. [?Andrew], naval officer: in Four Days Fight, 7/288

'BALL', Betty, actress: *see* Hall, Betty

BALL, [John], Treasurer to the London Commissioners of Excise: proposed as Treasurer for Tangier, 6/94 & n. 1; business with P, 6/130; 8/331; political news from, 8/410; dismissed, 8/557 & n. 3; 9/110; deplores state of country, 9/120; social: 9/331

BALL (Bell), Capt. [?Naphthali], naval officer: in Four Days Fight, 7/150; news from, 7/288

BALL, Sir Peter, Attorney-General to the Queen Mother: Brampton business, 2/28 & n. 2; 3/102, 176 & n. 3; also, 8/22

BALL, Dr Richard, Master of the Temple: preaches at St Gregory's, 3/252 & n. 2; anecdotes of sermons, 9/505–6 & n.

BALLADS [*see* Music: Songs; Musical Compositions]: on Rump, 1/114 & n. 2; 'To all you ladies', 6/2 & n. 1; on Albemarle, 8/99 & n. 2; Arthur of Bradley, 9/460 & n. 5

BALLAST OFFICE: 1/296 & n. 2

7/319, 327; improved by good clothes, 7/329; to replace Mercer, 7/299, 303, 304, 314, 319; dismissed, 8/212; musical: P admires her singing, 6/235; 8/165; out of practice, 7/299, 319; learns *It is decreed*, 7/420; 8/36, 50, 54, 142; sings with P/EP, 8/49, 97, 157; learns part-song, 8/113; social: accompanies EP on visits, etc., 7/329, 335, 351, 373; 8/37, 72, 158, 165, 202, 206; runs for wagers, 8/167; alluded to: 7/422

BARKING, Essex: timber shipped from, 3/170

BARKING CHURCH: *see* All Hallows

BARKING CREEK, Essex: ships sunk in, 8/263

BARKSTEAD, John, regicide: arrested, 3/45 & n. 1, 47; hanged, 3/66; treasure allegedly buried in Tower, 3/240–1 & n., 246, 248, 250; the search for, 3/240–2, 244, 250–1

BARKWAY, Herts.: P at, 2/146

BARLOW, [Thomas], former Clerk of the Acts: claims the office, 1/188 & n. 2–193 passim, 198; 2/55 & n. 2; agrees to annuity in compensation, 1/202 & n. 1, 205, 206; annuity paid, 1/305; 2/22, 103; 4/22, 232; P enquires about health, 2/55; supports P's claim to draft contracts, 3/100; gift to Sandwich, 4/323, 397; death, 6/33; payments to executors, 7/40; also, 4/96 & n. 4

BARNARDISTON (Barmston), [George], P's relative, of Cottenham, Cambs.: 8/466 & n. 2

BARNARDISTON (Bernardiston), Sir Samuel: arraigned before House of Lords, 9/192–3 & n.

BARNARD'S INN GATE, Holborn: 8/245

BARN ELMS, Surrey: P/EP visit(s), 7/235; 8/188, 202, 236, 256, 346, 400; 9/128, 271; duel, 9/27

BARNES, [William], of Cottenham, Cambs.: proposed as match for Paulina P, 8/261 & n. 2

BARNET, Herts.: rebels at, 2/8; P and others take waters, 5/200–1; 8/380–2; other visits, 5/64, 233, 299; 7/127; 8/475; 9/224; Red Lion, 5/299; 8/381

BARNET HILL, Herts.: 5/64

BARNETT, Mrs ——, shopkeeper, New Exchange: 9/534; ~ her assistant Betty, 9/534; ? also, 9/263, 511

BARNWELL, Robert, Sandwich's steward: ill, 1/205, 207; 2/3; to see coronation, 2/75; shows P alterations to Hinchingbrooke, 2/183; dies owing money to Sandwich, 3/101, 116; social: 2/135, 183

BARNWELL ABBEY, Cambridge: P visits, 9/213 & n. 1

BARON, Lt-Col. [Benjamin]: news from, 2/58 & n. 5; at Lord Mayor's banquet, 4/354; on Turkish government, 5/30; account of travel in Asia, 5/34

BARON, [Hartgill], clerk in the Privy Seal Office: dispute about clerkship, 1/207 & n. 2, 208, 211, 235, 236; month's service in office, 1/212; fees, 1/247

BARR, Peter, merchant: gift of wine to P, 7/175 & n. 2

BARROW, [Philip], storekeeper, Chatham: efficiency, 4/149; 6/183; discusses faults of yard, 3/154; quarrels with Clerk of Cheque, 3/155; criticises Batten, 4/134; Batten's enmity, 4/149; differences with colleagues, 4/149 & n. 2; 6/183; at launch, 4/225; and muster, 4/228; to visit Isle of Man, 4/240; threatens to resign, 5/5 & n. 1; grievances, 5/47, 50; sends P oysters, 5/88; house, 3/156; and 'antiquities', 4/225; social: 3/153; ~ his niece, 4/225

BARTHOLOMEW FAIR: *see* Entertainments; Fairs and Markets

BARTLET, Nick, servant to Sandwich: 1/33

BARTLET: *see* Berkeley

BARTON, ——, of Brampton, Hunts.: 2/204, n. 2, 205; 3/221, 286–7; 5/298

BARWELL, [John], saddler to the King: social: 3/172; 5/202; ~ his wife, 3/172; her maid, ib.

BASINGHALL ST: plague, 6/144

BASSETT, Sir Arthur, soldier: with Tangier garrison, 5/176 & n. 3; 9/272

BASSUM, John, servant to P's father: P's boyhood memory of, 9/3

BATELIER, Joseph, sen., wine-merchant: complains of embargo on French wines, 7/403; dies, 8/465

BATELIER, Joseph, jun., wine-merchant: on wine trade, 8/421; social: 7/421; 8/381; 9/303–4; ~ his wife [Eleanor], 7/421; 9/303–4

BATELIER, Mary, linen draper, Royal Exchange, daughter of Joseph sen.: P admires her beauty, 6/?73, 76, 128, 157, 170–1, 334; 7/15–16, 135, 265; closes shop in Plague, 6/174, 334; bridesmaid to Jane Birch, 9/500; social: 7/43, 110, 200, 233, 240, 246, 265, 322; 8/19, 421; 9/289, 296, 304, 327, 373, 393, 417, 455, 510, 521, 527, 529, 531, 536, 564; alluded to: 7/270; ~ her sweetheart, 9/531

BATELIER, Susan, daughter of Joseph, sen.: returns from France, 7/199; social: 7/200, 228, 240; 9/417, 464, 521

BATELIER, [Susanna], wife of Joseph, sen.: 'a fine woman', 7/240; angry at loss of dog, ib.; gives spaniel to EP, 9/296; also, 9/333, 417

BATELIER, William, wine merchant, son of Joseph sen.:

P'S OPINION: 7/228, 238, 358

CHRON. SERIES: his trick in buying claret, 7/256; gives EP puppy, 7/360; news of French fashions, 7/379; and of Clarendon's flight, 8/561; shop rent, 7/404; recommends cook-maid, 8/419; and EP's companion, 8/448, 456; talks of wine trade, 8/421; ?9/443; his post in customs, 9/18 & n. 4; supplies P with wine, 9/249; helps P draft letter to Duke of York, 9/304; visits Impington, 9/309, 315; and France, 9/342; returns with letters for King, 9/425; admires Louis XIV, 9/426; brings French wares for P and EP, 9/427, 428, 431, 450–1, 453, 464

SOCIAL: takes EP to dancing meeting, 7/238; dresses as woman at party, 7/246; attends dances, 7/362–3; 8/28, 104, 493, 511; 9/12, 42, 134, 289, 457–8, 464, 510–11; at Bartholomew Fair, 9/290; gives house-warming party, 9/333; also, 7/230, 233, 240, 249, 258, 358, 380, 403; 8/19, 100, 344, 378, 447, 537; 9/18, 19, 35, 36,

113, 145, 221, 278, 296, 297, 301, 327, 332, 337, 441, 453, 454(2), 455(2), 456, 463, 500, 506, 510, 521, 530, 555

ALLUDED TO: 9/334, 417

~ his black manservant, 9/464; black maidservant, Doll, 9/464, 510

BATEMAN, Sir Anthony, Lord Mayor 1663–4: commands bonfires for Queen's birthday, 4/382; quells riot, 5/99–100 & n.; present at fire, 5/248; alluded to: 4/353

BATERTON: see Betterton

BATES, Dr William, Vicar of St Dunstan-in-the-West c.1654–62 (d. 1699): objects to toasts, 2/105; his preaching, 3/161 & n. 2; farewell sermons before ejection, 3/166–7, 167–8 & n.; allowed to resume preaching, 8/265 & n. 6; also, 8/383; alluded to: 3/162

BATH, KNIGHTS OF THE: installation, 2/79 & n. 2; in pre-coronation procession, 2/82 & n. 4; at coronation banquet, 2/85

BATH, Som.: King and court visit, 4/272, 287, 288, 292; P and household visit, 9/231, 236, 238–9; description, 9/232–3 & n., 238–9; abbey tombs, 9/238–9 & nn.; Cross Bath, 9/233 & n. 2, 239; King's Bath, 9/239, 240; Queen's Bath, 9/239; [Bath-]chairs, 9/233; town music, 9/233–4; walls etc., 9/238

BATHS and bathrooms [see also Dress and Personal Appearance: washing]: P admires Povey's bathroom, 5/161 & n. 5; Lowthers' tub alluded to, 8/217

BATTEN, [Benjamin], son of Sir William: proposed as lieutenant, 7/301, 306

BATTEN, [Elizabeth], Lady Batten, wife of Sir William:

P'S OPINION/DISLIKE: her bad temper, 2/78; pride, 2/161; 3/93; hypocrisy, 3/284; ill-breeding, 8/408; he avoids, 2/16; 3/179; their mutual dislike, 6/131; pleased at her losing overshoe, 6/299; vexed at her claims to precedence, 3/54–5, 296; 4/426; and velvet gown, 4/400; also, 3/187–8

CHRON. SERIES: visits dockyards, ships etc., 1/315, 316, 317; 2/45, 57–8,

67–73 passim, 113, 116; 3/198; 4/204; 5/39, 307; sees regicides' corpses hanged, 2/26–7; at Walthamstow house, 2/50, 63, 74, 78; 3/180; 4/221; 6/102, 234; stories of former condition, 2/146; 4/233 & n. 1; 5/141; estranged from EP, 3/146, 249–50, 302; 4/71; 5/356; 6/46, 95; dislikes Commissioner Pett, 4/53, 253; friendly to P, 4/51, 218; 5/216; 8/105; offends Mennes, 6/233(2), 234; returns to London after Plague, 7/36; helps P in Fire, 7/272; left poor by husband's death, 8/462, 476–7; quarrels with children, 8/476–7; P's claim on her estate, 8/462, 477, 483, 561, 569, 579, 582, 584; 9/117, 119; made sole executrix, 8/483; and main legatee, 8/580; unable to pay husband's debt to Navy Board, 9/149–50; ill, 2/116; 7/332; 8/4; also, 8/159, 314, 523–4

SOCIAL: chooses Penn as valentine, 2/36; given parrot by Ph. Pett, 2/69; sees pre-coronation procession, 2/82; attends funeral, 2/131–2; celebrates wedding anniversary, 3/21–2; at daughter's wedding, 4/217–18; P escorts to church, 4/268; seasick on river trip, 4/296, 299; gives Christmas feast, 5/354, 356, 357; at Sheriff Waterman's dinner, 6/79; Sir W. Hickes's, 6/221, 222; friendly with 'Madam' Williams, 6/234; at christening, 8/403, 404–5; Penn's house, 2/19, 39; 3/4, 270; 5/7; 8/3; taverns, 2/61, 175, 218, 233; 3/31; at theatre, 2/127, 155; P/EP visit(s)/dine(s) with etc., 1/295; 2/31, 55, 56–7, 59, 94, 208; 4/13, 177, 188; 5/309, 322; 6/4, 5, 9, 78, 140; 8/314; at P's house, 2/22, 23, 53; 8/4, 433; also, 4/200, 236–7; 6/226; 7/69, 162; 8/112–13

ALLUDED TO: 1/280, 289; 2/190, 202, 232; 3/30, 70, 145; 5/176; 8/322

~ her maid Anne (Nan): 1/316; 2/72–3; 3/249; her kinswoman Mrs Hester, 2/215

BATTEN, [Elizabeth], wife of William, jun.: pretty, 2/30; foolish admiration of play, 2/191; son christened, 4/165; social: 2/78, 82, 109; 4/218

BATTEN, Martha: *see* Castle

BATTEN, [Mary]: *see* Leming

BATTEN, Sir William, Surveyor of the Navy 1660–7:

PERSONAL: physical appearance, 7/105–6; good humour, 7/131–2; good raconteur, 8/135; religious observances, 3/31, 54; death, 8/459, 462; burial, 8/475, 476

AS NAVAL COMMANDER: Penn's superior officer in Civil War, 1/226 & n. 3; opinion of Sandwich, 2/24, 169; reminiscences, 3/252; alleged cowardice in action (July 1648), 5/169 & n. 1; violent language about Dutch, 8/345; criticises naval tactics, 8/275, 306; also, 1/159

AS SURVEYOR OF THE NAVY:

APPOINTMENT: 1/191, n. 2; salary, 1/194 & n. 4, 253; sworn J.P., 1/252; fears dismissal, 3/158; Pett proposed as assistant, 3/237; 4/75 & n. 3; presents surveys, 7/316; fears Rupert's disapproval, ib.

CHATHAM CHEST: alleged malpractices, 3/172 & n. 3; 5/122, 141, 196, 301; 6/183; debt to, 9/149–50; also, 7/110

CONTRACTS AND STORES: drafts/helps to draft contracts, 4/61, 326, 380–1; 7/68, 233; favours Stacey, 4/187; and Wood, 5/6 & n. 2, 108; criticises Warren's contracts, 4/314, 380, 382, 383, 421, 423–4; 5/300–1, 303, 304; 7/2; shows P plank, 4/289; storekeeping criticised, 5/167, 318

DOCKYARD BUSINESS: Chatham: visits 2/11, 13, 67–73, 112, 116, 208; 3/68, 205; 4/314; pays at, 3/215, 290; surveys at, 1/204; 3/150–1; 4/118; dismisses clerk of survey, 5/36, 140–1; Deptford: visits, 3/19; 4/67, 203–4, 317–18; 6/169; 8/95; pays at, 1/290; ?2/94; 3/58, 124, 128, 129, 193; 4/175, 386; sales at, 2/45; 4/319; surveys at, 3/30–1; 5/35, 39; examines site of mast-dock, 5/202, 353; 6/96; Harwich: visits, 6/4, 5, 9, 83, 104, 131; Portsmouth: visits, 2/199, 202; 4/12, 389; 6/330; pays at, 3/280, 289; 4/253; surveys at, 4/141, 153, 156; Woolwich: visits, 1/313–16, 319; 2/50; 4/67, 203–4, 284; 5/182, 213; 8/95; sale at, 2/50; trial of yarn, 3/101;

wharf, 4/284; ~ almost drowned near Portsmouth, 3/253–4

FINANCIAL BUSINESS: at pays at Treasury Office, 2/227; 4/2, 291–2 & n.; 7/332; works on Treasurer's accounts, 3/240; 5/318; and Creed's, 3/279; 4/11; on commanders' pay, 4/7; also, 6/72; 7/314, 374; 8/20, 200, 274, 510

JUDICIAL BUSINESS: in Field's case, 3/280–1; 4/171, 172, 350, 421–2; at Court of Admiralty, 4/76

OTHER BUSINESS: visits wrecks, 1/313; 6/54; attends launches, 4/102–3; 5/307; visits ships, 4/203–4 & n.; 6/193–4; 7/352; arranges weighing-up of, 8/266, 325; buys Commonwealth arms, 2/69 & n. 2; has Commonwealth figurehead burnt, 4/418 & n. 2, 420–1; angered by pacifist sermon, 2/37; assaulted by seamen, 6/288; abused by seaman's wife, 8/268; part in Carkesse's dismissal, 8/60, 76, 100, 109, 146, 213, 215, 238, 385; unspecified: 1/239, 243, 253; 2/40, 206; 3/21, 22, 24, 62, 101, 146, 203, 229, 272; 4/4, 31, 43, 61, 177, 222, 243, 278, 322, 338; 5/138, 156, 156–7, 274, 299, 342; 6/13, 19, 98, 145, 222; 7/12, 105, 107–8, 115, 162; 8/25, 142, 181, 186, 278

PERQUISITES AND PROFITS [see also Reputation]: chest of drawers from ropemaker, 3/197; granted lighthouse patent, 5/314; 6/3 & n. 4; fails to obtain place in Prize Office, 5/322, 327, 328, 333; buys ketch, 7/105–6; given share in privateer (Flying Greyhound), 7/299, 300–1 & n.; her voyages and prizes, 7/316, 418, 424; 8/1, 8, 17, 180, 344, 349, 351–2, 369, 441–2; dispute with Swedish Resident about prizes, 8/21–2, 23, 27, 128, 130, 135, 135–6, 169; to become sole owner, 8/112; buys out P, 8/341, 385, 462; 9/119; alleged favour to crew, 9/99

RELATIONS WITH COLLEAGUES AND ASSOCIATES: with P: mutually critical, 3/59, 64, 145; 6/92; quarrel about warrants, 3/163–4; mate's appointment, 4/110; contracts, 5/115–16; 7/358–9; supplies, 5/157, 238; un-specified quarrels, 5/118; 7/232; ally in Field's case, 4/51–4 passim; and in Carkesse affair, 8/101–2, 105; high opinion of P, 8/419; also, 5/45, 341; 7/36; with others: mutual recrimination over Interregnum careers, 2/65; complains of colleagues' malice, 3/171; relations with Pett, 1/240; 4/53–4; 8/100; Warren, 2/78; 4/437; 5/318; Slingsby, 2/202; Waith and officers of Navy Treasury, 3/29; Carteret, 3/59; Mennes, 3/14, 227; 4/194; 5/235, 293; 6/233, 234; Cox, 4/149; Hewer, 4/337; Commissioner Taylor, 5/326, 350; 6/295; Penn, 6/66; 8/217; Brouncker, 7/410; 8/78, 80, 97, 126

REPUTATION: criticised by P for corruption, 3/145; 4/205, 325; 5/120, 121, 131, 143, 182; 6/298; for corrupt collusion: with hemp merchants, 3/101–2 & n.; flagmakers, 3/148 & n. 3; ropemaker, 3/155 & n. 3, 157; tar merchant, 4/182; Cocke, 4/194, 241, 284; Wood, 4/201; 5/117; Castle, 5/83 & n. 3; and Dr Walker, 8/123; criticised by P for inefficiency, 3/59; 4/2, 97, 98, 113; 5/120; 6/284, 330; 7/359; 8/12, 582; said to be more diligent, 3/174; corruption/inefficiency criticised: by Warren, 3/131; 5/131, 143; Capt. J. Allen, 3/155, 157; Coventry, 4/17, 194–5, 196, 341, 397; 5/169; 7/409; 8/570, 571; Carteret, 4/97; 6/74; P. Pett, 4/98; Barrow, 4/134; Hempson, 5/140–1; C. Pett, 5/109; Waith, 5/155; Gilsthorpe, 8/560, and in 'libel', 7/388

OTHER PUBLIC OFFICES: as M.P.: elected for Rochester, 2/55, 57, 58; attends Commons, 4/58; 6/274–5; Trinity House: defeated in election to Mastership, 3/93; elected, 4/185; rebuilds almshouses, 5/116–17 & n.; claims members' exemption from militia, 6/24–5 & n.; power in, 6/107, 298; unspecified business, 2/26; 3/29; dinners at, 2/4; 3/103, 187, 190; 4/209, 343; at Trinity Monday service, 5/172

NEWS FROM: naval: 6/115, 119; 7/151, 156, 225, 228, 395, 415, 416; 8/350;

political: 2/107; 4/53, 187, 207–8; 5/98–9, 104, 105, 313; 6/250, 274–5; 7/298, 330, 341–2, 401; 8/14, 49, 376, 422

PRIVATE AFFAIRS:

FINANCES: landed estate, 4/400 & n. 4; assessment for Poll Tax, 8/120; will, 8/483, 580; 9/149–50

HEALTH: ill, 2/30, 32; 3/43, 44, 234, 236, 239, 247; 5/119, 309; 6/32(2); 8/296, 298, 302, 459, 462; bled, 3/233; sprains foot, 8/95, 97

HOUSES: Seething Lane: takes up residence, 1/209; bricks up window, 1/269; storey added, 3/59, 66, 118, 127; roof-frames made, 3/102, 111; chimney fire, 8/28; Walthamstow, Essex: P visits, 1/279, 280; 2/78, 109–10, 145, 146; 4/217–18; 6/102, 190, 220; 8/423; description, 1/279 & n. 2, 280; 8/423; gardens, 2/109; wine from, 8/341–2

HOUSEHOLD: Dutch drawing, 4/109; removes goods during Fire, 7/272, 274; extravagance, 9/150

RELATIONS WITH P AS NEIGHBOUR [see also Surveyor of the Navy]: mutual dislike, 3/28–9, 149; 4/27, 161; 5/354; 6/131; Batten's friendly overture, 3/145–6; jealous of P, 3/189; 4/439; P unwilling to visit, 3/4, 52; also, 2/16, 145; 3/39, 67, 180; 4/165, 329; 5/244; 6/32(2)

SOCIAL: entertains colleagues at Walthamstow, 1/279, 280–1; 2/78, 109; 6/102, 220; 8/423; joke chair, 1/280 & n. 1; wedding breakfast for servants, 1/293; EP his valentine, 2/36, 40; tells ghost story, 2/68; sees pre-coronation procession, 2/82–3; in chariot race, 2/110; steals tankard as joke, 2/169, 178; wedding anniversary, 3/21–2; pleasure trip to Downs, 4/296, 299; Christmas feast for colleagues and families, 5/354, 356, 357; 7/422; dines with King, 6/170; wears favour for Brouncker's birthday, 6/285; at Royal Society club meeting, 7/43; sees Lely's portraits of flagmen, 7/102; at Gresham College, 7/281; parish dinner, 8/218; at his house (Seething Lane): 1/242, 243, 294, 309, 323; 2/24, 59, 62, 64, 66, 73, 77, 79, 88, 95, 125,

131, 132, 139, 160, 191, 193, 219, 220, 223; 3/7–8, 10, 42, 44, 79, 112, 180, 181, 261; 4/23, 54, 171, 188, 203–4, 221, 230, 242; 5/216, 307; 6/14, 37, 39, 40, 49, 66, 150, 186, 190, 199; 7/66, 80, 220, 226, 252, 278, 280, 282, 283, 286, 300, 317, 326, 376, 387, 422–3; 8/113, 121, 151, 197, 216, 272, 316, 318, 382, 401; at P's house: 2/22–3, 53, 126, 195, 218–19; 4/39; 8/441; at houses of other associates: 2/51, 66, 71, 90, 222; 3/88, 270; 4/200, 341, 405; 5/15, 102, 335; 6/56, 187, 191, 222, 226, 245; 7/36, 278, 299; 8/3, 4, 77; at taverns: 1/230, 283–4, 296; 2/210, 211; 4/22, 25, 58, 101; 6/95, 145; 7/63, 181, 289–90; 8/27, 49, 108, 112–13, 133, 220; at Dolphin: 1/264, 292; 2/44, 54, 61, 65, 155, 175, 218; 3/42, 279; 5/308; at coffee houses: 2/109–10, 146; 4/4, 60, 77, 184, 237; 7/36; 8/405, 435

ALLUDED TO: 1/159; 3/8

~ his black servant, Mingo, 2/36, 61, 69; 4/51; 6/288; 8/123; foot boy, 3/77

BATTEN, William, barrister, son of Sir William: consulted by P, 4/193; house admired by P, 4/218; story of Sedley's pranks, 4/209; remarks on homosexuality at court, 4/210; recommends charm for colic, 6/17; disinherited, 8/580 & n. 3; social: 2/191; ~ his son [William], 4/165 & n. 2, 218

BATTERS, [Christopher], naval officer: recommended as gunner, 1/81; asks P to adopt daughter, 6/37–8; commands fireship, 7/412; drowned, 7/413 & n. 1; 8/39; kind to P and EP, 7/417

BATTERS, ——, wife of Christopher: recommends maid, 7/121; widowed, 7/417; remarried, 8/39; social: 5/238; 6/37; alluded to: 8/99; ~ her daughter, 6/37

BATTERSBY, [John], apothecary, Fenchurch St: medical advice, 2/132; 4/39; social: 2/170; 4/6, 15; 7/236; ~ his wife [Ann], 4/6

BATTERSBY, ——, a minister: lends P money, 2/190–1, 215; 3/215; social: 3/138, 277, 294; ~ his pretty wife, 2/215

BATTS, Capt. [George], naval officer: Coventry's high opinion, 4/196; dismissed by Albemarle, 9/5
BAWDSEY, Suff.: P recalls eating oysters, 1/104
BAXTER, [Nicholas], Equerry of the Great Horse to the Duke of York: shows P Royal Mews, 5/70–1 & n.
BAXTER, Richard, Puritan divine and author (1615–91): to preach farewell sermon, 1/251–2 & n.; preaches at St Anne, Blackfriars, 3/92; P buys *Evangelium Armatum*, 4/111 & n. 4
BAYLES (Bales), Tom, lawyer: 7/383
BAYLIE, [Francis], shipbuilder, Bristol: new ship, 9/235 & n. 1
BAYLIE, Maj. [Matthew], Ordnance officer: 9/468
BAYNARD'S CASTLE: King at, 1/178
BEACH, Richard (later kted), naval commander: highly regarded by Coventry, 4/196; by P, 4/432; in command of *Leopard*, ib.; ~ his attractive wife, ib.
BEALE, [Bartholomew], Auditor of Imprests in the Exchequer, and relative of P: attends funeral, 4/432; house in Salisbury Court, 5/7; accountancy methods, ib.; work as auditor of P's Tangier accounts, 6/15; 8/52, 344; 9/58, 202, 477, 478, 479; house and office in Holborn, 9/477, 478; P tips clerks, 9/479; social: 3/279; 6/68
BEALE, [Charles], Deputy-Clerk of the Patents: issues P's patent as Clerk of the Acts, 1/197, 198, 199
BEALE, [Francis], P's landlord in Axe Yard: P's rent, 1/87; alluded to, 1/249; ~ his wife [Alice], 1/249 & n. 1
BEALE, [Simon], shipbuilder: 1/158
BEALE, Simon, Trumpeter to the King: 1/319; 9/317 & n. 3
BEANE, ——, merchant: 4/10
BEARD (Bird), ——, Huntingdon carrier: 1/87; 2/5, 172
BEAR GARDEN, Southwark: P sees bull-baiting, 7/245–6 & n.; and prize-fights, 8/239 & n. 1, 429, 430; 9/516–17
BEAR GARDEN STAIRS: 8/239

BEAR'S QUAY, nr Billingsgate: P visits granaries, 5/179
BEAR STAIRS [P often refers to the jetty as 'The Bear' or 'The Bear at the Bridge Foot': for the tavern of that name, *see* Taverns etc.]: 1/242; 2/114; 5/197; 9/304, 313
BEAUCHAM(P) (Beecham), [James], goldsmith: sells P tankard, 1/292, 296; serves on jury, 4/171; P consults ib., 4/394
BEAUFORT, Duc de: *see* Vendôme, François de
BEAUMONT, [Joseph], Master of Peterhouse and Canon of Ely: preaches at Whitehall, 6/5 & n. 2
BECKART: *see* Bicker
BECKE, Betty, of Chelsea: reputation, 4/270, 281, 303, 388; affair with Sandwich, 4/270–1, 281, 282, 286, 292, 303, 379, 387–8; 5/173–4; lodging in Axe Yard, 4/392; visits Lady Sandwich, 5/179, 184; P's impressions, 5/179; alluded to: 9/455
BECKE, ——, P's cousin: borrows from P, 1/30; visits London, 2/103
BECKE, Mr ——, father of Betty: at Little Chelsea, 4/160; visits Lady Sandwich, 5/179; alluded to: 4/114
BECKE, Mrs ——, mother of Betty: Sandwich lodges at her house, 4/114, 160, 419; also, 5/179; house described, 4/117; banqueting house, ib., 4/160
[?BECKFORD, Peter; Jamaican planter]: 2/6 & n. 3
BECKFORD, Capt. [Thomas], slop-seller to the navy, kted 1677: refuses to undertake victualling, 6/255 & n. 1; gifts to P, 9/81–2, 405; social: 6/329
BECKINGTON, Som.: P visits, 9/232
BECKMAN, Capt. [Martin], military engineer, kted 1685: map of Tangier, 8/37 & n. 2
BEDELL, [Gabriel], bookseller: 1/85
BEDFORD, Lord: *see* Russell, F.
BEDFORD, Beds.: P's visit and comment, 9/224
BEDLAM: (district): bookseller, 5/14; (hospital): Roger P's children visit, 9/454 & n. 1
BEDNALL, Bednell Green: *see* Bethnal Green

BEE, [Cornelius], stationer: dispute over *Critici Sacri*, 9/259 & n. 2

BEECHAM: *see* Beauchamp

BEESTON, [William], actor: in ?*The damoiselles à la mode*, 9/307 & n. 1; reads part in *The Heiress*, 9/436 & n. 1

BELASYSE, Sir Henry, son of the 1st Baron Belasyse; M.P. Grimsby, Lincs, kted 1661: on *Naseby*, 1/130; arrested for manslaughter, 3/34 & n. 2; defence printed, 3/35–6 & n.; in brawl at Lord Oxford's, 4/136; killed in duel, 8/363–4 & n., 377, 384; alluded to: 8/454–5 & n.

BELASYSE (Bella(s)es, Bellassis), John, 1st Baron Belasyse, Governor of Tangier 1665–7; Lord-Lieutenant of E. Riding, Yorks., and Governor of Hull:

AS GOVERNOR OF TANGIER: P's low opinion, 7/130; 8/100, 155; appointed, 6/6–7 & n.; asks for P's support, 6/9; supported by committee, 6/18; instructed in duties, 6/22, 25; attempts to reorganise victualling, 6/105; concerned for own profit, 6/306; 7/99; complains of shortage of money, 7/4; returns from Tangier, 7/129; profits 7/130 & n. 2, 265; anxious to increase garrison, 7/130; bills, 7/174, 264; professes friendship for P, 7/185, 320; dislikes Creed, 7/185; meets Excise Commissioners, 7/190, 191; cheated by Vernatti, 7/264 & n. 2, 338; proposal for payment of garrison, 7/320, 321; accounts, 7/330, 338; 8/22, 32, 52–3, 63, 103; passed by committee, 9/199; examined by Exchequer, 9/202, 429, 529; profits in currency exchange, 9/205; tricks Cholmley, 8/45, 100, 127; criticised in committee, 8/61; to resign or be dismissed, 8/103, 111, 117, 127; resigns to become Captain of Pensioners, 8/154, 160; to purchase navy treasurership (rumour), 8/222; supports P in dispute over paymastership, 9/417; unspecified business, 6/13, 27; 7/164, 417, 423; 9/272

MILITARY CAREER IN YORKSHIRE: stories of Civil War, 6/30–1 & nn.; visits Hull to prepare garrison, 7/185 & n. 1, 193, 266; to go to Yorkshire on militia

business, 8/154–5 & n.; offers P help concerning prize ship, 8/345–6 & n.

POLITICAL/COURT NEWS FROM: 7/342–3; 8/74–5, 155; 9/462, 467–8, 472

PRIVATE AFFAIRS ETC.: lodging in Lincoln's Inn Fields, 6/9, 28; new house [? in Bloomsbury Square], 9/202 & n. 2; pictures, 9/202 & n. 4, 434–5; ~ his wife [Anne], 7/171; 9/537; his daughter, 7/171

BELASYSE, John, son of the 1st Baron Belasyse: arrested for manslaughter, 3/34 & n. 2; defence printed, 3/35–6 & n.

BELASYSE, Mary, Lady Fauconberg, (b. Cromwell),wife of the 2nd Viscount: 2/83 & n. 1; 4/181

BELASYSE, Thomas, 2nd Viscount Fauconberg: at theatre, 4/181

BELL, Capt.: *see* Ball, Capt. [?Naphthali]

BELL (Aunt Bell), Edith, sister of P's father: birth-date, 5/360 & n. 1; dies of plague, 6/314, 342; social: 1/205; 2/141, 172; 4/272; alluded to: 1/11

[BELL, William], Rector of St Sepulchre, Holborn: sermon, 5/347 & n. 4

BELL ALLEY, Westminster: plague deaths, 6/132

BELLAMY, [Robert and Thomas], relatives of P and petty-warrant victuallers: debt owed by Navy Board, 4/374 & n. 2; 6/54, 59, 111

BELLAS(S)ES, Bellassis: *see* Belasyse

BELLS, ringing of [*see also* Music: church]: for Monck, 1/52; arrival of Queen, 3/83; peace with Dutch, 8/399

BELLWOOD, Mr ——, formerly clerk to John Turner, lawyer: conceit, 9/463; news from, 9/465

BELL YARD, Lincoln's Inn Fields: gaming house, 2/211–12

BENCE, Ald. [John]: (untrue) story of wife's death of plague, 6/187

BENCE (Bens), ——, [? the foregoing]: 1/323; 2/220

BENDISH, ——, son of Sir Thomas, distant connection of P: 1/259 & n. 1

BENDY, Mrs ——: 5/130

BENIER (Beneere), Tom, barber: shaves P, 3/108, 233; theatre gossip from, 3/233

BENNET, Sir Henry, cr. Baron

[BERE], forest of, Hants.: 3/69

BERGEN, Norway: Teddeman's attack on Dutch fleet, 6/193, 195–6 & n., 197, 213, 218 & n. 2, 229; 7/13, 17, 55; official account, 7/335 & n. 2; parliamentary enquiry, 8/494, 538, 549–50

BERGEN-OP-ZOOM, Netherlands: 8/80

BERKELEY, Sir Charles, cr. Viscount Fitzharding 1663, Earl of Falmouth 1664: low reputation, 4/331; 6/71, 123–4 & n.; Coventry's praise, 9/294; appointed Keeper of Privy Purse, 3/227 & n. 2; rumoured promotion to marquessate, 5/232; ambitious to become Captain-General, 5/345; enjoys King's favour, 3/303, 4/25, 137, 138, 256; 5/168; services to King as pimp, 3/282; gifts from King, 5/40 & n. 3, 50, 56; relations with Lady Castlemaine, 3/289; 4/38; 5/21; Duke of York's confidence in, 4/138; enmity to Clarendon, 5/345; and Rupert, 6/12; patronage of Fitzgerald, 4/116; 5/344–5 & n.; of H. Brouncker, 6/59–60, 61–2; and of Creed, 6/71; at Tangier committee, 5/61–2; 6/58, 61; claims to have enjoyed favours of Anne Hyde, 1/315; 4/138; offers Elizabeth Pearse £300 p.a., 3/227; death at Battle of Lowestoft, 6/123–4 & n.; 9/294

BERKELEY, Sir Charles, son of the 9th Baron Berkeley: 8/338 & n. 1

BERKELEY, [Elizabeth], daughter of the 9th Baron: at court ball, 7/372; admired by Louis XIV, 8/338 & n. 1

BERKELEY (Barkley, Bartlet), George, 9th Baron Berkeley (of Berkeley Castle), cr. Earl 1679 [usually Lord George Berkeley]: dines with Manchester, 1/75; on *Royal Charles*, 1/156; entertains royal party at Durdans, 3/184 & n. 2; at meeting of E. India Company, 5/76; and of Royal Society, 8/243; house in Piccadilly, 6/39 & n. 2; experiment in cart design, 9/328–9 & n.; alluded to in error, 6/316 & n. 4; ~ his wife, 8/338

BERKELEY, Sir John, 1st Baron Berkeley of Stratton; Navy Commissioner 1660–4; Ordnance Commissioner 1664–70:

CHARACTER: 6/118, 316

AS NAVY COMMISSIONER: appointed, 1/191, n. 2; relations with Sandwich, 3/122; 6/54; and with Coventry, 6/16, 118; examines Creed's accounts, 4/216; defends Warren's mast contract, 4/421; disagrees with P about flag supplies, 5/178; hostile to Hayter, 6/118; demands prize-money for navy, 8/144; part in *Lindenbaum* case, 8/181, 231; supports Carkesse in dispute with Board, 8/189; sells his place to Sir T. Hervey, 8/294 & n. 1; also, 4/331; 5/301, 333; ~ his clerk, Davis, 4/408

HOUSES: Navy Office lodgings, 1/197; chamber at St James's, 5/220

MILITARY CAREER: appointed Ordnance Commissioner, 5/316 & n. 1; boasts of prowess, 6/38 & n. 1; attends Privy Council, 8/112; to take charge of Suffolk militia, 8/255; defends work on Medway fortifications, 8/496

AS STEWARD TO DUKE OF YORK'S HOUSEHOLD: boasts of profits, 4/331; and financial acumen, 8/149; arranges for Milles's appointment as chaplain, 8/241; dishonest handling of Duke's revenues, 9/319 & n. 1

TANGIER BUSINESS: appointed to committee, 6/7; criticises Povey's accounts, 6/13, 38, 79; 9/371; friendly to P, 6/69, 118; proposals for victualling, 6/171; attends meetings/discusses business, 6/58, 61; 9/272, 316

SOCIAL: 4/155, 340, 341, 487–8; 5/11

MISC.: praises Louis XIV's government, 4/416; and discipline of Commonwealth, 6/45; P consults about case in Lords, 5/110; serves on commission for repair of St Paul's, 5/220; attends meetings of Royal Fishery, 5/336; 6/53; views on taxation, 6/69; praises P's parliamentary speech, 9/105 ~ his wife, 8/487

BERKELEY, Mary, Countess of Falmouth, widow of the 1st Earl: her beauty, 7/178 & n. 2; to marry H. Jermyn (rumour), 8/366, 368; social: 9/468

BERKELEY, Capt. William, kted
1665, naval commander: emissary in
negotiations with Turks, 4/369–70 &
nn.; account of Algiers, 4/386;
accused of avoiding action in Battle of
Lowestoft, 6/129 & n. 5; serves under
Penn, 6/147; offers marriage to
Lawson's daughter, 6/150; illegally
takes prize-goods from Dutch E.
Indiaman, 6/263; portrait by Lely,
7/102 & n. 3; killed in action, 7/169;
body displayed in The Hague, ib. &
n. 3; alluded to: 6/132
BERKENHEAD (Birkenhead), Sir
John (1617–69): P consults about tax
assessment, 3/283 & n. 5
BERKSHIRE HOUSE, Westminster:
occupied by Clarendon (1666–7),
7/375 & n. 1; 8/93; and by Lady
Castlemaine, 9/190 & n. 3
BERMONDSEY: Jamaica House,
8/167
BERNARD, Sir John, son of the
following; succ. bt. 1666; lawyer, of
Brampton Park, Hunts.: family's
electoral interest in Huntingdon,
1/86–7 & n.; elected M.P., 1/87, n. 1,
99; at Brampton church, 3/220; at
Brampton manorial court, 4/309;
arbitrates in dispute about Robert P's
will, 3/265; influence in Brampton
resented, 8/220 & n. 2; ~ his wife
[Elizabeth], 3/220 & n. 1
BERNARD, Sir Robert, Bt, Serjeant-
at-law, Huntingdon: advises P about
Robert P's will, 2/137, 194–5, 205;
3/220–1; presides over Brampton
manorial court, 3/222–3; 4/308–9;
attends arbitration meeting, 3/276;
distrusted by Sandwich, 3/281; re-
tained by P in dispute with Thomas
P, 4/28; arranges disposal of P's
reversionary interest, 5/36, 44; arranges part-payment of Piggot's debt,
5/149, 158; dismissed from recorder-
ship of Huntingdon, 4/30, 62; interest
in Brampton manor, 4/343; ~ his
wife (Lady Digby), 2/137 & n. 5
BERNARD, William, son of Sir
Robert: social: 2/208, 210, 213–14
BERNARDISTON: see Barnardiston
BERNARD'S INN GATE: see Barnard's Inn Gate

BERTIE (Bertus), [Edward]: on *Nase-
by*, 1/134 & n. 5
BERTIE, Montague, 2nd Earl of
Lindsey (d. 1666): in brawl, 4/136
BERTIE (Bertus), [Robert]: on *Naseby*,
1/134 & n. 5
BEST, Mrs —— (Goody Best), of
Gravesend: 8/313
BETHEL, Capt. [?Slingsby], army
officer: given new commission, 8/265;
social: 2/13
BETHNAL GREEN: P visits, 4/200;
5/132; Sir W. Rider's house, 4/200;
7/272, 282, 283; story of blind beggar,
4/200 & n. 6; naval guns heard,
8/254
BETTERTON, Mary ('Ianthe') (b.
Saunderson); actress, wife of Thomas:
P admires in *The Bondman*, 3/58 &
n. 3; 5/224 & n. 2; *The Duchess of
Malfi*, 3/209 & n. 1; Orrery's *Henry V*,
5/240 & n. 3; and *The Rivals*, 5/335 &
n. 1; marriage to Betterton denied,
3/233 & n. 1; her voice, 5/34; acts in
The valiant Cid, 3/273 & n. 1;
'ordinary' performance in *Mustapha*,
6/73; alluded to: 7/347
BETTERTON (Baterton), Thomas,
actor and dramatist: P admires in
The Bondman, 2/47 & n. 2, 56, 207;
Hamlet, 2/161 & n. 3; 4/162; 9/296;
The Duchess of Malfi, 3/209 & n. 1;
Orrery's *Henry V*, 5/240 & n. 3;
9/256–7; *The Rivals*, 5/335 & n. 1;
and *The mad lover*, 9/453 & n. 2; 'the
best actor in the world', 2/207;
sobriety, 3/233; marriage to Mary
Saunderson denied, ib. & n. 1; in
The valiant Cid, 3/273; compared with
Harris, 4/239; in *Mustapha*, 6/73;
laughs in serious part, 8/421; illness,
8/482, 499, 521; 9/63; returns to stage,
9/256; alluded to: 7/347
BETTON(S), Mrs ——: 7/110
BEVERSHAM, [Robert], grocer, Fenchurch St: P orders sugar from,
6/149; dies of plague, 6/298; ~ his
pretty wife, 6/149, 298
BICKER, family of, Amsterdam:
quarrel with House of Orange, 6/147
& n. 1
BICKERSTAFFE [Charles, later kted],
clerk in the Privy Seal Office: in

Food]: in St James's Park, 2/157 & n. 1
GENERAL: aviaries, 4/85, 272; 7/182;
8/404
NAMED VARIETIES: blackbird: P's, 4/150,
152; canaries: P's, 2/23; 6/8; cocks
and cockfighting: 2/44; 4/427–8;
9/154; eagle: P's, 5/352; geese: 8/68;
hawks: presented to King by Russian
envoys, 3/268, 297; in Russia, 5/272;
hen: experiment on, 6/84; [mina-
bird]: presented to Duke of York,
5/131–2; nightingales: P hears near
Woolwich, 4/151; 5/130; [?ortolans]:
7/200; parrots: P's, 3/174; also, 2/69;
3/105; 6/60; pigeons: P's at Axe Yard,
1/45, 189; Dr Williams's, 2/176; in
Russia, 5/272; burnt in Fire, 7/268;
sparrow (tame): 7/138; 9/225; starling:
once the King's, 9/99, 208, 209;
swallows: hibernation of, 4/412–13 &
n.; turtle-doves: EP's, 1/232; water-
fowl: in St James's Park, 2/157; 3/47;
8/68
BIRKENHEAD: *see* Berkenhead
BIRTHDAYS: P's, 1/65; 2/42; 3/34;
4/55; 5/62; 6/42; 7/53; 8/77; 9/457;
others', 2/142; 6/285
BISCAY, Bay of: 3/78
BISHOP, Sir 'Edward', *recte* Richard,
Serjeant-at-Arms: 8/564
BISHOPSGATE: Quaker meeting,
5/285
BISHOPSGATE ST [*see also* St
Botolph; Taverns etc.: Bull; Great
(Old) James]: harpsichord maker,
2/40, 44; Fire, 7/277–8; house blown
up, 8/119; terminus for Cambridge
coaches, 9/207, 209, 213, 306; alluded
to: 2/26; 7/368
BISHOP'S STORTFORD (Stafford),
Herts.: P at, 8/466–7; 9/209, 213;
Reindeer inn, 8/466–7; 9/209
BLACKBORNE (Blackeburne), [Rob-
ert], Commonwealth Admiralty offi-
cial:
CHRON. SERIES: fears restoration of
King, 1/91; issues P's warrant as
secretary to fleet, 1/94; reports
Restoration imminent, 1/103; advises
P on duties, 1/193; now drinks
healths, 1/263; dealings with P about
Hewer, 2/34, 97; 4/323, 353, 358, 367,
371–2; puritan views, 4/372–7 & nn.;

distrusted by Carteret, 3/5; informs
P of corruption in Navy Treasury,
3/28; sends official papers to Navy
Office, 3/37; low opinion of Penn,
4/375; secretary to E. India Company, 9/410; also, 1/96; 9/485
SOCIAL: 1/173, 174, 211, 213, 268, 301,
303; 2/97
ALLUDED TO: 1/27, 59, 81, 83, 84
~ his wife, 1/213, 215, 217, 218, 227,
268; her kinswoman, 1/227; his
brother, 1/303
BLACKBURY, [Peter], timber merchant: P visits yard, 4/176; consults
about masts, 4/261; also, 3/165; 6/195
BLACKFRIARS: St Anne's Church,
3/92 & n. 1; Fire ruins, 8/6; glasshouse,
9/457 & n. 2
BLACKFRIARS [Stairs]: 1/229
BLACKFRIARS THEATRE: *see*
Theatres
BLACKHEATH: P drives chariot,
6/213
[BLACK HEATH, Wilts.]: ?9/228 &
n. 4
BLACK LION (mercer's shop), Westminster: 9/454
BLACKE: *see* Blake
BLACKMAN, Capt. [James], Woolwich: 5/190–1 & n.
BLACKWALL DOCKYARD: P
visits, 5/202; 7/126, 138; 8/84, 124;
new docks, 2/14 & n. 2; petrified
trees, 6/236–7 & n.; Navy Board
plans mast-dock, 5/270; 6/96; prize-
goods to be stored, 6/236; soldiers
embark from, 7/141(3); ships repair-
ing, 8/124, 135; alluded to: 1/280;
3/156
BLAGGE (Blake), [Margaret], Maid of
Honour to the Duchess of York:
9/468 & n. 5
BLAGRAVE, [Thomas], court musician: sobriety, 7/128; P redeems lute
from, 1/91; plays flageolet, 1/180;
pew in Whitehall chapel, 1/313;
3/42; sings, 3/67–8; 5/126, 229, 236,
242; tells P of chapel rules, 5/267;
performance disparaged, 8/529–30;
house, 3/67; 5/107, 126, 229, 242;
recommends Tom Edwards, 5/234;
alluded to: 5/242; ~ his wife, 5/242;
his niece: sings, 3/67–8; 5/126, 242;

proposed as EP's companion, 5/107, 224, 229(2), 230, 236, 242

BLAKE (Blacke), Gen. Robert, military and naval commander (d. 1657): courage, 5/169 & n. 3

BLAKE, Capt. Robert, naval officer (d. 1661): made captain of *Worcester*, 1/109; given command of squadron, 1/119 & n. 3; death and burial, 2/73, 74; also, 1/324; 2/15, 16, 17

BLANCH APPLETON (Blanche Chapiton), Aldgate: 5/18

BLAND, John, merchant, first Mayor of Tangier: P's opinion, 5/266; 9/430; writings on trade and Tangier, 3/157–8 & n.; informs P about mercantile practices, 3/255; 4/10; attends Tangier committee, 4/21, 23; 5/105; foreign news from, 4/198 & n. 2; P acts for in freightage dispute, 4/398, 404 & n. 2, 424, 426; 5/19, 23, 26, 36, 139; provides pieces-of-eight for Tangier, 5/15, 226; in dispute about Portuguese customs dues, 5/43 & n. 2; interest in Tangier victualling, 5/212; anxious for post there, 5/226; at Tangier, 5/265, 270, 287–8, 291; 7/109; dispute with Norwood, 9/392 & n. 1, 430–1 & n.; proposals for civil government of Tangier, 9/430–1; unspecified business, 3/300; 4/13, 14, 18, 198; 5/232; social: 3/188; 4/41, 81, 85, 242; 5/265, 270; ~ his son [Giles], 6/65; his kinswoman: musical, 4/242; 6/28

BLAND, [Sarah], wife of John: her grasp of business, 3/300 & n. 2; 5/266; goes to Tangier, 6/28, 42, 43, 44

BLAND, 'one': 9/175

BLAND, ——, waterman: 9/313

BLANQUEFORT (Blancford, Blancfort, Blanfort): *see* Duras

BLAYNEY, Edward, 3rd Baron Blayney (d. 1669): commends Montaigne, 9/120

BLAYNEY, [Robert], secretary to Lord Ashley: 9/152

BLAYTON (Payton), [Thomas]: accompanies P to Audley End and Cambridge, 1/66, 68, 69, 71; gift to P on appointment as purser, ?6/190–1; social: 1/210

BLEAU: *see* Balue

BLENKINSOP, ——: 3/44

BLINKEHORNE, ——, miller, nr Wisbech, Cambs.: 4/311–12

BLIRTON: *see* Blurton

BLONDEAU, [Pierre], Engineer to the Mint (d. 1672): to introduce improvements, 2/38–9 & n.; stamps for new coinage, 3/265 & n. 2; secret process, 4/70, 147

BLOUNT (Blunt), Sir [Henry], traveller: talks about Egypt etc., 5/274 & n. 1

BLOUNT (Blunt), Col. [Thomas], inventor, Fellow of the Royal Society, of Wricklemarsh, Kent: experiments with chariot design, 6/94 & n. 2, 213; 7/20 & n. 2; house and garden, 6/94 & n. 3

BLOW (Blaeu), John, composer (d. 1708): 8/393–4 & n.

BLOWBLADDER (Blowblather) St: 8/371

BLOYS: *see* Boys, Sir J.

BLUDWORTH (Bluddell), Sir Thomas, Lord Mayor 1665–6: appointed sheriff, 3/162; presses seamen, 7/187, 190; incompetence, 7/190, 269(2), 280 & n. 4, 393 & n. 2

BLUNT: *see* Blount

BLURTON (Blirton), Mr ——: tells bawdy anecdote, 2/43; social: 2/125, 193; 3/48

BOATE, Mrs ——: 2/54

BOCKET (BOCHETT), Mrs ——: courted by Dr Child, 1/301 & n. 3; at Sandwich's 1/309; ~ her dirty children, 8/193

BODDILY, Bodilaw: *see* Badiley

BODHAM, [William], Clerk of the Ropeyard, Woolwich: Penn's clerk, 3/69, 75; clerk to Chatham Chest, 5/122; appointment to Woolwich, 5/231; complains of its cost, 5/231, 248; his stores, 5/325; story of Tom of the Wood, 8/270; inspects batteries with P, 8/284; alluded to: 3/156; 6/189

BODVILE (Brodvill), [John]: case in Lords, 5/140 & n. 1

BOEVE (Bovy), [James], merchant: 9/206 & n. 6

BOIS: *see* Boys

BOIS-LE-DUC (The Boysse), Netherlands: 8/80

BOLES: *see* Bowles, [J.]

BOLLEN, [James], Groom of the Privy Chamber: 2/234 & n. 2

BOLTELE: *see* Bulteel

BOLTON, [Richard], cornet: preaches mock-sermon, 9/554 & n. 3

BOLTON, Sir William, Lord Mayor 1666–7: sworn in, 7/346 & n. 2; suspended from Court of Aldermen, 8/562 & n. 1

BOMBAY (Bombaim): naval expedition to, 4/139 & n. 2, 204 & n. 1, 210, 291–2, 299; decay of Dutch trade, 4/139; English government deceived about, 4/299 & n. 2

BOND, [Henry], teacher of mathematics (d. 1678): instructs P on timber measurement, 3/105 & n. 2; 5/115

BOND, Sir Thomas, Bt, Comptroller of the Household to the Queen-Mother (d. 1685): 1/322 & n. 3

BONFIRES: in celebration of: Monck's action against Rump ('the Burning of the Rump'), 1/52 & n. 4, 53; 3/95; 7/136; readmission of secluded M.P.s, 1/63; Restoration, 1/89, 122, 163; 7/136; arrival of Henrietta Maria, 1/281–2; Gunpowder Plot, 1/283; 7/358; coronation, 2/87, 88; Queen's arrival, 3/83, 87; King's birthday, 3/95; anniversary of the coronation, 4/109; 7/109; 9/172; Queen's birthday, 4/382; Battle of Lowestoft, 6/123 (at Navy Office); 6/129 (by Dutch at Dunkirk); Four Days Fight, 7/152, 344; Holmes's attack on Dutch in Vlie, 7/249; P's comments: bonfires few for King's birthday, 3/95; few in city, 7/136, 358; none lit for peace, 8/399

BOOKBINDER, P's [*see also* Books]: 5/199; 9/32

BOOKER, [John], astrologer (d. 1667): criticises Lilly, 1/274 & n. 2

BOOKS [*see also* Booksellers (P); Languages; Musical Compositions]:
P's COLLECTION:
  GENERAL: history, vol. i, pp. xxxix, lxxi–lxxiv; removed from Sandwich's lodgings to Axe Yard, 1/59; French books bequeathed to EP, 1/90; collection moved to Seething Lane

and rearranged, 1/232, 241, 268, 302; dusted, 5/358; put in order, 7/37, 311, 316, 322; 9/24(2); removed to and from Deptford in Fire, 7/?273, ?276, ?278, ?285, 290–1; missing books found, 7/290 & n. 3, 292; to be limited to two bookcases, 9/18, 48; shown to guests, 9/411, 424; P consults Naudé's book on collecting, 6/252 & n. 1; books acquired from Holland, 1/140 & nn., 260; and France, 9/431–2 & n.

  BINDING [*see also* Nott, [W.]; and Richardson, [W.]: ordered, 5/199 & n. 2; 7/41; to be made uniforms, 6/14, 24, 31–2, 33; gilded, 7/243, 266, 303–4, 306, 307, 311; of maps, 5/55; of plays, 7/104–5; books bought ready bound, 1/140 & nn., 260; cost, 1/281; 4/240; 6/28; 9/166

  BOOKCASES (presses): made by Simpson, 7/214 & n. 4, 242, 243; delivered, 7/251, 252, 258

  CATALOGUES: books numbered and listed, 7/412 & n. 2, 416, 417, 419, 421; 8/8, 40(2), 45; 'titled', 9/49 & n. 2, 72; catalogued, 9/72, 559–60

  OTHER COLLECTIONS: Earl of Peterborough's, 4/270; Wisbech parish, 4/311 & n. 3; Earl of Arundel's, 8/6–7 & n.; Capuchin friary's, 8/26; Fouquet's, 9/173 & n. 3; Clarendon's, 9/480

  BOOKS AND PAMPHLETS MENTIONED IN THE TEXT [a single asterisk denotes that P read or 'looked over' a book, or part of a book; a second that he comments on it]:
  [ALLESTRY, R.], *The causes of the decay of Christian piety*: 9/10–11 & n. 2

  ALSTED, J. H., *Encyclopaedia*: 1/275 & n. 4

  ARETINO, PIETRO: 4/136–7 & n.

  ARISTOTLE: 4/267(2)

  [ASHLEY, A., *The mariner's mirrour*]: 4/240 & n. 1

  BACON, F., *Sermones Fideles (Faber Fortunae)*: 2/102** & n. 1; 5/39**; 7/72**, 129**, 242**, 346; *Novum Organum*: 1/140 & n. 4

  BARCLAY, J., *Argenis*: 1/231 & n. 1; 4/369*

  BARTAS, DU (trans. Sylvester), *Divine weekes and workes*: 3/247** & n. 1

[RHODES, R.], *Flora's Vagaries*: 8/463* & n. 5

RIDLEY, SIR T., *A view of the civile and ecclesiasticall law*: 7/112** & n. 2; 119*, 126*

ROSINUS, J., *Antiquitatum romanorum corpus absolutissimum ex variis scriptoribus collect*: 1/243 & n. 3

RUSHWORTH, J., *Historical Collections*: 4/395 & n. 1, 402*, 406*, 408*, 411*, 417** & n. 1, 421*, 434**, 435**; 6/10* & n. 3

RYCAUT, P., [*The present state of the Ottoman empire*]: 8/121 & n. 2, 156 & n. 2, 159**, 166*, 167**, 175**, 199**

SANDERSON, W., [*A complete history of the life and reign of King Charles . . .*]: 1/132 & n. 4

[SANDERUS, A.], *Flandria Illustrata*: 5/38* & n. 6

[SANTOS, F. DE LOS, *Descripcion breve del monasterio de S. Lorenzo el real del Escorial . . .*]: 9/353 & n. 1

SCAPULA, J., *Lexicon Graeco-Latinum*: 5/198 & n. 3, 199, 200

[SCARRON, P.], *The fruitlesse praecaution*: 1/135* & n. 2, 266**, 267*

SCOBELL, H., *Collection of acts and ordinances . . . made in the parliament . . .*: 4/395 & n. 2, 402

SCOT, R., [*The discovery of witchcraft*]: 8/383 & n. 2

[SCUDÉRI, MME DE], *Artamène ou le Grand Cyrus*: 1/312 & n. 2; 7/122; 8/225*; *Ibrahim, ou L'Illustre Bassa*: 9/89 & n. 2, 247(2)*

The second address from the gentlemen of the county of Northampton to his Excellency the Lord Generall Monck: 1/73 & n. 1

[SEDEÑO, J.], *Summa de varones illustres*: 9/173 & n. 3

SELDEN, J., *Mare Clausum*: 2/223 & n. 3, 226*, 227*, 234* & n. 1, 235*, 236*, 237*, 238*; 3/6* & n. 1; 4/105 & n. 2, 107 & n. 3

SENECA: 8/507

SHAKESPEARE, *Plays*: 4/410 & n. 4; 5/198 & n. 4, 199, 200; *Hamlet*, 5/320 & n. 4; *Henry IV* part 1: 1/325 & n. 1; *Othello*: 7/255**

SIDNEY, SIR P., [*Arcadia*]: 6/2* & n. 3

?[SMITH, J.], *The sea-man's grammar*: 2/53** & n. 4

SORBIÈRE, S.-J., [*Relation d'un voyage en Angleterre . . .*]: 5/297 & n. 2; 9/206*

[?SOUTHLAND, T.], *Love a la mode*: 4/235* & n. 2

SPEED, J., [his '*geography*' (? *A prospect of the most famous parts of the world*)]: 1/254* & n. 5; [*History of Great Britaine*]: 7/290 & n. 3; 8/91**, 387 & n. 3, 498; [*The theatre of the empire of Great Britaine*]: 3/114* & n. 4

SPELMAN, SIR H., [*Glossarium Archailogicum*]: 5/190 & n. 2, 198, 199, 200

SPENCER, J., [*A discourse concerning prodigies*]: 5/165** & n. 1

SPRAT, T., *History of the Royal Society of London*: 8/380 & n. 1, 387

STEPHENS/STEPHANUS: *see* Estienne

STILLINGFLEET, E., *Origines Sacrae*: 6/297** & n. 1; [*A rational account of the grounds of the Protestant religion*]: 7/336** & n. 2

STOW, J., *Survey of London*: 4/410 & n. 4

[STUBBE, E.], *Fraus Honesta*: 4/218 & n. 1

SUCKLING, SIR J., *Aglaura*: 5/263** & n. 1

SWAN, W., *The unlawfull use of lawfull things* (? not published): 2/235 & n. 2

[TATHAM, J.], *The Rump, or The mirror of the late times*: 1/289** & n. 2

TAYLOR, J., [Εὐμβολον Θεολογικόν: or *A collection of polemical discourses*]: 6/312* & n. 3

TAYLOR, S., [*A history of gavelkind*]: 1/63 & n. 4; *The Serenade, or Disappointment* (MS.): 9/546-7 & n.

TESAURO, E., *Patriarchae, sive Christi servatoris genealogica, per mundi, aetates traducta*: 2/22 & n. 3

[*Le testament du defunt Cardinal Jul. Mazarini, duc de Nivernois, premier ministre du roi de France*]: 4/411-12 & n.

[*To his excellency General Monck. A letter from the gentleman of Devon in answer to his Lordships of January 23 . . .*]: 1/34* & n. 3

[*A true and perfect narrative of the great*

BOREMAN, Dr [Robert], Rector of St Giles-in-the-Fields: sermon, 8/99

BOREMAN, Sir William, Clerk Comptroller of the Household: consulted about mast-dock, 5/353; measures against plague, 6/211 & n. 5; social: 6/208

BORFETT (Burfett), [Samuel], chaplain to Sandwich: social: 1/210, 285; 8/99

BOSCAWEN, [Edward], M.P. Cornwall: examines Navy Board accounts, 7/305 & n. 2; praises P's parliamentary speech, 9/109

BOSSE, [?A.], painter: copy of P's portrait, 9/261 & n. 4

BOSTOCK, ——, formerly clerk in the Exchequer: social: ?1/319; 2/162-3; 5/30

BOSTON, —— [?the foregoing]: 1/319

BOTELER: see Butler

BOTTOMRY (bummary): risky investment, 4/398 & n. 2; fraudulent claim concerning, 4/401 & n. 3

BOUGHTON, Northants.: Sandwich at, 4/307-8

BOULOGNE (Bullen, Bulloigne): storm near, 3/143; Dutch fleet off, 7/279, 281; alluded to: 8/380 & n. 2

[BOURBON, Henri de, Duc de Verneuil], French ambassador-extra-ordinary Apr.-Dec. 1665: arrives incognito, 6/76 & n. 1

BOURBON-L'ARCHAMBAULT (Bourbon): Henrietta-Maria takes waters, 6/142 & n. 3

BOURNE, Maj. [Nehemiah], Navy Commissioner 1653-60: 1/197 & n. 1

BOVY: see Boeve

BOW: P/EP visit(s), 1/280; 5/175; 7/113, 117, 120, 124, 151, 208, 240; 8/326, 377, 443, 447; 9/470, 528, 546; dancing meeting, 7/238; girls' school, 8/448, 451; King's Head, 3/169; Queen's Head, 8/112

BOW CHURCH: see St Mary-le-Bow

BOWCOCKE (Brecocke), [Richard], landlord of the Swan, Stevenage: 'the best Host I know', 8/475 & n. 1

BOWES, Sir Jerome, envoy to Muscovy 1583-4: anecdotes of, 3/188-9 & n.

BOWES (? Bewes), ——, shopkeeper: 3/52

BOWLES (Boles), [John], grocer: death and burial, 7/256; ~ ?his wife, 5/166; 7/394

BOWLES, John, of Brampton, servant to Sandwich: accompanies P to London, 8/474-5; explains hunting terms, 8/475; social: 2/105, 108, 138, 183; 8/477, 478, 481; 9/224

BOWLING ALLEY, Westminster: 7/123 & n. 3

BOWMAN, Mr —— [?Edward or Francis, Gentlemen-Ushers to the King]: 2/80 & n. 2

BOWRY, Capt. [John]: ship hired, 4/52-3 & n.

BOW ST: alluded to: 6/1; 9/62

BOWYER, [Elizabeth], wife of Robert: her remedy for cold, 1/85; social: 1/317; 2/21, 113; 3/61; alluded to: 1/166

BOWYER, Mary, daughter of Robert: sends maid to EP, 2/218 & n. 3

BOWYER, [Robert], ('father Bowyer') Usher of the Receipt in the Exchequer: EP stays with at Huntsmoor during P's absence in Holland, 1/84, 85, 131, 166; drowned in riding accident, 5/34; social: 1/229, 286; 2/21, 49, 86, 87, 113, 215, 241; 3/65; alluded to: 1/249, 251, 314, 323; ~ his daughters, 1/317; 2/113; 3/61; 258

BOWYER, William, son of Robert; doorkeeper in the Exchequer: escorts EP to Huntsmoor, 1/89; her valentine, 3/29; simple discourse, 3/145, 299; youthful appearance, 6/235; social: 1/88, 176, 192, 201, 244, 320; 2/232; 3/174; 5/262; alluded to: 1/209; 5/34

BOWYER, [William], tar merchant: supplies, 4/182, 187; gift, 4/182

BOYLE, Lady Anne: see Mountagu, Anne, wife of Edward, 2nd Earl of Sandwich

BOYLE, Lady Henrietta: see Hyde, Lady Henrietta, wife of Laurence Hyde

BOYLE, Richard, succ. as 2nd Earl of Cork 1643; cr. Earl of Burlington 1664: travels to Flushing, 1/?106,

?112; as Lord Treasurer of Ireland, 8/301 & n. 1; house in Piccadilly, 9/321 & n. 1; social: 8/498; 9/131 ~ his wife [Elizabeth]: 8/498; 9/322

BOYLE, Richard, son of the foregoing: killed in action, 6/122

BOYLE, Robert, scientist [see also Books]: at Royal Society, 6/36 & n. 5; recommends oculist, 9/248

BOYLE, Roger, Baron Broghill, cr. Earl of Orrery 1660, politician and dramatist [see also Plays]: influence with Richard Cromwell, 1/180; and King, 6/301 & n. 2; supports Sandwich, 6/301; 7/54; opposes Ormond, 9/185; as dramatist, 9/522; also, 1/260; 9/276

BOYLE, ——, [?Charles or Richard]: 1/106 & n. 3, 112

BOYNTON, [Katherine], Maid of Honour to the Queen: seasick, 5/306

BOYS (Bloys), Sir John: on *Naseby*, 1/106 & n. 4; supports King, 1/112 & n. 3; carries letters between King and Sandwich, 1/125; also, 1/136

BOYS, [John], wholesaler at the Three Crowns, Cheapside: marriage, 3/163; house burnt in Fire, 5/247–8; ~ his wife: 3/163

BRADFORD, [Martha], housekeeper, Hill House, Chatham 1661–9: P complains to about accommodation, 4/225 & n. 3

BRADLY, ——: at Graveley manorial court, 2/182

BRADSHAW, [John], regicide (d. 1659): Westminster lodgings, 1/13 & n. 4; body exhumed and displayed, 1/309; 2/24, 27, 31

BRAEMS (Brames, Breames), Sir Arnold, merchant: social: 1/293, 323; 2/192; 9/57

[BRAGG, Thomas], chaplain, Portsmouth dockyard: sermon 'full of nonsense and false Latin', 3/72 & n. 1

BRAHAM (Brames, Breame), Sir Richard, merchant: 3/43

BRAHE, Nils Nillsson, Graf, Swedish ambassador-extraordinary 1661: in dispute about striking flag, 2/212 & n. 3; 3/14; state entry, 2/187, 188, 189

BRA(I)NFORD: see Brentford

BRAMES, Breame(s): see Braems/ Braham

BRAMPTON, Hunts. [see also Ball, Sir P.; Barton, [J.]; Bernard, Sir R.; Day, [J.]; Dickinford, ——; Gorham, [M.]; Pepys, Robert; Pigott, [R.]; Prior, ——; Stankes, W.; Taylor, ——]:

P'S ESTATE [for his inheritance from Robert P and the subsequent disputes, see principally Pepys, R.; Trice, T.]: attempts to buy Norbury's house and land, 2/124 & n. 5; fails to unite scattered holdings, 8/282–3; income, 4/119 & n. 2, 121; 5/36, 44, 354, 360; his 'Brampton book', 3/48; 'Brampton papers', 4/121, 122; 5/31, 39, 195(3); 8/264

P'S HOUSE: alterations, 2/182–3; 3/94, 97, 219; Sandwich's plans, 3/206, 210; further alterations planned, 8/237, 471; parlour, 8/469; garden and summer-houses, ib.; P sends gold to in Medway crisis, 8/263–4, 272, 273; recovers gold, 8/472–5, 539; thinks of retiring to, 7/315, 332; 8/237, 469; 9/293; to be let, 9/212; also, 7/340

MANOR: sold to Sandwich, 3/102, 176; also, 4/343

MANORIAL COURT: P attends, 3/222, 223; 4/308–9; 5/281, 282, 298; his speech at, 4/308–9; also, 3/48, 199, 206, 208, 209–10, 211, 213, 219, 221; 4/300, 303, 305

PLACES IN: Bull inn, 4/309; church [St Mary's], 3/220; Green, 8/471; Portholme meadow, 2/135; 5/158; 9/210; river, 4/312; woods, ib.

P'S VISITS [for visits by other members of family, see under names]: 2/133–9, 180–4; 3/216–25; 4/307–14; 5/294–9; 8/453, 457, 460, 464, 465–75; 9/209–12, 223, 224; cost, 8/479; also, 3/127

MISC.: storm, 3/35, 42; parish feast, 3/144; 4/237

BRAYBROOKE, Robert, Bishop of London 1381–1404: tomb etc., 7/367–8 & n.

BREAD ST: 4/181

BRECOCKE: see Bowcocke

BREDA, Netherlands: Charles II at, 1/117; alluded to: 1/129

BREDA, DECLARATION OF: read

in Parliament, 1/118 & n. 2, 122; to Sandwich's Council of War, 1/123–4 & n.; welcomed by fleet, 1/124, 131; invoked by King, 4/58 & n. 3; alluded to: 1/127

BREDA, PEACE OF: see War, Second Dutch

BREDHEMSON: see Brighton

BREKINGTON: see Beckington

BRENTFORD (Branford, Brainford), Mdx: P visits Povey's house, 6/198, 214, 266, 267; market day, 1/20; plague, 6/225; church [St Lawrence], 6/199 & n. 1; inns, 6/199 & n. 1; 7/26; alluded to: 6/216; 7/54; 9/509

BRENTWOOD (Burntwood), Essex: plague at, 6/181

BRERETON, William, 3rd Baron Brereton: appointed to Brooke House Committee, 8/577 & n. 3; his manner, 9/10 & n. 1; plays organ, 9/11

BREST: French troops at, 8/1 & n. 3; engravings, 9/437

BRETT, Sir Edward, soldier: 1/264

BRETTON (Britton), Dr [Robert], Vicar of Deptford: P's opinion, 4/175; 6/107; preaches to Trinity House, 4/185; 5/172; 6/107

BREVINT (Brevin), Daniel, Canon of Durham (d. 1695): 3/85 & n. 1

BREWER, Capt. [William], painter: 4/15, 187

BREWER'S YARD, Westminster: 1/175; 5/212

BRIAN, Mr ———: 3/217

BRIDE LANE, Westminster: see Taverns etc.: Black Spread Eagle

BRIDEWELL [see also New Bridewell]: the house of correction, ?1/167; pressed men in, 7/187, 190, 191; building described, 8/6; the precinct: ?1/167; 2/116

BRIDGEMAN, John, Bishop of Chester 1619–52: armorial glass, 3/254 & n. 3

BRIDGEMAN, Sir Orlando, Lord Chief Baron of the Exchequer 1660; Lord Chief Justice of Common Pleas 1660–7; Lord Keeper 1667–72: charge to jury at regicides' trial, 1/263 & n. 2; appointed Lord Keeper, 8/410–11 & n.; popularity, 8/410; 9/375; P admires, 8/421; speech to Parliament,

8/476 & n. 2, 480 & n. 2; opinion on charge against Clarendon, 8/541; member of Cabal, 8/585; 9/425; friendly with Coventry, 9/41; opposes dissolution of Parliament, 9/360, 375; attempts reorganisation of Navy Board, 9/290, 291–2 & n., 321, 503, 550; illness, 9/425 & n. 4; his part in Coventry's petition for release, 9/475, 491; also, 8/412; 9/106; social: 9/352; alluded to: 3/254

BRIDGES, [Richard], linen-draper, Cornhill: calico contract, 5/292 & n. 1, 295, 351

BRIDGES, Sir Toby, soldier: praised by Albemarle, 5/310 & n. 1

BRIDGEWATER, Lord: see Egerton

BRIEFS (Chancery): frequency, 2/128 & n. 3

BRIGDEN, Dick, haberdasher, Fleet St: sells sword to P, 1/94; 2/24, 28; made captain of auxiliaries 2/24; house damaged in storm, 3/32; social: 3/165

BRIGGS, [Timothy], scrivener: gift to P, 6/83, 100, 101

BRIGHAM, [Thomas], royal coach-maker: complains of Duchess of Albemarle, 1/181 & n. 4

BRIGHTON (Bredhemson, Bright-hemson), Sussex: Charles II's escape from (1651), 1/156 & n. 1; 8/74; alluded to: 7/288 & n. 2

BRISBANE (Brisband, Brisbanke), [John], naval official: P admires, 6/176–7; talks of spells etc., 6/177–8; takes P to gambling at court, 9/2–3, 4; news from: 9/66, 86, 179; social: 6/179, 182; 7/326, 388; 8/164; 9/35, 87, 126, 188; alluded to: 7/387

BRISTOL, Earl of: see Digby

BRISTOL (Bristow), Som.: story of mayor, 3/180; Rupert surrenders (1645), 5/170 & n. 2; 6/30; ships built, 8/47 & n., 270 & n. 4; 9/235 & n. 1; P and family visit, 9/234–6 & nn.; dog-carts, 9/234 & n. 4; Bristol milk, 9/235–6 & n.; Cross, 9/236 & n. 3; Custom House, 9/235 & n. 3; Horse Shoe Inn, 9/234 & n. 2, 236; Marsh St, 9/235; Quay, 9/235; Sun Inn, 9/234 & n. 6, 235; Tolzey, 9/236 & n. 2; Three Cranes tavern, 9/234 & n. 5

BRITTON: see Bretton

BROAD ST [see also African House; Navy Treasury; Taverns etc.: Glasshouse]: dancing meeting, 1/253; Plague, 6/128; Fire, 7/289

BRODRICK, Sir Allen, M.P. Orford, Suff.: witty, 6/313; drunken speech in parliament, 7/416 & n. 3

BRODVILL: see Bodvile

BROGHILL, Lord: see Boyle, Roger

BROGRAVE, ——: 2/31

BROMBRIGE: see Bromwich

BROME (Broome), Alexander, poet: wit and conceit, 4/100 & n. 3; death, 7/193; social: 7/12 & n. 1

[BROME, ——], daughter of [Richard Brome], landlord of the Ship tavern, Billiter Lane: admired by P, 8/156, 345, 443; 9/51, 284, 485–6; marriage, 8/345, 346

BROMFIELD, Mary: see Harman

[BROMFIELD, Thomas], Common Councilman: 1/24 & n. 6

BROMWICH (Brombrige), [Francis], Capt.: murdered, 9/412 & n. 2

[BROOKE, Francis]: history of Abingdon hospital, 9/227 & n. 3

BROOKE, Lord: see Greville

BROOKE(S), Sir Robert, M.P. Aldeburgh, Suff.: ability, 8/493, 572; house at Wanstead, 6/102 & n. 4; 8/172, 197; appoints Milles rector, 8/241 & n. 1; proposes recall of Sandwich, 8/486; chairman of Committee on Miscarriages, 8/493, 537–8, 546, 560; 9/88, 142; praises P's parliamentary speech, 9/110; also, 8/540, 544, 572

BROOKE HOUSE, Holborn: Commission of Accounts at, 8/559 & n. 2; 9/254, 394 & n. 2, 562

[BROOKE HOUSE COMMITTEE]: see Brooke House, Holborn; Parliament (the Cavalier): seventh session

BROOKES, Capt. [John], Master-Attendant Chatham: grounds ship, 8/310 & n. 1; gives evidence against Commissioner Pett, 8/461 & n. 3; suspended, 9/258 & n. 3

BROOME: see Brome, A.

BROUNCKER (Brunkard), Henry, Groom of the Bedchamber to the Duke of York; M.P. New Romney, Kent, 1665–8; succ. as 3rd Viscount

1684: character, 8/69 & n. 3, 406 & n. 4; claims treasurership of Tangier, 6/59–60 & n., 61; pimp to Duke of York, 7/159; 8/286; supports Carkesse against Navy Board, 8/169, 178; dismissed by Duke of York, 8/406, 416, 447; misconduct at Battle of Lowestoft, 8/489–90 & n., 491–2; blamed by Committee on Miscarriages, 9/142; flees to France, 9/169 & n. 2, 170; expelled and impeached by Commons, 9/170; appeals to King, 9/178; returns to court, 9/348; duel, 9/470 & n. 1

BROUNCKER, Sir William, 1st Viscount Brouncker (d. 1645): anecdote of, 8/126 & n. 1

BROUNCKER (Brunkard, Brunker (d)), William, 2nd Viscount, Navy Commissioner:

CHARACTER: 5/341; 6/193; 7/96–7, 237; 8/311, 312;

AS NAVY COMMISSIONER:

GENERAL: appointment, 5/324 & n. 3, 341; ignorant of naval affairs, 5/341; instructed by P, 5/343; studies ship's drawing, 6/7; chairs Board, 9/365; neglects office for mathematics, 9/501; clerks, 8/104

CHRON. SERIES: visits fleet, 6/228; in charge of Dutch prize goods, 6/234, 236, 237, 242, 262, 263, 280, 300; 8/446; complains of pillage, 6/249; examines suspected pilferer, 6/309, 329, 333, 334; 7/22; to despatch fireships, 7/258; defends Carkesse, 8/76(2), 78, 80, 83, 97, 100–1, 103, 104, 105, 109(2), 126, 146, 178, 189, 203, 204, 213, 215–16, 217, 531; at Chatham in Medway crisis, 8/259, 268, 271, 296, 350; at Rochester, 8/306, 307; blamed for discharging ships by ticket, 8/271, 273; examined about tickets by Committee on Miscarriages, 8/504, 508, 509, 510, 538; 9/62, 69, 77; lobbies M.P.s, 9/79, 80, 83, 84; his defence, 9/100, 102, 103, 107; examined by Committee on Miscarriages about Chatham defences, 8/496, 501, 508; proposes reform of Board, 9/287–8, 341, 400; suspects P of writing Duke's letter criticising Board, 9/295; his reply, 9/305; resents powers of joint-Treasurers, 9/408;

reports rumours of appointments, 9/337 & n. 1; rumoured dismissal, 9/503

CONTRACTS: favours Warren's mast contract, 7/2–3; promotes Cocke's interests, 7/91, 115, 150, 184, 206, 221, 228

DOCKYARD BUSINESS: at Woolwich, 6/205–6; Deptford, 6/184; 7/20–1; Chatham and Harwich, 7/408; 8/296; discharges officers and seamen, 7/410(2)

FINANCIAL BUSINESS: approves P's memorandum on pursers, 7/9, 13, 14; comments on pursers' accounts, 7/106; part in proposed reorganisation of comptrollership, 7/361 & n. 2; 8/11–12, 20, 24, 25, 30, 32, 104, 586; objects to Penn's accounts, 8/50; criticised by Carteret, 8/110; offered half-share in Treasury by Carteret, 8/277; to take charge of Ticket Office, 9/383; also, 7/97; 8/4

PERQUISITES: promised plate by Cocke, 7/90, 91; secret understanding with Warren, 8/12, 31, 106, 115, 177; and Clutterbuck, 9/346 & n. 2

RELATIONS WITH P: their mutual dislike, 6/324; 7/78, 121, 131, 232–3, 258; 8/36, 220; annoys P by alliance with Warren, 8/12, 31, 115; baulked by P in payment of bills, 9/346 & n. 2; supports P in Hayter's case, 9/327, 328; and in Hewer's, 9/391, 394; also, 7/36; 8/342; 9/384 & n. 2

RELATIONS WITH PETT: 8/166, 311

COLLECTIVE BUSINESS (his part in discussions, decisions etc.): contracts and stores: 6/327; 7/68; dockyards: 6/216; financial: 6/74, 78, 203, 273, 327, 329, 336; 7/4, 76, 82, 284, 289, 295, 303, 311, 354; 8/111, 131, 372, 441, 460, 550; 9/109, 146, 174, 222, 445; ships/shipbuilding: 6/233, 281; 7/69; 9/100–1; tickets: 8/393; 9/15; victualling: 9/298, 303, 315, 316; misc. and unspecified: 6/193–4, 199, 200, 201, 211, 222, 334, 339; 7/71, 79, 82–3, 107–8, 304, 305; 8/87, 392, 394, 449, 460, 464, 479, 482, 494–5; 9/121, 130, 133, 150, 190, 454

AS COURTIER: supports Sandwich, 6/324; attends Queen's council as Chancellor, 7/303; cabals with Lady Denham, 7/323; omitted from commission on Duke of York's household, 8/592; also, 6/220–1

MUSICAL: examines claviorganum, 8/25; music meetings at his house, 8/54–7, 64–5; explains nature of sound, 9/147

POLITICAL: has conventiclers arrested, 6/199; views on war situation, 7/409, 411–12; supports attack on Clarendon, 8/401, 410; political news· etc. from: 7/152; 8/6, 424, 480; 9/17, 134, 173, 320, 446

PRIVATE AFFAIRS ETC. [for his liaison with 'Madam' Williams, see Williams, Abigail]: his two mistresses(?), 7/237–8; 8/226; infrequent attendance at church, 9/452; illnesses, 6/150, 156; 7/232–3; 9/223, 544, 546; houses/lodgings: in Piazza, Covent Garden, 6/2; 7/3, 4; coach-house, 7/224; at Greenwich, 6/204, 226; at Navy Office, 7/26, 296; 8/24, 31, 36, 40, 51; alterations, 8/226; 9/544; household poverty-stricken, 8/226; ~ his footman Tom, 7/232; his maid, 8/314

RELATIONS WITH P [see also above, Navy Commissioner; below, social]: admits P to Royal Society, 3/72 & n. 3; 6/36; their mutual regard, 6/237; 9/287–8; his gifts, 6/168 & n. 3, 212; 7/114, 293; recommends spectacles, 7/419; also, 7/378–9, 390; 8/12

SCIENTIFIC: President of Royal Society, 6/36; 7/96; 8/11; 9/333; at meetings of (business unspecified), 7/51; 9/113, 146, 248, 263; at Royal Society club, 7/148; 9/146–7, 334; as mathematician, 6/8; 9/191; helps to design yacht, 3/164, 188; and coaches, 6/94; 7/20; dismantles and reassembles watch, 6/337; discusses Wilkins's 'universal character', 7/12; his recipe for varnish, 7/147–8; discusses anatomy of teeth, 7/223–4; optics, 7/224, 225; sound, 9/147; visits King's laboratory, 9/416

SOCIAL: drives P in Hyde Park, 6/77; 7/106; 9/151; plays billiards, 6/190; gives birthday dinner, 6/285; and Twelfth Night party, 7/5–6; visits P's house, 7/66–7; Greenwich Palace,

7/105; friary, 8/25–6; godfather to Carkesse's child, 8/111; at theatre, 8/395, 509; 9/57, 148, 157, 166, 178, 310; Teddeman's funeral, 9/200; Bartholomew Fair, 9/301; parish dinner, 9/559; at houses/lodgings of naval associates in Greenwich and London: 6/186, 187, 191, 212, 220–1, 222, 228, 334; 7/18, 34, 38, 68, 279, 364; 8/3, 4, 77, 394, 482, 525; 9/34, 214, 283, 410–11, 505; at his house in Covent Garden, 6/2; 7/36, 40; 8/431; 9/104, 161; his lodgings in Greenwich, 6/204, 213, 217, 226, 227, 232–3, 332, 338, 339; 7/1, 3, 4; Madam Williams's lodgings, 6/302, 303; 7/77, 92–3, 341; 9/199; taverns etc., 6/38, 119; 7/43, 63, 74, 329; 8/49; 9/82, 115; elsewhere, 5/238; 7/253, 320; 8/180; 9/183, 198

ALLUDED TO: 9/309

~ his kinswoman, 9/146

BROWNE, [Alexander], drawing master: gives lessons to EP, 6/98 (2) & n. 1, 205, 282; to Peg Penn, 6/210; P jealous of, 6/246; objects to his presence at table, 7/116, 117; his painting, 9/261; his *Ars Pictoria*, 9/561 & n. 5; social: 7/134

BROWNE, Sir Anthony, of Weald Hall, nr Brentwood, Essex: 6/181 & n. 2 ~ his brother, ib.

BROWNE, Capt. [Arnold], naval officer: 5/30

[BROWNE, Frances], of the White Horse, Lombard St: her beauty, 7/68; commits suicide, 8/82 & n. 1; ~ her husband [Abraham], 7/68 & n. 3

BROWNE, John, Clerk of the Parliaments: social: 3/89; 9/1; ~ his wife [Elizabeth], 1/177 & n. 1; 2/15, 16; 3/89; his mother, 3/89

BROWNE, John, Deputy-Storekeeper of the Ordnance, Chatham: 4/260 & n. 3, 261; 5/30

BROWN(E), [John], mathematical-instrument maker, the Minories: sells P 'White's ruler', 4/84 & n. 2; pocket-ruler, 4/266, 267; slide-rule, 5/17 & n. 3, 237; Wren's drawing instrument, 9/537–8 & n., 548; also, 4/434; 5/14

BROWN(E) Capt. [John], naval officer: to sail to Jamaica, 3/150 & n. 3; quarrels with purser, 3/284 & n. 1; accidentally killed, 4/113; social: 2/36, 53; ~ his wife, 2/53; 4/113; his son baptised, 2/107, 109, 110, 146; his children, 4/113

BROWNE, [John], Storekeeper, Harwich: 1/196

BROWNE, Sir Richard, Clerk of the Privy Council: opposes new dock at Deptford, 3/18 & n. 1; explains quarantine order, 4/399 & n. 2; discusses freight charges, 4/430; clerk to Council's Committee for Retrenchments, 8/405, 406; his council work alluded to, 8/176, 278, 279; 9/350; political news from, 8/317; social: at Lord Mayor's dinner, 6/126; also, 8/552; 9/206, 502

BROWNE, Maj.-Gen. Ald. Sir Richard, kted May 1660, bt July 1660, M.P. London 1660, Ludgershall, Wilts. 1661–9; colonel in city militia; Lord Mayor 1660–1: resumes seat in parliament, 1/64 & n. 2; proclamation against repealed, 1/65; at ship's pay, 1/253–4; house, 1/275 & n. 3; his Lord Mayor's Day, 1/276–7; measures against Venner's rising, 2/8, 11; against riots, 5/99; 9/466 & n. 1; consulted about militia assessment, 3/283; sued for arbitrary arrests, 6/126; to pull down houses in Fire, 7/271; also, 5/114; social: attends Lord Mayor's dinner, 6/126; also, 2/105, 232

BROWNE, Sir Richard, son of the foregoing: at Lord Mayor's dinner with father Richard and son Richard, 6/126

BROWNE, Capt. —, of the Victualling Office: takes oath, 3/135

BROWNE, ——, nicknamed Colonel, of Brampton: 9/212

BROWNE, Mr ——, of St Malo: 7/133

BROWNLOW, [William], P's schoolfellow: 9/153 & n. 3

BRUANT: see Culan de

BRUCE, Robert, styled Lord Bruce, M.P. Bedfordshire 1661–3, cr. Earl of Ailesbury 1664: introduces test bill, 4/136; returns from Flanders, 7/142

BRUMFIELD: see Bromfield

BRUNKARD, Brunker(d): see Brouncker

BRYAN, Jacob, purser: 8/271–2

BRYDGES, William, 7th Baron Chandos (d. 1677): 3/288 & n. 1

BUAT, van: see Culan de

BUCK, [James], Rector of St James Garlickhithe Dec. 1661–86: preaches at St Gregory-by-Paul's, 2/192 & n. 5, 211

BUCK(E), Sir Peter, Clerk of the Acts 1600–25: P's pride in his knighthood, 1/318 & n. 2

BUCKDEN, Hunts.: Robert P's property, 2/183 & n. 3; EP at, 3/148; 7/93; Bishop of Lincoln's house, 9/35 & n. 3

BUCKHURST, Lord: see Sackville, Charles

BUCKINGHAM, Dukes of: see Villiers

BUCKINGHAM, Bucks.: P visits, 9/224–5; church and school, 9/225 & n. 1; bridge, ib. & n. 2

BUCKLERSBURY (Butlersbury): 1/210; 4/182

BUCKNELL, Ald. [William], kted 1670: 9/507 & n. 4

BUCKWORTH, Sir [John], merchant, Crutched Friars: P's regard, 6/145–6 & n.; ~ his wife [Hester], 5/259 & n. 4; 7/273; his son, 7/273, 419–20; his daughters, 9/533

BUCKWORTH, Hunts.: Backwell's estate, 9/185 & n. 2

BUDD, [David], Admiralty lawyer: 8/27

BUGDEN: see Buckden

BUGGINS, [John], of Stukeley, Hunts.: 3/176 & n. 2

BUGGINS, Mrs ——: 5/27, 94

[BULL, Nathaniel], Surmaster, St Paul's School: 2/238 & n. 2

BULLEN: see Boulogne

BULTEEL (Boltele), [John], secretary to Clarendon (d. 1669): social: 7/38, 68; 8/394

BUN(N), Capt. [Thomas], naval officer: gift to P, 1/231; helps to design Tangier jetty, 3/238 & n. 2; social: 2/120

BUNCE (Bunch), Sir James: recounts Cavaliers' grievances, 6/329–30 & n.

BUNTINGFORD, Herts.: P visits, 4/307

BURCHIN LANE: see Birchin Lane

BURFETT: see Borfett

BURFORD, Mr ——: social: 8/465–8 passim

BURGBY, Mr ——, writing-clerk to the Privy Council: news from, 5/72–3

BURGESS, [William], Exchequer clerk: P visits on Tangier business, 6/235; 8/295, 326, 329, 341, 377, 383, 440; 9/477

BURGLARY, robbery and theft [see also Law and Order etc.]:

GENERAL: increase allegedly due to disbanded soldiers, 1/256 & n. 3; Rotherhithe notoriously dangerous, 3/201; and road between Westminster and Kensington, 5/180; thefts by servants, 4/294 & n. 3; by disbanded Cavaliers, 4/374 & n. 1

PARTICULAR CASES: thefts from dockyards and ships: 1/316; 3/137 & n. 2; 4/76–7, 236; 6/184; attempted burglary, 1/305; tankard and cloak stolen from P's house, 2/140; EP's new waistcoat from coach, 4/28; horse stolen, 4/310; looting in Fire, 7/282; shoplifting, 9/285; also, 4/260; 5/10–11, 13; 8/316 & n. 2, 319, 321; 9/51

P'S FEAR OF BURGLARY AND LOOTING: leaves lighted candle in dining room, 3/101; fears looting in Fire, 7/285, 286; and by rioting seamen, 7/415; fears burglars, 1/305; 2/4; 5/201, 281, 282, 296; 6/25; 7/197–8; 8/552, 555

P'S FEAR OF ROBBERY AND THEFT: 2/158; 6/106, 200, 232, 235, 236; meets men with cudgels, 5/193; 9/172; fears attack in ruined streets after Fire, 8/60, 62, 371; 9/4, 8, 55; fears for EP's necklace at theatre, 7/412; fears pickpockets at Queen's Chapel, 8/588; and Bartholomew Fair, 9/313; armed guard on coach, 3/201; carries drawn sword in coach, 8/60, 62

POLICE MEASURES AGAINST: watch warns P of open door, 4/304; also, 7/363–4; 8/589; 9/134(2)

BURLINGTON, Earl of: see Boyle, Richard

BURNET, Dr Alexander, P's physician,

Fenchurch St: treats P for stone, 5/1 & n. 3, 191, 211; and ulcer, 5/194, 363; confines himself to house in Plague, 6/124, 125; accused of murdering servant, 6/165, 203; death, 6/203 & n. 1, 204, 226; social: 2/107; 3/178; 5/24; ~ his wife, 5/1

BURNTISLAND (Burnt Iland), Fife: Dutch bombard, 8/202 & n. 1

BURNTWOOD: *see* Brentwood

BURR, John, P's clerk: on voyage to Holland, 1/87; on board *Swiftsure*, 1/95, 96; at Gravesend, 1/98–9; annoys P by absence ashore, 1/103, 111, 116, 133; work for P, 1/111, 117; gifts to P and EP, 1/203, 232; also, 1/94, 104

BURRELL, ——: 1/47

BURROUGHS, [William], clerk to Sir W. Penn: 9/326

BURROWS, Lieut. [Anthony], naval officer: death, 6/336; pay-ticket, 7/168

BURROWS (Borroughs, Burroughs), [Elizabeth], of Westminster, widow of the foregoing: her good looks, 6/163; 7/168, 218; an old acquaintance, 6/336; amorous encounters with P, 7/168, 204–5, 240, 345, 392, 396; 9/158; breaks assignations, 7/380, 385, 386, 387, 392, 393; 8/12, 14, 71, 128; feigns grief for husband, 8/111; social: P's valentine, 9/158; also, 7/134, 232, 262, 394; 8/335, 375–6, 429, 478, 564; 9/118, 129, 142; ~ her children, 6/163; her aunt, 7/386

BURROWS, [John], slopseller to the navy: gift to P, 6/63

BURSTON, [John], chart maker, of Ratcliffe: engraves drawing of Portsmouth, 6/38, 46, 49, 50, 55; P buys engravings from, 6/111; ?9/266, 268

BURT, [Nicholas], actor: as Othello, 1/264; 9/438; in *Cataline*, 8/575 & n. 3

BURTON, [Hezekiah], Fellow of Magdalene College, Cambridge: suggested as tutor for W. Penn, jun., 3/21; also, 1/67, 68

BURTON, [Richard], locksmith, Chatham yard: his wife's gift to P, 7/351

BURY ST EDMUNDS, Suff.: beauty of women at, 4/186

BUSBY, Dr Richard, Headmaster,

Westminster School: his 'devilish covetousness', 8/199 & n. 1

BUSHELL, [Edward], merchant: in dispute about Portuguese customs dues, 5/43 & n. 2

BUTLER, (Boteler), family of: household, 1/217; emigrate to Ireland, 1/209

BUTLER, (Boteler), Frances ('la belle Boteler'), sister of Butler, ('Mons. L'Impertinent'): her beauty, 1/58, 176, 201–2, 208, 217; 2/125; 5/100, 286; 6/84; recovers from smallpox, 1/58–9; goes to Ireland, 1/209; courted by Col. Dillon, 1/217; 2/152; 3/299; 9/311 & n. 4; at Clerkenwell church, 5/286; has left Clerkenwell, 7/75; 9/311; ~ her sister; 1/207, 217; 5/101

BUTLER, James, Duke of Ormond, Lord-Lieutenant of Ireland 1661–9: position and wealth, 5/73, 183; 9/347 & n. 1; engraving of, 8/10 & n. 3; resents Albemarle's appointment as Lord-Lieutenant, 1/228–9 & n.; at coronation banquet, 2/85; visits Portsmouth, 3/70, 71; as Lord-Lieutenant, 3/79; Barker's action against, 8/404, 420 & n. 2; threatened impeachment, 8/518–19 & n.; 9/184–5 & n.; establishment reduced, 9/41 & n. 1; in England, 9/195, 204; influence over King, 9/204–5; dismissal, 9/346–7 & n., 375, 385, 446, 466 & n. 1, 478; to be succeeded by commission, 9/351; social: 2/100; also, 1/300; 8/326; 9/525

BUTLER, Lord John: suitor to Elizabeth Malet, 7/385; at theatre, 8/45

BUTLER, Lord Richard, cr. Earl of Arran 1662: hunts deer in St James's Park, 5/239; dances at court, 6/29; said to have given pox to wife, 6/167–8 & n.

BUTLER, Samuel, author of *Hudibras* (d. 1680) [*see also* Books]: dines with P, 9/265

BUTLER, Thomas, son of Duke of Ormond, styled Earl of Ossory: witness to Duke of York's secret marriage, 2/40–1; challenges Buckingham, 7/343 & n. 3, 350; at court ball, 7/372; quarrels with Ashley, 7/376 & n. 1

BUTLER, ——('Mons. L'impertinent'):

n. 1; election of proctors and taxors, 3/217–18 & n.; praevaricator, 5/278 & n. 1; parliamentary election: 1/108–9 & n.

COLLEGES: Christ's: factions, 1/63–4 & n.; P visits, 2/135, 180; Jesus: 9/213; manorial court, 2/182; King's: P walks in grounds, 1/68; visits chapel, 2/135–6 & n.; 3/224; 8/468; Magdalene: P visits, 1/67, 68; 9/212; remarks on 'old preciseness', 1/67; recalls undergraduate days, 1/67; 3/31, 54 & n. 1; 5/203, 361; 8/466, 468; 9/212; W. Penn, jun. to be entered for, 3/17 & n. 4, 21; gateposts, 8/469 & n. 1; buttery, 9/212; college beer, ib.; St John's: P visits library, 3/224 & n. 1; 8/468; Trinity: P visits, 3/224; 8/468; celebration of Monmouth's visit, 4/99; Trinity Hall: P entered at (1650), vol. i, p. xxi; visits, 2/146; 3/218; alluded to (in error): 8/133

CAMBRIDGESHIRE: parliamentary elections, 1/112 & n. 2; 8/85–6 & n.; Roger P's estate, 4/159; P's proposed purchase of land, 5/196; prestmoney, 8/85 & n. 2

CAM(P)DEN, Lord: see Hickes

CANARY COMPANY, the: patent criticised in parliament, 7/314 & n. 2, 342, 414; 8/2 & n. 5, 70; cancelled, 8/297 & n. 4

CANNON ROW, WESTMINSTER: 3/285

CANNON (Canning) ST: road widened, 4/77 & n. 3; Fire, 7/269, 270; subsidence, 9/288

CANTERBURY, Kent: King visits, 1/161; P visits cathedral, 1/172; remains of Becket's tomb, ib. & n. 3; list of archbishops in, 6/339 & n. 4; alluded to: 2/32; 4/25

CAPEL, Arthur, cr. Earl of Essex (d. 1683): 9/418

CAPEL, Sir Henry, M.P. Tewkesbury, Glos.: 9/418, 527–8

CARACENA, Don Luis de Benavides, Marques de, Governor of the Spanish Netherlands 1658–64: unpopularity, 9/396 & n. 3; confessor, 9/396–7

CARCASSE: see Carkesse

CAREW, [John], regicide: executed, 1/266 & n. 1

CARISSIMI, Giacomo, composer: songs, 5/217 & n. 2; alluded to: 8/56

CARKESSE (Carcasse), [James], clerk in the Ticket Office:

CHARACTER: 6/193; 7/366; 8/78, 94, 146

CHRON. SERIES: Brouncker's clerk, 6/193; servant to Marquess of Dorchester, 7/366; work in Ticket Office, 7/366, 418; injured in riot, 8/60(2); charged with malpractices, 8/63–4 & n., 76, 83–4, 97, 100–1, 103, 109; championed by Brouncker, 8/83, 97, 100–1, 103, 104, 178, 189, 203, 215, 217; dismissed, 8/103; case referred back to Board, 8/146; appeals to P, 8/109, 150, 169, 200, 204, 238(2), 302; Pett's attitude, 8/166, 200; case discussed, 8/178, 186, 198, 343–4; report on, 8/204–5, 212–18 passim, 343–4; referred to Council, 8/376, 379, 385, 386, 388; Carkesse reinstated, 8/555; gives evidence against Board to Committee on Miscarriages, 8/523, 524, 531; appears before Brooke House Committee, 9/43; hostility to P, 8/392; asks forgiveness, 8/555; makes allegations against, 9/99; P's MS. account of case, 8/186; case alluded to: 8/101–2, 105, 260

SOCIAL: watches Fire, 7/271; at parish dinner, 8/218

~ his wife, 7/67; his brother, 7/271; his child, 8/111

CARLETON, ——, coachman: 4/155

CARLINGFORD, Lord: see Taafe

CARLISLE, Earl of: see Howard, Charles

CARNEGIE, Anne, Countess of Southesk: Duke of York's mistress, 9/154; gives him pox, 6/60 & n. 2; 9/154–5 & n.; at theatre, 9/383

CARNEGIE, Robert, 3rd Earl of Southesk: revenge for wife's infidelity, 9/154–5 & n.

CARPENTER, [Richard]: preaches at St Bride's, 3/162 & n. 2

CARR, Sir Robert, M.P. Lincolnshire: attacks Sandwich in Commons, 9/174 & n. 5; social: 8/363

CARR, [William]: petitions Commons

against Gerard, 8/581 & n. 1; pun-
ished by Lords, 8/583, 587; 9/32;
tried for desertion, 9/55, 57
CARRICK, Mrs ——: 1/27
CARTER, Charles, Rector of Irthling-
borough, Northants., 1664–75: gift to
P, 1/321 & n. 4; chaplain to Bishop of
Carlisle, 8/51 & n. 2; news of Mag-
dalene friends, ib.; social: 1/45, 287;
2/123
CARTER, Mr —— [?the foregoing]:
visits P, 1/203
CARTER, Mrs ——: servant to Lady
Wright, 1/41, 288; 6/160; wants a
husband, ib.; social: 7/17
CARTERET, [Anne], daughter of Sir
George: marriage, 4/254 & n. 3
CARTERET, [Benjamin], son of Sir
George; naval officer: 4/433
CARTERET, Betty, daughter of Sir
George (mentioned in error): 4/254 &
n. 1
CARTERET, [Carolina], daughter of
Sir George: marriage, 4/254 & n. 1;
alluded to: 5/15
CARTERET, Sir Edward, Gentleman-
Usher to the King: 8/115
CARTERET, Elizabeth, Lady Car-
teret, wife of Sir George:
CHARACTER: P's regard, 3/60; 7/88,
295; 8/48
CHRON. SERIES: portrait by Lely, 5/104;
pleased at son's match with Jemima
Mountagu, 6/138, 153; kindness to
P/EP, 6/152–3, 156; fears Plague,
6/156; gifts to Jemima, 6/157, 158;
wedding visit to Dagnams, 6/167, 168,
173, 175–6, 179; gratitude to P as
matchmaker, 6/178, 182; fears for
husband's position at Court, 7/57, 88;
8/165; 9/339; laments state of nation,
7/325; 8/113; pleased at husband's
resigning Treasurership, 8/299; also,
6/161, 163, 212; 7/291; 8/149, 480
SOCIAL: in Hyde Park coach parade,
3/78; visits Lady Sandwich, 5/179; at
Sheriff Waterman's dinner, 6/79; P
and EP visit at Cranbourne, 7/54–7;
also, 3/85, 126, 179, 197; 5/105; 6/112;
7/89, 335; 8/42–3, 163, 450, 596;
9/10
CARTERET (Cartrite), Sir George,
Treasurer of the Navy 1660–7; Vice-

Chamberlain of the Household 1660–
70; Vice-Treasurer of Ireland 1667–
73; M.P. Portsmouth 1661–9:
CHARACTER: said to be diligent but
grasping, 5/73; P's view: incompetent, 4/132, 192, 233; 6/72, 95;
7/293; good-natured, 1/296; 5/104;
likeable, 8/117; honest, 8/165;
Coventry's view: able but lazy, 3/243;
8/47, 140, 164–5, 179, 290
AS TREASURER OF THE NAVY:
CHRON. SERIES: appointed, 1/191,
n. 2; his salary, 1/194, n. 4; 7/313 &
n. 2; his poundage, 3/106–7 & n.,
107–8, 174, 243; 4/302; reduced by
Additional Aid Act, 6/292 & n. 3,
311(2), 312–13, 323; 7/4, 5, 24; by
payment in course, 6/304; and by
Poll Tax, 8/30 & n. 3, 67; too power-
ful, 3/177; rarely attends Board,
8/162, 252; colleagues criticise his
officials, 3/28, 29–30; methods of payment, 6/75, 83, 95; accounts, 7/43, 64,
77; and dilatoriness in raising credit,
8/47, 140, 164–5, 179, 290, 327;
accounts examined by parliament,
7/260–1, 262, 287, 291, 292, 294 &
n. 1, 295, 313, 319, 321–2, 356;
attacked by 'libel', 7/342; in danger of
dismissal, 7/319; 8/304; to sell office,
7/334; 8/222, 277; defends himself,
8/2, 18, 247, 251, 295, 301; accounts
examined by Brooke House Committee, 9/117, 179, 214, 562; exchanges
offices with Vice-Treasurer of Ireland,
8/295 & n. 3, 297, 299, 301 & n. 1,
322; to retire, 8/597; also, 9/67
FINANCIAL BUSINESS: general: accounts examined/passed by Board,
3/14, 240; 4/96–7, 99; 5/104, 105, 318,
329; 6/119(2), 257; 7/289; 8/141,
169–70, 449, 458, 460, 497, 598;
9/222, 250; complains of lack of
money, 3/104, 108; 6/293(2); 7/284,
331; 8/41, 73, 205; applies to Lord
Treasurer, 3/278, 279; 6/74, 78; 7/48;
surplus, 4/305, 317; cash supplied from
customs, 7/11; to obtain cash from
Prize Office, 8/58, 144; opposes loan
from city, 7/160; uses officials' credit,
8/48, 327; and his own, 8/180, 290;
successful in raising loans, 8/140;
9/448; complains of bankers' refusal

to lend, 8/143, 149; to pay in course, 4/75 & n. 2; pays with own money, 6/150; particular items: scheme for paying seamen, 1/308; cashes/certifies bills, 2/61, 62, 96; 4/283, 414; 6/24; at pays, 3/58, 66, 69–75 passim, 193, 203, 290; 7/132–3, 196, 308; victuallers' accounts, 3/62; 4/389; Creed's, 4/192, 197, 198, 204, 207, 215–16, 219; Dunkirk money, 3/269 & n. 3; customs dispute, 5/54–5, 76; purchase of tar, 5/134; estimates for parliament, 5/329; pay tickets, 6/72, 74; 8/110; Board's expenses, 6/74; marine insurance, 6/112; Warren's bills, 7/354; method of paying bills, 8/89

OTHER BUSINESS: Navy Office premises, 1/194; sale of stores, 2/45; appointment of ships' masters, 2/108, 111; projected dock, 2/198; shipping, 2/202; 3/40, 59–60, 81, 85; trial of yarn, 3/102; contracts, 4/241, 327, 383; 9/542; mast-dock, 5/202, 353; appointment of Commissioner Taylor, 5/350; surveyorship of victualling, 6/266; enquiry into victualling, 7/260; Board's report to Duke of York, 7/375–6; Carkesse case, 8/102, 103, 215; also, 1/192, 242; 4/314; 5/7; 6/149; 7/319; 8/153, 154, 155; unspecified: 3/22, 48, 51, 53, 101, 106, 148, 192, 280, 284; 4/4, 12, 81, 105, 106, 152, 175, 258, 322; 5/333; 6/105, 324; 7/291, 312, 369; 8/131, 141, 189, 277, 281, 355, 405–6, 429, 524

RELATIONS WITH COLLEAGUES AND OTHERS: tries to get colleagues appointed prize commissioners, 5/327, 333; supports P's appointment as Clerk, 1/192; P helps him set office in order, 1/194; cultivates his goodwill, 3/75, 79, 210; 6/75; 7/57, 61–2, 66, 67; his esteem for P, 3/81, 108, 171, 172; 7/334; supports P over contracts etc., 3/100; 4/327, 380, 383; 6/116(2), 138; they exchange confidences, 3/59; 4/397; 7/78, 131; P supports him in dispute with Coventry, 3/107; advises P on prize-goods, 7/219; angry with him, 8/69; distrusts Batten, 3/59, 157; 4/182; 6/74; annoyed with Penn, 3/79; his complaints/accusations against Coventry,

3/79, 104 & n. 3, 107–8; 4/170, 330–1 & n.; Coventry's hostility, 7/27, 41, 42, 43, 83; they are reconciled, 6/147; 7/196, 325; also, 3/5; 9/339

OTHER APPOINTMENTS: Governor of Jersey 1643–51: 3/243 & n. 2; alleged malpractices, 4/195 & n. 1, 305–6; 8/161 & n. 4; on Tangier commission: 3/238; displeased at P's appointment as Treasurer, 6/60; signs bills, 6/191–2; attends meetings, 4/335; 5/308; 6/58; 7/156; Master of Trinity House: 5/172, 5/210; on appeal tribunal for prizes: 8/181, 231

NEWS FROM: political/parliamentary/ court news, 3/79; 4/103, 212; 6/291; 7/172, 303, 308–9, 370; 8/126, 207, 229–30, 277, 355, 416, 418, 479–80, 525, 573, 596–7; 9/9, 67; naval, 3/79; 5/275, 352, 353; 6/198; 7/143, 159–60; 8/41–2; foreign, 4/198; 7/250

AS POLITICIAN: deplores court's immorality, 6/167; 8/355; believes in 'show of religion', 8/355; comments on approach of war, 5/175, 353; despairs of war and state of nation, 7/24, 62, 83, 131, 160, 196, 281, 307, 334, 370, 383; 8/161, 222–3, 573, 596–7; 9/67; visits fleet, 7/124, 159–60; 8/514; criticises naval tactics, 7/143, 159–60, 188; 8/148; and naval unpreparedness, 8/117; dislikes Treasury commission, 8/244; his influence, 6/190, 323; 7/6, 8; 8/18, 69, 166–7; supports Clarendon, 4/195; 5/205, 212, 213, 218–19; 8/406, 418; envious of Sandwich, 4/117, 219; allies with, 6/277, 313, 323; 7/54; 8/462(2); supports in prize-goods affair, 7/262; 9/87, 96; attends Cabinet/Council, 5/317; 8/117, 278; also, 2/82; 3/240; 8/18, 217

FAMILY: pleasure in son's marriage, 6/137, 138, 141, 153, 161, 167, 168, 173, 178, 179, 182, 200; reports approval of King and Duke of York, 6/144–5, 148; marriage settlement, 6/148, 180 & n. 3, 191; attends wedding, 6/175–6, 179, 182; wedding gifts, 7/358; 8/207, 221; arranges Hinchingbrooke's match, 8/190 & n. 4, 208, 216; 9/28; daughter Poppet, 8/155; daughters (unidentified), 3/197;

Moll Davis, 9/219; seriously ill of fever, 4/337, 339, 342, 344, 347, 348, 352, 356, 358, 363, 378, 407, 439; 5/4; looks ill, 5/107; takes physic, 7/87; visits Tunbridge Wells, 4/240, 251; 7/214; Bath, 4/292; Oxford, 4/315, 321; movements in Plague: at Salisbury, 6/172; Wilton, 6/189; Hampton Court, 7/46; returns to Whitehall, ib.

HOUSEHOLD: her Maids of Honour: their beauty, 4/230; 7/347; dress, 3/92 & n. 2; 5/188; 7/162, 325; complain of drinking water, 3/92 & n. 3; stories of, 3/177 & n. 1; 4/37 & n. 4, 37–8; some return to Portugal, 3/234–5; attend launch, 5/306; play cards, 7/48; 8/70; visit Tunbridge Wells, 7/214; also, 3/299; 4/142; 5/107; court ill-attended, 3/197, 299; 4/49; physician(s), 3/235; 4/345; closet, 5/188 & n. 3; council, 7/303

SOCIAL AND CEREMONIAL: listens to music, 3/90; 8/534; 9/322–3; entertained by Lord Berkeley, 3/184; Lord Mayor, 4/193–4; Buckingham, 4/238; at court ball, 3/300, 301; 7/371–3; at ambassador's audience, 3/297; banquet at Windsor, 4/113; military review, 4/216; her birthday, 4/382; 7/341 (error), 371–3; at opening of parliamentary session, 5/93; visits fleet, 5/193, 196; at launch, 5/306; 9/101; court lottery, 5/214, 215; plays cards, 7/48; 8/70; dines in public, 8/161, 404, 428; 9/320; receives Duchess of Newcastle, 8/163; also, 4/229–30; 5/163, 348; 8/551, 570; 9/294, 323, 331

AT THEATRE: at Cockpit, 3/260, 273; Whitehall, 7/325, 347; 9/219, 456; Theatre Royal, 8/167; 9/203

ALLUDED TO: 8/464; 9/276

CAVALIERS: alleged plots against Commonwealth, 2/204, 225; 5/264; unjust treatment, 3/42–3 & n.; act for relief of, 3/199 & n. 2; cause indiscipline in fleet, 4/169; unfit for employment, 4/196; importune King, 4/373; danger to law and order, 4/374 & n. 1; grievances, 6/303, 329–30 & n.; manners, 9/478

CAVE, [John], Gentleman of the

Chapel Royal: killed in street quarrel, 5/32 & n. 3

CAVE, ——, of St Bride's parish: boards Tom P's child, 5/114; imprisoned, 5/114, 252–3; demands money, 5/82, 154, 158, 167–8

CAVENDISH, Margaret, Duchess of Newcastle (b. Lucas, d. 1673), wife of the 1st Duke [see also Plays]: eccentric dress and behaviour, 8/163–4 & n., 186–7, 196, 243; attracts crowds, 8/163–4, 196, 197, 209; visits Royal Society, 8/243 & n. 3; house at Clerkenwell, 8/209; Life of husband, 9/123 & n. 3

CAVENDISH, William, styled Lord Cavendish, 4th Earl (1684), and 1st Duke (1694) of Devonshire (d. 1707): on Naseby, 1/134

CAYUS: see Caius

CECIL, Robert, 1st Earl of Salisbury (d. 1612): tomb, 8/381 & n. 5

CECIL, William, 1st Baron Burghley (d. 1598): letters, 8/313 & n. 3

CECIL, William, 2nd Earl of Salisbury (d. 1668): 'simple', 5/298–9 & n.; report of expulsion from Lords, 1/127 & n. 1; ~ his gardener, 1/59; 2/139

CENTEN (Seaton), Capt. Bastiaan, Dutch naval officer: killed in action, 6/122 & n. 5

CERVINGTON (Servington), [Charles], tally-cutter in the Exchequer: 2/241

CHAMBERLAIN, Mr and Mrs ——: their singing, 6/316, 338

CHAMBERLAYNE (Chamberlin), Sir Thomas, Governor of the E. India Company: news of Dutch in India, 5/49–50 & n.; supports war, 5/108–9

CHANCERY [see also Justice, administration of]: Rolls Chapel: P hears case, 1/50 & n. 2; orders stationery from, 1/88–9 & n.; hears sermon, 6/80; examines patents in, 9/480, 483; Six Clerks' Office: P visits for patent as Clerk of Acts, 1/197; about agreement with Barlow, 1/205; and dispute with Trice, 2/210; 4/221, 242, 345, 346, 351

CHANCERY LANE [for buildings,

Braganza. For his mistresses *see* Davis, Moll; Gordon, Eleanor, Lady Byron; Gwyn, Nell; Haslerigg, Mrs; Stuart, Frances, Duchess of Richmond; Villiers, Barbara, Countess of Castlemaine, Walters, Lucy; Weaver, [Elizabeth]]: story of proposed match with Frances Cromwell (1654),5/296–7 & n.; speculations about choice of bride, 2/37–40 passim & nn., 45, 52 & n. 1; Dutch oppose Portuguese match, 2/65 & n. 3; letters from Catherine of Braganza, 3/51; her arrival, 3/83, 87, 97; quarrels with over Lady Castlemaine's appointment to Household, 3/147 & n. 2; neglects her, 3/234–5; 4/439; 5/56; 8/558; grieved by her illness, 4/339, 342; 9/204–5; gives away part of dowry, 5/50 & n. 4
MUSICAL: guitar, 1/172; comments on anthems, 1/220, 265; beats time to, 4/394; liking for French music, 1/297–8 & n.; 8/73 & n. 3
NAVY BOARD AND ADMIRALTY BUSINESS ETC.: visits Woolwich, 3/265; 4/103; helps design *Henrietta*, 4/123 & n. 1; derides Petty's double-keeled ship, 4/334; 5/32–3 & n.; at launches, 5/306, 353; 9/101; commends A. Deane's *Rupert*, 7/127; patronises van Heemskerck's design, 9/171; visits Dutch E. Indiaman, 4/204; inspects fleet, 5/156, 193, 196; 6/170; 7/168; appoints prize commissioners, 5/333; orders about sale of prize goods etc., 8/16, 446; attends Navy Board meetings, 6/55; 7/201; 8/126; appoints commanders, 6/148; orders Board to Greenwich, 6/195 & n. 1; issues merchantmen's passes too freely, 7/349; orders money for fleet, 8/57–8, 68; inspects Sheerness, 8/84, 126–7; plans for campaign (1667), 8/97–8; action in Medway raid, 8/260, 263; plans criticised, 8/306; blames Board, 8/315; consulted by Board about ticket controversy, 9/101; with Duke of York adjudicates dispute between commanders, 9/107 & n. 3; and makes appointments, 9/128, 131; with Duke authorises payment of navy creditors, 9/149, 150, 152, 153; overrides Duke in replacement of Penn, 9/349–50,

551; orders Duke to suspend Anglesey, 9/340–1, 351, 362; orders fitting out of fleet, 9/425–6; and report on Board's constitution, 9/444 & n. 2, 519, 551; reassured about navy debts, 9/447; also, 4/360; 5/291; 8/477–8, 515
PARLIAMENT [omitting formal occasions]: sends message about Catholic priests, 4/92 & n. 3; holds conference with Commons on supply, 4/183 & n. 1; condemns attempted impeachment of Clarendon, 4/229 & n. 3; obtains repeal of Triennial Act of 1641, 5/93, 112 & n. 4; promotes merchants' complaints against Dutch, 5/105, 137; appeals for war effort, 6/270 & n. 1; power reduced by scrutiny of accounts, 7/307, 308; libel against circulated in Commons, 7/342; orders M.P.s from theatres etc. to vote, 7/399–400; threatens dissolution, 7/404; appoints commissioners to examine accounts, 8/2 & n. 3, 6, 193–5 & n., 251–2 & n.; quarrels with Commons over dispensing powers, 8/6, 9–10 & n., 18–20 passim; relations strained, 8/38, 125; to recall parliament, 8/292–4 passim; against recall, 8/362; allows enquiry into miscarriages of war, 8/424–5, 485; thanked for Clarendon's dismissal, 8/479, 480; to hold elections (rumour), 9/71; to meet parliament about religion, 9/104; attends Lords' debate on precedence, 9/106–7; urges Commons to vote supply, 9/141 & n. 2; message about adjournment, 9/174
ENCOUNTERS WITH P: calls P by name, 6/82, 104–5; high opinion of, 6/91, 292; 7/26, 27, 28, 31; grants him *Maybolt*, 8/477–8; appealed to on Hayter's behalf, 6/115–16; and on A. Joyce's, 9/33; congratulates on parliamentary speech, 9/105, 122; grants leave of absence, 9/558, 560; also, 3/191; 8/365–6
PICTURES: collection, 1/257–8 & n.; 3/82 & n. 2, 292; 4/319, 393 & n. 1; 7/97, 102 & n. 3
POLITICAL FAVOURITES [for appointment and dismissal of ministers, *see* under names]: Clarendon, 2/142; 'old

CHELSEA COLLEGE: proposed grant of, to Royal Society, 8/537 & n. 3

CHESHIRE: antiquity of families, 9/280 & n. 2

CHESTERFIELD, Lord: see Stanhope

CHESTERTON, Cambs.: P's old walk, 9/212; church (St Andrew's), ib.; ferry, ib.

CHESWICKE, ——, musician: 5/194

CHETWIND (Chetwin, Chetwynd), [James], Chancery clerk: P's regard, 3/275; his office, 1/50; P consults on Garter fees, 1/162; his pictures and lute, 1/182–3; chews tobacco, 2/128; his dog, 3/3; dies rich, 3/275 & n. 2; news from, 1/61; social: at old club in Bull Head, 2/127; 7/375; also, 1/50–3 passim, 74, 80, 92, 95, 244, 248; 3/49

CHEVERTON: see Chiverton

CHEVINS: see Chiffinch

CHICHELE, Henry, Archbishop of Canterbury 1414–43: portrait, 9/226 & n. 2

CHICHELEY, Sir Henry, of Wimpole, Cambs.: on *Naseby*, 1/130

CHICHELEY, Sir John, naval officer: begs prize-ship from King, 8/508; to give evidence to Committee on Miscarriages, 8/527, 549; social: 7/401; 8/433, 575; 9/281

CHICHELEY, Thomas, kted 1670; Ordnance Commissioner and M.P. Cambridgeshire:

PUBLIC CAREER: appointed to Ordnance Board, 5/316; attends Navy Board, 7/104; 8/215 ['Cholmley' ed.'s error]; attends Privy Council committee, 8/112; reports on gun-trials, 7/183 & n. 1; disappointed of Comptrollership of Household, 8/185 & n. 1; a 'high-flyer' in Parliament, 8/85–6; opposes comprehension bill, 9/112; praises P's parliamentary speech, 9/105; parliamentary news from, 8/501, 527

PRIVATE AFFAIRS ETC.: house in Great Queen St, 9/112 & n. 1; high style of living, ib.; social: plays tennis with King, 8/418–19; also, 5/330; 9/281

[CHIDLEY, Samuel], scrivener: 4/344, 345 & n. 1, 351

CHIFFINCH (Cheffins), Thomas,

Keeper of the Private Closet to the King: death, 7/94

CHIFFINCH (Chevins), William, page of the Bedchamber to the King: shows P King's pictures, 8/403; his lodgings, 9/557–8; social: 9/198, 507, 560; alluded to: 7/374

CHILD, Josiah, merchant, cr. bt 1678: P's regard, 6/255 & n. 1; declines Tangier victualling, ib.; bids for navy victualling, 9/287, 288, 316, 323; proposed appointment as Navy Commissioner, 9/507, 509, 550; complaints of, 9/549, 551; social: 9/543

CHILD, [William], organist: suitor to Mrs Bockett, 1/301 & n. 3; to be made doctor of music, 4/199 & n. 1; plays organ, 1/292 & n. 3, 297; 4/428; 8/145; sets music for P, 1/302, 324; 3/33; 7/227; 8/167; plays lute, 1/324; and viol, 2/39; takes P to rehearsal, 2/41; takes P and EP to service, 7/57–8; social: 1/234, 276, 285; 2/96–7; 7/59–60

CHILDREN, P's attitude to [for his foot-boys, see Birch, W.; Edwards, T.; Servants]:

HIS CHILDLESSNESS: disappointed of hopes of children, 1/1; finds new use for nursery, 2/127; considers possibility of childlessness, 3/16; 4/365; 5/277, 281; sorry to have no heir, 8/49; given advice on curing infertility, 5/222; asked to adopt child, 6/37; wishes cousin's boy were his own, 8/442

HIS AFFECTION FOR/INTEREST IN: jokes with, 2/72; enjoys company of Mountagu boys, 2/158; takes children to zoo, 3/76; pleased to see Bridewell children at work, 5/289; children dance to his singing, 9/196; admires child at Lamberts', 2/123; Cocke's boy, 2/218; Sir T. Crew's children, 3/76; Gauden's, 4/244; 'stout witty' Dick Penn, 6/35; roguish wit of young J. Pearse, 6/317–18; 7/70, 100; 8/103, 188; pretty boy in church, 7/169; Buckworth's children, 7/273, 419–20; 9/533; the seven children of Sir S. Fox, 7/406; pretty daughter of Mrs Knepp, 8/57; quick wit of boys on trial, 8/319; 'false tone' of shepherd-boy reading Bible aloud, 8/338; intelligence of Mountagu twins, 8/472; Princess Mary's dancing, 9/507

CHILLENDEN (Chillington), Capt. [Edmund], soldier: 1/7 & n. 4

CHITTERNE, Wilts.: P visits, 9/231

CHIVERTON, Ald. [Sir Richard]: his hemp, 6/77

CHOLMLEY, Hugh, succ. to baronetcy 1665, engineer, Gentleman-Usher to the Queen 1662–c. 79:
PERSONAL: duel, 3/157; 4/47; house in Pall Mall, 8/99 & n. 4; ill, 9/95, 99, 122
TANGIER: appointed to committee, 3/238; attends committee, 5/154; 7/321; distrusts Irish, 5/302; hopes to become Governor, 7/99; 8/45, 103–4, 111, 116–17, 127; victualling business, 6/101–2; 7/121; 8/445, 461, 491; mole business: contracts for construction, 4/13 & n. 1, 26–7, 35–6, 45, 88 & n. 3; his gifts to contractors, 8/592–3; to be appointed Surveyor-General, 9/199 & n. 2, 364; accounts/money for, 5/344; 6/103; 7/18–19, 98–9, 323, 403; 8/63, 77, 205, 212–13, 298, 344, 377, 440–1, 482, 518–19, 522, 592–3, 596; 9/197, 199, 214, 388; also, 9/455; unspecified business: 7/132; 8/106, 205, 449; 9/492
COURT/PARLIAMENTARY NEWS FROM: 5/153; 7/163, 336–7, 403; 8/61–2, 93–4, 100, 106–8, 167, 244, 282, 292, 329–30, 412, 438, 446–7, 478, 482, 518–19; 9/53, 185, 530
OPINIONS: of court, 8/331; government by army, ib.; monarchy's prospects, 8/378; Anglesey, 8/301; Coventry, 8/518
RELATIONS WITH P: P's regard, 8/99–100, 331; 9/326; P opposes him over Tangier mole, 5/303; P's annual retainer from, 6/306; 8/593; also, 7/407 & n. 4
RELATIONS WITH SANDWICH: 5/343; 9/326; gift to, 8/592–3
SOCIAL: 5/215; 7/308, 375; 8/557; 9/22, 328–9, 465, 518

CHRIST CHURCH, Newgate St: P attends service, 7/169; Fire, 7/309

CHRISTENINGS: P/EP godparent(s) at private ceremonies: 2/109(2), 216; 5/176; 6/152; 7/49, 128, 129, 329–30; 8/202, 404–5, 540; 9/260; also, 1/42; 2/171, 230; 4/82–3; 5/265; 6/102; 7/129, 394; 8/438; 9/84; public service, at French church, 3/296; Roman Catholic, 7/329–30; customs: 2/109–10, 216; 4/82–3; 5/200, 211; 7/49, 329–30; 8/202, 405

CHRISTIAN, Prince of Denmark, later King Christian V 1670–99: installed as Knight of Garter, 4/108 & n. 3

CHRISTIANIA, Norway: timber from, 3/118 & n. 3

[CHRISTINA OF BOURBON], Dowager-Duchess of Savoy: court mourning for, 5/18 & n. 3

CHRISTINA, Queen of Sweden 1644–54: 8/164 & n. 1

CHRISTMAS, Mr ——, P's schoolfellow: remembers P as 'a great Roundhead', 1/280; mimics preachers, ib.; social: 2/62

CHRISTMAS [see also Drink; Food; Twelfth Night]: wassail bowl, 2/239; boxes, 4/426; 7/422; 8/589; 9/403; gifts (to P's father), 5/344, 346; wedding, 6/338; Catholic ceremonies, 8/588–9; gambling during, 9/2, 4

CHRIST'S HOSPITAL, Newgate St: P buys fairings at, 2/166; boys attend Spital sermon, 3/57–8 & n.; children boarded out after Fire, 7/17 & n. 7

CHURCHILL, Arabella, Maid of Honour to the Duchess of York and mistress of the Duke (d. 1730): 9/413 & n. 2

CHURCH OF ENGLAND [see also Christenings; Funerals; Nonconformists; Presbyterians; Religion (P); Sermons; Weddings]:
CHRON. SERIES:
RESTORATION 1660–2: disputes between Presbyterian and Episcopalian clergy, 1/204 & n. 2; consecration of bishops, 1/276 & n. 2; Worcester House Conference, 1/271 & n. 3, 278 & n. 2, 282–3; bishops restored to Lords, 2/82 & n. 7, 111, 216; Savoy Conference, 2/141; restoration of lands, 1/152; restoration of services: 1/190 & n. 1; at Westminster Abbey, 1/190, 261, 283, 324; Whitehall, 1/176, 195, 210; St Margaret,

CLARENDON PARK, Wilts.: sold by Albemarle to Clarendon, 5/61 & n. 1; dispute over timber, 5/203–6 passim, 210, 212–14 passim, 216, 218, 219, 238, 318, 321; alluded to: 9/321

CLARGES (Clerges), Sir Thomas; Muster-Master General; M.P. Westminster 1660; kted 1660: Sandwich's low opinion, 1/129; army's envoy to King, 1/128 & n. 2, 129; report on navy's debts, 1/288 & n. 1; criticises Navy Board, 8/510; 9/62; alluded to: 1/184

CLARKE: see Clerke

CLARKE, [Frances], wife of Timothy: P admires, 1/214; 3/75–6, 99; witty but conceited, 3/299; 4/14; 5/197; a poor housewife, 4/142; 8/58–9; proud, 7/100; 8/157; slanderous anecdote of, 7/100; painted, 8/58; social: 4/88 89, 97; 5/245, 291; 8/101, 421; alluded to: 3/298; 4/42; ~ her cousin, 4/14; her kinswoman, 5/197

CLARKE, [Julian] (Aunt Kite): fatally ill, 2/172 & n. 2; disposes of property, 2/173 & n. 1; burial, 2/178, 179; P as executor, 2/179; goods valued, 2/190

CLARKE (Clerke), Capt. Robert, naval officer: arrests Cavalier, 1/99; gift to P, 1/104; kindness to P, 1/257; serves on *Antelope*, 6/19; and *Gloucester*, 7/148; conduct in Dutch raid criticised, 8/310; criticises sinking of *Monmouth*, 8/327–8; social: 1/115; 2/74, 210

CLARKE, [Timothy], royal physician: CHRON. SERIES: P's regard, 1/134; 5/245; on Dutch voyage ('the Doctor'), 1/134, 135, 136, 145, 153–4, 156, 157; tells P story, *The fruitless precaution*, 1/135 & n. 2, 266; at The Hague, 1/138; discusses nature of tragedy, 1/236 & n. 3; visits Portsmouth, 3/69–72; tells bawdy stories, 3/69; to nominate P as Fellow of Royal Society, 3/72 & n. 3; at Royal Society club, 6/36; part in P. Carteret's marriage negotiations, 6/136, 137; criticism of Davenant, 8/59; writes play, 8/59–60; also, 8/159

AS PHYSICIAN: attends Capt. Ferrers, 2/103; Sandwich, 4/17; and King,

5/197; dissects cadavers before King, 4/132; prescribes for P, 4/407, 441; experiment with opium, 5/151; discusses arrangements for war wounded, 5/332 & n. 5; also, 7/177; 9/254

COURT NEWS FROM: 1/143; 3/282; 4/19; 7/48–9; 8/35, 47

SOCIAL: entertains P to poor dinner, 8/58–9; also, 1/173, 211, 214; 3/73, 74, 230, 299; 4/14, 142; 8/157; 9/200, 413; ~ house, 3/76

ALLUDED TO: 1/159; 4/10, 97

CLARKE (Clerke), Sir William, kted 1661, Secretary at War 1661–6: orders troop movements, 1/86; P asks favour from, 6/169; news from, 6/280–1 & n.; a 'brisk blade', 7/84; Sandwich's low opinion, 7/203; fatally wounded in action, 7/147, 149, 154; alluded to: 6/121 & n. 2, 122–3; 9/317

CLAXTON, [Hammond], of Booton, Norf., P's relative: advises P over Robert P's will, 2/181; 3/218; social: 2/146, 147

CLAXTON, [Paulina], wife of Hammond, housekeeper to Roger P: 3/219; 4/159

CLAYPOLE, John ('Lord') (d. 1688): enquires for lease of P's Axe Yard house, 1/218 & n. 1; ~ his footman, ib.

CLAYTON, Sir Thomas, Warden of Merton College, Oxford 1661–93: 9/352 & n. 2

CLEGGAT, Col. [?Thomas], Greenwich: political news from, 6/286; social: 6/245, 316

CLEMENT IX, Pope 1667–70: election, 8/336 & n. 1

CLEMENTS [?John], bo'sun: 3/155

CLEOPATRA: alluded to in sermon, 5/97; picture, 9/430

CLERGES: see Clarges

CLERK OF THE ACTS, the [i.e. P's principal activities as Clerk. References to his attendance at the Board and to his share in its collective decisions are indexed under Navy Board. *See also* Royal Exchange; for his relations with colleagues and associates, *see* under names.]:

GENERAL: career summarised, vol. i,

134, 239, 291; 6/24, 32, 338; 9/562; attitude to giving receipts, 4/436; 5/271; 6/83; 'mighty merry' with Warren over 'our ... tricks', 7/24; falsifies record, 7/295 & n. 1; nervous of parliamentary enquiry into, 9/73, 81–2, 90, 99, 562 & n. 1

HIS SUCCESS [for his love of work, *see also* Vows. For his repute with others, *see* under names]: his pleasure in work and prospect of wealth, 3/40; 4/66; 6/145, 319; 7/215, 249; 8/246; recognises he was appointed by 'chance without merit' and that 'only diligence' keeps him in, 6/285; growing reputation, 2/51; 3/120, 150, 205, 210, 302; 4/1, 289, 296–7, 386; 5/80; 6/324; less unpopular than colleagues in war crisis, 8/297–8, 302, 315, 490(2); said with Coventry to do all work of office, 3/290; 4/19–20; fears distractions of music and cards, 4/104–5, 107; 8/57; realises severity may make him unpopular, 4/256; upbraids himself for idleness, 5/273, 280, 288, 289; 6/92; 7/62, 65, 126, 136; 8/527; 9/173; fears being thought idle, 4/3; 5/341; 6/89; 8/113, 232, 260, 411, 552, 576; 9/78, 144, 155, 170; unwilling to delegate, 6/272; guilty at going to theatre, 8/171, 173, 552; at neglecting Navy Office for Tangier business, 6/107, 109; expected to become Lord High Admiral's secretary, 8/419; alone attends Duke's meeting about expedition to Algiers, 9/516; also, 3/45, 49, 114, 125, 131, 132, 139, 144, 146, 151, 159, 209, 233, 284; 4/23, 71, 166, 188, 205, 257; 5/30, 31, 62, 173, 227, 285, 305, 360; 6/8, 62, 307; 7/107, 123, 286; 8/77, 204, 311–12, 442; 9/8

HIS OFFICE/CLOSET/STUDY IN NAVY OFFICE: alterations, 3/36 & n. 1, 113, 190; 4/282, 284, 286; 5/143 & n. 1, 144, 145; 6/111; 8/522 & n. 3, 523; cleaned, 3/113; 4/285; 7/124; 8/240; bores holes to see into general office, 3/126, 134; table, 3/158; alters position at, 9/547; engravings in, 6/111 & n. 5, 144; 7/124; temporary office at Greenwich, 6/200, 201, 227; study alluded to, 3/266

OFFICE STATIONERY: orders paper from France, 1/201 & n. 1; acquires file, scissors, etc., 2/171; 3/17, 115; buys memorandum-book, 3/115; has paper ruled, 7/98(2), 100. 101, 105, 110, 115

OFFICE RECORDS [The many occasions on which P 'sorts' his papers are not indexed. *See also* Navy Board: records]:

GENERAL: makes inventory, 1/195; buries papers during Fire, 7/274; demonstrates office methods, 9/527

COLLECTIONS [omitting letters, memoranda etc. written for particular occasions]: Admiral's Instructions, abstract of, 3/148 & n. 1; contract book(s): 3/65 & n. 2, 83, 105, 106; 4/214, 220; 5/117; 6/43; 8/353, 540, 545; 9/43–4; entered monthly, 6/43; neglected, 8/350; carried in pocket, 8/540; bound, 8/551; day books, 5/117 & n. 4; 9/444; letter book(s), 3/281 & n. 2; 7/266 & n. 1; 8/258, 314; mast prices, list of, 3/256; memorandum book(s), 4/241 & n. 3, 421, 423; 5/36; 9/91, 406; collection for history of Navy, 9/501 & n. 2, 502, 506, 507; 'Navy MS' or precedent book: 4/11 & n. 1, 14, 15, 23, 29, 36, 65, 96, 107, 188, 191, 214, 218, 219; borrowed by Coventry, 4/264; 'Navy White Book', 5/116 & n. 1, 287; office notes, 5/174; order books, 8/539 & n. 4, 540; ships, list of, with dimensions, 9/26 & n. 2; tables of naval matters, 7/148; varnished paper book, 7/199, ?304, ?305

HIS CLERKS [*see also* Edwards, T.; Gibson, R.; Hayter, T.; Hewer, W.]: purchase price of a clerkship, 1/194; their right to sign warrants, 3/106 & n. 2, 138, 163–4; 4/72; extra provision for, 5/228 & n. 1; 8/593–4 & n.; their profits, 5/320; P's appreciation of, 8/553; their help with pay tickets, 9/100, 102; dine with P [?working dinners], 8/297, 528, 539–40, 540, 546, 565, 569, 584, 588, 594; 9/8, 26, 42, 79, 100, 110, 125, 126, 137, 145, 147, 158, 164, 166, 167, 168, 178, 198, 201, 207, 209, 216, 221, 223, 307, 310, 312, 314, 327, 339, 342, 357, 381, 408, 413, 416, 437, 458, 481

303–4 & n.; 5/215–16 & n., 333 & n. 1; 7/2–3 & n.; deals, 4/232 & n. 4, 233; tar, 4/364 & n. 1; 5/136 & n. 3; glazing, 5/44 & n. 4; hammocks, 6/40 & n. 2; plank, 6/99 & n. 6, 185 & n. 2; defends Warren's contracts, 4/326, 421 & n. 3; 7/2–3 & n.; 9/254, 255; criticises Winter's, 4/326; and Murford for alleged breach of, 4/353 & n. 1; makes calculation about Wood's masts, 5/51 & n. 4, 52

DOCKYARDS [for his work at individual yards *see* Blackwall; Chatham; Deptford; Portsmouth; Woolwich]: drafts letter 'of reprehension and direction', 3/164 & n. 5; introduces new call-book, 3/234 & n. 2, 289 & n. 2; 4/14–15; to visit Deptford and Woolwich at least once a week, 4/425; defends his administration, 4/256; proposes employment of workmen in fire-fighting, 7/274

FINANCIAL [*see also* Exchequer; Navy Board; Treasury; Warwick, Sir P.]: *general*: prepares statement on debts for parliament, 1/211, 214 & n. 4, 226 & n. 4, 227, 228, 246 & n. 3, 247, 288 & n. 1; drafts scheme for paying off seamen, 1/309 & n. 5; makes estimates for boats, 3/52; drafts statement of navy estimates, 3/179 & n. 4; prepares answer to Lord Treasurer, 3/250, 258, 261, 280 & n. 1; and account of expenses (1660–2), 4/49 & n. 2; calculates debts, 4/304; introduces new method of accountancy, 5/7; proposes separation of posts of deputy-treasurer and muster-master, 5/8 & n. 1; drafts letter to Lord Treasurer on cost of war, 5/325, 326, 329; inflates estimate, 5/330 & n. 2; to be fully informed by Treasury, 6/46; works on accounts, 6/256 & n. 3, 257 & n. 4; 7/76(2); comments on proposal to pay bills in course, 6/304 & n. 3; and on value of Additional Aid (1665), 6/327, 334; 7/4, 87; presents statements of need for money: to Lord Treasurer, 7/48 & n. 2, 294 & n. 1, 295; to Duke of York, 7/122(2) & n. 1, 205–6 & n., 373 & n. 2, 374(2), 381; 8/138 & n. 2, 274 & n. 3; 9/49, 94; to Cabinet/

Council, 7/311–12 & n.; 8/111(2), 111–12 & n., 114 & n. 3; enquires about loans at Guildhall, 7/72 & n. 2, 76, 88 & n. 2; prepares statement on cost of war for Commons, 7/233, 285–8 passim & nn., 291–4 passim & n., 300, 301–2 & n., 308 & nn., 310, 314; 8/90; compares costs of First and Second Dutch Wars, 7/307 & n. 5, 308; calculates extraordinary charges, 7/310; his imprests authorised by Board, 7/328, 330; prepares accounts for parliament, 7/417; examines petty warrant accounts, 8/50; attempts to get creditors paid, 8/203(2); 9/140, 146, 149; works on report to Treasury Commission on accounts (1660–7), 8/250, 349, 372 & n. 1, 373 & n. 2; consults Treasury about commanders' pay, 8/398; works on Navy Treasurer's accounts, 8/448 & n. 4, 458 & n. 2; drafts Council order about Exchequer certificates, 9/152–3; applies to city for cash, 9/169; ordered by Council to calculate charge of summer fleet, 9/216; reforms storekeepers' accounts, 9/300, 374 & n. 1, 474; defends Board against criticisms from new Treasurers, 9/447; examines old accounts, 9/479; prepares estimates, 9/493–4 & n., 501, 530; also, 4/305, 306; 6/75; 7/77; 8/89, 273, 274, 277, 524; 9/40, 109, 110, 119, 271

pays [*see also* Navy Treasury; and under names of dockyards]: signs tickets, 6/158; 7/366; 8/280; discusses order of pay, 7/308, 327; and methods of expediting, 8/433 & n. 1, 558 & n. 3; inspects Ticket Office, 7/76, 418; to draw up rules for issue of tickets, 9/15 & n. 4

pursers: plans reform of, 6/325, 341; memorandum on, 7/1(3) & n. 1, 2(3), 5, 9, 10 & n. 1, 13; plan adopted, 7/27, 28, 105, 106 & n. 2; offers to help Mennes with pursers' accounts, 7/421 & n. 2; new proposals, 9/459, 460 & n. 2

JUDICIAL/DISCIPLINARY BUSINESS [*see also* Carkesse, [J.]; Field, [E.]]: memorandum on bill empowering Principal Officers as city magistrates,

COMMISSIONER OF THE SICK AND
WOUNDED AND PRISONERS OF WAR:
appointed Treasurer, 5/329 & n. 1;
business, 8/112; also, 6/217

HIS SHARE IN SANDWICH'S PRIZE-GOODS:
bargains and agreements with P and
others, 6/230, 238 & n. 4, 241, 243,
245, 297; acquires certificate from
Sandwich, 6/247; goods threatened
with seizure, 6/243, 252, 256, 259,
260–5 passim, 269–70; profit, 6/313–
14, 327, 328, 329, 334, 340, 341;
7/65; affair investigated by Brooke
House Committee, 9/48–50 passim
& nn., 57, 61, 63, 66, 72; also, 6/228,
234, 239, 246, 247, 248, 271–2, 272,
312, 318; 7/6

POLITICAL VIEWS ETC.: on Dutch war,
5/35, 105; 6/282; 7/286–7; fears parliament will withold supply, 2/196–7;
8/68–70; pessimism about government and state of nation, 6/210–11,
218, 245; 7/14, 375; 8/125, 409; 9/96;
believes active King the only solution,
8/37; on danger of civil war, 8/70;
help to Coventry, 9/303; news from,
7/220, 287, 309, 311, 317, 402; 8/18, 24,
37, 68–70, 80, 105, 153, 176, 275–6,
409, 447, 535, 568, 572; 9/278

COMMERCIAL NEWS: about Guinea
trade, 4/363; loss of rents in Fire,
7/286 & n. 2; bankers' wartime credit,
8/285

HOUSES: at Greenwich: P visits, 3/142,
143; 6/233, 291, 297; stable, 6/233;
garden, 6/291, 297; door by the
water, 6/297; in London: 8/441, 497

RELATIONS WITH P: gifts of fish etc.,
2/225; 3/81; silver plate, 7/90, 91, 121,
132, 405, 409, 416–17, 420; money,
7/132; lends coach, 7/269; warns
against Brouncker, 8/203; asks for
loan, 8/598; praises parliamentary
speech, 9/105, 113; advises about proposed reform of Board, 9/290; also,
7/305; 8/572; 9/285

SOCIAL: drunk, 2/?232, 238; 3/4;
6/290; atheistical talk, 5/335–6; on
river trip, 3/30–1; talks of Poland,
3/154; of Roman history, 4/362; of
Cromwell's betrayal of Charles I,
5/335 & n. 2; plays billiards, 6/190;
enjoys Mrs Penington's company,

6/273, 297, 299, 308, 310; at Twelfth
Night party, 7/6; dance, 7/18; taverns, 2/208, 218, 219, 233; 6/325;
7/68, 74, 89; 8/95; houses/lodgings of
associates in London and Greenwich,
2/211, 218–19; 3/10, 88; 5/277;
6/186, 187, 204, 209, 217, 236, 237,
275, 285, 303, 307–8, 311, 313, 317;
7/14, 67, 376; 8/65, 66; 9/410; at his
Greenwich house, 3/142, 143; 6/191,
192, 212, 220, 222, 227, 228, 275, 291,
296, 316, 324, 335–6, 339; London
house, 7/34, 38, 404, 408; 8/394–5,
441, 497; 9/15; also, 2/220, 223–4;
?4/212; 6/226, 248, 303

ALLUDED TO: 9/286, 501

~ his son: 2/218; at school, 6/223; his
black footboy (?Jack) dies of suspected
plague, 6/232, 233, 236, 244, 283, 285;
his servant Jacob, 6/259; his maid,
7/63

COCKE, [Robert], navy victualler at
Lisbon: gift to P, 4/290 & n. 2;
accounts, 4/325

COCKE, ——, ?a prostitute, Fleet
Alley: P entertained by, 5/225–6

COCKER, [Edward], calligrapher
and engraver: P's regard, 5/237–8 &
n.; engraves P's slide-rule, ib.; sells
him reading glass, 5/290, 291–2

COCKPIT, the: see Whitehall Palace

COCKPIT, the new, King's Gate,
Holborn: P at, 9/136, 141, 154

[COENDERS, Rudolf], Dutch naval
commander: killed in action, 7/229 &
n. 3, 231 & n. 4

COFFEE-HOUSES:

GENERAL: political talk/debate in [see
also below, Miles's]: 5/30, 228, 321;
8/304; Presbyterians' bold talk, 4/15;
literary/scientific talk, 5/14, 27–8, 37,
108, 123; music, 5/12; in Plague, 7/45;
chocolate drunk, 5/329

P VISITS [business talk/transactions not
noted]: [Miles's, the 'Turk's Head',
New Palace Yard, Rota Club at], 1/13,
14, 17, 20–1, 61, 63, 288; Grant's,
4/64–5; coffee-house(s) near Navy
Office [all or most in Cornhill],
1/318; 2/11, 108, 111, 151; 3/2, 35;
4/340, 353, 371, 378, 380, 434, 438;
5/1, 12, 34, 293, 295; in Covent
Garden, 5/37 & n. 2 (the 'great' coffee

political/court news from, 7/353–4; 8/11, 86, 368–9, 544, 597; alluded to: 2/97; 9/139; ~ his brother, 1/206

COLLADON (Collidon), Sir John, physician: patent for smoky chimneys, 4/315 & n. 1

COLLAR: see Collier

COLLETON (Collidon), Sir John, merchant: report on Fishery lottery, 5/299–300 & n.

COLLIER, [?John] ('Blacke Coller'): Hawley's case against, 1/199–200 & n.

COLLINS, [Jerome], surgeon: to sail with Rupert, 5/275 & n. 1

COLLINS, ——: employed by Brooke House Committee, 9/43

COLNBROOK, Mdx: 9/243

COLVILL(E), John, goldsmith banker, Lombard St:

BUSINESS WITH P: Tangier: cashes tallies, 6/108, 115, 163, 164; 7/214, 242; and bills of exchange, 6/169; 7/66; his accounts settled, 6/204–5, 325; also, 9/265; private: sells salts, 6/131; arranges loan on Treasury warrants, 7/85, 89–90 & n., 230, 243, 244, 251; advances money for Paulina P's portion, 9/97; unspecified: 6/184, 297; 9/214

HIS NEWS/OPINIONS: critical of ministers, 7/244; news of Dutch fleet, 6/184; of court and parliament, 7/323; low view of government credit, 6/268; 7/171; praises P's parliamentary speech, 9/109; also, 6/318

MISC.: credit survives Fire, 7/323; moves to Lime St after Fire, 7/323; new house in Lombard St, 9/112

~ his beautiful wife: 6/131–2

COLWALL, [Daniel], Treasurer of the Royal Society: supports Carkesse in dispute with Navy Board, 8/555; at Royal Society, 9/147, 334

COMBERFORD, [Nicholas], chartmaker, Ratcliffe: P admires his methods, 4/240

COMETS and meteors: see Science and Mathematics: astronomy

COMINGES, Gaston Jean-Baptiste, Comte de, French ambassador 1663–5: at review of troops, 4/217; takes offence at Lord Mayor's banquet,

4/355; house [Exeter House, Strand], 5/103 & n. 4

COMMANDER, [Henry], scrivener, Warwick Lane: draws up deed for Sandwich, 4/343; and P's will, 5/20, 25, 26, 29, 31, 192; negotiates P's purchase of land etc. for coachhouse and stable, 8/209, 224, 225, 246, 250

COMMON GARDEN: see Covent Garden

COMMONWEALTH, the:

GENERAL: P reproached for service to, 6/329–30; return predicted, 8/337–8, 390, 556; 9/373; political/military efficiency, 3/90; 6/45–6; 8/250, 377–8, 390–1

POLITICAL HISTORY: successive régimes in 1659, 5/8 & n. 2; Committee of Safety (1659), 1/39, 51; 2/92; Council of State (1660): clerks dismissed, 1/23; members chosen, 1/65 & n. 4; appoints Sandwich general-at-sea, 1/71; orders Cavaliers and disbanded soldiers to leave London, 1/91 & n. 2; prepares agreement with King, 1/103 & n. 2, 111; also, 1/48

ARMY: high repute abroad, 4/215 & n. 3; and at home, 4/217, 373–4 & n.; disbandment, 1/242 & n. 1, 249, 257, 295 & n. 3, 304; political activity: officers submit to Rump, 1/1, 13, 14; soldiers mutinous, 1/36 & n. 4, 36–7 & n., 38 & n. 1, 40 & n. 3, 59 & n. 4; officers' attempted remonstrance to parliament, 1/81–2 & n., 88 & n. 1; soldiers said to be anti-royalist, 1/86; Dunkirk garrison royalist, 1/101; army's engagement to support parliament, 1/108 & n. 3; envoy sent to King, 1/128 & n. 2; also, 1/121

FINANCIAL ADMINISTRATION: coinage, 4/148 & n. 2; efficient collection of excise, 4/374–5 & n.; revenue, 5/68 & n. 3

NAVAL ADMINISTRATION: alleged corruption, 1/308; praised, 6/45; compared with Navy Board, 7/307 & n. 5, 308; 9/444, 484 & n. 3; methods, 9/485; creditors to be paid (1663), 4/158–9 & n.; promotion by sanctity, 4/375; Cromwell's expenditure, 5/59 & n. 4

COMPTON, James, 3rd Earl of

Northampton (d. 1681): in Chancery case, 1/48, n. 1; introduces bill banishing Clarendon, 8/565

COMPTON, Sir William, Master of the Ordnance: carries letter from Sandwich to King, 1/129–30; watches gun trial, 3/130 & n. 4; compares contemporary fleet with that of 1588, 3/187 & n. 2; appointed to Tangier Committee, 3/238, 272; attends meetings, 4/21, 23, 269, 335, 338; death, 4/338–9; high repute, ib.; social: 3/242

CONDÉ, Louis II de Bourbon, Prince de (d. 1686): Bristol's falsity to, 4/213, n. 2; bravery, 5/171

CONNY, [John], surgeon: 9/495, 497

CONSTABLE, Lord High, office of: rumour of Albemarle's appointment, 8/269 & n. 3, 270

CONSTANTINOPLE: ambassador sails to, 1/217, 224, 250; peace with Algiers confirmed from, 4/369–70 & n.

COOK, John, regicide: trial, 1/263 & n. 1; head displayed, 1/270

COOKE [Edward], underclerk to the Council of State: 1/25, ?203, ?207

COOKE, Capt. Henry, Master of the Choristers, Chapel Royal: anthems sung/conducted/composed by, 1/220, 260; 2/41; 3/84, 85, 190, 197; 4/428; singing and compositions admired by P, 8/59; claims to have taught Davenant, ib.; at music meeting, 8/532; introduces Tom Edwards to P's household, 5/162, 234, 255; 6/77; social: 1/223; 2/103, 142; 7/412; 8/58; alluded to: 7/383

COOKE, [John], clerk to Secretary Morice: 5/62 & n. 2

COOKE, Capt. [Thomas], Master of the Tennis Court, Whitehall: plays with Rupert, 8/418–19 & n.

COOKE, Mr ——, servant to Sandwich: as messenger, 1/101, 109, 111, 118, 128, 131, 132, 137, 162, 165, 166, 167, 170, 179, 238, 239, 264; 8/582; 9/51; troubles P (? for employment), 1/207 (doubtful reference); repays debt to, 2/109; to negotiate match for Tom P, 3/176, 183, 185, 195, 202, 203, 205, 207, 228, 232, 233; 5/252; at

Brampton and Cambridge, 3/219, 223, 224, 226; 9/212; asks for post at Tangier, 4/66; past kindness to P, 5/252; at Hinchingbrooke, 7/131, 234; social: plays ninepins, 4/160; also, 1/151, 174, 176, ?203, 221; 3/138; 7/83

COOKE, [?Samuel], bookbinder: makes bosses for P's Bible, 1/281

COOKSHOPS and cooks [For cooks named in the text, see Gentleman, ——; Levitt, [W.]; Phillips, [?J.]; Slater, ——; Starkey's; Robinson, ——; and Wilkinson's [W.]. Cooks who were domestic servants appear under the names of their employers]: P dines at Welsh cook's at Charing Cross, 4/12; ?6/40, 79; at other cookshops, 1/14, 195 & n. 3; 2/116, 160, 190, 196, 197; 4/34; 7/320; 9/391, 480, 494, 509; food supplied from, 1/10 & n. 6, 16, 17, 190, 202, 270; 2/89, 146, 234, 237; 3/62, ?251, 293; 4/281, 326, 384; 5/126; 6/75; 7/274; food cooked at, 4/334; 7/199; cooks hired from, 2/28; 3/53; 4/13; 7/388, 389, 392; ?9/423–4; wedding party at, 7/262

COOLING: see Coling

COOPER, Sir Anthony Ashley, cr. Baron Ashley 1661, cr. Earl of Shaftesbury 1672, Chancellor of the Exchequer, Treasurer of the Commission for Prizes, and Treasury Commissioner:

CHARACTER: ability, 4/137, 158–9, 176; 5/174; 6/13; 7/121; 8/231; 9/199; alleged corruption, 6/218; 7/128 & n. 3, 129, 137, 156, 163, 167; 8/445, 446

PRIVATE AFFAIRS: claims Whitehall lodgings, 1/17, 22, 23; house [Exeter House, Strand], 8/445, 553; operated on for abscess, 9/246 & n. 1; portrait by Cooper, 9/139 & n. 3

AS POLITICIAN (GENERAL): appointed to Privy Council, 1/171; enemy of Clarendon, 4/137; 5/34; to be Lord Treasurer (rumour), 4/137–8; ally of Buckingham, 4/137; 9/444–5; quarrels with Ossory, 7/376 & n. 1; opinion on status of judges in Lords, 8/445 & n. 4; to be dismissed (rumour), 8/596 & n. 1, 600; speech on bill establishing Brooke House Committee, 9/8

AS CHANCELLOR OF THE EXCHEQUER: navy business, 4/158–9; 5/321; Tangier business, 6/91(2) [*see also* below]; alluded to: 8/180

AS TREASURER OF THE COMMISSION FOR PRIZES: orders payment to navy, 6/319; resists Navy Board's request for ships, 7/80; accounts, ˑ 7/309; 8/446; quarrels with Board over sale of goods, 8/16, 20, 144; sits as Commissioner of Appeal, 8/231; alluded to: 8/252

AS TREASURY COMMISSIONER: appointment, 8/223, 229–30; low view of˚ colleagues, 8/244; and unpopularity with them, 9/205; proposes method of paying off fleet, 8/456; opposes Navy Board's application for money, 9/152, 171, 174, 444–5; unspecified business, 9/525; alluded to: 8/249

AS MEMBER OF TANGIER COMMITTEE: examines Povey's accounts, 6/13, 14, 15–16, 33, 77–8, 79; 9/371, 449; Rutherford's, 6/95; Yeabsley's, 7/121, 156; bribed by Yeabsley, 7/128, 129, 137; supports his claims, 7/156, 167; 8/445, 446, 461; cool with Peterborough, 7/156, 163; examines Belasyse's accounts, 9/199; approves P's fees, 9/340; attends meetings, 5/174; 6/58; 8/347; unspecified business, 6/71 8/197; 9/152

~ his wife [Margaret], 8/446; for his clerk, *see* Blany, R.

COOPER, [Henry], officer of the King's Works: 1/314; provides seat for P at coronation, 2/83

COOPER, [Richard], sailing master: P's opinion, 4/84; 'one-eyed', 4/133; mate of *Royal James*, 3/128; master of *Reserve*, 3/159, 160; quarrels with Holmes, 4/67, 78, 81; dismissed, 4/84; teaches P mathematics, 3/128, 131–4 passim, 136, 140, 148, 149; ships' rigging etc., 3/138, 149, 152, 158, 160, 161, 163; and cartography, 4/133–4; 5/303

COOPER, Samuel, miniaturist (d. 1672): painting of EP, 9/138 & n. 3, 253, 256, 258, 259, 261, 263, 264, 267, 268, 276–7; its cost, 9/277; other

paintings by, 9/139–40; his house, 9/139 & n. 1; musical and other talents, 9/259–60; good company, 9/256; social: 9/265; alluded to; 3/2; ~ his cousin Jack [Hoskins], 9/265

COOPER, [William], timber purveyor to the Navy Board: report by, 3/169; his dullness, 4/231

COOPER, Maj. ――: 7/68, 404

COPENHAGEN: 1/140; 4/69 & n. 2

COPPIN, Capt. [John], naval officer: transferred from *Langport* to *Newbury*, 1/109; killed in action, 7/154

CORBET, Miles, regicide: arrested in Delft, 3/45 & n. 1, 47–8 & n.; in Tower, 3/47; executed, 3/66

CORBET, Mrs ――: social: 7/362; 8/384, 502; 9/12, 128, 133, 186

[CORBETTA], Francesco, court musician: 8/374 & n. 3

CORDERY, Mr ――: 6/108

CORDERY, Mrs ――: 2/153, 157

COREY, [Katherine], ('Doll Common'), actress: performance in *The scornful lady*, 7/422 & n. 6; quarrels with Lady Hervey, 9/415 & n. 1

CORNBURY, Viscount: *see* Hyde, L.

CORNHILL [*see also* Coffee-houses; Taverns etc.: Globe; Pope's Head; Three Golden Lions; White Bear]: coronation arch, 3/138 & n. 2; Fire, 8/151–2 & n.; Backwell's building development, 9/517 & n. 1; stocks, 1/314; carrefour at conduit, 3/268

CORNWALL, rebellion in (1549): 9/167 & n. 5

CORNWALLIS, Charles, 2nd Baron Cornwallis, Gentleman of the Privy Chamber 1660–d. 73: pimps for King, 9/264

CORNWALLIS, Frederick, 1st Baron Cornwallis, Treasurer of the Household 1660–d. 62: distributes medals at coronation banquet, 2/84; death and funeral, 3/10 & n. 4; character, ib.

CORNWALLIS, [Henrietta Maria, of the Queen-Mother's Household]: 9/23

CORONEL(L), [Sir Augustine], financial agent of the Portuguese government: in dispute over customs dues, 5/43 & n. 2

CORRESPONDENCE (P) [omitting

cookmaid: (wages) 6/29; E. Knepp: (signing herself 'Barbary Allen') 7/4; Lambert: (a simple letter) 1/183; Lanyon: (news) 6/8 & n. 2; R. Matthews: (pay) 1/33; Moore: (news) 1/113, 170; (lawsuit) 3/83; J. Pearse: (invitation) 4/10; Mrs J. Pearse: (social) 8/25;

EP: (health) 1/128; (family news) 1/166; (her loneliness) 3/257–8; 4/9; (country life) 4/199; (quarrels with father-in-law) 4/210; (quarrels with Ashwell) 4/262; (journeys) 7/93; 8/272; (stay at Roger P's) 9/310; (unspecified) 1/106, 137; 4/221; John P, sen.: (Brampton business) 2/180, 194, 195; 3/212, 240; 4/15; 7/80; (storm) 3/35; (family news) 3/106; 4/271; 5/154; 6/314; 9/308–9; (employment for relative) 3/119; (Ferrer's fight) 3/196; (Tom's match) 4/12; (Tom's children) 5/154, 158; (household arrangements) 4/180; (Pall's match) 7/78; (illness) 8/119; (J. Trice's difficulties) 8/158; (EP's return) 8/286; (unspecified) 9/18; John P, jun.: (request for books) 1/243; (asks favour) 2/26; (his ordination; in Latin) 7/50; (mother's illness) 8/122, 129; (and death) 8/134; (unspecified; in Latin) 1/137; Paulina P: (mother's illness), 3/103; Robert P: (asks favour) 2/96; (land purchase) 2/117; (unspecified) 1/218; Roger P: (Pall's match) 9/18–19; Tom P: (family news) 3/107; Tom P the turner: (Robert P's will) 3/48;

Sandwich: (shipping), 1/302; (alterations at Hinchingbrooke) 1/313–14; (Lisbon news) 2/209; (Tangier news) 2/221; 3/33 & n. 2; (requests visit) 3/240; (comet) 5/352; (return) 6/41; (Lady Jem's marriage) 6/163, 202; (return) 6/237; (prize-goods) 6/269, 309; (rebuke) 9/217; J. Scott: (Tom P's estate) 5/124, 149–50; (unspecified) 1/22 (in cipher); 1/44 (in cipher); 2/163; 5/225

CORTENAER, Egbert Meüssen, Dutch naval commander: sails from Holland, 6/108 & n. 3

COSIN (Cosens), John, Bishop of Durham 1660–d.72: votes for Clarendon's impeachment, 8/542 & n. 1

COTTENHAM, Cambs.: Pepys family in, 8/261 & n. 4, 274 & n. 2 ~ 'Cottenhamshire', 8/517

COTTERELL, Sir Charles, courtier, (d. 1702): story of Russian diplomatists, 8/428 & n. 3; at Danckert's, 9/504; ~ his son [Clement], ib. & n. 3

COTTINGTON, Francis, 1st Baron Cottington (d. 1652), diplomatist: advises Charles I to seize Spanish bullion, 7/253 & n. 1; stories of disinheriting nephew, 8/566–7 & n.; and of mission to Spain, 9/256 & nn.

COTTLE (Cuttle), [Mark], registrar of the Prerogative Court of Canterbury: house at Greenwich, 6/339 & n. 2; at Twelfth Night party, 7/5; alluded to: 6/334; 7/68; ~ his wife, 7/5

COTTON, Cambs.: 2/148

COUNCIL OF TRADE: see Privy Council

COUNTER, the, city prison (in the Poultry): prisoners sent to, 2/73 & n. 3; 3/44; 5/114; and conventiclers, 4/129; also, 4/421

COUNTRY, Capt. [Richard], naval officer: sails with P to Baltic (1659), 2/185 & n. 5; gift of fruit, 2/185–6

COUNTRYSIDE, P's appreciation of [his visits to the country are indexed under place names]: expresses enjoyment of pastoral scene near Brampton, 3/221 & n. 2; nightingales near Woolwich, 4/151; 5/130; walks/rides: near Rotherhithe, 4/112; Woolwich, 4/149; Epsom, 4/245–9; 8/335–40; Brampton, 4/312; Islington, 5/132–3; 8/175; Kingsland, 8/211–12; and Hatfield, 8/381; river outing, 8/236; journey in West Country, 9/229, 231, 232, 234; and Medway valley, 9/495; would rather take trips to country than own country retreat, 8/339–40 & n.

COURLAND, Duke of [? Jacob, Duke 1642–82]: method of hunting, 4/413–14

[COURTIN, Pierre], French ambassador-extraordinary 1665: arrives incognito, 6/76 & n. 1

other news of 1666 campaign, 7/181, 224, 228, 288, 304; Dutch raid on Medway: disapproves of reduction of fleet, 8/140; orders fireships, 8/256 & n. 2, 259, 260 & n. 1; discharges ships at Chatham, 8/271 & n. 1; blamed for disaster, 8/298; criticises Deane and Spragge, 8/358, 379; defence against parliamentary criticism, 8/490 & n. 2, 492 & n. 2, 497–8, 524, 536; examined on use of tickets, 8/497; incriminating letter suppressed, 8/507 & n. 1; also, 5/321; 6/112

ACCUSATIONS OF CORRUPTION: criticised for selling offices, 3/104 & n. 3; for selling offices and charging excessive fees, 4/156 & n. 4, 166, 169 & n. 3; defence, 3/243, 4/330–2 & n., 383; 7/306–7; takes salary in lieu of fees, 4/331 & n. 4; 9/92; cases cited, 4/71; 5/231 & n. 4, 235, 248–9 & nn.; to be attacked in Commons, 8/18, 69–70; examined by Committee on Miscarriages, 8/504, 505, 507; to be attacked in Commons, 9/87, 92, 98 & n. 2, 108 & n. 2, 128–9, 169; Sir F. Holles's part in attack, 9/92, 129, 173; and Tatnell's, 9/108; petition against him, 9/87 & n. 2, 129, 173; fears Brooke House Committee, 9/258, 277; accused of treason. 7/242 & n. 1

OTHER APPOINTMENTS:

AS TREASURY COMMISSIONER: appointed, 8/223, 229–30; asks for P's help, 8/230–1; dominates colleagues, 8/398; depressed by lack of money, 8/290, 591; 9/101, 248; reorganises Wardrobe, 9/7; concentrates on Treasury work, 9/316, 447; praises Southampton, 9/448; dismissed, 9/478–9 & n.; also, 9/465

AS TANGIER COMMISSIONER: appointed, 3/171, 238 & n. 3; critical of Povey, 3/177; supports P in disputes, 5/279; 9/418; encourages him to accept treasurership, 6/60, 106; other business: Povey's accounts, 5/48, 52, 123, 124, 127, 132, 135, 139; shipping, 5/177; victualling, 5/210; new commission, 5/229; reduction of garrison, 5/310; and of costs, 8/347; P's report on lack of money, 7/383; reform of

government, 8/160, 201; Belasyse's profits, 9/205; construction of mole, 9/364; puts low value on overseas possessions, 8/347–8; misc. and unspecified business, 3/272, 287; 4/335, 341; 5/168, 204; 6/154; 7/156, 166, 167; 8/210

AS M.P.: opposes motion to farm administration of navy, 7/304; defends Carteret, 7/322; libel against, 7/342; assures House King will disband army, 8/353; speaks in defence of clergy, 9/121 & n. 2

AS PRIVY COUNCILLOR: business: Lord Treasurer's accounts, 7/295; state of navy, 7/312; report on Navy Board, 7/374; on Tangier, 7/383; Navy Treasurer's accounts, 8/449; naval bounties, 8/460–1; manning fleet, 9/121; size of fleet, 9/216–17; unspecified, 7/354; 8/317

ON FISHERY COUNCIL: attends meeting, 3/269–70; anxious for its success, 4/366

RELATIONS WITH P: regard for/kindness to, 2/24; 3/134, 151, 171, 183, 185, 202, 210, 216, 272, 282, 302; 4/39, 232, 289; 6/63, 64(2), 172; 7/26–7, 28, 67–8; 8/420; 9/502–3; with P/Pett dominates office, 3/284, 290; P fears his reforming zeal, 3/83; welcomes it, 3/105; supports P's reform of victualling, 6/279–80; of pursers, 7/1 & n. 1, 5, 9 & n. 3, 10, 13, 28, 106; of office in general, 9/205, 253, 293–4, 312, 523 & n. 2; shows him MSS, 5/177 & n. 2; 9/523 & n. 2; supports claim to purveyorship, 2/54; gives silver pen, 4/263–4 & n., 268; suggests he write war history, 5/177–8; proposes increased pay for his clerk, 5/228 & n. 1; advises on dealing with parliamentary critics, 8/303–4, 524, 560; 9/79, 178; and with Brooke House Committee, 9/42, 79, 117; provides office papers for his defence, 9/255; urges him to lend to government, 8/392, 393; helps obtain *Maybolt*, 8/477; congratulates on parliamentary speech, 9/104–5; urges him to enter parliament, 9/454; when in Tower and afterwards advises on office matters, 9/481, 488, 503–4, 523, 563; P values his favour, 7/248; 8/113, 175, 203, 255; fears he has lost it, 4/27; 6/166; 7/65–6, 67, 69; their talks rare, 8/20, 206; also, 4/135, 136, 140, 322; 8/131, 141; 9/33, 255

RELATIONS WITH SANDWICH: enmity, 2/170; 3/121, 122; criticises in prize-goods affair, 7/10, 27, 34, 41, 52, 67, 68; 9/165; prejudiced report of Battle of Lowestoft, 6/121 & nn., 134, 135 & n. 1, 276, 301; their consequent estrangement, 6/230, 276, 287, 291, 301; friendly, 3/177; 6/139; 8/572

RELATIONS WITH OTHERS: criticises Mennes, 4/97, 219, 341; 8/586; 9/131; and Batten, 4/97, 219, 437; 5/169; defends Batten, 4/194; criticises Carteret, 4/195; 7/43, 65–6, 83; 8/140, 164–5, 179–80, 247, 290, 301; friendly to, 7/325; admires Jolliffe, 5/300; criticises Commissioner Pett, 8/230–1, 278; Deane, 8/358 & n. 1; and Anglesey, 8/567; praises Brooke House Commissioners, 8/586

AS POLITICIAN: made knight and Privy Councillor, 6/137, 141; 'now a great man', 7/248; fears fanatics' rising, 3/186; allegedly disloyal to Clarendon, 4/195–6; believes Catholics and Cavaliers incapable of business, 4/196; impatient with inefficiency, 4/267; unpopular, 8/270, 298, 304, 317–18; 9/41; to be Secretary of State, 8/118–19 & n., 120; distrusted by Clarendon, 6/276; 7/55; low opinion of Clarendon and Southampton, 9/40, 256, 486; high opinion of Falmouth, 9/294 & n. 1; leads attack on Clarendon, 8/409 & n. 2, 410, 413–15 & nn., 417, 504, 506, 507, 550, 560; his MS. account of, 9/475–6; loses favour of King and Duke of York, 8/424, 530, 570, 592; no longer in cabal, 8/585, 597; reconciled to Duke of York, 8/413–15, 485, 486, 535, 550–1; 9/79, 342; dependent on him, 9/336; will accept office only in commission, 8/505; ousted by Buckingham and Arlington, 9/67, 323; weary of office, 9/386–7, 447, 471; satirised in *The country gentleman*, 9/471 & n. 2; challenges Buckingham to duel, 9/462–3 & n.,

467–8 & n., 471 & nn., 472; dismissed from Council and sent to Tower, 9/466 & n. 2, 468, 470, 484; petitions King, 9/475; his dismissal unpopular, 9/478; his visitors at Tower, 9/473, 493; released, 9/490, 491, 493; returns to court, 9/515, 523; dislikes French treaty, 9/536; also, 7/325; 9/417

NEWS FROM [select. Coventry was one of P's main sources of information]: 3/44; 4/347, 352; 5/127, 264; 7/308, 318, 321, 364; 8/20, 397, 570; 9/86–7, 92–3, 279, 290–1, 293–4, 415, 489–90

HOUSES: lodgings in Old Palace Yard, 2/222; in Whitehall Palace (in winter): 1/226 etc.; little new chamber, 3/229; in St James's Palace (in summer): 3/136; his plate, 5/120; picture, 7/183; new closet, 7/227; new house in Pall Mall: 8/504 & n. 5, 507–8, 559; closet, 9/255; round table, ib. & n. 2; chimney pieces, 9/267; dining room, 9/303; hangings, 9/330; surrenders claim to Turner's lodgings in Navy Office, 8/24

SOCIAL: sings on barge, 2/77; gives dinners to naval associates, 2/222; 5/11, 102, 111, 166; dines at Trinity House, 3/103, 187; 5/172; at Africa House, 5/48; with Sandwich, 3/139; Batten, 3/148, 181; 5/216, 357; Sheriff Meynell, 3/200; Foley, 3/266; Mennes, 4/28; Carteret, 5/15; and Chicheley, 9/112; dines impromptu with P, 3/285–6; his amusing stories (alluded to), 4/346, 406; 7/135; at theatre, 8/167; at races with King and Duke of York, 8/203–4

MISC.: reads psalms in shorthand, 2/76 & n. 3; his mistress, 5/7; on varieties of courage, 5/169–71; unwell, 5/81, 223; 7/332; 9/563; defends father's reputation, 7/261 & n. 3; goods removed from St James's during Fire, 7/279; anecdote of Fire, 7/282; keeps diary, 9/475; also, 9/276

ALLUDED TO: 1/313; 2/95, 185; 8/324

~ his clerk(s), 3/138, 237 [see also Robson, [T.]]; his footboy, 4/15; 8/260

[COWDREY, Walter], Keeper of

Newgate prison: malpractices, 8/562 & n. 2

COWES, Capt. Richard, naval officer: gift to P, 1/114

COWES, Isle of Wight: 5/304

COW LANE: coachmakers, 9/333, 352; also, 7/395 & n. 1; 8/464

COWLEY, Abraham, poet: new book of poems, 4/386 & n. 3; ill, ib. & n. 4; death, 8/380 & n. 3; repute 8/380, 383 & n. 3; alluded to: 7/400

COWLEY, Thomas, Clerk of the Cheque, Deptford: tells P of abuses, 3/128; bookkeeping, 3/129, 234; 4/80; gives P Cowley's poems, 4/386; ~ his clerk, 8/39

COWLING: see Coling

COX, Capt. [John], naval officer; Navy Commissioner 1669–72; kted 1672: quarrels with Storekeeper, 4/149 & n. 2; alleged bribe to Batten, 5/141; action in Battle of Lowestoft, 8/489–90 & n., 491(2), 492; Guinea business, 9/350; proposed as Penn's successor, ib.; appointed Navy Commissioner, 9/441, 499; also, 4/226; 8/188; 9/549–50; social: at Trinity House as Elder Brother, 7/72; at parish dinner, 9/559; also, 2/229, ?232; ?4/212; 9/469; alluded to: 9/381

COX, [Thomas], Colonel of city militia: narrow escape in Venner rising, 7/190 & n. 4

COYET, Peter Julius, Swedish ambassador-extraordinary 1666–7: intermediary in peace negotiations, 8/80 & n. 4, 92, 155, 177, 317, 349

CRAFFORD: see Crawfurd

CRAFTS: breadbaking (French), 6/48 & n. 3; heraldic painting, 4/424–5 & nn.; modelling in plaster, 9/442 & n. 2, 449, 487–8; jewelry (Woolwich stones), 8/84 & n. 2; mason's work, 5/63 & n. 2, 449, 487–8; needlework, 2/123; 4/74, 180; picture framing, 9/538; shellwork, 1/148 & n. 2; 4/293, 295, 298–9; 5/45; varnish and lacquer work, 4/153 & n. 2; 6/97; 7/147–8 & n., 184–5 (imitation tortoise-shell), 9/531–2 & n.

CRAGG, Mrs ——: Betty Martin's

landlady, 8/128, 435; P's valentine, 9/126; social: 8/323; 9/551

CRANBOURNE LODGE, Windsor Park: P/EP visit(s), 6/197–8; 7/52, 54, 56; rebuilt, 6/197 & n. 4; view from, 6/198; alluded to: 6/190, 191; 8/42

CRANBURNE, ——, of Fleet Lane: association with Tom P, 5/82

CRANFIELD, Anne, Countess of Middlesex (b. Brett), widow of Lionel Cranfield, 1st Earl (d. 1670): her accident at court, 1/181–2

CRANFIELD, Lionel, 3rd Earl of Middlesex (d. 1674): on *Royal Charles*, 1/156

CRANMER: error for Grindal, q.v.

CRAVEN, William, 1st Earl of Craven, courtier and soldier: chairman of Fishery Corporation, 5/251, 299–300, 323; 6/53; coxcomb, 6/258; high opinion of P, 6/197, 239, 305; covets Navy Treasurership, 7/6, 14; commands riot troops, 9/129; house at Hampstead Marshall, Berks., 9/242 & n. 2; also, 6/264, 298; 8/278; social: at theatre with Queen of Bohemia, 2/156; at Trinity House dinners, 4/185; 5/172

CRAWFURD (Crafford), John, 17th Earl of Crawfurd (d. 1678): on *Naseby*, 1/134 & n. 3

CRAWLY, ——: 5/114

CREED, Elizabeth (b. Pickering), wife of John: lacks wedding portion, 1/295; well-bred but fat, 4/308; P plans match for, 6/18, 21; at court masque, 6/29; courted by Creed, 6/88, 89–90; marriage, 9/269, 279, 318, 322, 332 & n. 3, 335; with child, 9/562; also, 5/32, 53; 9/345, 487; social: at P's house, 5/95; 9/408, 409; on river trip, 5/180; P/EP visit(s), 9/379–80, 430, 519–20

CREED, John, servant to Sandwich and naval official:

CHARACTER: able but false, 4/11, 192, 197, 198, 204, 206; 5/74, 108, 119, 189, 238, 302; 6/15, 71; 7/156, 242; 8/203; 9/247; mean, 1/223 & n. 2; disliked by P, 7/310, 381; 9/248, 264; Sandwich, 2/99; 5/74; Howe, 5/74; Lord Belasyse, 7/185; and Povey, 9/247; also, 7/167, 168

at meetings, 4/13, 27, 31–2, 102; 5/97, 105, 124, 139, 154, 210, 339; 6/13, 22, 61, 134, 151; 7/95, 121, 228, 254, 265; 8/61, 210; 9/355, 562; also, 3/238
SOCIAL [on some of these occasions, e.g. visits to dockyards, Creed may have transacted Tangier business]: at Trinity House dinners, 1/177; 3/246; 6/35; coronation banquet, 2/86; walks round Tower, 2/213–14; at funerals, 3/269; 6/114, 127; 8/101; christening, 4/82; visits Epsom, 4/245–9 passim; at Bartholomew Fair, 4/298; 5/265; Lord Mayor's banquet, 4/354–6; visits Greenwich, 5/178; Rochester and Chatham, 8/306, 307, 311–14 passim; sees freaks at Charing Cross, 8/326; prize fight, 8/429, 430; and cockfight, 9/154; calls on P with his bride, 9/408; at Twelfth Night party, 9/409; inhospitable to P and EP, 9/520; at taverns/coffee-houses etc., 1/75, 174, 207, 217, 221, 263, 267, 284, 303; 2/36, 63, 79, 88, 95, 101, 103, 116, 117; 3/94, 152, 248, 298; 4/12, 23–4, 58, 130, 179, 196, 349, 353, 361, 371, 427, 435; 6/115, 251; 9/163, 164, 169; at P's house, 1/173; 2/113; 3/91, 116, 132; 4/32, 40, 55, 133, 141, 157, 164, 188, 214, 266, 389; 5/128, 155, 175, 185, 242, 256, 259, 282, 304, 321, 323, 344; 6/41, 61, 109, 118; 7/131, 168; 8/130, 209, 232, 255, 362, 451, 511, 578; 9/51, 57, 61, 116, 197; at theatre, 1/224, 264; 2/34, 35, 54, 56, 66, 80, 89; 3/260; 4/4, 6, 16, 55–6, 162, 163; 5/240; 6/73, 83; 7/421–3; 8/399, 486; 9/162, 186, 248; at houses of other colleagues and associates, 1/268; 5/257; 6/63, 68–9, 87, 172–3; 7/29–30, 191; 9/130, 165, 176; at Sandwich's lodgings, 2/100; 3/288, 299; 4/5, 21–2, 101, 160; 9/334; at his own, 3/226–7, 281, 282; 4/22; 9/345; walks with P in St James's Park, Whitehall, to Deptford, Woolwich etc., 4/30–1, 37, 87, 113, 131, 151, 286, 297, 348; 5/47, 127, 133, 155, 186, 198, 215, 269; 6/118; 7/144, 148–9, 155, 221, 242, 265, 375, 376; 8/94, 368, 412, 464, 544, 545, 590; 9/141–2, 206–7, 215; on pleasure trips to Hackney/Islington/Vauxhall etc., 5/176, 180–1,

190; 6/74, 136; 7/136, 223; 8/240–1, 249–50; also, 4/124, 125, 142, 163
MISC.: admires France, 2/33; at Backwell's, 3/94; belittles Lawson's achievements, 4/73; proposed as joint-secretary to Fishery corporation, 5/251; at Fire, 7/269, 271; at riot, 9/129–30
ALLUDED TO: 1/190; 9/272, 487
~ his footboy, 4/12; 5/45, 180
CREED, Richard, brother of John: his Puritan views, 1/91 & n. 2; alluded to: 1/86
CREEVEY, Thomas, diarist (d. 1838): opinion of P's diary, vol i, p. lxxxiii
CREIGHTON (Creeton), Robert, Dean of Wells 1660–70, Bishop 1670–d. 72: P admires his preaching, 5/96; comical sermon, 3/42–3 & n.; preaches against nonconformity, 4/92–3; 5/96–7; and (in King's presence) against adultery, 8/362–3, 366; social: 8/417
[CRÉQUI, Charles Duc de], French ambassador to the Papacy 1662, 1664–5: 4/24 & n. 1
CRESSET, ——, 8/425 & n. 3
CREW, Jemima, Lady Crew (b. Waldegrave), wife of John Crew, 1st Baron: her 'saintly questions', 7/17; also, 1/41; 3/2; 5/209; ~ her page, 8/333
CREW, John, cr. Baron Crew of Stene 1661:
PUBLIC AFFAIRS: his part in return of secluded M.P.s, 1/18, 57, 60, 62; elected Councillor of State, 1/65, 82; and M.P., 1/116; created baron, 2/80; views: on constitution of House of Lords, 1/118, 125–6; contribution of Presbyterian clergy to restoration, 3/290–1; Dutch War, 5/244; 6/6; 7/125, 387; poll tax, 7/387–8; Brooke House Committee, 8/193–5; management of royal finances, 8/195; dissolution, 8/558; Dutch alliance, 9/1, 30; toleration, 9/31; the court, 9/190; also, 8/99, 251
PRIVATE AFFAIRS: new house in Lincoln's Inn Fields, 2/153 & n. 2, 213; ill, 9/265, 268, 550
RELATIONS WITH P: their mutual regard, 2/124–5; 3/55, 265; 7/355–6; 9/1; his advice about fees etc., 1/122 & n. 1; offers bargain of land, 5/196; also, 3/11

CRITZ (Cretz), Emanuel de, Ser-jeant-Painter to the King (d. 1665): shows P royal collection of sculpture, 1/188–9 & n.; copies Lely's portrait of Sandwich, 1/272, 273, 290, 292, 301–2; other copies, 3/80 & n. 1; social: 5/84

CROCKFORD, ——, ?porter: 1/92 & n. 2; 2/87

CROFTON, Zachary, Presbyterian minister (d. 1672): imprisoned, 2/58–9 & n.

CROFT(S), Herbert, Bishop of Here-ford 1661–d. 91: his preaching, 1/265; 8/116 & nn.; convert from Catholi-cism, 8/116 & n. 4; votes for Claren-don's impeachment, 8/532 & n. 3

CROFTS, [?Thomas], clerk in the Signet Office: 1/208, 211

CROFTS, William, 1st Baron Crofts: 3/149 & n. 5; 9/336, n. 4

CROFTS, Mr: see Scott, James, Duke of Monmouth

CROFTS, Mrs ——, shopkeeper, of Westminster: her shop, 9/129, 142; social: 6/115, 163: 7/392

CROMLEHOLME (Crumlum), Samuel, High Master of St Paul's School: a conceited pedagogue, 6/53; advises on John P's exhibition, 1/27; given book for school by P, 2/239 & n. 3; 4/33, 132–3; 5/38; his drinking a warning to P, 3/199–200; losses in Fire, 7/297; also, 1/44; 3/142; social: 2/238; ~ his wife, 4/133

CROMWELL, Elizabeth, widow of Oliver: 1/248 & n. 1

CROMWELL, Frances, daughter of Oliver: her impending marriage, 1/248 & n. 1; proposed marriage to Charles II, 5/296–7 & n.

CROMWELL, Mary: see Belasyse

CROMWELL, Oliver:

CHRON. SERIES: at meetings of Eastern Association, 3/224 & n. 3; attitude to Charles I (1648), 5/335 & n. 2; to Charles II, 5/296–7; story of his tampering with royal tombs, 5/297 & n. 2; storm at his death, 3/32 & n. 2; body exhumed, 1/309 & n. 4; 2/24 & n. 3, 26–7, 31; effigy hanged, 4/418 & n. 2, 420; portrait by Simon, 4/70

REPUTATION: praised for: strong govern-ment, 4/376; promotion of trade, 5/52; 8/426; encouragement of navy, 5/59 & n. 4; Irish settlement, 5/346; financial credit, 6/78; prestige abroad, 8/249, 332; sobriety of court, 8/355; and intelligence service, 9/70–1; a 'coquin', 5/264; a 'rogue', 8/355; biography, 8/382 & n. 2

ALLUDED TO: 1/12; 3/46

~ his family, 5/297

CROMWELL, Richard: downfall, 1/21 & nn. 3, 4; rumours of restora-tion, 1/74, 76, 79; Sandwich's advice to in 1659, 1/180; life in exile, 5/296 & n. 2; 7/94 & n. 6

CROONE, [William], physician: de-scribes blood transfusion experiment, 7/370–1 & nn.

CROPP, ——, waterman: appointed government waterman, 1/37 & n. 2; also, 7/319

CROUCHED FRIARS: see Crutched Friars

CROW, Capt. [?George], naval officer: 8/266–7

CROW, ——, footman to John Claypole: 1/218

CROWE, Ald. [William], upholsterer in St Bartholomew's: denied title of alderman, 4/404 & n. 1; P/EP inspect(s) tapestries, 9/329, 330; and beds, 9/333, 334, 356; also, 1/269; 9/362

CROWLAND, Abbot of: P's family connection with, 8/261 & n. 4

[CROWTHER, Joseph]: unnamed clergyman who married Duke and Duchess of York, 2/40–1 & n.

CROXTON, [?Jane], of Salisbury Court: P consults on flags, 3/205 & n. 1; also, 5/86

CRUMLUM: see Cromleholme

CRUTCHED (Crouched) FRIARS [see also Taverns etc.: Three Tuns]: 7/152; 9/188, 519

CUCKOLD'S POINT, nr Deptford: 4/50

CULAN, Henry Fleury de, Heer van Buat: executed, 7/315 & n. 1

CUMBERFORD: see Comberford

CUMBERLAND, [Henry], tailor, of Salisbury Court: burial, 4/32 & n. 2

CUMBERLAND, Richard, P's con-temporary at St Paul's and Magdalene,

Bishop of Peterborough 1691–
d.1718: in London, 1/43 & n. 1; P
visits, 1/54; P's regard, 8/118; 9/17,
56 ~ his brother, 8/118
CURLE, Capt. [Edmund], naval officer: gifts to P and EP for captain's
commission, 1/180
CURSITORS' ALLEY, Chancery
Lane: 9/140
CURTIS, Capt. [Edmund], naval
officer: to go to Mediterranean, 1/119
& n. 3; social: 2/33
CUSTIS (Custos), [Edmund], merchant: dispute about freightage, 4/404;
5/23, 36
CUSTOM HOUSE: P visits, 3/163;
new site, 7/280; alluded to: 4/163;
8/566
CUSTOM HOUSE (STAIRS): 3/119,
180; 4/144
CUSTOMS DUES: navy expenses
charged on, 4/206; merchants' cheats
(unspecified), 7/31; farmers of: listed,
3/188 & n. 3; dine with Lord Mayor,
4/341; farm criticised by Treasury,
8/373 & n. 4; officers attempt to
seize prize-goods, 6/256, 258, 259
CUTLER, Sir John, merchant: story
of beer and thunder, 4/365; on commission for repair of St Paul's, 4/430;
social: 4/22, 65, 100, 256
CUTLER, [William], merchant: P's
opinion of, 4/188, 322; 5/136; 6/166,
331; his regard for P, 4/296–7; his
rise, 5/52; contracts for hemp, 3/114,
116; 6/77; for tar, 5/136; discusses
navy victualling, 4/181, 398; breaks
with Cocke, 5/51; opposed by P,
5/352; provides cash, 6/191; bargain
for freight to Tangier, 7/65; unspecified business, 4/296; 5/332, 354;
foreign news from, 4/322; 5/51, 141,
343; house in city, 4/398; in Hackney,
6/331; housing property in city,
5/282–3; social: 4/216; 5/19, 23, 62,
159, 186, 255, 336, 341; 6/25, 83, 166;
~ his wife and mother [?]-in-law,
4/398; 6/331
CUTLER, P's: 8/136, 232
CUTTANCE, Capt. Henry, naval
officer: receives commission for *Cheriton*, 1/121; on *Royal Charles*, 1/160;
also, 1/221

CUTTANCE, Capt. Roger, kted
1665, naval commander:
CHRON. SERIES: supports Mountagu
(Sandwich) as parliamentary candidate, 1/103 & n. 4; loyalty to Mountagu questioned, 1/107; transactions
concerning ships' pay, 1/162, 167;
3/128; part in prize-goods affair,
6/230, 240, 241, 247, 313; 9/91, 402 &
n. 3; at council of war, 6/230; news
from, 6/306–7; 8/549–50 & n.; influence with Sandwich, 7/19; out of
favour with Coventry, 7/34; criticised
by Sir J. Chicheley, 8/549; gifts to
Sandwich and P, 1/57, 130, 232; also,
2/15–16, 16–17
TANGIER: appointed to committee,
3/238; attends meetings, 3/272; 4/319,
335; his design for jetty, 3/238; to
visit, 4/132
SOCIAL: 1/56, 265, 267, 321; 2/22, 23,
45, 49, 72, 74; 3/269; on *Swiftsure*,
1/97, 98; on *Naseby*, 1/113, 114, 119,
123, 141, 159, 160, 164
ALLUDED TO: 1/101, 104, 158, 161, 166,
179
CUTTLE, Capt. [John], naval officer:
killed in action, 6/219, 225; also, 2/33,
50
CUTTLE, lawyer: *see* Cottle
CUTTS, Sir John, of Childerley,
Cambs.: proposed match with Lady
Jemima Mountagu, 4/174 & n. 2

DAGENHAMS (Dagnams), Essex: P
visits for wedding, 6/175–7; his other
visits, 6/158–61, 167, 180–1; 7/17–18;
gallery, 6/159, 160; gardens, 6/160;
buttery, 6/180; also, 6/163, 173, 188,
193, 225
DAKING (Deking), Capt. [George],
naval officer: discharged, 1/109 &
n. 2, 110; (?the same), 3/50
DALMAHOY (Dormehoy), [Tho-
mas]: on *Naseby*, 1/134 & n. 6
DALTON, [Richard], Serjeant of the
Wine-cellar to the King: buys lease of
P's house in Axe Yard, 1/235, 244–8
passim; social: 4/4
[DALZIEL, Lt-Gen. Thomas]: defeats
Scots rebels, 7/390 & n. 6
DAMFORD, ——: anecdote about,
1/262

DAMPORT: *see* Davenport

DANCING: P dances for first time, 2/61, 71; 7/18; dislikes/disapproves of, 2/212; 4/176; 6/79; admires at court, 3/300–1; 6/29; takes lessons/ practises, 4/111, 122, 124, 126, 129, 132, 133, 134, 141, 149, 150, 153, 161, 265; finds useful for a gentleman, 4/122; Sandwich's dancing-master, 2/117; dancing at court, 3/300–1; 5/56; 6/29; 7/341, 371–3; 9/507; King's French dancing-master, 9/507; dancing schools: in Broad St, 1/253; Fleet St, 2/212; in city, 4/107; Bow, 7/238; at private parties: 6/262, 279, 284; 7/73, 230, 263, 360, 362, 363, 422; 8/28–9, 104, 493, 511; 9/8, 12–13, 42, 128, 134, 172, 227, 458, 464, 511; at schools: 8/392, 396; theatres: 3/32; 8/27, 101, 171, 375, 388, 440, 451, 487; 9/24, 48, 107, 144, 183–4, 219, 420, 459; particular dances: branle, 3/300; 7/372; coranto (courant), 3/300; 4/122, 124, 126; 6/88 & n. 1; 7/372; Cuckolds all a'row, 3/300–1; country, 3/300–1; 4/126, 149, 150, 161; 8/232; 9/464; French, 7/372; jig, 6/79; 7/246; 8/101; 9/120, 219, 464; La Duchesse, 4/141, 265; military, 8/451; 9/459; morris, 4/120; Spanish, 9/440

DANCKERTS (Dancre), [Hendrick], painter (d.? 1680): paintings for P's dining room, 9/421, 423 & n. 1, 434, 487; of Greenwich Palace, 9/438, 445, 465, 485; Rome substituted for Hampton Court, 9/504; painting of Windsor, 9/539; of Tangier, 9/541 & n. 2

DANIEL, [Richard], of the Victualling Office: 1/249; death, 5/286

DANIEL, [Samuel], naval officer: wife solicits commission for, 6/335; 7/417; 8/367; on *Royal Charles*, 7/141; brings news of Four Days Fight, 7/145–7; social: 8/76; alluded to: 6/336

DANIEL, Mrs ——, of Greenwich, wife of Samuel: fondled by Lord Rutherford, 6/274; with child, 6/274, 336; dogged by P, 6/332(2); asks favour for husband, 6/335; 7/417; 8/233, 244, 367; P kisses, 6/336;

7/202; ?brings news of plague, 7/236; fondled by P, 7/417; 8/233, 244, 282; 9/132, 248; tries to borrow money from, 9/306; also, 7/7; social: at Greenwich, 6/315, 333, 338; 7/141; at P's house/office, 7/211, 341; 8/45, 76; 9/265; ~ her son, 7/128; ?her mother-in-law, 7/341

DANVERS, Col. [Henry], Fifth-Monarchist: arrest and escape, 6/184 & n. 3

DARCY, [Marmaduke], Cavalier: on *Naseby*, 1/154, 157; alluded to: 2/29

DARCY, Sir William: Fishery business, 3/269–70 & n.

[DARLING, Edward and Thomas] *see* Taverns etc.: Three Tuns, Charing Cross

DARNELL, [?Richard, jun.], musician: P buys music from, 8/24–5

DARTFORD, Kent: P visits, 2/15, 16, 17, 57, 72; 6/242; 9/495, 499; post-house, 2/17; alluded to: 2/32

DARTMOUTH, Devon: Straits fleet at, 8/345

DASHWOOD, Ald. [Francis]: 6/182

DA SILVA, Don Duarte, merchant: 3/114 & n. 2

DAVENANT, Sir William, playwright and producer [*see also* Musical Compositions; Plays]: reinstates Harris, 4/239 & n. 3, 347; opera *The siege of Rhodes*, 6/284 & n. 1; 8/25, 59; allegedly taught by Capt. H. Cooke, 8/59; criticised by Dr Clerke, ib.; death and burial, 9/156 & n. 1, 158 & n. 3; ~ his sons, 9/158 & n. 4

DAVENPORT, [Frances], actress: leaves stage, 9/156 & n. 2

[DAVENPORT, Hester] ('Roxalana'), actress: leaves stage to live with Earl of Oxford, 3/32 & n. 6, 58 & n. 3, 86; alluded to: 3/273, 295

DAVENPORT (Damport), [?John], of Brampton, Hunts.: social: 2/24, 137, 208, 210, 213

DAVIES, [John], Storekeeper, Deptford: character, 1/286; 4/151; P stays with, 2/12; complains of treatment under Commonwealth, 1/308; his stores, 3/111, 173; bookkeeping, 3/129, 234; in disputes over contracts, 4/73 & n. 2, 151 & n. 1; also, 2/13;

alluded to: 4/318; ~ his wife, 2/12; his kinswoman, 3/129

DAVIES, [Thomas], bookseller and P's schoolfellow: heir to T. Audley, 3/264 & n. 2; knighted as sheriff, 8/497

DAVIS (Davy), [John], clerk to Lord Berkeley of Stratton: P's dislike, 2/26; 3/259; attempted burglary at house, 1/305; news from, 2/10; to go to Ireland, 2/55; alluded to: 1/289, 291, 315; 2/9; 4/408

DAVIS, Jack, son of the foregoing, Navy Office clerk: lends Tower Hill lodgings to P, 3/182, 188–209 passim; alleged fraud by, 4/152; Batten wants dismissed, 5/32; social: ?1/289; ?2/8, 26; ~ his Tower Hill landlord, 3/200

DAVIS, [Jane], ('Lady Davis'), wife of John, clerk to Berkeley: P's dislike, 2/55; 3/259; annoys P by closing gate to leads, 1/277; resents EP's neglect, 2/10; to go to Ireland, 2/55; social: 2/25–6; alluded to: 2/114

DAVIS, Mary (Mall), actress: (untrue) rumour of death, 7/102 & n. 1; role in *Richard III*, 8/101 & n. 4; in *Love-tricks*, 8/375 & n. 2; her dancing, 8/101, 375; 9/24, 219; leaves stage to become King's mistress, 9/19 & n. 3, 24 & n. 2, 219, 388, 422, 450; alleged parentage, 9/24 & n. 2

DAVIS, [Thomas], messenger, Admiralty office: 1/103

DAVIS, Mr —— : employs Wayneman Birch, 4/382

DAVY: *see* Davis, [John]

DAWES, [Henry], merchant: shipping business, 1/267 & n. 4; a slave in Algiers, 2/34

DAWES, Sir [John], merchant: clandestine marriage, 4/121–2 & n., 269, 355; baronetcy, 4/269

DAWS, Mr —— [?identical with Henry Dawes]: 1/147

[DAWSON, William], naval officer: 9/488 & n. 2

DAY, [John], of Leverington, Cambs., P's great-uncle by marriage: P's claim on estate, 4/231 & n. 1, 300 & n. 2, 310–12

DAY, [John], 'old Day', fishmonger: 5/53

DAY, ——, carpenter: 1/78

DEAL, Kent: fleet off, 1/105–34 passim; forts near, 1/105 & n. 3; provisions from, 1/107, 134, 136; P visits, 1/119 & n. 4; Fuller's tavern, 1/119; Poole's, ib.; royalist demonstrations, 1/121(2), 129, 163; naval guns heard, 6/65; plague, 7/241 & n. 3; alluded to: 1/134; 5/212; 6/29

DEAN, Forest of: storm damage, 3/35 & n. 5; (1362), 3/165; ironworks, ib. & n. 1; 'forbid' trees, ib. & n. 2; timber, 4/20; alluded to: 3/114

DEANE, Anthony, kted 1675, shipwright:
CHARACTER: able but conceited, 3/170 & n. 1; 4/124, 176, 236, 381; 5/130; 9/152; a fanatic, 5/203

RELATIONS WITH P: instructs P in timber measurement, 3/151, 163, 169; 4/189–90; demonstrates slide-rule, 4/124; gives P ship model, 3/163 & n. 1, 208; instructs about ships/ship-building, 4/157, 172, 236, 262, 396; 5/29–30, 144, 146, 159, 189, 309; 8/489; 9/250; 'Doctrine of Naval Architecture' written at P's request, 9/531 & n. 1; tells of abuses in yards, 4/19, 79, 219; 8/489; 9/249; gift to P, 6/338; offers money, 9/528; P's gift to, 9/531

NAVY BOARD BUSINESS: rivalry with Petts, 3/170; complains of timber, 4/326; of timber contract, 4/381; and of colleagues, 4/384, 433; to fell Clarendon's timber, 5/203, 205, 210, 214, 238; discusses shipbuilding with Brouncker, 6/281; his *Rupert* praised by King and Duke of York, 7/119, 127; his drawing of, 8/142 & n. 2; and of *Resolution*, 9/262 & n. 4; his calculations of ship's draught, 7/127–8 & n.; his fireship design, 8/358 & n. 1; and gun design, 9/528 & n. 1; also, 5/155, 308–9; 8/39; unspecified business, 4/176, 425; 5/137; 9/175

SOCIAL: 4/141, 318; 5/185; 6/282

DEBUSSY (Debusty), [Lawrence], merchant: his tallies, 6/224 & n. 2; letter of credit, 7/174; poor English, 7/404; ~ his house and fine tapestry, 7/174

DEKING: *see* Daking

DEKINS: *see* Dickons, [J.]

DELABARR, [Vincent], merchant: social: 1/212; 2/65 & n. 2

DELAUNE, [George], merchant, Lothbury, and wife [Dorothea]: death, with family, in fire, 3/296 & n. 4

DELFT: P visits, 1/145–7; description, 1/145–6 & nn.; regicides arrested, 3/45, 47

DELKES 'old', waterman: appeals to P against son-in-law's impressment, 6/187, 202

DELL, [William], formerly Rector of Yelden, Beds.: his puritanism, 3/123 & n. 1

DENHAM, Sir John, poet and Surveyor-General of the King's Works: alterations at Hinchingbrooke, 1/313, 314 & n. 1; attends coronation, 2/83; as friend of Mennes, 4/436–7; pox cured by Mennes, 5/242; builds Burlington House, Piccadilly, 6/39 & n. 2; 9/321; death, 9/491 & n. 1

DENHAM, [Margaret], Lady Denham, wife of Sir John: liaison with Duke of York, 7/158–9 & n., 297, 315, 320, 323, 404–5; cabals with Coventry and Brouncker, 7/323; with Bristol, 7/404–5 & n.; rumoured poisoning by Duchess of York, 7/365 & n. 2, 366, 405; 8/6 & n. 2; postmortem, 8/8; house in Scotland Yard, 7/158

DENMARK [see also Copenhagen; Frederick III; Zeeland]: peace with, 8/399 & n. 1, 426 & n. 2; also, 1/41, 43, 83; 6/229

DEPTFORD, Kent [see also Baddiley, W.; Carteret, Sir G.; Cowley, T.; Davis, John; Pett, Christopher; Trinity House; Uthwayt, J.]:

TOWN: storm, 4/317–18; Plague, 6/253, 294, 331–2; 7/236 & n. 3, 239, 241, 285; pretty woman at, 8/141, 170 & n. 6; Balty St Michel lives at, 9/195, 261, 349; P to live with him, 9/349, 369; church [St Nicholas], 2/12 & n. 1; Globe, 1/254; 2/12, 77; 3/274; 6/96, 201; 7/285; ferry, 6/167; King's Head, 6/295; upper town, 6/331; Halfway tree, 8/188

DOCKYARD:

GENERAL: guard, 2/11, 12–13, 15; royal yachts at, 2/14, 120; ships built,

2/14 & n. 4; 5/24–5 & n.; launched, 7/160 & n. 3; project for new dock, 3/18 & n. 1, 29, 30 & n. 1, 32–3; timber frames for Navy Office houses built at, 3/111, 179, 188, 203; abuses, 3/128, 135–6, 274; 4/289 & n. 1, 293; 7/176(2); fire, 5/257; Navy Board meets at during Plague, 6/173, 184; plague in ships, 6/189, 204; workmen sent to fight Fire, 7/274, 276; P stores goods at during Fire, 7/273, 276, 278, 285, 290; Elizabethan wreck discovered, 8/188; measures taken against Dutch raiders, 8/256–7 & n., 259, 270, 282, 313; *Maybolt* at, 8/503–4; 9/29

VISITS BY P (sometimes with colleagues) on official business: pays: 1/253–4, 283, 286 & n. 2; 3/53 & n. 1, 58, 124, 179–80 & n., 185 & n. 1, 192, 193 & n. 2, 195, 198, 200–1 & n.; 4/7, 386 & n. 1, 425; 7/339; sales: 2/45 & n. 3; 3/185–6 & n.; criticises method, 4/319 & n. 2; shipping: ships fitted out/provisioned/despatched: 2/104, 112, 127; 3/31, 51, 63; 4/103–4; 5/165, 176; 7/157, 158, 162, 176(2), 177, 181; 8/176; measured, 5/217; 7/69; built, 8/124; launched, 9/101 & n. 2; inspects stores, 3/129, 173, 188; 4/79(2), 219; flags, 3/149; 4/151; 5/182; masts, 3/273–4; plank, 4/266; ironwork, 5/16; 7/119; canvas, 5/106, 155; poop lantern, 5/116–17; cordage, 5/287; timber, 5/312; and wet dock, 8/188; at musters, 3/160 & n. 1; 4/15, 50, 80, 222; consults officers about callbooks, 3/234; 4/7, 15, 80; investigates fire risks, 4/7; leases ground for mastdock, 5/231 & n. 1; also, 1/287; 2/12–13, 36, 45, 75–7, 104, 112, 127, 204; 3/19, 31, 111, 129, 135–6, 137, 140, 149, 160, 173, 179, 188, 192, 203, 211, 214, 227, 234, 273–4; 4/20, 67, 87, 103, 253, 277, 283, 288–9, 322, 425; 5/29, 39, 54, 72, 75, 80, 95, 138, 146, 156, 192, 213, 263, 303, 347, 351, 357; 6/74, 93, 118, 125, 128, 162, 201, 278; 7/19, 20, 21, 31, 115, 125, 126(2), 129, 134, 137, 138, 149, 166, 168, 175, 186, 191, 198, 249, 255, 319, 352, 358; 8/23, 39, 84, 95, 99, 124, 141, 162

579; 9/28, 331, 372, 455, 460, 473, 482, 500, 545

P'S COMMENTS WHILE WRITING: hears bellman's cry, 1/19; notes mistakes in entries, 1/92–3, 94, 207; 9/349, 353, 357, 363, 515; notes striking of clock, 2/14; receives funeral invitation, 2/73; makes entry for future reference, 3/3–4; writes 'slubberingly' in poor light, 3/236 & n.*c*; writes shakily because shocked, 8/208 & n.*a*; consults it, 4/296; makes entries for his justification, 7/331, 331–2; 8/548–9; values it, 8/264; confesses to tiredness, 6/16; 7/74

INCIDENTS AND PHRASES [i.e. some memorable passages which are difficult or impossible to retrieve by the use of the rest of the Index]:

CHILDHOOD: 'But Lord, how in every point I find myself to overvalue things when a child', 5/132

CHURCH: 'And when the parson begins, he begins "Right Worshipfull and dearly beloved" to us', 2/147

DEATH: 'all die alike, no more matter being made of the death of one then another', 4/339; 'but Lord, to see how the world makes nothing of the memory of a man an hour after he is dead', 5/91; 'This day Sir W. Batten, who hath been sick four or five days, is now very bad, so as that people begin to fear his death – and I at a loss whether it will be better for me to have him die, because he is a bad man, or live, for fear a worse should come', 6/32; 'Sir Wm. Petty came, among other things, to tell me that Mr. Barlow is dead; for which, God knows my heart, I could be as sorry as is possible for one to be for a stranger by whose death he gets 100*l* per annum', 6/33; '[Sir W. Batten] is so ill, that it is believed he cannot live till tomorrow; which troubles me and my wife mightily, partly out of kindness, he being a good neighbour, and partly because of the money he owes me upon our bargain of the late prize', 8/462; 'And here do see what creatures widows are in weeping for their husbands, and then presently

leaving off; but I cannot wonder at it, the cares of the world taking place of all other passions', 8/483

FOOD: 'And strange it is, to see how a good dinner and feasting reconciles everybody', 6/295

LONDON LIFE AND MANNERS: 'I sat up till the bell-man came by with his bell, just under my window as I was writing of this very line, and cried, "Past one of the clock, and a cold, frosty, windy morning." I then went to bed and left my wife and the maid a-washing still', 1/19; 'And here, I sitting behind in a dark place, a lady spat backward upon me by a mistake, not seeing me. But after seeing her to be a very pretty lady, I was not troubled at it at all', 2/25; 'But Lord, to see the absurd nature of Englishmen, that cannot forbear laughing and jeering at everything that looks strange', 3/268; 'But it is very pleasant to hear how [Will Stankes of Brampton] rails at the rumbling and ado that is in London over it is in the country, that he cannot endure it', 4/118; 'it being very pleasant to see how everybody [on Epsom Downs] turns up his tail, here one and there another, in a bush, and the women in their Quarters the like', 4/246; 'I went out, and running up (her friend however before me) I perceive by my dear Lady's blushing that in my dining-room she was doing something upon the pott; which I also was ashamed of and so fell to some discourse, but without pleasure, through very pity to my Lady', 5/129; 'I lacked a pot but there was none, and bitter cold, so was forced to rise and piss in the chimny, and to bed again', 5/357

LOVE AFFAIRS: 'When weary, I did give over, and somebody having seen some of our dalliance, called aloud in the street, "Sir, why do you kiss the gentlewoman so?" and flung a stone at the window – which vexed me', 4/203; 'a strange slavery that I stand in to beauty, that I value nothing near it', 5/264; 'Up, and to the office (having a mighty pain in my forefinger of my left hand, from a strain that it received last night in struggling avec la femme que je mentioned yesterday)', 6/40; 'I am not, as I ought to be, able to command myself in the pleasures of my eye', 7/110; 'into St Dunstan's church. . . . And stood by a pretty, modest maid, whom I did labour to take by the hand and the body; but she would not, but got further and further from me, and at last I could perceive her to take pins out of her pocket to prick me if I should touch her again; which seeing, I did forbear, and was glad I did espy her design', 8/389

MARRIAGE: 'myself somewhat vexed at my wife's neglect in leaving of her scarfe, waistcoat, and night-dressings in the coach today that brought us from Westminster, though I confess she did give them to me to look after – yet it was her fault not to see that I did take them out of the coach', 4/6; 'Coming home tonight, I did go to examine my wife's house-accounts; and finding things that seemed somewhat doubtful, I was angry, though she did make it pretty plain; but confessed that when she doth misse a sum, she doth add something to other things to make it', 5/283; 'To church in the morning, and there saw a wedding in the church, which I have not seen many a day, and the young people so merry one with another; and strange, to see what delight we married people have to see these poor fools decoyed into our condition, every man and wife gazing and smiling at them', 6/338–9; 'high words between us. But I fell to read a book (Boyle's *Hydrostatickes*) aloud in my chamber and let her talk till she was tired, and vexed that I would not hear her; and so become friends and to bed together', 8/250–1

MONEY: 'talking long in bed with my wife about our frugall life for the time to come, proposing to her what I could and would do if I were worth 2000*l*; that is, be a Knight and keep my coach – which pleased her', 3/39–40; 'it is high time to betake myself to my . . . vows, . . . so I may for a great while do my duty, as I have well begun, and encrease my good name and esteem in the world and get money, which sweetens all things and whereof I have much need', 4/6–7; 'And I bless God, I do find that I am worth more than ever I yet was, which is 6200*l* – for which the holy name of God be praised', 7/348–9; 'but it is pretty to see what money will do', 8/123

MUSIC: 'However, music and women I cannot but give way to, whatever my business is', 7/69–70; 'music is the thing of the world that I love most, and all the pleasure almost that I can now take', 7/228; 'but that which did please me beyond anything in the whole world was the wind-musique when the Angell comes down, which is so sweet that it ravished me; and indeed, in a word, did wrap up my soul so that it made me really sick, just as I have formerly been when in love with my wife; that neither then, nor all the evening going home and at home, I was able to think of anything, but remained all night transported, so as I could not believe that ever any music hath that real command over the soul of a man as this did upon me', 9/94

PLEASURE: 'I do think it best to enjoy some degree of pleasure, now that we have health, money and opportunities, rather then to leave pleasures to old age or poverty, when we cannot have them so properly' 3/86; 'I . . . do look upon myself at this time in the happiest occasion a man can be; and whereas we take pains in expectation of future comfort and ease, I have taught myself to reflect upon myself at present as happy and enjoy myself in that consideration, and not only please myself with thoughts of future wealth, and forget the pleasures we at present enjoy', 7/57; 'We eat with great pleasure, and I enjoyed myself in it with reflections upon the pleasures which I at best can expect, yet not to exceed this – eating in silver plates, and all things mighty rich and handsome about me', 7/388; 'they being gone, I paid the fiddler 3*l* among the four, and so away to bed, weary and mightily pleased; and have the happiness to reflect upon it as I do sometimes on other things, as going to a play or the like, to be the greatest real comforts that I am to expect in the world, and that it is that that we do really labour in the hopes of; and so I do really enjoy myself, and understand that if I do not do it now, I shall not hereafter, it may be, be able to pay for it or have health to take pleasure in it, and so fool myself with vain expectation of pleasure and go without it', 9/13; 'I did, as I love to do, enjoy myself in my pleasure, as being the heighth of what we take pains for and can hope for in this world – and therefore to be enjoyed while we are young and capable of these joys', 9/134

PUBLIC AFFAIRS: 'But methought it lessened my esteem of a king, that he should not be able to command the rain', 3/140; 'I see it is impossible for the King to have things done as cheap as other men', 3/143; 'He showed me a very excellent argument to prove that our Importing lesse then we export doth not impoverish the kingdom, according to the received opinion – which though it be a paradox and that I do not remember the argument, yet methought there was a great deal in what he said', 5/70; 'While we were talking, came by several poor creatures, carried by by constables for being at a conventicle. They go like lambs, without any resistance. I would to God they would either conform, or be more wise and not be ketched', 5/235; '[He] did . . . inform me mightily in several things; among others, that the heightening or lowering of money is only a cheat, and doth good to some perticular men; which, if I can but remember how, I am now by him fully convinced of', 7/304; 'by bringing over

one discontented man you raise up three in his room', 7/311; 'Most things moved were referred to committees – and so we broke up', 7/321; 'Englishmen on board the Dutch ships . . . did cry and say, "We did heretofore fight for tickets; now we fight for Dollers!"', 8/267; 'some rude people have been . . . at my Lord Chancellor's, . . . and a Gibbet either set up before or painted upon his gate, and these words writ – "Three sights to be seen; Dunkirke, Tanger, and a barren Queen"', 8/269; 'But it was pretty, news came the other day so fast, of the Duch fleets being in so many places, that Sir W. Batten at table cried, "By God!" says he, "I think the Devil shits Dutchmen"', 8/345; '[Coling] told us his horse was a Bribe, and his boots a bribe; . . . and that he makes every sort of tradesman to bribe him; and invited me home to his house to taste of his bribe wine', 8/369

SERVANTS: 'To the office, where . . . I sent my boy home for some papers; where, he staying longer then I would have him and being vexed at the business and to be kept from my fellows in the office longer then was fit, I became angry and boxed my boy when he came, that I do hurt my Thumb so much, that I was not able to stir all the day after and in great pain', 7/19; 'coming homeward again, saw my door and hatch open, left so by Luce our cookmaid; which so vexed me, that I did give her a kick in our entry and offered a blow at her, and was seen doing so by Sir W. Penn's footboy, which did vex me to the heart because I know he will be telling their family of it, though I did put on presently a very pleasant face to the boy and spoke kindly to him as one without passion, so as it may be he might not think I was angry; but yet I was troubled at it', 8/164

SOCIAL OCCASIONS: 'Went to hear Mrs. Turner's daughter . . . play on the Harpsicon; but Lord! it was enough to make any man sick to hear her; yet was I forced to commend her highly', 4/120; 'They have a kins-woman they call daughter in the house, a short, ugly, red-haired slut that plays upon the virginalls and sings, but after such a country manner, I was weary of it, but yet could not but commend it', 4/242; 'We were as merry as I could be with people that I do wish well to but know not what discourse either to give them or find from them', 4/427; 'A very good dinner among the old Sokers', 6/36

SUCCESS: 'There was also [a letter] for me from Mr. Blackburne, who with his own hand superscribes it to *S.P. Esqr.*, of which, God knows, I was not a little proud', 1/96–7; 'Lay very long in bed, discoursing with Mr Hill of most things of a man's life, and how little merit doth prevail in the world, but only favour – and that for myself, chance without merit brought me in, and that diligence only keeps me so', 6/285; 'We had much talk of all our old acquaintance of the College, concerning their various fortunes; wherein, to my joy, I met not with any that have sped better then myself', 8/51; 'my Lord Chan-cellor did say . . . that no man in Eng-land was of more method nor made himself better understood then my-self', 8/60

THEATRE: 'Burt acted the Moore; by the same token, a very pretty lady that sot by me cried to see Desdimona smothered', 1/264; 'I sitting behind in a dark place, a lady spat backward upon me by a mistake, not seeing me. But after seeing her to be a very pretty lady, I was not troubled at it at all', 2/25; 'And it was observable how a gentleman of good habitt, sitting just before us eating of some fruit, in the midst of the play did drop down as dead; but with much ado, Orange Mall did thrust her finger down his throat and brought him to life again', 8/516–17; 'It pleased us mightily to see the natural affection of a poor woman, the mother of one of the children brought on the stage – the child crying, she by

force got upon the stage, and took up her child and carried it away off of the stage from Hart', 8/594; 'I was prettily served this day at the playhouse-door; where giving six shillings into the fellow's hand for us three, the fellow by legerdemain did convey one away, and with so much grace face me down that I did give him but five, that though I knew the contrary, yet I was overpowered by his so grave and serious demanding the other shilling that I could not deny him, but was forced by myself to give it him', 9/90

WORK: 'having so many [letters] to write . . . that I have no heart to go about them', 1/215; 'here I had a most eminent experience of the evil of being behind-hand in business; I was the most backward to begin anything, and would fain have framed to myself an occasion of going abroad . . . but some business coming in . . . kept me there, and I fell to the ridding away of a great deal of business . . . and . . . I could have continued there with delight all night long', 7/249

WORKMEN: 'At home all the after-noon looking after my workmen in my house, whose lazinesse doth much trouble me', 1/243; 'All the after-noon at home among my workmen; work till 10 or 11 at night; and did give them drink and were very merry with them – it being my luck to meet with a sort of Drolling work-men upon all occasions', 1/255; 'a poor fellow, a working goldsmith, that goes without gloves to his hands', 8/437

MISC.: 'Lay long; that is, till 6 and past before I rose', 3/190; 'so home to dinner, where I find my wife hath been with Ashwell at La Roches to have her tooth drawn, which it seems akes much. But my wife could not get her to be contented to have it drawn after the first twitch, but would let it alone; and so they came home with it undone, which made my wife and me good sport', 4/97; 'By and by news is brought us that one of our horses is stole out of the Stable; which proves my uncles, at which I was inwardly glad; I mean, that it was not mine', 4/310; 'the fellow coming out again of a shop, I did give him a good cuff or two on the chops; and seeing him not oppose me, I did give him another; at last, found him drunk, of which I was glad and so left him and home', 4/342; 'it is not greatest wits but the steady man that is a good merchant', 5/300; 'where a Trade hath once been and doth decay, it never recovers again', ib.; 'one Mr Tripp, who dances well', 7/362; 'He told me also a story of my Lord Cottington: who wanting a son, entended to make his Nephew his heir, a country boy, but did alter his mind upon the boy's being persuaded by another young heir (in roguery) to Crow like a cock at my Lord's table, much company being there and the boy having a great trick at doing that perfectly – my Lord bade them take away that fool from the table, and so gave over the thoughts of making him his heir from this piece of folly', 8/566–7

DICK (Dike) SHORE: *see* Duke Shore

DICKENSON, Esther ('Widow'): *see* Pepys, Esther

DICKONS (Dekins), [John], hemp merchant: dies of grief, 3/213, 233; social: 3/19

DICKONS, [Elizabeth], ('my Morena'): at St Olave's, 2/192; illness and death, 3/213, 233; alluded to: 3/19

DIGBY, Lady Anne, daughter of the 2nd Earl of Bristol: jilted, 4/208–9 & n.

DIGBY, Capt. [Francis], naval officer, son of the 2nd Earl of Bristol: opinion of 'tarpaulins', 7/333

DIGBY, George, 2nd Earl of Bristol, succ. 1653 [occasionally referred to by his original title of Lord Digby], politician: a Papist, 4/224; 9/17; said to have turned Protestant, 5/58; 9/120; a public danger, 9/120; responsible for failure of Treaty of Uxbridge (1645), 4/212 & n. 1; sells

Irish peerage (1646), 8/126; in France and Flanders during Interregnum, 4/212–13 & nn.; enmity to Clarendon: 2/142; opposes over bill of uniformity, 3/49 & n. 1; brings articles of impeachment against (1663) 4/115, 219–20, 223–5 & nn., 229, 231 & n. 2, 367; 8/445 & n. 4; renews attack (1664), 5/34, 60 & n. 4, 73, 85, 89, 137, 208; influence over King, 4/137; part in scheme for parliamentary management, 4/200, 207, 207–8 & nn., 211 & nn., 213; supports marriage alliance with Parma, 4/224 & n. 1; flees to escape arrest, 4/271 & n. 1, 272, 298 & n. 4; 5/85, 89 & n. 3; Lady Denman supports him, 7/405; his faction, 7/261; appears in Lords, 8/362; recovers King's favour, 8/530, 532, 533, 597; ~ his chaplain, 5/58–9 & n.

DIKE: *see* Dyke

[DILLINGHAM, Theophilus], Master of Clare Hall and Vice-Chancellor, Cambridge: 3/218 & n. 4

DILLON, Col. Cary, succ. as 5th Earl of Roscommon 1685: courtship of Frances Butler, 1/209 & n. 3, 217; 2/152; 3/299 & n. 1; 9/311; duel, 3/171 & n. 1; alluded to: 1/214

DILLON, [William]: hanged, 4/60 & n. 1

DIPLOMATS [for individuals, *see* under personal names]: disputes about precedence among in London, 2/187–9 & nn.; in Paris, 4/419–20 & n.; (rumour of) in Madrid, 8/36 & n. 2

DIVES: *see* Dyve

DIXON, Mr ——: matchmaker for Tom P, 4/19, 21

DIXWELL, Col. [Basil], cr. bt 1660, of Broome, Barham, Kent (d. 1668): 1/172, 176, 182

DOBBINS, Capt. [Joseph]: feast as Elder Brother, Trinity House, 6/155

DOCTORS' COMMONS, St Benet's Hill: P visits, 1/229; 2/216; 4/368; 5/351

DOLBEN, Catherine, wife of John: story of, 9/89 & n. 5; ~ her two children, 9/89

DOLBEN, John, Dean of Westminster 1662–83, Bishop of Rochester 1666–83,

Archbishop of York 1683–d.86: sermon before King, 7/245 & n. 4; rumoured suspension, 8/587 & n. 2; slanders against, 8/596 & n. 2; dismissed from court office, 9/53 & n. 2, 89

DOLING, Thomas, messenger, Council of State: news from, 1/14 & n. 4; P's letters to, 1/116, 126 & n. 2; to go to Ireland, 1/311; visits Overton in prison, 1/319; social: 1/37, 38, 80, 92, 95, 174–5, 208, 230, 282

DOLL, milliner at the New Exchange: see Stacey

DOMESDAY BOOK: P to consult, 2/236 & n. 3

DONCASTER, ——, waterman: 3/156

DONNE: see Dunn

DONNE, John, poet (1573–1631): takes holy orders, 9/215 & n. 2

DORCHESTER, Lord: see Pierrepont

DORMEHOY: see Dalmahoy

DORMER, Charles, 2nd Earl of Caernarvon (1632–1709): on value of timber, 8/201 & n. 3

DORRINGTON, [?Francis, ?John], merchant: compensation for loss of ship, 9/69 & n. 1; bid for victualling contract, 9/288 & n. 2

DORSET, Earl of: see Sackville, R.

DORSET HOUSE, Salisbury Court: Clarendon at, 1/173, 184

DOUCE: see Doves

DOUGLAS, James, 2nd Marquess of Douglas (d. 1700): at court ball, 7/372; commands troops, 8/306, 308, 309, 311

DOUGLAS, William, 9th Earl of Morton (d. 1681): 9/534 & n. 2

DOVER, Kent: parliamentary elections, 1/96–7, 111(2), 167, 179 & n. 1, 183; clerk of castle, 1/97; jurats visit *Naseby*, 1/130; mayor welcomes King, 1/158; Dutch ships brought into, 5/326; Rupert's fleet at, 7/143–5 passim; Governor prepares against invasion, 7/187 & n. 1; squadron to be stationed at, 8/149 & n. 1; Dutch attack feared, 8/327 & n. 1, 328; Duke of York as Lord Warden, 9/280 & n. 4; also, 1/134, 279; 7/300

DOVES (?Douce, ?Dowes), Capt. ——: 2/207

DOWGATE [see also Taverns etc.: Swan]: Fire, 7/270

DOWNE(S), [Elkanah], Vicar of Ashtead, Surrey, 1662–d.83: dull sermon, 4/247 & n. 1

[DOWNES, John], actor and writer: in Davenant's *Siege of Rhodes*, 2/131 & n. 3

DOWNES, [John], regicide: reprieved 3/16 & n. 1

DOWNING, [Frances], b. Howard, wife of Sir George: praises Holland, 1/249; alluded to: 1/153

DOWNING, George, kted 1660, cr. bt 1663; Teller of the Receipt in the Exchequer 1656–60; reappointed 1660; envoy to United Provinces, 1657–60, 1660–7, 1671–2; Secretary to the Treasury Commissioners, 1667–71; M.P. Morpeth, 1660, 1661–79, 1679, 1679–81, 1681

CHARACTER: parsimonious, 1/186 & n. 2; 8/85; rogue, 3/45; vain, 8/425; efficient, 8/238, 240

AS ENVOY TO UNITED PROVINCES: offers P clerkship, 1/18, 31; P writes ciphers for, 1/28, 30, 31; leaves for Holland, 1/23, 25, 29, 31, 33; returns, 1/136 & n. 1, 249; knighted, 1/153; has regicides extradited, 3/44–5 & n., 48; news from, 5/121 & nn.; 6/103 & n. 2; protests against Dutch detaining English cargo, 5/321; assists in relief of English prisoners of war, 7/201 & n. 1, 380 & n. 3; 8/407–8 & n., 425; complains of peace terms, 8/425–7 & nn.; intelligence service, 9/401–2 & nn.

IN EXCHEQUER: as P's master, 1/2 & n. 1, 83, 107–8, 238; offers P council clerkship, 1/22 & n. 5, 35; lawsuit against Squibb, 1/31 & n. 1, 33–6 passim, 40, 45, 48, 49; encourages loans on Additional Aid (1665), 6/322, 327, 330, 334; 7/9, 23, 87, 124 & n. 2; 8/131–2, 397–8, 407

AS M.P.: part in drafting Additional Aid bill (1665), 6/292 & n. 3; 7/122; 8/30; project for leather trade, 8/425 & n. 4; introduces bill for Treasury orders, 8/520 & n. 2; parliamentary news from, 7/380; 8/520

AT TREASURY: appointed secretary, 8/238, 240; Tangier accounts, 8/249

SOCIAL: Christmas dinner for poor neighbours, 8/85 & n. 1; also, 7/215, 216

ALLUDED TO: as chairman of Council of Trade, 2/20; also, 1/10, 67

~ his child, 1/249; his mother [Lucy], 8/85

DOWNING, [John], anchor-smith: P returns *douceur*, 7/119, 138

DOWNING, Capt. [?John], soldier: gives evidence to Committee on Miscarriages, 8/538 & n. 3; social: 7/362, 363

DOWNS, the, off Kent [entries concerning use of roadstead by English warships are not indexed]: Batten's trip to, 4/296; Dutch fleet in, 6/258; Smyrna fleet, 7/404

DOYLY, Sir William, M.P. Great Yarmouth, Norf., 1660, 1661–77: parliamentary commissioner for paying off fleet, 1/255, 286 & n. 2; Commissioner for Sick and Wounded 6/217 & n. 4; 8/407; warrant for bucks, 6/220–1 & n.; 8/248; social: 6/218; 8/224

[DRAGHI, Giovanni Battista] (Seignor Baptista; Seignor Joanni), musician: compositions, 7/352 & n. 4; 8/54–5 & n.; feat of musical memory, 8/55–7 passim; ?his singing, 9/322 & n. 2

DRAKE, Mr ——, of Hackney: house and garden, 7/181 & n. 3

DRAMMEN (Dram), Norway: timber from, 3/118 & n. 3

DRAWWATER, Dorothy: 8/468 & n. 2

DRAWWATER, [James]: at P's Twelfth Night party, 1/10 ~ his wife [Jane], b. Strudwick, ib.

DRAYDON: *see* Dryden

DREAMS (P): bedwetting, 1/162; EP's death, 1/285; accident to EP, 2/226; swollen testicle, ib.; plots, 3/250; W. Swan the fanatic, ib.; lawsuit, 4/15; St John's Isle, 4/43; J. Cole, 6/145; Lady Castlemaine, 6/191; fire, 7/287, 296, 299; ?8/87, 128; death of mother, 8/129, 303; defending Navy Board in Parliament, 9/88; reflects on nature of, 6/191; EP suspects him of dreaming of Deb Willet, 9/384, 439

DREBBEL (Dribble), [Cornelis] van: his mine, 3/46 & n. 1; 4/378

DRESS AND PERSONAL APPEARANCE (MEN AND BOYS) [*see also* Prices; Watches etc.]:

GENERAL (P): importance of good linen, 3/216, 228; 8/121; and neatness, 2/199 & n. 1; to dress fashionably, 4/343, 357; 5/269, 302; 6/100; concerned at expense, 2/47, 129; 4/356, 357; 6/104; concerned not to over-dress, 9/551

GARMENTS AND ACCESSORIES:

APRONS: worn by apprentice weavers, 5/222

BANDS: King's lack of, 8/417; (P): 1/85; 3/61, 228; 4/234, 235, 354; 5/128, 139, 338; 6/73, 76; 7/61; lace/fine bands, 3/215, 219–20, 228, 236; 6/100, 128; 9/6; in plain band mistaken for servant, 8/115; band strings, 2/80

BELTS (P): sword belt, 4/80; 7/26, 353; 8/83, 321–2; 9/201, 537

BOOTS (P): riding-boots, 1/279; 2/132; 3/204, 217; 4/28

BREECHES: two legs through one knee of, 2/66 & n. 2; (P): baize linings, 1/268; close-knee'd, 3/106; white linings, 4/130; rabbit skin prevents galling, 5/298; silk, 6/218; camlet, 9/533

CANNONS (tops) (P): 1/156; black silk, 4/357, 400

CAPS: montero, 1/120; toilet, 1/239; Venetian, 1/324; fur, 8/22; (P): fur, 1/31; EP makes, 1/85; velvet studying, 1/120; velvet montero, 1/227, 232; 7/346; nightcap, 6/175

CHEMISE (P): 8/158

CLERICAL: 3/224; surplices, 3/215; cassock, 7/299 & n. 3, 310, 313; catholic priest in lay clothes, 7/329 & n. 3; hair shirt and sandals, 8/26; 'plain country parson dress', 8/118

CLOAKS: silk, 1/14; velvet-lined, 5/241; Colchester bays at Spanish court, 8/79; (P): camlet, 1/190; 7/7, 15; 8/525, 580–1, 599–600; velvet, 3/84; velvet-lined, 4/343, 344, 353, 357, 400; 5/125; lined with moiré, 5/142, 144; with plush, 5/302, 308, 309; cloak-coat, 7/106;

'common riding-cloak', 7/208; cloak made into suit, 1/118; 8/314; to be worn if without sword, 3/241 & n. 2

COATS: children's, 1/250; Duke of York's buffcoat, 6/51; (P): jackanapes, 1/193; velvet, 1/194, 221, 227, 232; 2/81, 100, 231; 7/7, 15, 25; camlet, 1/198; 4/112; camlet riding-coat, 3/42, 85; short black made from cloak, 1/251; trimmed from EP's petticoats, 2/120; 5/44; short, 5/240; as part of suit, 6/175; 7/353

CODPIECES: 8/421, 596

COLLARS: see scallops

COMB-CASE: 1/239

CRAVATS: 2/229; (P): 1/95; 7/25

CUFFS (hands) (P): 8/412, 440; laced, 6/125, 175; 9/201 & n. 1, 540

DOUBLETS (P): 3/181; slashed, 3/116

DRAWERS: holland, 5/222; (P): 7/280

FACINGS (P): 2/120

FROCK: 3/116

GARTERS (P): 4/131

GLOVES: working goldsmith without, 8/437; (P): buckskin, 1/166; kid leather, ib.

GOWNS (P): Indian, 2/130; 7/85; 8/462; morning, 3/77, 82; shag, 4/357, 360; dressing gown, 8/522

HABIT, RIDING (P): 3/288

HANDS: see cuffs

HANDKERCHIEVES ('han(d)kaychers'): as neckcloth, 7/269; King's lack of, 8/417; (P): (with strawberry buttons), 1/94

HATS: beaver, 2/80; plumed, 1/142; 2/172, 229; cocked, 8/249; (P): montero, 1/92, 227; beaver, 2/127, 203; 3/67, 71; 4/360; low-crowned beaver, 4/274, 280; velvet riding hat, 4/360; hatbands, 1/94, 247; wearing of: at meals, 5/277 & n. 3; during toasts, 7/246; by puritan preachers, 3/207 & n. 3; as mark of respect etc., 2/19 & n. 1; 4/114; 5/205; 6/14 & n. 2, 339; 8/319 & n. 2

JEWELRY: ring with Woolwich stone, 8/84 & n. 2; (P): Portuguese rings, 3/139

LACE: see Textiles etc.

LININGS: see breeches

LIVERY: Sandwich's servants', 2/79; Penn's and Batten's, 3/77; others',

8/115, 186; (P): servants', 3/47, 50 & n. 3, 77; 9/372, 378

MITTENS: fur, 8/22

MONTEROS: see hats

MUFF (P): 3/271

NECKCLOTH (P): 6/175; 8/486

NIGHTGOWNS (dressing gowns): 6/228; 7/378; 9/4; silk, 3/242; (P): 6/175; 7/268, 272

PANTALOONS: 5/255 & n. 1

POWDER (for head) (P): 3/96

RIBBONS [see also Marriage: wedding ceremonies]: green for birthday, 6/285; black for leg (new fashion), 7/324; (P): 9/165, 230

SASH (P): 8/462

SCALLOPS (collars): (P): 3/216, 220, 235

SHIRTS (P): wears two, 7/291; half-shirts, 1/231; 2/195; 4/360; 5/191

SHOES: shepherd's iron-shod, 8/339; (P) [see also Wootton, W.]: first wears buckles, 1/26; 'in shoemaker's stocks', 7/107 & n. 2; shoe strings, 9/188

SLEEVES: butchers', 5/222; (P): laced, 6/125; 9/201

SOCKS: (P): 8/105

STOCKINGS: shepherd's woollen, 8/339; (P): knitted, 1/85; grey serge, 1/94; linen, 1/156; silk, 1/164; 4/80; 9/193, 449 & n. 1.; short black, 1/251; thread, 2/138; 6/334; 8/105; woollen, 2/138; cotton, 6/73; leather, 6/309

SUITS: Sandwich's coronation, 2/83; his gold-buttoned, 4/187; Duke of York's riding, 2/213; silk, 5/24; (P): bombazine, 7/172, 182; 9/215, 217; camlet, 6/104, 106, 114, 125, 152; 8/295, 314, 315; 9/533, 534, 537, 540, 548; cloth: grey riding, 2/120; 3/42, 85, 106, 116; 4/243; moiré lined, 5/142, 144; also, 4/130, 316, 369; 5/125, 302, 308, 309–10, 322; 7/39; farandine, 6/124, 125, 175, 210; silk, 3/190, 196; 2/105; stuff, 6/127–8; 9/197, 201, 210, 540; misc.: with great skirts, 1/3, 38; skirts shortened, 1/121; white, with silver lace coat, 1/38; made from cloak, 1/118; old black new-furbished, 3/54; close-kneed coloured suit, 4/105; new fashion (vest, coat, belt, sword), 7/353; changes in September from silk to cloth suit, 8/455

SWORDS: Prynne's basket-hilt, 1/62; (P): rapier stick, 1/95, 138; sword 'refreshed', 2/24; smallsword with gilt handle, 4/80, 105; silver-hilted, 7/353; gilded for May Day, 9/537; wears to escort Sandwich, 1/93; starts wearing 'as manner among gentlemen is', 2/29 & n. 2; 3/241 & n. 2; equips footboy with, 3/77 & n. 2; 9/537

TOPS: *see* cannons

TRAVELLING-CLOTHES: 8/233

TUNICS: (P): velvet, 8/489; laced, 9/201 & n. 2; coloured camlet, 9/540

TURBANS: 7/378; worn by giant, 5/243

VEILS: at synagogue, 4/335 & n. 2

VESTS: new fashion, 7/315; first worn by Duke of York, 7/320; description, 7/324, 328; Louis XIV puts footmen into, 7/379 & n. 4; also, 8/154; (P): first wears, 7/346, 353(2), 362, 366; made from old suit, 8/295, 314, 341, 404; his new laced vest, 9/201; and flowered tabby, 9/533, 540

WAISTCOATS (P) (outer garments): green watered moiré, 1/298; false tabby with gold lace, 2/195; black baize faced with silk, 4/360; thin silk, 7/172; (under garments): leaves off/puts on according to season, 2/116, 195, 198; 3/138; 5/198; 6/67; 7/182; 8/235; 9/175, 180, 400, 549

WALKING STICKS (canes) (P): knotted, 1/104; rattan, painted and gilded, 1/244; buys at cane shop, 5/117; varnished for walking, 7/211; silver-headed Japan, 8/84

COMPLETE OUTFITS (P): 4/105, 400; 6/175; 9/201, 533

FASHION: changes at Easter, 8/63; King's new, 7/315, 320–1; description, 7/324 & n. 3, 328; worn by M.P.s, 7/324; hat 'cocked behind', 8/249; French ambassador's unfashionable dress, 9/284 & n. 3; (P): buys/ wears to keep up with: buckled shoes, 1/26 & n. 2; short cloak, 1/260; coat and sword, 2/29; longer hair, 2/97; new coat, 2/203; suit with linings

showing under breeches, 4/130; low-crowned beaver, 4/280; suits in new fashion, 7/353(2); 8/295; suit with shoulder belt for sword, 9/201

COURT/CEREMONIAL/PROFESSIONAL [*see also* clerical, above]: coronation robes, 2/80, 82, 84; regalia, 2/84; costumes at court ball, 7/372 & n. 3; Russian envoys' costumes, 3/297; 8/428; Persian envoy's, 9/17; Garter robes, 8/184–5; academic, 9/544

MOURNING: purple worn by King, 1/246; (P): hat band, 1/247; short black stockings, 1/251(2); rings, 2/74 & n. 2; 3/269; 4/21; belt, 2/203; shoes blacked, 5/90; white gloves, 5/90 & n. 2; servants', 8/134

BEARDS: Spanish fashion, 8/453 & n. 1; (P): shaves off beard/moustache, 3/97; 5/22–3 & n.

HAIRDRESSING: wigs worn at court, 4/136; King and Duke of York start wearing, 4/360; 5/49, 126; and W. Howe, 4/390; Rupert's, 8/146; (P): hair cut by: barber, 2/97; 4/237; 5/352; EP, 5/72; 8/35; 9/424; maids, 8/280; 9/201; and sister-in-law, 9/175; close-cropped, 7/112, 302; because lousy, 9/424; foul with powder, 3/96; combed by maids, 3/96; 6/21, 185; 8/531; 9/20, 37, 48, 73, 109, 277, 328, 337; head inspected, 9/239; finds difficulty in keeping hair clean, 3/96, 196; 4/130; to wear periwig, 4/130, 290, 343, 350, 357, 358, 378; first appearances in, 4/362, 363, 365, 369; periwig cleaned, 5/212; repaired, 6/74; fears to wear one made during Plague, 6/210; refuses to buy infested periwig, 8/133, 146; buys from French wigmaker, 8/136, 137, 138, 146, 177; 9/334; barber to keep in repair, 9/217; catches fire in candle, 9/322; periwig case, 4/363; also, 6/89, 97

SHAVING (P): trimmed by barber, 1/90, 113, 136, 142, 148, 152, 162, 200, 208, 214, 219, 224, 252, 298, 308; 2/32, 76, 97, 112, 135, 180, 241; 3/24, 41, 64, 71, 81, 187, 201, 215, 220, 233, 289, 299; 4/16, 20, 23, 43, 96, 130, 154, 186, 190, 258, 261, 312; 5/246; 6/257, 266, 288, 303, 306, 322, 331, 334; 7/6, 278,

293; 9/234, 496; employs barber on giving up pumice-stone, 3/196; for first time for a year, 6/233; pays barber, 9/225; shaves with pumice, 3/91, 97; shaves off beard/moustache, 3/97; begins using razor, 5/6; shaves off beard/moustache, 5/22–3 & n.; cuts himself, 5/29; shaves after week's growth during Fire, 7/288; shaves himself, 5/52, 55, 87; 6/159, 228, 311; 8/247

WASHING (P): washes regularly, 5/320; washes on hottest day of year, 3/75; and at EP's request, 6/44; washes feet/legs, 3/47; 4/165; 7/172, 206; catches cold, 7/207; ears washed, 6/21; lousy, 9/424

DRESS AND PERSONAL APPEARANCE (WOMEN AND GIRLS):

GARMENTS AND ACCESSORIES:

APRONS: Queen Catherine, 9/557

BANDS: lace, 6/172

BODICE: Nell Gwyn, 8/193; (EP): pair, 4/357

CAPS: Duchess of Newcastle's velvet, 8/186, 196

COATS (EP): velvet, 4/316

CUFFS (EP): laced, 8/392–3, 396

DRAWERS: 9/194; (EP): 4/140 & n. 1, 172

DRESS: lying-in, 6/55; 7/329; 'paysan', 8/375; riding, 6/162; 7/162; travelling, 7/142

DRESSING-BOX: 8/46, 53; (EP): 9/91

FANS (EP): 4/172

FARTHINGALES: Portuguese ladies-in-waiting, 3/92 & n. 2

GALLOSHES: 6/299

GARTERS: valentine gift, 9/449; (EP): valentine gift, 2/40

GLOVES: embroidered, 2/38; white, 2/38; 4/68; 7/344; Jessamy, 7/344; 9/449; (EP): valentine gift, 2/40; painted leather, 4/100; with yellow ribbons, 5/264; perfumed French, 9/427

GORGET: 4/279

GOWNS: velvet, 3/299; 4/2, 400; silver-laced, 5/188; flowered tabby, 9/521; (EP): black silk, laced with black gimp, 2/117; moiré to replace taffeta, 3/298; 4/10, 13; trimmed with point, 4/337; Indian, 4/391; 5/8;

Japanese, 4/415; laced, 5/100, 110, 118; 9/455–6; morning, 5/103; 8/465, 468; light coloured silk, 6/76; similar to Lady Castlemaine's, 7/298; coloured flowered tabby, 7/302; 9/540; cloth, 8/242

HANDKERCHIEVES ('han(d)kirchers'): ('lace', worn as collar), 7/341; 8/576; (EP): 2/211, 212, 214; 7/243, 379; 9/6

HATS: plumed, 4/230; straw, 8/382; (EP): straw, 8/382

HOODS: black, 1/42; (EP): yellow bird's-eye, 6/102 & n. 2; white, 8/124; French, 9/453

JEWELRY: posy ring, 1/39; diamonds and pearls at court ball, 7/371–2; (EP): pearl necklace, 1/240; 6/200–1; 7/108, 111, 112, 113, 412; pendants, 4/100; 5/196; diamond ring, 6/190–1; 9/67–8, 78, 88–9

JUSTE-AU-CORPS: black, 8/187; gold laced, 9/213

LACE: see Textiles etc.; when worn as collar, see above, handkerchieves

MANTLE: frieze, 1/60–1; white flannel, 8/79; (EP): 1/320

MASK [see also below, vizard]: at theatre, 8/71–2; at Vauxhall, 9/220; travelling 2/91 & n. 1; (EP): 5/28

MUFF (EP): 1/320; 3/271; 4/7; 7/39

NECKCLOTH: 8/224

NIGHTGOWN: Lady Castlemaine's, 8/404; (EP): 7/18; 8/210, 424, 458

PATCHES: worn by Dutch ladies, 1/138; shop girl, 3/239 & n. 2; Duchess of Newcastle, 8/186; Peg Lowther, 6/9; 8/196, 197; Lady Castlemaine, 9/186; Lady Sandwich and daughter, 1/269; (EP): first wears, 1/234, 283, 299

PATTENS (EP): 1/27

PETTICOATS: satin, 3/83; linen, trimmed with lace (Lady Castlemaine), 3/87; short crimson (Queen Catherine), 4/229; (EP): paragon, 1/82; trimmed with silver lace, 1/225; 5/239; 8/242; and gold lace, 5/44; sarcenet, trimmed with black lace, 3/65; yellow, 3/85; 5/264; green flowered satin trimmed with gimp lace, 3/125; silk striped, 4/199; silk, 5/114; 7/296; blue, 8/124; laced, 9/400

PINNER: (Lady Castlemaine), 5/126;

white (Queen Catherine), 9/557; (EP): 7/243; point-de-Gesne, 8/413 & n. 2

RIBBONS: on hat, 6/172; (EP): 2/235; on gloves, 5/264

SACK (SAC) GOWN (EP): brought from France, 9/464

SCALLOP (EP): 2/228

SCARF (EP): 4/6; laced, 5/274

SHOES: white, 6/299; shoe-strings as valentine present, 9/449; (EP): brought from France, 9/453

SLEEVES: hanging sleeves, 4/254; 9/507; smock sleeves, 8/193

SMOCKS: 3/87; 8/404; (EP): linen, 1/88

STOCKINGS: valentine gifts: silk, 7/70; green silk, 9/449 & n. 1; (EP): valentine gift, 2/40

SUITS: lustring, 2/38; flowered satin, 2/192; coloured silk with silver lace, 5/325; (EP) (in some cases already indexed under 'gown'): black sarcenet with yellow petticoat, 3/85; country suit, 4/155; riding, 4/184; laced, 5/125; moiré, 5/274; flowered ash-coloured silk, 6/53; with laced cuffs, 8/396; flowered tabby, 9/134

TRAIN: fashionable, 7/325; held up by page, 3/126; 8/302

TUNIC: 8/576

VEST (EP): velvet, 8/469

VIZARD [see also above, mask]: worn at play, 4/181 & n. 3; and in court masque, 6/29; (EP): 4/181; 8/423

WAISTCOATS: Queen Catherine's white laced, 4/229; (EP): slashed, 3/99 & n. 3; farandine, 4/28; white satin, 8/124; black moiré, 8/242

WHISK: 8/325; (EP): white, 1/299; lace, 6/55; scallop whisk, 3/285

COMPLETE OUTFITS: (Queen Catherine), 4/229–30; (EP): 8/124, 242

FASHION: velvet gowns, 4/2; moiré gowns for winter, 3/298; vizards in theatre, 4/181 & n. 3; masculine riding dress, 6/172 & n. 4; 7/162; Queen's fashion for skirts above ankle with train, 7/325, 335; fashions change at Easter, 8/63; importance of, 2/226, 230; painting of face unfashionable, 3/89; and Spanish farthingales, 3/92 & n. 2; (EP): to be in fashion

wears false hair, 3/51; moiré winter gown/suit, 4/10; hood, 6/102; immodest décolletage, 7/379

MOURNING: white scarves, 1/24 & n. 5; black, plain hair and no patches, 7/106, 306; Lady Falmouth's 'second or third', 7/178 & n. 2; hoods, scarves and gloves, 8/134; Duchess of York's black gown trimmed with ermine as second mourning, 8/570; (EP): for Duke of Gloucester, 1/246, 248, 251; mother-in-law, 9/134; gown laced for second mourning, 8/210, 211, 242; also, 2/202

MISC.: undress/deshabille, 3/99; 6/297, 335 & n. 1; tight-lacing, 5/222; servants' dress, 6/238 & n. 3; 7/329; antic dress (Duchess of Newcastle), 8/243; apron and pinner 'like a woman with child', 9/557

COSMETICS: paint used by Queen Catherine, 3/89 & n. 3; Mrs Williams, 6/204; E. Pearse, 8/439, 454, 503; 9/202; Knipp and Nell Gwyn, 8/463; Lady Carnegie, 9/383; orange-flower water, 4/229; (EP): puppy-dog water, 5/78; May-dew, 8/240; 9/549, 551

HAIRDRESSING: Princess Henrietta Maria 'frized short up to her ears', 1/299 & n. 4; Queen Catherine wears 'à la négligence', 4/229–30; false hair worn by F. Stuart, 8/44; Knipp's hair 'tied behind', 8/389; (EP): has hair dressed, 1/287; false hair: 'perruques', 3/51; white locks, 6/55; 7/346–7; 8/210–11; 9/454

WASHING: (EP): 6/44; for court visit, 1/298 & n. 3; after house has been redecorated, 9/372; for May Day parade, 9/538; visits hot house, 6/40 & n. 1, 41

DRIBBLE: see Drebbel

DRINK:

P'S DRINKING HABITS [see also Vows]: drinking club, 1/208; 6/148 & n. 1; headaches from drinking wine, 1/46, 84, 120, 218, 219, 307, 313, 321, 323; 2/34, 65, 99, 115, 186, 191, 211; 3/61, 151; 4/186; 8/5; 9/193; gets drunk, 2/51, 87, 175, 186; advised to drink less, 2/17; effects of abstinence, 3/18, 31; abstains from wine, 3/107, 112, 118, 119; 4/254; 5/312; drinks wine in moderation, 3/130, 151, 163, 197; 4/235; mixes wine with beer, 4/343, 410; 5/236; relaxes vow during Plague, 6/226; 7/49; alleged to be a drinker, 6/243; drinks sack despite oath, 7/23; and burnt wine, 8/130; first morning visit to tavern for seven years, 9/220

HEALTHS: puritan objections, 2/105 & n. 5; 5/172 & n. 4; French method, 4/189; loyal toast accompanied by gun salute, 1/152; drunk kneeling, 1/121, 122; 2/87; ladies toasted, 2/220; 7/246; 8/130–1

VARIETIES:

BRANDY: 9/103, 498; burned, 8/20

BRISTOL MILK: see wine

BUTTERMILK: 5/152

CHOCOLATE: 1/178; 3/226–7; 4/5; 5/64, 139; at coffee house, 5/329

CIDER: 3/300; 4/28, 121; 7/115; 8/315; French, 4/254

COFFEE: 5/76, 77, 105

ELDER SPIRITS: 4/221

GRUEL: 4/40

HIPPOCRAS: see wine

JULEP: 1/181

LAMB'S WOOL: see ale

MEAD: 8/460

METHEGLIN: 1/72; 7/218

MILK: 4/29; 7/207; 9/224; from milkmaid on Epsom Downs, 8/339; from Keeper's Lodge, Hyde Park, 9/142 & n. 1, ? 154, 175, 184, 222, 260, 533–4

MUM: see ale

MUSCADINE: see wine

ORANGE JUICE: 9/477 & n. 3

POSSET: 3/274; 4/40, 202, 319; 5/77; sack posset: 1/9, 10, 11; 4/14, 38; 9/13; in Davenant play, 9/134

PURLE: see beer

SACK: see wine

STRONG WATERS: EP for fainting fit, 4/307; also, 2/24; 4/284; 6/40, 198; 7/157; 8/412, 504, 544; 9/99

TEA: 'cupp of tee', 1/253 & n. 5; also, 6/328 & n. 1; 8/302

WATER: [for spa water, see Health]: public supply, 3/92 & n. 3; 4/295 & n. 3; 8/370 & n. 2; also, 4/265; 6/23

WHEY: 3/116; 4/164 & n. 2, 175,

179–80, 286; 5/152; 6/120; 7/170 & n. 4; 8/215; 9/215

WINE: Bristol milk: 9/236 & n. 1; burnt: 7/295, 425; 8/47, 120, 130, 589; canary: 2/211; 6/151; claret: 1/277; 2/25; 4/65, 171; 6/151; 7/175, 375; 8/393; burnt, 5/90; 7/386; 8/124; English: from Walthamstow, 1/317; 8/341–2; Florence wine: 1/324; 2/8; Haut Brion ('Ho Bryan'): 4/100 & n. 4; hippocras ('hypocras'): 4/354; 5/118; Malaga (see also sack): 3/14; 6/151; muscadine: 1/296; Navarre: 9/443 & n. 1; Rhenish: 2/125; 8/156; with sugar, 2/38; 3/24; Bleakard, 4/189 & n. 3; sack: with wormwood, 2/9; raspberry sack, 2/212; Malaga, 4/235; 6/151; mulled, 6/266; 7/424; 9/103; anecdote of its killing toad, 7/290; also, 1/57, 230, 292, 308; 2/25, 217, 219, 224; 5/32, 37; 6/224; 7/23, 166; 8/5; 9/227; sherry: 3/14, 180; tent: 4/405; 5/11, 222; 6/151; wormwood: 1/301; 4/25, 58; misc.: wine and sugar, 1/167; 4/179; mulled white, 1/292; wine traders' tricks, 7/256

WINE CELLARS: P orders jointly with colleagues, 3/14 & n. 3; crested bottles, 4/346 & n. 1; pride in stock, 6/151; cellars at Audley End, 1/70 & n. 1; 8/467–8; Whitehall palace, 1/193, 246, 247; 2/175; and at Povey's, 4/18 & n. 2, 298; 5/161

DRUMBLEBY (Drumbelly), ——, flageolet maker, Strand: the best in town, 8/53; supplies flageolets, 8/53, 87; 9/30, 51, 160; recorder, 9/157; moulds for eye tubes, 9/278; ~ his boy, 9/364

DRURY LANE [see also Coffee-houses; Taverns etc.: Bear; Theatres]: plague in, 7/72–3; milkmaids in, 8/193

DRYDEN (Draydon), John (1631–1700) [see also Plays]: known to P at Cambridge, 5/37 & n. 2; share in authorship of Sir Martin Mar-all, 8/387 & n. 1, 468, n. 2; alluded to: 8/363

DUBLIN: Castle Plot, 4/168 & n. 2, 170; packet boat, 4/256; alluded to: 3/162

DUCK LANE: booksellers in, 2/131; 6/332; 9/85, 86, 121, 148, 167, 260, 265, 543

DUCKINFORD, ——: 4/343

DUCKING-POND FIELDS: 5/101 & n. 1

DUDLEY, Robert, 1st Earl of Leicester (d. 1588): letters, 6/308 & n. 2

DUDLEY, [?William]: 1/83

[DUELL, Fleetwood], sexton, St Olave's, Hart St: 2/6 & n. 5; ?also, 3/3; 7/425; 9/21

DUELS: see Law and Order, offences against

DUGDALE, John, son of William; kted 1686 (d. 1700): 7/297 & n. 2; social: 2/221–2 & n.

DUGDALE, William, kted 1677, antiquarian (d. 1686): losses of books in Fire, 7/297 & n. 2; his *Origines Juridiciales*, ib.

DUKE, [George], secretary to Fishery Corporation: 5/223, 262, 314

DUKE (Dick, Dike) Shore, Limehouse: P visits, 2/14; 7/126

DUMFRIES: 7/377 & n. 4

DUNCOMBE, [Sir Edward], of Battlesden, Beds., father of Sir John: 8/245 & n. 1

DUNCOMBE (Duncum, Dunkum), Sir John, M.P. Bury St Edmunds, Suff., 1660, 1661–79, Ordnance Commissioner 1664–70, Treasury Commissioner 1667–72:

CHARACTER: able, 8/178; proud, 8/178 & n. 2, 244, 249, 251, 496, 501; profane, 9/93; unpopular, 9/205

AS ORDNANCE COMMISSIONER: appointed, 5/316; loan to Navy Board, 8/178; proud of office's efficiency, 8/178–9 & nn.; fears Commons, 8/179; supports Navy Board against Carkesse, 8/215; defends in Commons, 8/495–6; also, 8/112

AS TREASURY COMMISSIONER: appointed, 8/223, 229–30; Navy Board business, 8/433 & n. 1; 9/101, 122 & n. 1, 444–5; unspecified business, 9/465

AS PRIVY COUNCILLOR: 8/233–4, 278

GENERAL AND MISC.: regard for P, 8/179; 9/105, 493; for Coventry, 9/41; jealous of Clifford, 8/185; sudden rise, 8/234 & n. 1, 245, 249; ridiculed

in play, 9/471 & nn. 2, 3; dismissal expected, 9/478 & n. 2; lodgings, 8/178; reminiscences of France, 9/93

ALLUDED TO: 9/415

DUNKIRK: sale to French: disapproved of by merchants, 3/229 & n. 1; by P, 3/230; Sandwich's part in, 3/237 & n. 2; 7/55 & n. 4; proceeds, 3/262 & n. 3, 265 & n. 1, 269, 271; 5/59; 6/326 & n. 2; Clarendon blamed for, 4/223 & n. 3; 6/39; 7/55 & n. 4; 8/265, 269 & n. 2, 270, 402; parliamentary enquiry, 8/485; sale alluded to: 3/245, 272; 8/348; coveted by Spain, 3/115; French troops at, 8/265; also, 1/101; 6/129; alluded to: 1/105; 5/170; 7/146; 9/492

DUNN (Donne), [?Thomas]: 1/114, 115, 118, 121–2, 134, 171, 226; social: 3/138; alluded to: 1/162

DUNSTER, [Giles], merchant: on Brooke House Committee, 9/254

DUPORT, [James], chaplain to the King (d. 1679): preaches at Whitehall, 4/36–7 & n.

DUPPA, Brian, Bishop of Salisbury 1641–60, Winchester 1660–d.62: preaches at Whitehall, 1/210 & n. 1; also, 1/259

DUPUY, [Lawrence], Yeoman of the Robes to the Duke of York: knave, 5/279 & n. 2; also, 8/374

DURAS, Louis, Marquis de Blanquefort (d. 1709), succ. as 2nd Earl of Feversham 1677, Household officer of Duke of York: influence, 7/163 & n. 2; flatters Lady Castlemaine, 8/404; at court, 9/468–9; also, 8/412 & n. 2; social: 6/29

DURDANS, the, nr Epsom, Surrey: Lord Berkeley entertains royal party, 3/184; P visits, 4/246; P's boyhood memories, 3/184; 4/246

[DUREL, John], pastor of French church at the Savoy (d. 1683): 3/207 & nn.

DURHAM YARD: Brooke House Committee in, 9/43; fire, 9/534–5 & n.

DURY, Madam: 1/300

DUTCH CHURCH, the, Austin Friars: exchange of congregations with French church, 3/277 & n. 1; alluded to: 4/398

ETHELL, Robert, of Huntingdon: 2/137

ETHEREGE (Etherige), Sir George, playwright (d. 1691) [*see also* Plays]: critical of actors, 9/54

ETON COLLEGE: P visits, 7/59–60 & nn.

EVANS, [Lewis], harpist: dies in poverty, 7/414

EVANS, Mr ——, butler to Lady Wright: 1/29; plays lute, 1/29, 288

EVANS, Mr ——, the tailor: 2/165

EVANS, Capt.: *see* Ewen(s)

EVELYN, John, diarist:
CHARACTER: P's regard, 6/243, 289–90; 7/26, 29, 49, 112, 297; 9/484
POLITICAL OPINIONS: laments state of court/nation, 7/29, 297, 406; 8/181–4 *passim*, 248–9, 278, 377; 9/484; stories of Louis XIV's power, 8/182–3; believes republic imminent, 8/556
AS COMMISSIONER FOR SICK AND WOUNDED etc.: attends on Navy Board, 6/239, 243; consulted by P, 6/253; proposed infirmary, 7/29 & n. 1, 49; also, 6/275, 278
HOUSE (Sayes Court, Kent): admired by P, 6/94–5 & n.; P visits, 6/94–5, 243, 253, 289–90, 331; 7/112; garden, 6/97 & nn., 253 & n. 3; also, 9/449
WRITINGS, INTELLECTUAL INTERESTS ETC.: impromptu nonsense verse, 6/220; translation of Naudé's *Advis pour dresser une bibliothèque*, 6/252 & n. 1; book on painting, 6/286 & n. 2; *Elysium Britannicum*, 6/289 & n. 4; plays, ib. & n. 5; *hortus hyemalis*, 6/289 & n. 6; Leicester MSS, 6/308 & n. 2; collection of paintings, mezzotints etc., 6/289 & n. 3; admires Clarendon House, 7/32; also, 6/243
MISC.: proposes Thomas P of Hatcham as J.P., 7/112; news of Plague from, 7/241; scheme for making bricks, 9/314 & n. 3; purchase of land near Deptford yard, 9/484 & n. 1
SOCIAL: stories of Frances Stuart, 8/342–3; also, 6/217, 218, 291, 324

EVELYN, Mary, wife of John: her paintings, 6/243

EVELYN, [Richard], brother of John (1622–70): his house (Woodcote Park), nr Epsom, 8/338 & n. 1, 339 & n. 1; ~ his wife [Elizabeth], ib.

EVERTSEN, [Cornelis], jun. Dutch naval officer (d. 1706): captured in naval action, 6/81–2 & n.; ~ his father (d. 1679) ib.

EVERTSEN, [Jan], Dutch Admiral: his squadron, 6/108 & n. 3; suspected of disloyalty, 6/122 & n. 6; killed in action, 7/229 & n. 3, 231, 233

EVETT, Capt. [?Philip, naval officer]: in search for Barkstead's treasure, 3/242, 246, 248, 256, 285, 286

ÉVORA, Portugal: recaptured by Portuguese, 4/215 & n. 2

EWELL (Yowell), Surrey: P/EP visit(s), 4/248, 249; 6/235, 244–5, 304; soldiers quartered at, 6/245; ~ 'my Besse' at inn, 6/304

EWEN(S) (Evans), Capt. [Thomas], naval officer: Elder Brother's dinner at Trinity House, 3/246 & n. 1; reports on Tangier mole, 4/319

EXCHANGE: *see* New Exchange; Royal Exchange

EXCHANGE ALLEY: coffee-house, 4/162; Backwell's building scheme, 4/214 & n. 3

EXCHANGE ST, Westminster: 7/369 & n. 4

EXCHEQUER, the:
CHRON. SERIES: shortage of cash, 1/117; Lord Treasurer sworn in, 2/31; proposed payment of Navy Victualler by, 3/106–7, 107–8; attempted reorganisation of expenditure, 3/297 & n. 1; management of credit under Additional Aid Act and Eleven Months Tax, 3/312; 8/132 & n. 1, 269, 590; unsuitability as commercial bank, 8/132; also, 6/65
BUILDINGS: 7/325; Upper Bench, 1/47; at Nonsuch in Plague, 6/186, 188; and after Fire, 7/278
COURT OF: Squibb's case, 1/48, 49; Field's case, 4/51–2, 192–3; Lord Mayor sworn in, 7/346; *distringas* from, 9/535
CLERKS: Monck's gift to, 1/118; new appointments, 1/128; 2/4; fees, 6/100; 7/398; 8/74; inefficiency, 6/157; 7/125, 126, 168; social: St Thomas's Day feast, 1/320 & n. 1; 2/236; also,

2/241; 6/106; 8/435; alluded to: 4/46

OFFICERS: holidays, 1/320 & n. 1; 8/73, 132; auditors: consulted by Navy Board, 4/158–9; dine with, 3/279; 5/318; alluded to: 6/79

P'S SERVICE IN: clerk to Downing, vol. i, p. xxiii; 1/2 & n. 1; salary/fees, 1/10, 33; 2/9; payments, 1/6, 9, 14–15, 33, 37; accounts, 1/61; hopes for vice-chamberlain's place, 1/80; replaced temporarily, 1/83, 107–8; resigns, 1/238; 2/108; stores money etc. at, 2/19; also, 1/26, 45, 59; 4/126

P'S TRANSACTIONS WITH: Tangier business: 6/106; 7/240, 241–2, 255, 385, 389, 396, 398, 407; 8/102, 122, 295, 299, 329, 344, 390, 434–5, 439, 440; 9/30, 36; accounts, 8/180, 508; Navy victualling business: 8/432; Tangier or Navy victualling business: 6/100, 187–8, 234, 235, 244–5, 304, 311, 312; 7/38, 39, 45, 71, 81, 118, 137, 164, 168, 265, 299, 304; 8/422, 444; 9/295, 376, 477, 486

EXCISE, the [see also Taxation]: office building [Bartholomew Lane], 7/79; new office [Aldersgate St], 9/265, 269; new farmers appointed, 8/557 & n. 3; P's business with [mostly to cash tallies as Treasurer for Tangier; occasionally on Navy Office business]: 6/133, 136, 163; 7/79, 131, 133, 134, 164, 190, 214, 378, 402, 407; 8/63, 64, 77, 193, 198, 223, 329, 331, 341, 445, 518, 545; 9/64, 110, 120, 269, 278, 376, 513, 514, 520, 534, 543, 545, 562, 562–3; also, 1/8, 192

EXECUTIONS: see Justice, administration of

EXETER HOUSE, Strand: sermons in chapel, 1/3 & n. 1; 5/103; residence of French ambassador, 5/103; of Lord Ashley, 8/445, 553; used by Tangier Committee, 6/15; Doctors' Commons, 8/22, 23; and Admiralty Court, 8/130 & n. 1, 579; also, 2/189; 4/295; 8/128, 129

EXTON, Dr [John], Judge of Court of Admiralty, 1649–d. 68: gives charge, 4/76

EYRES (Ayres), Col. [William]: his regiment, 1/64

FAGE (Fyge), Valentine, apothecary: consulted by P, 1/9 & n. 2, 49, 55; political news from, 1/9, 16, 25, 47, 49, 55; social: 1/257

FAIR(E)BANKE, ——: dispute with Coventry about fees, 1/240–1 & n.

FAIRBROTHER, William, Fellow of King's College, Cambridge: good natured, 3/224; 4/266; drinks King's health, 1/67; verses on Prynne, 1/69; arranges P's M.A. ceremony, 1/195, 222; made D.C.L., 1/258; also, 1/68, 265; 2/25; 3/21, 186; social: at P's house, 1/221; 2/28; 3/166; 5/351; at John P sen.'s, 1/173, 220; 2/75, 81; 3/161; in Cambridge, 2/136; 3/217, 224

FAIRBROTHER, ——: 1/172

FAIRFAX, Sir Thomas, 3rd Baron Fairfax: political intentions, 1/4 & n. 5; disbands troops, 1/8; ordered to London by Rump, ib.; signs address to Monck, 1/55 & n. 4; at The Hague, 1/147; given army command in Medway crisis, 8/265 & n. 5; bust at Swakeleys, 6/215 & n. 1

FAIRS AND MARKETS: Abingdon (Oxon.): custard fair, 9/227 & n. 2; Baldock Fair (Herts.): P and EP visit, 2/183 & n. 6; Bartholomew Fair, Smithfield [see also Entertainments]: P/EP visit(s), 2/166 & n. 2, 172; 4/288, 298, 301; 5/260, 265; 8/405, 408–9, 421, 423; 9/290, 293, 296, 297, 299, 301; opening ceremonies, 4/288; performing monkeys, 2/166; 4/298; clockworks, 4/298; 8/423; rope dancing, 2/172; 5/260, 265; 9/290, 293, 301; puppet plays, 8/408–9 & n., 421 & n. 2; 9/293, 296, 299 & n. 2, 301; misc. sideshows, 2/172; 4/288, 301; 9/293, 296, 297, 301; alluded to: 1/242 & n. 2; Leadenhall: P visits market, 4/290–1; 9/285; also, 7/280; Mile End Green: market established after Fire, 7/280; Southwark Fair: P visits, 1/242 & n. 1; 9/313; puppet play and rope dancing at, 9/313; St Ives Market (Hunts.): 3/220; St James's Fair: 1/208 & n. 3; St James's Market: 9/514; Sturbridge Fair (Cambs.): P and EP at, 2/181 & n. 3; EP to visit, 9/253, 301, 306, 309;

Tower Hill: market established after Fire, 7/281

FAITHORNE, [William sen.], engraver and printseller: P buys from, 1/174 & n. 2; 3/2; 7/173, 359, 393; 8/10; engraving of Lady Castlemaine, 7/359 & n. 3, 393; instrument for drawing perspectives, 9/513

FALCONBRIDGE: see Belasyse, Thomas, Lord Fauconberg and Fauconberg, Edward

FALCONER, [Edward] (ed. error): see Fauconberg, [Edward]

FALCONER, [Elizabeth], widow of John: formerly his maid, 4/67; claims compensation on his death, 5/231, 248 & n. 2, 249, 253; ill, 5/213; social: 5/155, 192

FALCONER, [John], Clerk of the Ropeyard, Woolwich: marriage, 4/67; gift to EP, 5/45, 47; P inspects ropeyard with, 5/54; illness and death, 5/109, 125, 130, 137, 155, 213, 217, 248 & n. 2; stories of gifts to Penn and Coventry, 5/231 & n. 4, 248, 249, 253; 8/228; social: 2/121, 155, 227; 3/19, 102, 142, 159, 179; 4/103; 5/156, 182, 192; ~ his friend, 5/155

FALMOUTH, Viscount: see Berkeley, Sir C.

FALMOUTH, Cornwall: 7/397

FANATICS [P uses both 'fanatics' and 'sectaries' to describe the extreme Puritans. See also Anabaptists; Fifth-Monarchists; Nonconformists; Plots and risings, minor]: strength in London, 1/109, 111; 4/373 & n. 3; blame King for persecution, 3/127; rising feared, 3/186, 236, 303; prophesy end of world next Tuesday, 3/266–7; want court and church purified, 3/275; alleged loyalty, 4/373; 5/264 & n. 1; rebel in Yorkshire, 4/391 & n. 1; riot in churches, 9/96 & n. 1

FANCHURCH ST: see Fenchurch St

FANSHAWE, Anne, Lady Fanshawe, wife of Sir Richard: 3/126; 7/379–80

FANSHAWE, [Henry], brother of Thomas Fanshawe, 2nd Viscount Fanshawe: seeks place in navy, 9/86 & n. 3

FANSHAWE, [Lyonel], 2/163 & n. 3; 3/57

FANSHAWE, Sir Richard, diplomatist: drafts preambles to patents of nobility, 1/188 & n. 1, 189; ambassador to Portugal, 2/163 & n. 3; 3/2 & n. 3, 57; death, 7/214 & n. 1, 380

[FARRINER, Thomas], King's Baker, Pudding Lane: Fire alleged to have started at his bakery, 7/268 & n. 1; 8/81, 82

FAUCONBERG (Falconbridge etc.), [Edward], Deputy-Chamberlain of the Receipt at the Exchequer: agrees to P's resigning, 1/80; consulted by P, 2/236; alluded to: 7/303, 304, 314, 319; 8/212; social: 1/24; 2/239–40, 241; 6/162, 235; 7/398; ~ his kinsman, R. Knightley; his kinswoman, Barker, EP's companion (qq.v.)

FAUNTLEROY (FONTLEROY), [?Thomas]: 1/294

FAVERSHAM, Kent: 8/358

FAZEBY, Capt. [William], naval officer: 7/141–2

FÉCAMP (Feckam): King lands at (1651), 1/156

FEE LANE: see Fleet Lane

FELTON, Sir Henry, Bt, M.P. Suffolk (d. 1690): 6/118

FELTON, [John], assassin of Buckingham: 2/93 & n. 2

FENCHURCH ST [see also Taverns, etc.: Mitre]: Plague, 6/124, 128, 225; Fire, 7/276; P shops in, 8/173; 9/322; St Gabriel's church, 6/76 & n. 2

FENN, John, Paymaster to the Navy Treasurer: financial business: with P, 4/422; 6/192(2); 8/259; Penn, 7/65; and B. St Michel, 8/153, 162, 163; also, 7/169, 312; 8/121–2, 177, 281, 285; 9/169, 362, 428; malpractices: 6/40, 117; enquired into by Brooke House Committee, 9/82; rudeness, 7/89; a tool of Backwell, 7/214; P warns Carteret against, 6/190; usefulness to Carteret, 8/48 & n. 1, 180, 327; dismissed, 9/357 & n. 2; news from, 8/299, 354, 416; social: 3/14; 6/187, 198; 7/48, 74, 89, 404; 9/337; ~ his pretty wife, 9/337; his son, 6/24

FENNER, family of: dine at P's father's, 1/266; at funeral, 2/179

FIFTH MONARCHISTS: support Lambert, 1/7; rising under Venner, 2/7–11 passim & nn., 18; belief in Second Coming, 2/10–11; also, 4/375
FINANCES (P) [i.e. his private finances. *See also* Banks etc.; Brampton; Clerk of the Acts: perquisites etc.; Prices; Wills (P)]:
GENERAL: early poverty, 1/2; ambition to save £2000, keep a coach and become knight, 3/39–40; to save £1000, 3/99, 302; 5/3, 225; to save £3000, 7/367; has plate and goods worth £250, 6/207; also, 4/416
ACCOUNTS:
    PERSONAL: vows to keep/bring up to date, 3/40, 125; 6/336; 7/86; complicated by Tangier entries, 6/113; comparison of, for 1665 and 1666, 7/425–6; works on (no amounts given): 1/3; 2/98, 106; 4/316, 360, 424; 6/1, 192, 258, 339, 340, 341; 7/34, 82, 85, 86, 88, 89, 101, 109, 175, 188, 213, 244, 323, 338, 345, 397; 8/139, 191, 192, 210, 242(3), 508; 9/1, 7, 403, 492, 564; in arrears, 6/265, 339; 7/85, 86, 192, 342, 396; 8/192, 570; 9/180, 404, 424, 559, 564; petty bag book, 4/350
    FAMILY: payments to father and brother John, 1/205; 7/170, 225
    HOUSEHOLD (kitchen): P audits, 4/183; 5/3, 283; 8/444, 455
EXPENDITURE [items mentioned in connection with his accounts only. Asterisks denote entries at which amounts are given]: worried about, 2/213, 224, 242; 3/2–3, 39*; vows to reduce, 3/40, 125, 302; on journeys, vol. i, pp. c, ci; 9/160–8*, 224–43*; his clothes, 2/129; 3/95, 236; 4/320*, 337, 357*; 5/284*, 310; EP's clothes, 4/320*, 357*; 5/284*, 310; mourning clothes, 8/146, 192; EP's dancing lessons, 4/166; jewelry, 7/112–13*; house/household, 3/271*, 289*; 4/301, 320*, 337; 5/284*; 7/112–13*; pays bills (mostly to shopkeepers), 3/36, 78, 79, 82; 4/111; 7/425–6; 8/153, 189, 367, 443, 580, 599; 9/121, 126, 127, 177, 332–3, 404; likes to pay promptly, 4/282; 5/192, 193, 195
LOANS: borrowed: £10 from Lord

Crew, 1/14; 30s. from Cooke, 2/109; £40 from Batten, 2/145, 167; 3/39; £50 from Battersby, 2/190–1; lent: to Beck, 1/11, 30; £80 to Sandwich, 1/269; £500, 2/61; a further £200, 4/286, 290, 438; 5/131, 175; £60, 9/51; £500, 9/321; £100 to Lady Sandwich, 9/194, 211; £350 to Andrews, 6/85, 86; £350 to A. Joyce (proposal), 9/16–17; £1000 to Roger P on mortgage, 9/357–8, 369, 377; stands security for cousin Thomas P's loan of £1000 to Sandwich, 2/62; 5/186, 187; refuses to lend £1000 to Morland, 8/420
SAVINGS:
    AMOUNT OF PERSONAL WEALTH IN CASH (recorded at monthly/annual reckonings): £40, 1/32, 58, 130 & n. 1; c. £80, 1/164; c. £100, 1/168, 169, 209; £120, 1/210; c. £200, 1/240, 256; £150, 1/279; £200, 1/305; £240, 1/315; £300, 2/1; £350, 2/37; £500, 2/106; c. £600, 2/175; £500, 2/241; 3/39; £530, 3/95, 97, 99, 115; £650, 3/125, 151; c. £686, 3/182; £680, 3/209; £679, 3/236; £660, 3/271; £630, 3/296; £650, 3/301; £640, 4/29, 62; £670, 4/88; £700, £4/112; £726, 4/166; £719, 4/202; c. £700, 4/205; £730, 4/255; £750, 4/291; £760, 4/320; £717, 4/357, 358; £770, 4/401; c. £800, 4/438; £850, 5/31; £890, 5/71; c. £900, 5/106; £908, 5/137, 138; £930, 5/163; £951, 5/193; £1014, 5/227, 228; £1020, 5/258; £1203, 5/284; £1205, 5/310; £1209, 5/334; £1349, 5/359; £1257, 6/26; £1270, 6/47; £1300, 6/71; £1400, 6/92, 116; £1900, 6/179–80; £2164, 6/190; £2180, 6/205, 207; £4400, 6/341(2); £4600, 7/65; £5000, 7/90(2), 112–13; £5200, 7/138, 139; c. £5600, 7/192–3; £5700, 7/231; £6200, 7/348–9, 350; £6200, 7/425–6; £6800, 8/87; £6700, 8/192; £6900, 8/245
    RATE OF ACCUMULATION: saves £500 in 1664, 5/359; £100 in one month, 6/92; £3100 in 1665, 6/341
    CASH IN HOUSE: £300, 3/148; c. £1000, 5/281; £1800, 6/205, 207; c. £2000, 7/251; c. £2350, 7/275;

£2800, 7/367; takes measures for its safety in Fire, 7/275, 336, 340, 367; during Dutch raid, 8/262–4 passim, 264, 273, 280, 281, 296, 472–4, 487, 539; also, 1/57–8, 168, 178–9, 183; 2/50

CASH AT BANKERS: withdraws £200 from Backwell, 2/76; deposits £2000 with Vyner, 7/34; withdraws it, 7/84, 85; withdraws £2000, 7/196; given advance by Colvill, 9/97; also, 6/193; 7/230, 242; 8/151

CASH ELSEWHERE: at Rawlinson's, 1/221; in Exchequer, 2/19

INVESTMENTS: in bottomry, 1/294; Portuguese trade, 2/76; land, 2/127; 5/196; 8/517; loans to government 5/323; 6/330; 7/85, 88–90 & n., 201–2, 205, 230, 243–4, 251; 8/38, 87, 397, 407, 420 & n. 1

TAXES: assessment/payment: poll-tax (1660), 1/315–16 & n.; (1667), 8/30 & n. 1, 120 & n. 2, 152–3, 192; royal benevolence (1661), 2/167–8 & n.; relief of indigent officers (1662), 3/199 & n. 2, 283 & n. 5, 285; Militia Act (1662), 3/275 & n. 1, 283

FINCH, [Francis], Excise Commissioner: P consults about Tangier, 6/136; political news from, 7/191–2

FINCH, Heneage, 2nd Earl of Winchilsea, ambassador to the Ottoman Empire 1660–9: on *Naseby*, 1/133; to go to Constantinople, 1/217; alluded to: 1/134, 135; 7/326

FINCH, Sir Heneage, Solicitor-General, cr. Earl of Nottingham 1681: eloquence, 5/140 & n. 2, 324; 8/22; 9/529; chairman of Commons' Committee for Public Debts, 1/214; administers oaths to P and Batten, 1/252; entertains King at Inner Temple, 2/155 & n. 2; business with Tangier Committee, 3/172; 4/45; with Navy Board, 9/146 & n. 1, 148; rumoured appointment as Attorney-General, 8/412; speeches in court, 9/85 & n. 2, 529 & n. 2, 531–2 & n.; praises P's parliamentary speech, 9/104, 113, 146; his garden, 5/179 & n. 1; alluded to: 9/122, 340; ~ his son, 9/203; his coachman, 4/431

FINCH, [?William], mercer, the

Minories: ?7/303; 8/224 & n. 5, ?525, 529, 580–1; 9/?136, 221; ~ his pretty wife, 8/224; 9/221

FINES: see Fiennes

FIRE: P's fear, 2/100; 5/249; 6/49; false alarm, at P's house, 6/27; outbreaks: in the Piazza, Covent Garden, 3/11; Lombard St, 3/94; 5/71; Lothbury, 3/296 & n. 4; Wood St, (false alarm), 4/6; Lady Castlemaine's lodgings, 5/27; Cheapside, 5/247–8, 249; Deptford Yard, 5/257; Horse Guard House, 7/362–3 & n.; Westminster, 7/363; Southwark, 7/363; 8/191 & n. 1; Bishopsgate St, 8/119 & n. 3; in city, 8/164, 201; Aldersgate St (arson), 8/316, 320; Durham Yard, 9/534–5 & n.; and Bridgetown, Barbados, 9/243 & n. 2; counter-measures: buckets etc., 5/27, n. 1; houses pulled down, 5/248; blown up, 7/362; 8/119; 9/534–5; fire-engines, 8/191, 320; ~ chimney fires, 8/28; 9/534

FIRE, the GREAT (1666):

GENERAL: 7/267, n. 2; follows drought, 7/269; P writes up diary entries, 7/282, 318, 402; sermon on, 7/283; fast day for, 7/316 & n. 3; 8/413; 9/297; prophesied by: Mother Shipton, 7/333 & n. 2; Nostradamus, 8/42 & n. 2; anon. prophet, 8/42–3; Tom of the Wood, 8/270; P dreams of, 7/287, 296, 299; fears renewed outbreak, 7/366; 8/28, 87, 126, 128; alluded to: 8/191

ORIGIN: in Pudding Lane, 7/268 & n. 1; attributed by rumour to enemies, 7/275 & n. 3, 277 & n. 2, 279, 366, 405 & n. 3, 406; 8/42; enquiry into by Commons' committee, 7/343 & n. 4, 356–7 & n.; 8/439 & n. 4, 444–5; trial and execution of Hubert, 7/357 & n. 2; 8/81–2

OUTBREAK AND SPREAD: 7/267–79 passim; 8/5; fires persist, 7/288; smoking ruins, 7/393, 401, 406; 8/17, 87, 114; Fish St, 7/268(2), 270; Pudding Lane, 7/268; 8/5; St Magnus Church, 7/268; Steelyard, 7/268, 269; Thames St, 7/270; Dowgate, ib.; Cannon St, ib.; Fish St Hill, 7/272; Tower St, 7/273–4, 274–5, 393; Trinity House, 7/274; Pie Corner, 7/275; Old

6/294–5; instructs about pursers' business, 6/325; granted £5000, 7/377; advised by P on allowances, 8/113, 118(3); criticised by Rupert and Albemarle, 8/513; 9/107, 142; new contract, 8/567 & n. 3; 9/8(2), 47, 252, 253, 288, 312, 315(2), 316 & n. 1, 317–18 & n., 323, 393 & n. 1; Penn a partner, 9/348, 399 & n. 4; also, 2/221; 7/29, 118; 8/344, 382–3; 9/429; unspecified business, 4/89; 6/265; ?7/232; 8/43, 110, ?197; 9/25, 393, 427–8, 429

AS VICTUALLER FOR TANGIER: attends meetings, 3/300; 4/21, 23; 5/97; discusses victualling, 4/26; fails to obtain contract, 5/204, 210, 212, 271; account with Teviot, 5/339 & n. 3; awarded contract, 6/157, 171, 204; accounts [see also 'as Navy Victualler'], 6/251; gifts to P: £60, 6/251; £500 6/322, 324, 325, 341; promises commission, 7/8; £100, 8/35, 36, 37, 44; £250, 8/372; P willing for him to reveal gifts, 9/99; also, 7/402; unspecified business: 6/253–4; 7/24, ?232; ?8/197; also, 5/171 & n. 3

AS ALDERMAN AND SHERIFF: in Fire, 7/277; appointed non-resident Sheriff, 8/432, 458; also, 8/583; 9/33, 111

SOCIAL: entertains associates, 4/337; 7/373; 9/34, 214, 432; visits Coventry in Tower, 9/104; also, 1/187; 2/222; 3/42, 107; 4/26, 242; 5/338; 6/329; 8/348, 374, 584; 9/222

MISC.: house at Clapham, 4/244 & n. 1, 249; 6/172, 312; 7/29; at Smithfield, 9/34; to advise Penn about house purchase, 8/197; news from, 8/269 ~ his children, 2/54; 4/244; 6/172; 7/29–30, 88; his man, 8/267; his clerk, 9/342

GAUDEN, [Elizabeth], Lady Gauden, wife of Sir Denis: 4/244, 245; 9/34; ~ her spaniel, 4/246

GAUDEN, [Elizabeth], widow of John: her conversation, 4/244 & n. 4, 245; alluded to: 4/251

GAUDEN, John, Bishop of Exeter 1660–2, Worcester 1662: death, 4/244 & n. 2; social: 1/187 & n. 3

GAUDEN, [Samuel], son of Sir Denis: 4/245 & n. 1

GAUDEN, [Sarah], daughter of Sir Denis: 6/172; 7/30, 88 & n. 4

GAULTIER (Gotier), Mons. ——: teaches singing, 4/242 & n. 4

GAULTIER, Mrs; the Queen's tire-woman: 9/454

GAYET, Susan: see Guyat

GAYLAND: see Guyland

GEERE, [John]: 1/184 & n. 2

GENOA: terms of doges' appointment, 3/7–8 & n.; alluded to: 8/374, 548

[GENS, Jan de], captain of the Mary: 4/157 & n. 2

GENTLEMAN, Jane, P's servant: recommended, 4/274, 276; enters service, 4/290, 292; deaf, 4/292; angers EP/P, 4/337, 354; wishes to leave, 4/356; accused of lying, 4/361; to leave, 5/101; also, 4/362, 389, 399, 438; 5/9, 71, 185; ~ her father, 4/389

GENTLEMAN, Mr ——, cook: 9/116, 373–4; ~ his wife and son, 9/373–4

GENTRY, the: ignorant of corn trade, 9/1; antiquity of in Cheshire, 9/280 & n. 2; rate of decay, 9/550

GEORGE, P's 'old drawer' at the Sun tavern, King St: 1/229; 2/178; 4/217

GERARD, Sir Charles, 1st Baron Gerard of Brandon, cr. Earl of Macclesfield 1678 (d. 1694): friend of Lady Castlemaine, 4/1; favourite of King, 4/68; enemy of Clarendon, 8/525; sells commission in Life-guards, 4/371; 8/436; 9/308; criticised by King, 4/334; dress, 8/154; dispute with Carr, 8/573–4 & n., 581 & n. 1, 583, 587; 9/31–2, 55 & n. 1, 57; dispute alluded to, 9/85; case against Fitton, 9/83–4 & n.; dispute with Newcastle-upon-Tyne, 9/359 & nn.; praises P's parliamentary speech, 9/106

GERARD, [Jeanne], Lady Gerard, wife of Lord Gerard: slanders Lady Castlemaine, 4/68

GERMAN PRINCESS, the: see Moders

GERMANY [i.e. the territory of the Holy Roman Empire]: advance of

and P's, 9/59; praises Sandwich as ambassador, 9/59–60; and P's parliamentary speech, 9/105; stories of Spain, 9/118; news of Sandwich, 9/164, 320; also, 9/65; social: 9/116, 162, 176, 321–2, 423–4

GOFFE (Gough), Stephen, divine: anecdote of, 7/290 & n. 2

[GOGH, Michiel van], Dutch ambassador 1664–5: arrives, 5/175 & n. 3; conciliatory, 5/181 & n. 3; audience with Duke of York, 5/264; and King, 5/301; imprisoned (rumour), 6/273 & n. 1; also, 5/283

GOLD (Gould), [Elizabeth], Lady Gold, widow of Sir Nicholas: wealth, 5/1; marriage to T. Neale, 5/1, 184 & n. 2; 6/126; ~ her brother, 5/184

GOLD (Gould), [John], hemp merchant: his knavery, 5/117

GOLD (Gould), [?John, ?Edward], merchant: 9/421

GOLD (Gould), Sir Nicholas, merchant: attends Rota Club, 1/14 & n. 3; death, 5/1

GOLDEN EAGLE, New St (?shop): 1/205

GOLDING, Capt. [John], naval officer: killed in action, 6/82

GOLDING, ——, barber, Greenwich: plays fiddle, 3/164; 6/227 & n. 3, 263, 279

GOLDSBOROUGH, Mrs ——: debt to Robert P, 2/195–6 & n., 197, 198; 3/44; estate, 3/232; 4/203, 362; alluded to: 9/451; ~ her son, 3/232; 4/203, 362

GOLDSMITH, Capt. [Ralph], naval officer: 9/160 & n. 5

GOLDSMITHS: see Banks and Bankers

GOLDSMITHS' HALL, Foster Lane: funeral, 6/114

[GOLOVIN, Mikhail], Russian envoy: 8/428 & n. 2

GOMBOUST, [Jacques]: map of Paris, 7/379 & n. 2

GOMME (Gum), Sir Bernard de, military engineer: advises King on Medway defences, 8/126 & n. 2

[GONSON, Benjamin], Treasurer of the Navy 1549–1577: ledger, 6/307–8 & n.

GOODENOUGH, [Edward], plasterer: sends P gift, 2/32 & n. 2; consulted about rooms at Navy Office, 3/197

[GOODFELLOW, Christopher], Reader, Inner Temple (d. 1690): 9/465–6 & n.

GOODGROOME, [John], musician: gives P/EP singing lessons, 2/126 & n. 2, 130, 144, 145, 190; 7/397; 8/411, 424; teaches P to trill, 8/424; P critical of, 8/109, 378; given copy of *Beauty Retire*, 7/397; sings with P and EP, 8/171; social: 3/108, 298; 7/412; 8/209; 9/414

GOOD HOPE, CAPE OF: stories of natives, 3/298 & n. 3

GOODMAN, ——: 1/236

GOODS, John, servant to Lord Sandwich: on *Naseby*, 1/105, 108, 110, 116, 134, 151, 160; also, 2/16, 26; 4/210; social: 2/3, 90

GOODSON, [William], naval commander: P's regard, 5/30

GOODWIN [SANDS], the (off the E. Kent coast): 6/29; 7/145

GOODYEAR, [Aaron]: 8/171 & n. 5; 9/13; ~ his sister [Hester], 8/171 & n. 5

GORDON, Eleanor, Lady Byron: King's gift to, 8/182 & n. 1

GORHAM (Gorrum), Goody [Margaret], alehouse keeper, Brampton: P visits alehouse, 2/138 & n. 1, 148; 4/309; 9/212; lease, 3/222; 8/471 & n. 4

GORING, George, 1st Baron Goring and Earl of Norwich (d. 1663): returns from France, 1/106 & n. 2; stories of, 2/29 & n. 3; 7/290

GORING HOUSE, St James's Park: wedding at, 1/196; P admires, 7/203 & n. 1

GOSNELL, [?Winifred], companion to EP; later an actress: to enter EP's service, 3/256 & n. 2, 258, 260, 261, 263, 267, 269, 270, 271; arrives, 3/276; leaves, 3/277, 278; sings well, 3/256, 260, 276; dances, 3/263; at theatre, 3/294; becomes actress, 4/162 & n. 5; 7/422; 9/219; in *The slighted maid*, 4/163; 9/268; *The Rivals*, 5/267 & n. 2; *The Tempest*, 9/422; ~ her sister, 3/256, 260, 294; her mother, 3/260, 261, 269, 278

GOSPORT, Hants.: P visits, 3/70

GÖTEBORG (Gothenburg, Gottenburg), Sweden: masts from, 5/215; Dutch ships wrecked at, 5/279; shipping to/from, 7/287, 390, 408, 420, 424 & n. 3; convoy for, 7/216 & n. 1; insurance for shipping, 7/25

GOTIER: *see* Gaultier

GOUGE, [Thomas], Presbyterian divine (d. 1681): refuses to use Prayer Book, 3/161 & n. 4

GRABU (Grebus), [Luis], court musician: appointment, 8/73 & n. 3; performances criticised, 8/458, 530; at rehearsal, 9/163

GRACE, Mrs, servant to Lady Sandwich: 2/16

GRACECHURCH (Gracious) ST: conduit in carrefour, 3/268; St Benet's church, 6/225 & n. 2; Fire, 7/276; road reconstructed, 9/285

GRAFHAM, Hunts.: 4/312

[GRAHAM, James, 2nd Marquess of Montrose]: poem by, 1/33 & n. 1

GRAMONT, Antoine, Duc de (d. 1678): Bristol's ingratitude, 4/212–3 & n.

[GRAMONT, Armand de], Comte de Guiche (d. 1673): praises English in Four Days Fight, 7/222 & n. 4

GRANDISON, Viscount: *see* Villiers, G.

GRANGER, [Abraham Gowrie]: forgeries, 5/12 & n. 5; 9/83–4 & n.

GRANT, ——, coffee-house keeper: 4/64–5

GRAUNT, Capt. John, statistician [*see also* Books]: collects Barlow's annuity, 2/103; 4/22; 7/40; his prints, 4/106; reports to Royal Society on Petty's ship, 4/263; social: on growth of population, 4/22; and music, 5/12; stories of suicides, 9/175; at Royal Society music meeting, 5/290; also, 4/100, 256, 334, 437; alluded to: 3/2

GRAVELEY, Cambs.: dispute over Robert P's land, 2/136, 148, 156, 174, 178, 180, 182, 205; Cotton closes, 2/148; courthouse, 2/182

GRAVES, ——: a drowsy preacher, 3/264

GRAVESEND, Kent: P/EP visit(s), 1/172–3; 2/67; 3/153, 156; 4/258, 260, 261; 5/190; 6/119, 181, 182, 183, 240; plague, 6/195, 249; naval action off, 8/349, 350, 351; ships, 8/379; defences, 8/257–8, 276, 313 & n. 1, 351; White's, 6/240; Swan Inn, 3/153 & n. 1, 156; Ship Inn, 8/258, 351; 9/300

GRAY: *see* Grey, [T.]

GRAY'S INN: P visits, 7/184; 9/311, 480; students' rebellion, 8/223 & n. 3; garden, 3/275

GRAY'S INN FIELDS: 7/72, 169; 8/453; 9/311

GRAY'S INN WALKS: 1/176; 2/98, 125, 128, 152; 3/60, 64, 77; 4/101; 9/311

GRAYS (Grayes-market), Essex: 1/104; 6/240; 8/257

GREAT LEVER HALL, Lancs.: 3/254 & n. 3

GREATOREX, [Ralph], mathematical-instrument maker, Strand: his armillary sphere, 1/14; waterpump in St James's Park, 1/263–4 & n.; lampglasses, 1/273; varnish, 4/153 & n. 2; schemes for fen drainage, 4/356 & n. 2; diving experiments, 5/268–9 & n.; to visit Tenerife, 2/21 & n. 4; sells P drawing pen, 1/273; and weather glass, 3/203; 4/84; teaches him mathematics etc., 2/112; mends his ruler, 3/266; engraves almanac on, 4/270, 277; social: 1/174; 2/110; 3/105; alluded to: 2/55; 4/152; ~ his apprentice, 9/437 & n. 3

GREBUS: *see* Grabu

GREEN(E), Major [John], fishmonger: 5/312

GREEN, [John], merchant: in customs dispute, 5/43 & n. 2

GREENE, [John], of Brampton: 2/138; 3/223

GREENE, [Levi], naval officer: dismissed for drunkenness, 9/5–6 & n.; made captain against Duke of York's wishes, 9/39

GREENE, [William], tar merchant: 3/137 & n. 3

GREENLAND: whale fishing, 4/125

GREENLEAF (Greenlife), Mrs ——: 1/190

GREENWICH, Kent [omitting

maid for, 4/284; in search for Barkstead's treasure, 3/242; advises P on coachhouse, 9/39, 46; also, 1/278, 298, 314; 3/199, 264; 4/54, 113, 154, 363; 6/27, 224, 258; 7/202, 305; 8/217; 9/43; ~ his wife [Alice], 8/226; son [William] dies, 4/416 & n. 2; son [Thomas] christened, 5/176 & n. 1; maidservant: 5/249; 7/124; P attracted by, 3/126; 8/120

GRIFFITH, ——, courtier: at court ball, 7/372

GRIFFITHS [Griffin], [William], ward of Sir W. Batten: 4/296; 8/433

GRIMSBY, Lincs.: M.P.s for, 8/454–5

GRIMSTON, Sir Harbottle, M.P. Colchester, Essex: chosen Speaker, 1/115–16 & n.

[GRINDAL, Edmund; 'Cranmer' in error], Archbishop of Canterbury 1576–d. 83: letter to Queen Elizabeth, 4/329–30 & n.

GROCERS' COMPANY: *see* London: livery companies

GROCERS' HALL: 1/71

GROOME, ——, clerk in the Signet Office: 1/212

GROVE, Capt. [Edward], river agent for the Navy Board: character, 4/73 & n. 1; defends P against Exchequer Court bailiffs, 4/52; appointed shipping agent for Tangier, 4/85, 93; gifts to P, 4/93, 120; wife's death, 5/38, 42; match projected with Paulina P, 5/42–3; cowardice in Battle of Lowestoft, 6/130 & n. 2; social: 4/157, 231, 365, 406; 5/95

GUERNSEY, Channel Is.: garrison, 6/142–3

GUILDFORD, Surrey: P/EP visit(s), 2/93–4; 3/69, 75; 9/273–5 passim; King visits, 3/86; places: Red Lion inn, 2/93–4 & n.; 3/69; 9/274–5; Abbot's Hospital and grammar school, 2/93–4 & n.; 9/273 & n. 3; Holy Trinity church, 2/94 & n. 2; 9/274 & n. 1; St Catherine's Hill, 9/275

GUILDHALL (Yildhall): seamen paid off, 2/45, 50, 53, 55; trials, 3/120; 4/402, 403; 9/382; Lord Mayor's banquet, 4/354–6; P consults officials, 7/72; 9/33; rebuilt after Fire, 8/583 & n. 1; 9/545–6 & n.

GUINEA: ships to, 1/313, 316; Anglo-Dutch rivalry, 5/115, 160; Dutch intentions, 5/121 & n. 2; conflicting news from, 5/127 & n. 2; Holmes's attack on Dutch, 5/160 & n. 4, 283 & n. 1, 285, 341; de Ruyter's counterattack, 5/352–3 & n., 355 & n. 1; 6/42 & nn., 43, 46; English losses, 9/401; fleets sail to: Dutch: 5/225, 231, 242, 273 & n. 1, 283, 295 & n. 2; English: 5/242, 246, 248, 250, 258, 264, 265, 295; also, 2/160; 4/363

GUINEA COMPANY: *see* Royal African Company

GUINEA HOUSE: *see* Africa(n) House

GUMBLETON, Mr ——: 9/289, 458

GUNFLEET, the, shoal off Essex coast: fleet in, 6/99; 7/139, 140; alluded to: 7/178, 300

GUNNING, Peter, Master of Clare College, Cambridge 1660; Master of St John's and Regius Professor 1661; Bishop of Chichester 1669–75, of Ely 1675–d. 84: his London congregation, 1/42; weekly fast, 1/58; sermons, 1/3 & n. 1, 11, 32, 60, 76; 2/239; administers communion to Commons, 2/107; active against puritans, 2/147 & n. 2

GUNPOWDER PLOT DAY: observation of, 1/283; 2/208; 5/314; 7/358

GUNS, pistols [*see also* Ships: guns]: P's pistol, 2/9; his French gun, 8/137 & n. 1; repeater guns, 3/310 & n. 4; 5/75 & n. 1

GUY, Capt. [Thomas], army officer: 1/101; social: 1/116, 182

GUY, Capt. [Thomas], naval officer: 7/344–5 & n.

GUYAT (Gayet), Susan: P takes to Islington, 9/197; theatre, 9/198–9, 203; and Vauxhall, 9/216; sings with, 9/202, 217

'GUYLAND' ('Gayland', 'Guildland') [*recte* 'Abd Allāh al-Ghailān], Moroccan warlord: relations with, 3/172 & n. 2; 4/283 & n. 1, 337 & n. 1; 7/167 & n. 3; overthrown, 7/214 & n. 2; 8/347–8 & n.

GWYN, Nell, actress:
CHRON. SERIES: P's admiration, 6/73 &

HAMILTON, James, Bishop of Galloway 1661–d. 74: besieged in house, 4/130–1 & n., 138
HAMILTON (Hambleton), [James, George and Anthony], courtiers: 5/21 & n. 1; alleged liaisons with Lady Castlemaine, 5/21; 'Hamilton' [?Anthony], a favourite of King's, 5/56; 'Mr Hamilton' at court ball, 7/372
HAMMERSMITH: 9/531, 557
HAMMON(D), [Mary]: 6/212; 7/255 & n. 2; death, 9/161
HAMPSTEAD, Mdx: P visits, 6/155; Belsize House, 9/281 & n. 4
HAMPTON COURT: Queen-Mother at, 2/4; court at: on Queen's arrival from Portugal, 3/89, 95, 97, 99, 100, 127, 146, 150, 157, 175; during Plague, 6/142 & n. 1, 166–7; 7/24, 26; Sandwich and family visit, 2/25; 3/94, 96, 103, 104, 120; P visits, 3/81–2 & n.; 6/153, 154, 156, 166, 171; 7/24–7 passim; Charles I's escape from (1647), 6/316–17 & n.; painting by Danckerts, 9/423 & n. 1, 504; rooms etc.: furniture and pictures, 3/82 & n. 2; chapel, 6/166; council chamber, ib.; garden, ib.; alluded to: 8/430
HAMPTON WICK, Mdx: P's lodgings, 7/26, 28, 29
HANBURY, [?Lucy], of Brampton: 3/220
HANES, Joseph: see Haynes
HANES, Lettice: see Howlett
HANNAM, Capt. [Willoughby], naval officer: in St James's Day Fight, 7/222 & n. 2; Coventry's regard for, 7/409–10 & n.
HANSON (Henson), [Edward]: bullet clock, 1/209
HARBING, ——, a poor fiddler: to marry Jane Welsh, 6/16, 19, 22, 74–5; 7/103
HARBORD (Herbert), Sir Charles, sen.: 3/57
HARBORD (Herbert), Sir Charles, jun.: brings letters from Sandwich to King, 3/57 & n. 1; knighted, 6/275 & n. 3; serves in Tangier, 9/374 & n. 2, 418–19 & n., 422; his painting of Tangier, 9/541 & n. 2; social: at P's dinner for Sandwich, 9/423–4; and

for Hinchingbrooke, 9/552, 553; also, 7/54; 9/345
HARBY (Harvy), Sir Job, Bt, customs farmer, d. 1663: 3/188
HARDING, [John], court musician: sings at party, 1/10–11 & n.
HARDWICKE, old: 5/272
HARDY, Nathaniel, Dean of Rochester 1660–d. 70: at The Hague, 1/144; sermon on death of Duke of Gloucester, 1/245; poor sermon on Fire, 7/283
HARE, Mrs [Alice]: see Taverns etc: Trumpet
HARGRAVE, [Richard], cornchandler, St Martin's Lane: 1/182–3
HARGRAVE, Mrs: see Taverns etc: Dog, New Palace Yard
HARLEY (Harlow), Sir Edward, ex-Governor of Dunkirk: to be Governor of Tangier, 9/492 & n. 2
HARLEY, Maj. [Robert], brother of Sir Edward: at The Hague, 1/147 & n. 2
HARLINGTON, Mdx: P at, 6/216; Arlington's title taken from, ib. & n. 1
HARMAN, Capt. John, kted 1665, naval commander: made rear-admiral, 6/129; serves under Allin, 6/147; convoys ships from Baltic, 6/328; conduct in Four Days Fight, 7/143, 154; voyage to W. Indies, 8/132, 147, 156; (untrue) story of capture of Dutch E. Indiaman, 8/374, 375; victory over French, 8/430 & n. 1; award of bounty to, 8/460–1 & n.; conduct at Battle of Lowestoft, 8/491, 492; 9/80 & n. 3, 142, 158–9; committed by Commons, 9/166–7 & n. 167; released, 9/170; portrait by Lely, 7/102; also, 7/97, 110; 8/130, 149; 9/142
HARMAN, Mary (b. Bromfield), wife of Philip: marriage. 4/345 & n. 2; P admires, 4/265; 5/223, 228, 229, 347; 6/164; 7/15; dies in childbed, 6/125, 152, 164; social: 5/266, 280; ~ her father [Thomas], 6/152
HARMAN, [Philip], upholsterer, Cornhill: P's regard, 7/15, 73; marriage, 4/345 & n. 2; son christened, 6/152; proposed match with

Fight, 7/152 & n. 3; Lady Castlemaine lodges with, 8/366 & n. 1,
376, 377

HARVEY, [Elizabeth], Lady Harvey,
wife of Sir Daniel: 2/193; 3/12;
offended by Doll Common's mimicry, 9/415 & n. 1, 417

HARVEY, Sir Thomas: *see* Hervey

HARVEY'S: *see* Taverns etc.

HARVY, Sir Job: *see* Harby

HARWICH, Essex: lighthouse, 5/314;
6/3 & n. 4; English/Dutch ships at/off,
6/76, 86, 90, 104, 126, 296; 7/146, 148;
8/254(2), 281, 345, 357; hailstorm,
7/208; Duke of York inspects fortifications, 8/115 & n. 2, 125, 126;
militia raised, 8/255; Dutch attack,
8/317 & nn., 322 & n. 2; Duke of
York visits, 8/328; dockyard [*see also*
Deane, Anthony; Taylor, Capt.
John; Taylor, Capt. Silas]: visits by
Batten, 6/83, 115, 119; Brouncker,
7/408; pay at, 6/90; also, 6/330

HASLERIG: *see* Heselrige

HASLERIGGE, Mrs ——: her child
attributed to King or Duke of York,
3/227, 255

HASTINGS, Sussex: parliamentary
election, 1/102 & n. 2

HATCHAM, Surrey: 4/235

HATFIELD, Herts.: P/EP visit(s),
2/138–9, 149; 4/314; 5/298–9; 8/381–
2; places: Hatfield House: gardens
and vineyard, 2/139 & n. 2; 8/381;
chapel (St Etheldreda), 2/139 & n. 3;
5/298–9 & n.; 8/381 & n. 1; Salisbury
Arms: 2/138, 139; 8/381, 382

HATTON, Christopher, 1st Baron
Hatton (d. 1670): 2/221

HATTON, Sir Thomas, of Long
Stanton, Cambs., royalist agent: joins
King at Breda, 1/117 & n. 1

HATTON GARDEN: P visits, 8/110,
167, 597; Wardrobe moves to after
Fire, 8/597 & n. 1

HAVANT, Hants.: 3/69

[HAWKINS, Christian]: marriage,
4/121–3 & n., 260, 355

HAWKINS, Mr ——, shopkeeper, of
Rochester: P kisses wife, 8/312

HAWKYNS, [William], Canon of
Winchester: preaches at St Paul's,
5/66–7 & n.

HAWLES (Hollis), [Anthony], chaplain to the King: 1/157

HAWLEY [Haly], Francis, 1st Baron
Hawley (d. 1684): 6/110 & n. 2

HAWLEY, [John], Exchequer clerk:
PERSONAL: witnesses P's will, 1/90;
moves from Bowyers', 1/244; lives in
Westminster, 5/185; proposed by P
as match for Betty Lane, 4/431; 5/9,
41, 42, 71, 113, 242; also, 1/94

CAREER: P's substitute during absence,
1/18, 83, 238; 2/9; hopes for promotion, 1/35; accounts, 1/41–2, 61;
offered bribe, 1/77–8; said to have
resigned, 1/186; legal action against
Collier, 1/199–200 & n.; unspecified
Exchequer business, 1/13–14, 30, 33,
43, 49, 65; to serve Bishop of London,
2/9; refuses post as Sandwich's
steward, 5/185; becomes parish underclerk, 7/211

SOCIAL: visits/dines with P, 1/6, 10, 31,
57, 58, 189; 3/255; 4/51, 66; 5/25, 287,
304; gives P cane, 1/244; also, 1/8, 25,
88; 2/40, 227

HAYES, [James], secretary to Prince
Rupert: victualling business, 7/265,
266; fees, 7/323–4 & n.; news from,
7/339, 340; also, 7/84; 8/34, 52

[HAYES, Walter], mathematical-
instrument maker, Moorfields: compasses from, 5/271 & n. 3

HAYES, ——: to marry Jane Welsh,
6/16–17

HAYLS (Hales), [John], portrait painter:
GENERAL: to paint P and EP, 7/42–3 &
n.; looks at pictures in Whitehall,
7/97–8; and at S. Cooper's portraits,
9/139–40; P compares with Lely,
8/129; dines with P, 9/265; his house,
7/70 & n. 1, 396; 9/175

HIS PORTRAITS:
HENRY HARRIS: 9/138 & n. 2, 140, 175,
206; P criticises, 9/299

THOMAS HILL: P admires, 7/42–3 &
n.; displeased with finished version,
7/52, 53; buys copy, 7/125

ELIZABETH PEARSE: 7/93 & n. 1, 97,
108; a poor likeness, 7/111, 117, 120,
131; her son James, 8/439; 9/188; and
daughter Betty, 9/188

P'S FATHER: sittings, 7/151 & n. 2,

8/149; 9/476; for fever/cold, 2/163; 4/17, 55; 5/197 & n. 3, 198; in pregnancy, 8/164; for smallpox, 8/524; for eye-strain, 9/261; amounts recorded, 3/76–7 & n.; 9/261

MAGIC: hare's foot, for colic, 5/359 & n. 1; 6/17, 18, 67; charms for staunching blood, etc., 5/361–2 & nn.

OPHTHALMIC: P tries globe light, 5/290, 291–2; green spectacles, 7/406, 419, 420, 424–5; new spectacles from Turlington, 8/486 & n. 3, 519; paper tubes, 9/270 & n. 3, 277, 278, 279, 286, 337, 384, 451, 482–3, 516; plaster vizard with tube, 9/463, 533, 547

SWEATING: for inflammation/itching, 4/39, 57, 89, 300; 5/260, 261; for pox, 8/217; in Russia, 5/272

MISC.: suitable clothing, 2/129; 5/240, 359; 6/66–7, 101; removal of earwax, 3/124; fluxing, for pox, 6/12; head shaved in smallpox, 4/339; gargling, 4/339; ten rules for curing infertility, 5/222

HEART, ——, landlord of Abingdon inn: 9/228

HEATH, [John], Attorney-General of the Duchy of Lancaster: to examine Chatham Chest accounts, 3/257 & n. 2

HEBDON, Sir John, merchant, agent for the Tsar of Muscovy: supplies hemp, 4/175 & n. 5; views on English court, 4/176; admires Lord Ashley's efficiency, ib.; and Dutch efficiency, ib. & n. 1

HEEMSKERCK, Laurens van, naval officer: in Holmes's Bonfire, 7/247; his ship design, 9/171 & n. 2, 198, 206, 488; dispute with lieutenant, 9/488

HELLEVOETSLUIS (Helversluce): 1/127

HELY, Mrs ——: gave P his 'first sentiments of love and pleasure', 4/247

HEMPSON, [William], Clerk of the Survey, Chatham: house, 2/70; cunning, 4/226; criticises Comm. Pett, 5/28; dismissed, 5/36, 140–1; stories of Batten's corruption, 5/141; also, 3/153; social: 2/68, 125, 126; ~ his wife, 2/68, 69, 125, 127; 5/141

HENCHMAN, Humphrey, Bishop of Salisbury 1660–3, London 1663–d.75: consecrated, 1/276 & n. 2; preaches at Whitehall, 7/99 & n. 1; at Maundy ceremony, 8/150 & n. 1; his patronage of city churches, 8/151–2 & n.; severity as landlord, 9/23 & n. 1; also, 1/259; 2/9; 5/67 & n. 2; 6/87

HENLEY, Sir Andrew: assaulted in court of Common Pleas, 7/391 & n. 1

HENRIETTA, Princess, Duchess of Orleans, sister of Charles II (d. 1670): marriage to Duc d'Anjou, 1/240 & n. 3; 2/56 & n. 1; dines in public, 1/299; appearance, ib. & nn.; sails to France, 2/1, 23; has measles, 2/11, 14; also, 4/26, 430 & n. 1

HENRIETTA-MARIA, Queen Mother (d.1669):

PERSONAL: appearance, 1/299; in debt, 5/59; portrait by Van Dyck, 6/222 & n. 2; 8/181 & n. 3; by Huysmans, 5/254; piety, 7/384; marriage negotiations (1624–5), 3/253–4 & n.; rumoured marriage to St Albans, 3/263 & n. 3, 303; 5/57–8 & n.; 8/564 & n. 1

CHRON. SERIES: returns to England, 1/260, 278, 279, 281, 282 & n. 2; to France, 1/302, 303, 322; 2/1, 3, 23, 93; to England, 3/128, 139, 143, 148; at public functions etc., 3/297; 4/216; 5/193, 196; relations with Frances Stuart, 4/366; 8/184; ill and goes to France, 6/142 & n. 3; 9/508 & n. 3; promotes peace/alliance with France, 7/420 & n. 2; 9/536 & n. 2; enmity to Secretary Nicholas, 8/534 & n. 1

HER COURT: dines in public, 1/299; at Somerset House, 3/191; keeps great state, 3/299, 303; 4/48–9; new buildings, 4/127 & n. 3; 5/63 & nn., 300; paintings, 6/17 & n. 3; also, 5/56

SOCIAL: at court lottery, 5/214, 215; dines with Lord Mayor, 4/193; seldom at public theatre, 8/55–6 & n.; dancing, 9/507; also, 1/297; 4/229

MISC.: sells reversion to Brampton manor, 3/176 & n. 3; her liking for pears, 8/417; also, 2/33; 4/20

ALLUDED TO: 3/82; 7/253; 8/161

~ her servants, 5/58 & n. 3; confessor, 4/111 & n. 3; Capuchins, 7/329

HENRY, Duke of Gloucester, son of Charles I: on *Naseby*, 1/152, 153; sails to England, 1/154, 157, 158; at theatre, 1/171; entertained by Speaker, 1/174 & n. 1; ill with smallpox, 1/240, 243; dies, 1/244, 245, 248; buried in Westminster Abbey, 1/249 & n. 2

HENRY VIII: portrait: at Audley End House, 1/70; 8/467 & n. 4; at Barber-Surgeons' Hall, 4/59 & n. 3; tomb, 7/58 & n. 6; 'King Harry's chair', 1/280 & n. 1; alluded to: 5/69

HENSHAW, Joseph, Bishop of Peterborough 1663–d.79: preaches at Whitehall, 9/563 & n. 2

HENSON: *see* Hanson

HERALDRY: P's arms, 3/50 & n. 3; 8/128 & n. 1; armorial glass at Great Lever, Lancs., 3/254; arms etc. of Duke of Monmouth, 4/107 & n. 2; 5/318 & n. 4; of Royal African Co., 4/152–3 & n.; hatchments etc. at funeral, 4/424–5, 427, 432; arms and title of Sandwich, 5/319; loss of Heralds' rolls in Fire, 7/410 & n. 3; book on, 8/422 & n. 4; also, 4/175

[HÉRAULT, Louis], minister of the French Church, Threadneedle St: sermons by, 3/296 & n. 2; 5/342

HERBERT, Sir C. sen. and jun.: *see* Harbord

HERBERT, Capt. [Charles], naval officer: 6/237, 238

[HERBERT], John, servant to Tom P: 4/183 & n. 2; servant to P. Honywood, 5/88, 244, 252; character, 5/241

HERBERT, Philip, 5th Earl of Pembroke (d. 1669): rumoured expulsion from Lords, 1/127 & n. 1; a founder of Royal African Company, 1/258 & n. 2; inefficient in financing Royal Fishery, 5/294 & n. 1; plays tennis, 9/150; views on Genesis, 9/150–1 & n.; alluded to: 9/230

HERBERT, William, styled Lord Herbert, 6th Earl of Pembroke 1669 (d. 1674): suitor to Elizabeth Malet, 7/385

HERBERT, [William], landlord of the Swan, New Palace Yard [*see also* Taverns etc.]: unwell, 8/124; finds P

tumbling Frances Udall, 8/224

HERBERT, Mrs ——, of Newington Green: 5/132

HERCULES PILLARS ALLEY: 9/42

HERMITAGE, the: 3/163

HERRING, John, Vicar of St Bride, Fleet St: preaches, 1/26 & n. 1; extruded, 3/162 & n. 1, 167; farewell sermon, 3/168; social: 1/229

HERRING, [Michael], merchant: lends money to Sandwich, 1/56 & n. 5, 72, 75, 80

HERRINGMAN, [Henry], bookseller at the New Exchange: P visits shop, 8/380 & n. 3, 383, 597–8; 9/248, 367

HERTFORDSHIRE: parliamentary election, 9/150 & n. 2

HERVEY (Harvey), Sir Thomas, Navy Commissioner 1665–8:

CHARACTER: 6/119; 7/359–60; 8/531–2

AS COMMISSIONER: appointed, 6/37 & n. 2; absent during Plague, 7/39; expects dismissal, 8/293–4 & n.; at pay, 7/359–60; in Carkesse affair, 8/76, 215; examines Gauden's accounts, 8/322; at Ticket Office, 8/531–2; in enquiries of Committee on Miscarriages, 8/494–5, 538; 9/80, 83, 84, 103; at launch, 9/100–1; unspecified business, 8/77, 178, 180, 314–15, 328, 479, 581

HOUSE: to occupy Turner's lodgings, 6/37 & n. 2; 7/105, 296, 359

NEWS FROM: 7/152; 8/328

SOCIAL: 6/77; 7/364; 8/65, 77, 220, 563–4; 9/82, 104, 115

HESELRIGE (Haslerig), Sir Arthur, Bt, republican politician (d. 1661): his quarrel with City of London, 1/16 & n. 1, 53 & n. 2, 60; and parliament, 1/50, 74 & n. 4, 81 & n. 1; raises support against army leaders, (Dec. 1659), 2/92 & n. 3

HETLEY, [William], of Brampton, Hunts.: on *Royal Charles*, 1/162, 168; gifts to P and Howe, 1/182; death, 2/18; property at Brampton, 2/28 & n. 2; social: 1/163, 177, 324; alluded to: 1/172

HEWER, [Ann], wife of Thomas: P meets, 1/268; moves to Islington after Fire, 7/275; 'well-favoured',

8/24; social: 8/48, 101, 158, 193, 197, 254; 9/417; alluded to: 1/215
HEWER, [Thomas], printer and stationer: P meets, 1/268; dies of plague, 6/225, 235; alluded to: 2/96; 4/106, 114
HEWER, Will, P's clerk in the Navy Office [P spells the name variously: Eure, Ewere, Ewre, Hewers]:
P'S OPINION: favourable, 1/202–3; 5/255; 8/207; 9/75, 368–9; unfavourable, 2/199, 201; 3/105; 5/301; 9/53
PERSONAL: ailments, 1/215, 216; 2/96; 4/28, 106, 114, 194, 291; 6/174, 175; 9/242; money etc. stolen, 1/233; 2/140; banking account, 8/263; hears common prayer for first time, 1/245; in mourning for father, 6/235; suggests Mercer as EP's companion, 5/229, 257, 258, 265; tries to negotiate her return, 7/300, 301, 303; admires EP, 9/398; gives her diamonds, 9/7; criticises P to EP, 8/171; P jealous of, 5/13, 19, 29, 44, 301; refuses proposal to marry Paulina P, 8/17; brideman to Jane Birch, 9/500; intermediary in Deb Willet affair, 9/367–71 passim, 373, 379, 411, 413, 518; also, 9/19
HIS WORK IN HOUSEHOLD:
GENERAL: arrives, 1/204; sent to church, 4/43; misdeeds, 1/219, 254–5; 2/34, 63, 79, 97; 3/35; 4/97, 171, 356, 358, 365; 5/13; P thinks of dismissing, 3/4–5; 4/318, 323; ears boxed, 3/105, 180; 4/166; to lodge elsewhere, 4/358, 363, 367, 371–2, 381, 382
ERRANDS/MESSAGES: 1/226, 232, 237; 2/10, 191, 212, 221; 3/80; 7/176; 9/405, 420
ESCORTS/ACCOMPANIES P/EP ON HOUSEHOLD/NAVAL BUSINESS IN LONDON: 1/212, 213, 218, 289, 324; 2/8; 4/435; 9/32, 256, 259, 382–4 passim, 401, 406, 408, 417, 421, 422, 430, 451, 465, 474, 484, 493, 519, 520; on journeys: Brampton etc., 3/206, 217–23 passim; 5/200–1; 7/92–3, 137; 8/381, 465, 468, 471–2, 474–5, 479; 9/145, 306, 310; Woolwich, 8/240; West Country, 9/223, 224, 226, 228–30 passim, 233, 234; Deptford, 9/335
MISC.: helps with accounts, 1/209;

9/564; puts P to bed, 3/182; reads Latin testament, 4/189, 190, 193, 204, 236; examined in Latin, 4/271; reads to P, 9/372, 387, 506; copies words of song, 9/242; helps to store cash, 7/367; 8/473–4; gives first aid to P's father, 8/237; in mourning for P's mother, 8/134; witnesses P's will, 8/266; also, 3/152; 4/166; 6/141; 9/209
HIS MOVEMENTS: his new chamber, 4/320, 323; lodges at Mercers', 5/256 & n. 1; his rooms, 7/152; returns to P's house in Plague, 6/154, 156, 174, 175; lodges at Greenwich, 6/233, 251; moves to Woolwich after Fire, 7/275, 280; returns to P's house, 7/287; in lodgings again, 9/458 & n. 2
NEWS FROM: 8/269–70, 297, 538; 9/99–100, 104, 397
HIS WORK IN NAVY OFFICE: allowance, 1/305 & n. 5; 4/353, 358; accused of leaking information, 3/5; fraud, 4/152; receiving gift, 9/283; and conspiring to get contract, 9/288 & n. 2, 389–91 passim, 393, 394; at Deptford, 2/95; 3/111, 180; Portsmouth, 3/69–75 passim; 7/75; Harwich, 6/90; accounts/estimates, 1/226–7; 6/205, 256, 271; 7/305; 8/48, 372; 9/260, 376; other financial business, 2/54–5; 4/20, 337; 7/25; 8/259; 9/376, 377, 486, 513; at launch, 5/305; in Carkesse affair, 8/94, 204, 212; inspects sunken ship, 8/293; organisation of office, 9/151; parliamentary business, 9/99, 102–3; clerical business (general): writes shorthand notes, 7/374; 9/480, 483; also, 3/119; 5/257; 6/108, 109; 7/100; 8/503, 557; 9/344, 478, 479; unspecified business, 6/32, 201, 202; 9/281, 282, 325, 364, 392, 547; ~ Tangier business, 5/267; 7/255; 9/267, 414
SOCIAL: sees pre-coronation procession, 2/83; on river trips, 3/95; 6/119; to see E. Indiaman, 4/210; entertains P/EP and others at lodgings, 6/130; 7/152; 9/458, 459; and Barnet, 8/382; at riotous party, 7/246; on trips to Islington, 7/317; and Epsom, 8/337–9 passim; at theatre, 7/423; 8/158, 435, 481, 521; 9/249, 296, 326, 521–2; in

3/219, 220, 223; 4/307, 308(2), 313; 5/298; 8/469–72 passim; 9/211; King to visit, 4/324; alterations, 1/313–14 & n., 324; 2/8, 27, 35, 48–9 & n., 79, 135, 183; 3/110, 220 & n. 5; 4/308; 5/298; 8/470; cloister, 2/183; courtyard, 4/313; garden (crooked wall, the Mount), ib.; 8/472; waterworks, 5/298; summer house, 8/472; park, 8/472; grove, ib.; drawbridge, ib.; Nuns' Bridge, ib.; chapel, 9/211; alluded to: 9/495

HIND COURT, off Fleet St: 1/199

HINDHEAD, Surrey: P and EP at, 9/274

HINGSTON (Hinxton), [John], organist: sets bass to *It is decreed*, 7/414 & n. 1, 420; court news from, 7/414; P consults, 8/574

HINTON, [Edmund], goldsmith: 6/332

HINTON, [John], physician in ordinary to the King: 6/332 & n. 2

HISTORY: P comments on uncertainty of historical knowledge, 8/99

HOARE, [James], sen., joint-Comptroller of the Mint: shows Mint to P and Mennes, 4/143–8 & nn.; social: 7/22; alluded to: 9/410–11 & n.

HOARE (Whore), [James], jun., Joint-Comptroller of the Mint: 9/410–11 & n.

HOARE (Whore), [Richard], clerk in the Prerogative Court of Canterbury: his calligraphy, 1/132–3 & n.; 6/339 & n. 3; also, 2/145

HOARE (Whore), [William], physician: social/musical, 1/10–11 & n.; 4/18; 5/174; 6/61; ~ his wife [Hester], 6/61

[HOBART, Sir Richard], Groom Porter: rebuked in sermon, 3/292–3 & n.

HOBELL, Mrs ——, of Banbury: proposed wife for Tom P, 3/176 & n. 1, 183, 192, 195, 201, 207, 210, 226; match broken off, 3/231 & n. 1, 232–3; 4/12, 253

HODDESDON, Herts.: P at, 9/213

HODGES, [?Edmund], of Lincoln's Inn Fields: 2/125

HODGES, [Thomas], Dean of Hereford (d. 1672): Lady Sandwich stays with at Kensington, 5/178 & n. 5

[HODGKIN, Roger], Fifth-monarchist: executed, 2/18 & n. 2

HOGG, Capt. [Edward], commander of privateer *Flying Greyhound*: captures prizes, 7/418, 424; 8/7, 115–16, 341, 344; his knavery, 8/159 & n. 1, 352, 385; ordered to sea, 8/180; alluded to: 8/392

HOGSDEN: *see* Hoxton

HOLBEIN: portraits of Henry VIII at Audley End, 1/70; 8/467 & n. 4; and in Barber-Surgeons' Hall, 9/293 & n. 1; work at Nonsuch House attributed to, 6/235 & n. 3

HOLBORN [*see also* Taverns etc.: Black Swan; Chequer; George]: subsidence in, 5/82–3 & n.; Fire, 7/282; bearded lady, 9/398; Conduit, 3/148; 9/265, 375, 438; terminus for Brampton coach, 5/200; and York coach, 5/234; Cockpit at King's Gate, 9/154; alluded to: 4/44

HOLBORN CONDUIT HILL: 8/448; 9/520

HOLCROFT, John, P's cousin: 2/109, 111, 114

HOLDEN (Holding), [Joseph], haberdasher, Bride Lane: P buys hats from, 2/25, 104, 127; 4/274, 280, 300, 411; alluded to: 7/394

HOLDEN, [Priscilla], wife of Joseph: to recommend maid for EP, 4/279; finds nurse for Tom P, 5/82; at his death and funeral, 5/86, 87, 91; godmother, 7/394 & n. 2

HOLDER, [Thomas], Auditor-General to the Duke of York and Treasurer of the Royal African Company: 6/170; 8/27; 9/313 & n. 4

HOLDER [?Holden], ——: 7/394 & n. 2

HOLE HAVEN, Essex: quarantine harbour, 4/399 & n. 2; Dutch ship aground, 8/306

HOLINSHED, ——, tobacconist: marries widowed Kate Joyce, 9/127, 195

HOLLAND, Gilbert: gift to P, 1/95; social: 1/94

[HOLLAND, John], Rector of Holy Trinity, Guildford: 2/94 & n. 2

HOLLAND, Capt. Philip, naval

officer: advises P on perquisites, 1/82; commission renewed, 1/167 & n. 2, 168; political news from, ib.; P pays debt to, 2/116; attempts suicide and turns Quaker, 4/109; social: 1/15, 17, 56, 59, 196, 205; alluded to: 1/313, 316 & n. 2; 3/163; ~ his mother, 2/116; sons, 9/184

HOLLAND, ——, wife of Capt. Philip: a plain dowdy, 2/116; her mother a Quaker, 4/109; social: 1/17, 205

HOLLAND, Earls of: see Rich

HOLLAR, Wenceslaus, engraver (d. 1677): appointed royal scenographer, 7/378–9 & n.; engraving of city after Fire, ib.

HOLLES, Denzil, cr. Baron Holles 1661, ambassador to France 1663–6: Privy Councillor, 1/171; (untrue) rumour of dismissal, 8/596, 600; and of affronts to, 4/419–20 & n., 5/59–60 & n.; plenipotentiary in peace negotiations, 8/61, 63, 138 & n. 4, 175, 189 & n. 2, 216, 218, 249, 352; bewails state of country, 7/370; said to be wise, 8/70

HOLLES, Sir Frescheville, naval officer, M.P. Grimsby, Lincs.: conceited, 8/275, 292, 304; 9/516; service with fireships, 8/256 & n. 4, 272, 275, 379; at odds with Coventry, 8/304; 9/76, 92, 108–9, 129, 173; defends Brouncker in Commons, 9/62; attacks Sandwich, 9/68; his family in parliament, 8/454–5 & n.; Sir J. Smith's enmity to, 9/118; parliamentary news from, 9/135

HOLLES, [Gervase], father of Sir Frescheville: as M.P. for Grimsby, 8/454–5 & n.

HOLLIER (Holliard, Holyard), [Thomas], P's surgeon:
AS SURGEON: treats P for stone, 2/17; 4/327, 345–6; 5/162, 165, 241; colic, 4/280, 328, 329, 332, 345, 385–6; and deafness, 4/319, 320; bleeds P, 3/66, 76–7; his laxative pills, 4/153, 386; and draught, 4/332; consulted about sore, 4/252; general advice, 2/17, 201; 3/10; on diet, 4/280, 345–6, 385–6; treats EP for earache, 3/124; and abscess, 4/379, 382, 383–4, 385; 5/145;

8/584; his bill, 4/435; examines Tom Edwards for stone, 3/329; treats P's father for rupture, 8/110, 213–14, 237; denies efficacy of touching for King's Evil, 1/281; supports claims of naval surgeons, 5/261 & n. 1; also, 9/558
GENERAL: praises Luther and Calvin, 4/386; anti-Catholic, 5/256; 8/586, 587; 9/16; losses in Fire, 8/87 & n. 4; house in Hatton Garden, 8/110
SOCIAL: fuddled, 4/386; 5/309; 9/142; talks Latin, 4/386; 9/142, 279; also, 4/434; 6/9; 7/127; 8/64; 9/72–3, 356, 561

HOLLINS, [John], Fellow of Magdalene College, Cambridge, physician: P visits, 1/67; also: 9/212

HOLLIS: see Hawles

HOLLOND, [John], Surveyor of the Navy 1649–52: scheme for paying off seamen, 1/306 & n. 1, 308; MS. discourse(s) on naval administration, 3/145 & n. 1, 280, 285; 9/489 & n. 2

HOLLOWAY: P at, 2/184

HOLLWORTHY, [Mary], widow of Richard: spurns advances of Spragge, 8/141; reputation for gossip, 8/544; conceited, 9/13; social: 9/220, 245; alluded to: 8/172 & n. 3; 9/433

HOLLWORTHY, [Richard], merchant, of St Olave's parish: dies in fall from horse, 6/296

HOLMES, Gabriel: tried for arson, 8/319–21 passim & nn.

HOLMES, Capt. John, kted 1672, naval officer: P's low opinion, 9/157; wounded, 7/155; under Harman's command, 7/409–10 & n.; marriage, 9/157 & n. 2

HOLMES, Margaret (b. Lowther), wife of John: pretty, 8/241; marriage, 9/157 & n. 2; at Lady Penn's, 7/96

HOLMES, [Nathaniel], Rector of St Mary Staining 1643–62, and preacher to the Council of State (d. 1678): preaches at Whitehall, 1/53; n. 1

HOLMES, Capt. Robert, kted 1666, naval commander:
CHARACTER AND REPUTATION: 2/169; 4/196; 6/129; 7/180, 344, 409–10
CHRON. SERIES: friend of Sandwich, 2/169; fails to enforce salute from Swedish ambassador, 2/212 & n. 3,

222, 229; 3/14; returns from Mediterranean, 4/67; quarrels with sailing master, 4/67, 78, 81, 83, 84, 91–2; violent words against Mennes, 4/92; returns from Tangier, 4/299; voyage to Guinea, 5/160 & n. 4, 341; 6/42 & n. 2; sent to Tower, 6/6 & n. 2, 56; in Battle of Lowestoft, 6/122; resigns commission, 6/129 & n. 2; in Four Days Fight, 7/143; quarrel (?duel) with Sir J. Smith, 7/339–40 & n., 348; 9/107 & n. 3, 118, 123; influence in fleet, 7/158, 178, 332, 333; alliance with Rupert, 7/332; and with Buckingham, 9/382, 467; criticised, 7/204; attack on Dutch ships in Vlie ('Holmes's Bonfire'), 7/247 & n. 1, 257; in St James's Day Fight, 7/344–5; appointed 'land admiral', 8/149; his part in Buckingham – Shrewsbury duel, 9/26–7; also, 7/409–10; 9/148, 352
SOCIAL: 1/317; 2/175, 240; 3/14, 22
MISC.: brings ape from Guinea, 2/160; his advances to EP, 2/237; 3/4; offered king's wife in Guinea, 3/11; objects to brother's marriage, 9/157
ALLUDED TO: 1/176, 182
HOLT, Mr ——, of Portsmouth: 3/70
HOLYARD: see Hollier
HOLYHEAD, Anglesey: 4/256
HOMEWOOD, [?Edward], Navy Office clerk: victualling business, 7/139; social: 3/5
HOMOSEXUALITY: increase of, 4/210; P's innocence of, ib.
HONYWOOD, Col. Henry: good natured, 3/9 & n. 2; killed by fall from horse, 4/25 & n. 2; alluded to: 3/7
HONYWOOD, Michael, Dean of Lincoln: good natured, 3/9; 4/167 & n. 1; 5/192, 233; P's gift to, 4/171–2, 173; alluded to: 3/7
HONYWOOD, Peter: lodges with P's parents, 2/5 & n. 3; demonstrates 'Prince Rupert's drops', 3/9 & n. 3; lame, 5/20; pays allowance to John P, 5/142 & n. 3; 6/49; social: at P's stone feast, 5/98; 6/124; also, 4/167; 5/91; 7/173; alluded to: 3/7
HONYWOOD, Col. Philip, kted ?1662: 1/130; 9/74
HONYWOOD, Sir Robert, M.P.

New Romney, Kent: 1/199 & n. 3; ~ his wife, ib.
HONYWOOD, Sir Thomas: 1/181 & n. 1, 220; ~ his daughter, 1/220
[HOOGSTRATEN, Samuel van] painter (d. c.1678): perspective painting, 4/18 & n. 1, 26; 5/277
HOOKE, [Robert], curator of experiments to the Royal Society [see also Books]: P's admiration, 6/36–7, 95; at Royal Society, 6/36–7 & n.; lectures on comet, 6/48 & n. 1; and felt-making, 7/51 & n. 3; experiments in coach design, 6/94–5; 7/12, 20 & n. 2; borrows book of naval terms, 7/148; explains nature of sound, 7/239 & n. 1; 9/147; and blood transfusion, 7/373; social: 8/64; 9/544
HOOKE, [Theophilus], clergyman, P's contemporary at Cambridge: 2/44
HOOKER, Ald. Sir William, merchant, kted 1666, Sheriff 1665–6: drafts plague regulations, 6/211 & n. 5; story of child saved from plague, 6/212; dirty house, 6/328 & n. 3; supplies tallow, 7/41; criticises Penn, 9/170; alluded to: 8/152
HOOKER (of the Privy Seal): see Hooper
HOOPER, [William], minor canon of Westminster: 2/240 & n. 2
HOOPER (Hooker), ——, of the Privy Seal: 1/208, 212
HOPE, the, reach of the Thames: P at, 5/197(2), 317; 6/287; Coventry at, 7/70; fleet/ships in, 1/98; 2/95; 5/190, 193, 196; 6/65, 103; 8/251, 257, 263, 266, 298, 349; Rupert sails from, 5/291; pontoon bridge, 8/254 & n. 4
HORACE: ode recited, 8/472
HORE (Whore), Philip: dispute about Irish estate, 5/324 & n. 1
[?HORNECK, Anthony], German minister: his preaching, 8/580 & n. 1
HORSE DEALERS: tricks, 4/120; 9/384, 391
HORSE GUARD HOUSE: fire, 7/362–3 & n.
HORSE SAND, off Portsmouth: 2/11
HORSLEY, Mrs —— [also Horsfall, Horsfield]: P admires ('my new Morena'), 5/349 & n. 3; 7/135–6 &

n.; takes to Vauxhall, 7/136; married, ib.; house burnt, 8/168; at theatre, 9/203; her silly talk, 9/204; widowed, 9/322; alluded to: 7/235, 269; ~ her husband, 9/204

HORSLEYDOWN, Bermondsey: P at, 7/22

HOSIER, Francis, Clerk of the Cheque and Muster-Master, Gravesend: gift to P, 8/526 & n. 1; advises on store-keepers' accounts, 9/300 & n. 2, 374 & n. 1; his methods approved, 9/444, 445, 474 & n. 1; ~ his wife, 9/300

HOSIER LANE, Smithfield: 9/521

HOTTENTOTS: stories of, 3/298 & n. 3

HOUBLONS, the brothers, merchants, sons of James [see also below]: P's regard, 6/337; 7/36, 39, 370; 9/68; send ships to Tangier, 7/20, 36, 38, 44–5, 45, 64, 98; gift to P, 7/64, 66; unspecified business, 7/52, 371; bewail state of nation, 7/371; discount rumours of invasion, 8/1–2 & n.; social: 6/336–7; 7/368; 8/337; 9/405

HOUBLON, Isaac, merchant, son of James, sen.: 7/270

HOUBLON, James, sen., merchant: 9/68 & n. 3

HOUBLON, James, jun., merchant, son of James, sen.: P's affection for, 6/27, 337; 7/64; sends goods to Tangier, 6/27, 28; news from, 8/151, 162; 9/65, 68; social: 6/63, 336–7; 8/1, 337; ~ his wife [Sarah], 9/65–6

HOUBLON, Peter, merchant, son of James, sen.: at Epsom, 8/337

HOULE: see Howell, W.

HOUNDSDITCH: 5/18

HOUNSLOW, Mdx: P visits, 6/197, 198; Priory, 6/198

HOUSEHOLD GOODS AND DOMESTIC ANIMALS [see also Servants (P)]:

FURNITURE, FURNISHINGS ETC.:

BEDS: press beds at The Hague, 1/139; truckle/trundle beds at inns, 3/75; 4/245; 9/231; at Brampton, 8/470, 474; down bed, 6/218; corded, 8/311 & n. 2; curtains, 4/226; 7/286; (P): green, 2/119; 4/329; red, 3/267; 4/329; settle-bed, 9/464; beds/bedsteads bought, 1/257; 3/261; 4/273;

camlet, 9/330, 334, 356, 367, 368; also, 6/147

CABINETS (P): with secret drawers, 5/152 & n. 2; walnut, 9/405, 406

CARPET, TURKEY (P): 1/232

CHAIRS: joke chair, 1/280 & n. 1; with reading desk, 8/25; turkey work, 8/167; gout chair, 9/215 & n. 3; (P): turkey work, 4/329; set, 7/112; also, 5/251

CHESTS: Duke of York's oriental, 2/79; (P): iron, 5/323; 6/205; 7/272; 8/487; plate, 7/367, 405

CHEST OF DRAWERS: 3/197; (P): 2/130

COUCH (P): 7/112

CURTAINS (P): green say, 2/124

DESK: with secret till, 5/9; with bookshelves, 5/64

HANGINGS FOR WALLS/BEDS: suits of, 5/214–15; 8/470; (P): green serge, 1/269; chintz, 4/299 & n. 1; counterfeit damask, 7/7(2), 10, 14, 19, 24; purple serge, 7/255, 256, 257, 258; tapestry, 8/455; 9/287; 'suit of Apostles', 9/329 & n. 4, 330; also, 9/296

LOOKING GLASS: at Hampton Court, 3/82; 'counterfeit windows', 8/25–6; (P): 5/347, 348; 8/213; 9/423

PRESSES (P): for papers, 2/25; cloaks, 4/353; books, 7/214, 242, 243, 251, 252, 258, 300, 311; 9/18, 48; tools, 7/319

TABLES: with leaf, 6/109 & n. 4; inlaid, 8/128–9; round table with recess, 9/255 & n. 2, 471 & n. 3; (P): side table, 2/110; dining table, 4/6, 14; also, 5/251, 253

P'S SILVERWARE: his pride in 7/35, 37, 39; 8/4 (2), 157, 580; basin (engraved), 8/548; candlesticks, 5/47; chafing dishes, 7/10, 34; drudger, 7/34; flagons, 5/216, 225, 234, 266, 301; forks, 7/358; plates, 7/409, 413, 426; porringer and spoons (christening gift), 2/109; salts, 5/266; 7/71; snuff dish, 8/40; snuffers, 1/15; state cup and cover, 5/45, 47; sugar box, 5/358; tankards, 2/140; 5/45, 47; tumblers, 5/302; 8/339

OTHER HOUSEHOLD GOODS: provision of in friary, 8/26–7; tableware at Lord Mayor's banquet, 4/354–5; bath,

politician, M.P. Stockbridge, Hants. (d. 1698) [*see also* Plays]: his proviso to poll bill, 7/399–400 & nn.; speech against royal prerogative, 8/9 & n. 1; adherent of Buckingham, 8/342; unpopular in Commons, 9/71 & n. 2; his phrase 'rowling out', 9/76; favours Penn's impeachment, 9/165; moves to have Sandwich recalled, 9/176; caricatured as Sir Positive At-All, 9/186 & n. 3, 190; caricatures Coventry in *The country gentleman*, 9/467, 471 & n. 2

HOWARD, Thomas, 2nd Earl of Arundel (d. 1646): 8/6–7 & n. 11

HOWARD, Thomas, 2nd Earl of Berkshire, Gentleman of the Bedchamber to the King (d. 1669): in 'dirty pickle', 7/218 & n. 2; Moll Davis his daughter, 9/24 & n. 2

HOWARD, Thomas: in duel, 3/171; flatters Albemarle, 8/147, 148

HOWE, Jack, brother of Will; deputy-clerk in Patent Office: 9/?202, 480

HOWE, Will, servant to Sandwich and Muster-Master:

CHARACTER: P's opinion: favourable, 3/90; 6/333–4; unfavourable, 4/390; 5/41; 6/50, 79, 231, 301; 7/22; disliked by Sandwich, 5/108; 6/54, 301

PERSONAL: ill, 1/178, 212; wears periwig, 4/390; his chamber and books in Gray's Inn, 9/480

AS SANDWICH'S SERVANT: accompanies to Holland, 1/85, 95, 143, 147–8, 173; and to Mediterranean, 2/120–1; 3/90; 5/302; as messenger, 1/93; 5/36; dislikes Creed, 1/101; 5/65, 107; his chamber in Whitehall, 1/222; at coronation banquet, 2/86; in Becke affair, 4/270, 281, 313, 379, 390, 395, 402, 419, 429; 5/36, 65, 70, 74; claims credit for P's appointment as Sandwich's secretary, 5/174; unspecified business, 4/173; 5/187; 7/52; 9/402; also, 1/191, 197, 267; 4/38

MUSTER-MASTER ETC. TO FLEET: appointed, 6/54–5 & n.; accounts, 6/62; 7/7, 31, 42; in prize-goods scandal, 6/230, 231, 299–300, 301, 303; arrested, 6/306, 309, 329; examined by Navy Board, 6/333–4; and by

Brooke House Committee, 9/91, 92, 363–4; scandal alluded to, 7/20, 22; also, 7/19

OTHER APPOINTMENTS: in Patent Office, 9/372 & n. 2, 480; asks for loan, 9/492 & n. 4; shows P Patent Office records, 9/479–80

MUSICAL: sings, 1/111, 113, 118, 144, 162, 164, 185–6, 194, 215, 285; 2/118, 121; 3/281; 4/63, 84, 149; 8/413, 429; 9/202; plays viol/violin, 1/104, 107, 114, 129, 285; 3/184, 187, 216, 281

SOCIAL: at taverns, 1/75, 259; 2/102; 3/248, 298; on *Swiftsure*, 1/96, 98, 100(2); and *Naseby*, 1/103, 105, 110, 115, 116, 120, 131, 166; visits Deal, 1/119; and The Hague, 1/149; at Wardrobe dinner, 2/104; dines with/visits P, 1/195; 5/162, 196; 8/5, 223, 365, 464, 570; 9/138, 255, 260, 279, 286, 464, 482, 533; at Sandwich's lodgings, 2/37, 41; 3/266, 282; 4/21–2, 117; 5/40; in Hyde Park, 4/119–20; at Vauxhall, 9/219; at theatre, 9/304, 322; also, 1/71, 74, 208, 209; 2/102–3

HOWELL, [Richard], turner to the navy: supplies files, 2/171; tells P of malpractices, 6/117 & n. 1; also, 2/231, 232; 3/298; 6/309 & n. 1; 7/274; ~ his widow, 9/311 & n. 1

HOWELL (Houle), [William], historian, Fellow of Magdalene College, Cambridge, 1652–?60 (d. 1683): news from, 4/274–5 & n.; at coffee-house with Dryden, 5/37; social: 1/45

HOWET: *see* Hewet

HOWLETT, Betty: *see* Mitchell

HOWLETT, Lettice (Lissett), P's aunt: to live with P's father at Brampton, 2/183; visits P, 8/442 & n. 1, 448; 9/195 & n. 1; at theatre, 8/450; ~ her son, 2/183

HOWLETT, Mr ——, shopkeeper, Westminster Hall: as tax-collector, 8/121; social: 5/41; 7/123, 197; 8/34, 72, 236; 9/99; alluded to: 4/234, 368; 5/71; 7/284, 337, 338, 378, 418

HOWLETT, Mrs ——, shopkeeper, wife of the foregoing: ill, 8/120, 121, 151; complains of son-in-law, 8/479; social: at her shop, 4/242; 5/41; 7/61, 378; 8/47; at christenings, 7/394; 8/202; also, 7/123; 8/34, 72;

9/99, 594; alluded to: 4/234; 8/400; 9/103

[HOWORTH, John], Master of Magdalene College, Cambridge 1664–8 and Vice-Chancellor 1667–d.68: 8/469 & n. 1

HOXTON, Mdx: P visits, 5/272; 9/197, 513; Baumes House, 5/272 & n. 2; 9/197

HUBBARD (Hubbert, Hulbert), Capt. [John jun.], naval officer: reputation, 7/333–4; 8/485–6 & n.; refuses to strike flag to French, 9/560 & n. 2

[HUBERT, Robert]: hanged for starting Fire, 7/357 & n. 2; 8/81 & n. 4

HUDSON, [James], wine cooper: 6/151; 8/265–6

HUDSON, [?John], of Westminster: 1/10, 17

HUDSON, [Michael], chaplain to Chatham Dockyard: his preaching, 4/258 & n. 2

HUDSON, [Nathaniel], scrivener, the Old Bailey: 5/114, 168

[HUGHES], Peg, actress: 9/189 & n. 3

HUGHES, [William], ropemaker, Woolwich: reports on yard, 3/101 & n. 3; dismissed, 3/197; to swear against Coventry, 4/170; a rogue, ib.; also, 5/256–7

HUGHES, ——, housekeeper to Parliament: 7/305

HULBERT: see Hubbard

HULL, Yorks.: garrison prepared against invasion, 7/185 & n. 1; prize ships at, 8/341, 344, 349, 352, 369, 385

HUMFREY, Pelham, composer (d. 1674) [see also Musical Compositions]: returns from France, 8/515 & n. 5; disparages King's music, 8/529–30; conducts at court, 8/532, 534

HUNGARY: Turkish advance into, 4/316 & n. 1, 321, 372 & n. 2

HUNGERFORD, Margaret, Lady Hungerford, widow of Sir Edward: 9/534–5 & n.

HUNGERFORD, Wilts.: P visits, 9/228

HUNT, [Elizabeth], of Axe Yard, wife of John:
CHRON. SERIES: P's regard, 4/3; 6/142; 7/92, 219; ill, 2/15; birth of son, 2/234,

235, 236; fat, 7/52; related to Cromwells, 7/94; returns from Cambridge, 7/219 & n. 2; also, 1/94, 254, 257; 2/10, 35, 53; 3/180; 4/361; 5/174
SOCIAL: at P's house, 1/6, 37, 202–3; 3/36, 75; 4/4, 114, 293, 365; 5/146, 340; 6/37; P/EP visit(s) etc., 1/217; 2/55, 87, 207, 240; 3/7, 51; 4/182, 274, 276; 5/51, 79; in Hyde Park, 4/73; 5/126; at P's stone feast, 5/98

~ her cousin, 5/146

HUNT, [?George], musical-instrument maker, Paul's Churchyard: alters theorbo, 2/201, 203; brings bass viol, 4/104–5; makes viol, 4/282, 284; lends lute, 5/258; alluded to: 2/209

HUNT, [John], of Axe Yard, friend and neighbour of P; sub-commissioner of the Excise:
CHRON. SERIES: P's regard, 4/3; 7/219; political news from, 1/58, 77; troubled at return of secluded members, 1/63 & n. 5; dismissed (temporarily) from Excise, 1/254 & n. 4, 257 & n. 2; 2/53 & n. 2; returns from duties in Cambridge, 7/44, 219 & n. 2; 8/84–5 & n.; prospers, 7/92; informs P of Betty Becke, 4/392; stands bail for Hayter, 6/116
SOCIAL: at P's house, 1/6, 37, 49, 53; 2/216; 3/25, 36, 75, 86, 105; 4/83, 118, 293; 5/72, 174, 340; 7/132; in Hyde Park, 5/126; also, 1/8, 27; 2/67, 87; 3/76, 191; 4/231; 9/165
ALLUDED TO: 4/42; 5/167

~ his kinswoman, 5/174

HUNT, John, son of John: birth and christening, 2/234, 235, 236; EP's gift as godmother, 3/7; also, 4/276, 293; 5/146

HUNT, Mrs ——, of Jewen St, Deb Willet's aunt: her conversation, 8/569; 9/332; also, 9/346, 520

HUNTINGDON, Maj. Robert: intermediary between Charles I and Cromwell, 5/335 & n. 2

HUNTINGDON, Hunts.: P visits, 2/137, 148; 3/220; 4/312, 313; 9/212, 224; at school, 1/87 & n. 4; town waits, 8/474; parliamentary elections, 1/86–7 & n., 99 & n. 1; assizes, 2/145, 148; Sandwich appointed Recorder, 4/30 & n. 1, 62; anecdote about

INGRAM, Sir Arthur, merchant: 6/108; 7/169

INGRAM, Sir Thomas, Privy Councillor: courteous, 7/20; appointed to Tangier Committee, 6/7; financial business, 6/33, 121, 133; 9/371; victualling business, 6/117, 171; attends meetings/unspecified business, 6/58, 61, 166; at Council committee, 8/278; ~ his clerk, 1/186

INGRAM, Mrs ——: 5/304

INNER TEMPLE: Reader's Feast, 2/155 & n. 2; 9/465–6 & n.; revels, 4/32 & n. 1; gaming in hall, 9/3 & n. 1; riot, 9/465–6 & n., 511–12

INNS: see Taverns etc.

INNS OF COURT: see under names

INSECTS: spontaneous generation, 2/105 & n. 4; bees: in Baltic, 4/413; apiary, 6/97 & n. 3; fleas: in P's bed, 5/260; also, 3/70; glow-worms: 8/340; gnats (?mosquitoes): at Brampton, 2/135, 138; in Fens, 4/311 & n. 1; lice: P suffers from, 9/231, 424; lice or nits: in P's hair/periwig, 5/212, 8/133, 146; 9/239, 424; moth: courtiers chase, 8/282

INSURANCE (marine): peacetime rates, 4/395 & n. 3, 394–7 passim; wartime, 5/126; story of fraud, 4/401, 403; also, 6/202, 328, 329; 7/25

INVENTIONS and machines [see also Entertainments: clockworks; Guns; Royal Society; Scientific and Mathematical Instruments; Ships; Watches and Clocks]: calculating machine, 9/116–17 & n.; chimney design (to prevent smoking), 4/315 & n. 1; claviorganum, 8/25 & n. 4; coins with milled edges, 4/147; diving bell, 5/268–9 & n.; false teeth, 5/293; fire-engines, 8/191, 320; fountain pen, 4/263–4 & n., 278; glass apiary, 6/97 & n. 2; glass coach, 8/396, 446; joke chair, 1/280 & n. 1; lamp glasses, 1/273; 5/237, 291–2; lighthouses, 5/314; 6/3 & n. 4; mechanical organ, 2/115–16 & n.; mine, 3/45–6 & n.; 4/378; sawmill, 3/118; smoke jack, 1/273; theatrical machinery, 2/155 & n. 1; 4/126 & n. 2, 182 & n. 3; 7/76, 77; varnish, 4/153 & n. 2; 7/147–8; waterwheel, 1/263–4; windmill, 9/520

IPSWICH, Suff.: 6/217

IRELAND: appointment of Lord-Lieutenant, 1/227–8 & n.; his establishment reduced, 9/41 & n. 1; declaration against nonconformity, 2/67 & n. 2; troops transported to Portugal, 3/85; land settlement, 4/66 & n. 1, 80, 82, 223 & n. 4, 295; 5/61, 324, 346; 9/119; rumour of dissolution of parliament, 4/80; Castle Plot, 4/94 & n. 2, 100, 285 & n. 3; controversy over cattle trade, 7/313–14 & n., 343; free quartering of soldiers, 8/518–19 & n.; Irish as French recruiting agents, 8/601

IRETON, Henry, regicide (d. 1651): body exhumed and hanged, 1/309 & n. 4; 2/24, 27; head displayed, 2/31 & n. 4

IRETON, [?Jerman, of Gray's Inn]: 9/464

IRETON, John, republican (d. 1689): imprisoned after Yarranton plot, 2/225 & n. 1

IRONGATE [Stairs], Little Tower Hill: 7/273

IRONMONGERS' HALL, Fenchurch St: funeral, 3/268

ISACKSON, ——, linendraper at the Key in Cheapside: 1/277

ISHAM, Capt. [Henry]: accompanies Sandwich to Holland, 1/95, 96, 102, 115, 126, 136, 137 & n. 2; to go to Portugal, 2/161, 163; brings letters from Lisbon, 3/51; social: 1/92, 97; 2/142

ISLE OF DOGS, the: P and party spend night on, 6/168; stranded on, 6/175; also, 6/331

ISLE OF MAN, the: 4/240

ISLE OF WIGHT [see also St Helen's Point; Newport]: 7/334; Charles I's escape to (1647), 6/316

[ISLEWORTH, Mdx]: P at, 6/199 & n. 1

ISLINGTON: P/EP visit (their 'grand tour'): 5/132; 6/86; 7/108, 122, 126, 129, 167, 170, 202, 223, 265, 267, 317; 8/211; 9/251, 271–2, 521, 558; plague in, 6/175–6; the fields/ponds: P visits, 3/57, 59; 9/32; boyhood memories, 5/101 & n. 1; Katherine Wheel, 7/167, 261; King's Head ('the old house', 'the great house'): boyhood

9/418, 422; unspecified, 3/272, 282, 300; 4/4; 5/177, 223; 6/58, 134; 7/82, 166, 321; 8/60–1, 347, 459, 521, 591, 600; 9/135, 316, 449
MILITARY CAREER: in Flanders (1658): 5/170–1 & n.; 6/302; 8/75; reminiscences, of, 9/396; rumoured appointment to new army, 3/15 & n. 2; 6/277 & n. 2, 302; 7/395; and as general of land and sea forces, 6/321 & n. 1; commands troops during Fire, 7/269, 271, 273; favours standing army, 8/355, 361, 366–7; reviews troops, 4/216–17 & n.; 9/308, 557 & n. 1; Governor of Portsmouth, 2/199 & n. 2; Lord Warden of Cinque Ports, 9/280 & n. 4
OTHER PUBLIC WORK: patron of R. African Company, 1/258; 4/335; 5/11; 9/350; and of E. India Company, 2/228; profits from wine licences, 9/132 & n. 1, 319 & n. 1; low opinion of new Council of Trade, 9/549 & n. 2
POLITICS [*see also* below, Court]:
  GENERAL: favours papists, 2/38; prefers Irish to English subordinates, 5/345; fears/resents Monmouth's claims, 3/238, 290, 303 & n. 1; 4/123, 138; 5/21, 58; 7/411; 8/434; advises tax by prerogative, 8/292–3; favours government by army on French model, 8/332; political news from, 5/13; 8/186, 384; 9/173–4, 310
  RELATIONS WITH KING AND MINISTERS: attitude to Clarendon's dismissal, 8/406, 409, 410 & n. 1, 412, 414, 416, 419, 420, 424, 476, 506; power reduced by, 8/434, 597; relations with King deteriorate, 8/431, 480, 482, 530, 532, 535, 558, 596, 602; improve, 8/568; 9/153; fears Clarendon's impeachment, 8/518; rumours of his own impeachment, 8/532, 533–4; reconciled with Coventry, 9/79, 336; power weakened by Buckingham's rise, 9/340, 341, 361, 373, 472, 550–1, 558; relations improve, 9/319, 490–1
  AS PRIVY COUNCILLOR: discusses state of navy, 7/311–13; money for navy, 7/377; 8/112; 9/216, 220; flag-officers' pensions, 9/257 & n. 2; attends cabinet meetings, 8/117, 138,

600; other council meetings, 7/26, 353; 8/111; 9/87, 122
  PARLIAMENT: candidate defeated, 7/337 & n. 2; attends Lords, 7/406; 8/46; 9/176; opposes recall, 8/292–3 & n.; members attend on, 8/477; instructions to friends, 8/482
  FOREIGN AFFAIRS: relations with Algiers, 3/121–2 & n.; 9/473, 516; favours Dutch war, 5/107, 111, 212, 242, 355; warns Dutch ambassador, 5/264 & n. 4; favours French alliance, 9/536; also, 8/452
COURT: reconciled to Queen-Mother, 2/2–3 & n.; association with Fitzharding and Muskerry, 4/116; 5/345; dislike of E. Mountagu of Boughton, 5/207; laughs at Sir R. Howard, 9/190–1; chides Bab May, 9/336–7; fears King may marry F. Stuart, 8/438; allies with Lady Castlemaine, 9/417; resents disgrace of H. Savile, 9/466, 469, 493; dines in public, 4/407; 8/161; attends Garter ceremony, 8/177; 9/246; and court balls, 3/300–01; 7/372; drunk at Cranbourne, 8/446–7; also, 3/191
MARRIAGE [for his mistresses, *see* Carnegie, Lady; Chesterfield, Lady; Churchill, Arabella; Denman, Lady; Hamilton, Lady Anne; Stuart, Frances]: rumours of, 1/260–1 & n., 273, 275, 284 & n. 1, 315, 319; publicly acknowledged, 1/320; 2/1; the ceremony, 2/40–1 & n.; dalliance with wife, 4/4; her jealousy, 4/138; his mistresses, 8/6, 286; henpecked (nicknamed 'Tom Otter'), 8/368 & n. 2; 9/342; marriage said to have 'undone the nation', 8/367; alluded to: 7/261; 8/287
FAMILY [*see also* Stuart]: children, 4/238, n. 1; untroubled by death of son Charles, 2/95 & n. 1; plays with daughter, Princess Mary, 5/268; also, 1/247–8; 2/213
RELIGION: friend of Catholics, 2/38; 'silly devotions', 9/163–4; attends Whitehall chapel, 3/42; 4/31, 401
SPORTS [for his yacht, *see* Ships: *Anne*]: plays pell-mell, 2/64; 9/542; hunts, 3/76, 198, 247, 260; 4/167, 192; 7/136–7, 228, 388; 8/382, 446–7;

9/442, 443, 455; 'a desperate hunts-
man', 4/371; injured hunting, 7/239;
hunts thrice weekly, 7/320; skates,
3/282; watches footrace, 4/255; races
horses at Putney, 8/204; visits Newmarket, 9/209, 340–1, 473
HOUSES AND HOUSEHOLD [seasonal
moves from Whitehall to St James's
are not indexed]:
WHITEHALL: Lely's portraits of flag
officers to hang in chamber, 7/102 &
n. 3; dressing chamber, 8/115; 9/491;
closet burgled, 9/489 & n. 3; little
chapel, 9/163–4
ST JAMES'S: hangings, 4/217; dressing
room, 8/374; pictures, 9/284; P
admires chamber, 8/198; moves to for
Duchess's lying-in, 6/19; and own
illness, 8/524
HOUSEHOLD: clerk of kitchen dismissed, 3/214 & n. 1; H. Killigrew
jun. banished, 7/336–7 & n.; H.
Brouncker dismissed, 8/416, 447;
corruption/extravagance, 5/120; 7/
191–2; 8/286, 287, 434; commissioners of, 8/287; 8/592 & n. 1; 9/290;
appoints Milles chaplain, 8/241, 248;
tenants include brothel keepers, 9/132
& n. 1; P admires 'little pretty
squinting girl', 9/295
SOCIAL: entertained by Speaker, 1/174;
Sir H. Finch, 2/155 & n. 2; Berkeley,
3/184; and Carteret, 6/169–70; at
Hinchingbrooke's wedding, 9/51;
plays 'I love my love', 9/468–9; at
theatre, 1/171; 2/80, 164, 174; 4/431;
5/33; 7/347; 8/91, 167, 388, 487;
9/183, 398; walks etc. in parks, 3/47,
60, 288; 8/68; 9/118, 414
MISC.: his horse Pen, 5/71; elected
Fellow of Royal Society, 6/6 & n. 1;
views ruins of St Paul's after Fire,
7/367; rules for forecasting weather,
9/150; recommends sauce, 9/443;
love of Navarre wine, ib.; in coach
accident, 9/474
ALLUDED TO: 9/425
JAMES, porter: news from, 1/36, 38
JAMES, Mrs —— (Aunt James): piety,
4/164–5; 5/266; P ashamed of neglecting, 4/163–4 & n.; 5/263; at Brampton, 5/263, 266, 282; breast amputated, 6/97 & n. 5; death, 7/36; social:

5/288, 289; 6/125, 133
JANE (Seymour), third Queen of
Henry VIII (d. 1537): tomb, 7/58 &
n. 6
JAPANNING: *see* Crafts
JEFFERIES, [Thomas], apothecary,
Westminster; P's kinsman: 8/517 &
n. 2
JEFFERY, Francis, Lord Jeffery, editor
of the *Edinburgh Review* (d. 1850):
opinion of Diary, vol. i, p. lxxxii
JEFFERYS, Capt. [?John]: on *Naseby*,
1/166
JEFFERYS, ——: a 'fumbler', 3/50 &
n. 1
JEFFREYS, ——: 6/65
JEGON (Jiggins), [Robert], Westminster magistrate: 3/278
JENIFER, Capt. [James], naval
officer: political gossip from, 8/118–19
& n.; account of St James's Day
Fight, 8/357–60 & nn.
[JENKINS], Eliezer (Ely), P's footboy: hired, 1/87; on Dutch voyage,
1/95, 96, 100, 101, 134, 135, 138, 139,
140, 143, 147; sad to leave P's service,
1/232; P meets again, 9/117; also,
1/89, 233; ~ his father, 1/87, 233
JENKINS, Leoline, kted 1670; judge
of the Court of Admiralty; Secretary
of State 1680–4 (d. 1685): character,
8/131, 133; his appointment, 8/133 &
nn.; hears prize case, 8/130–4 passim
JENKINS, [Capt. William], soldier:
killed in duel, 9/26–7 & n.
JENNENS (Jennings), Sir William,
naval commander: P's low opinion,
9/430; courage in Four Days Fight,
7/148; ill-government of fleet, 7/332;
quarrel with Le Neve, 7/380 & n. 2;
conduct at Gravesend criticised, 8/351,
379; also, 9/430 & n. 1
JENNINGS, ——, of the Privy Seal:
social: 1/206, 217; ?5/330
JENNINGS, ——, clerk to quarter-
master of Sandwich's troop: business,
1/14; social: 1/13; ?5/330
JENNINGS, Frances: her prank, 6/41
& n. 1
JENNINGS, Capt. W.: *see* Jennens
JERMYN (Germin), Henry, 1st Earl of
St Albans, courtier and diplomat:
PERSONAL: character, 1/307; rumoured

marriage to Queen Mother, 3/263 & n. 3, 303; 5/57–8 & n.; 8/564 & n. 1; new buildings in St James's Fields, 4/295–6; 7/87–8 & n.; dress, 7/328; reckless gamester, 8/190 & n. 2; fine coach, 8/196; also, 6/316 & n. 4
PUBLIC CAREER: ambassador to France, 1/300, 307; rumoured appointment as Lord Treasurer, 3/227; negotiations with France, 8/107 & n. 1; 9/530 & n. 2, 536; also, 2/33; 8/294
SOCIAL: 2/32; 4/229
JERMYN, Henry, Master of the Horse to the Duke of York; cr. Baron Dover 1685: rumoured marriage to Princess Dowager, 1/320; duel, 3/170–1; attempt at abduction, 5/58 & n. 2; at sea with Rupert, 5/311; affair with Lady Castlemaine, 8/366, 368; wealth, 8/196, 563–4; also, 9/473; ∼ his brother [Thomas], 8/563–4
JERSEY, Channel Is.: Carteret's government during Civil War, 3/243 & n. 2; 4/195, 306; Sir T. Allin's flight to (1650), 8/161 & n. 4
JERVAS (Gervas), [Richard], barber, New Palace Yard: trims P, 1/90; 4/130, 290; his man hired for Dutch voyage, 1/90; P inspects periwigs, 4/130, 290, 350; 5/224; 6/74; other visits, 5/246, 257, 260, 267–8, 275, 287, 316, 332, 340; 6/1, 6, 9, 16; 8/177; supplies infested periwig, 8/133, 146; sees diving experiment, 5/268–9; ∼ his wife [Grace], 4/261–2; 5/268–9; 6/6, 16; child [Ann] buried, 5/221; mother-in-law, —— Palmer, ventriloquist, 4/261–2
JESSOP, [William], Clerk of the House of Commons 1660: 'an old-fashion man of Cromwell's', 9/44; parliamentary business, 1/29; 2/32 & n. 3; secretary to Brooke House Committee, 9/30 & n. 1, 44, 298
JESUITS, the: Leopold I's reliance on, 4/350 & n. 2
JEWEN ST: Deb Willet lodges in, 9/543; also, 9/332, 520(2)
[JEWKES, Roland], lawyer: tomb, 8/545 & n. 2
JEWS: P attends synagogue, 4/335 & nn.; story of new Messiah, 7/47 & n. 4

JIGGINS: see Jegon
JIJELLI (Gigery), Algeria; captured by French, 5/295 & n. 1
JOHN GEORGE II, Elector of Saxony 1656–80: made Knight of Garter, 9/246 & n. 2
JOHNSON, [Henry], shipbuilder, Blackwall: story of petrified trees, 6/236 & n. 4; repairs ships, 8/135; social: 1/280
JOHNSON, Mrs ——, servant to Sandwich: 1/38
JOHNSON, Mrs ——, sister of Lady Mordaunt: 9/476 & n. 5
JOLLIFFE (Jolly), [George], physician: 4/60 & n. 3
JOLLIFFE, [John], merchant: 5/300
JONES, Anne, of St Olave's parish: social: 7/136; 8/29, 104, 150; 9/197
[JONES, John]: elected M.P. for London, 2/57 & n. 1
JONES, Col. John, republican: impeached, 1/34 & n. 2
JONES, Col. [Philip], parliamentarian: influence over R. Cromwell, 1/180 & n. 4; ∼ his son, 2/34 & n. 2, 56
JONES, Sir Theophilus, Scoutmaster-General of Ireland 1661–d.85: 2/173
JONES, ——, a young merchant: 8/76
JORDAN, Joseph, kted 1665, naval commander: in Battle of Lowestoft, 6/122; serves under Penn, 6/147; at council of war, 6/230; poor tactics in St James's Day Fight, 8/354 & n. 3, 357–60; portrait by Lely, 7/102 & n. 3
JORDAN, Mrs —— [?Mary, wife of Joseph]: as godmother, 2/109
JOURNAL: see Diary
JOWLES, Lieut. [Henry], naval officer: P's low opinion, 4/229; 5/1; marriage to Rebecca Allen, 4/229 & n. 1; challenges his captain to duel, 8/140–1; ∼ his mother, 4/227
JOWLES, Rebecca (b. Allen), wife of Henry: P admires, 2/68, 71, 72; 5/1; dallies with, 9/495, 497; married, 4/229 & n. 1; churched, 4/227; pleads for husband, 5/1; 8/140–1; social: 2/69, 125, 126, 127; 3/153; ∼ her pretty cousin, 9/497
JOWLES, Capt. [Valentine], naval officer: commissioned, 1/100; gift to P, ib.

KEMBE, Harry, Navy Office messenger: damages awarded against, 3/280; dies, 7/412

KEMPTHORNE, [John], naval commander; kted 1670: in Downs, 8/43; presides over court martial, 9/488, 497 & n. 1, 505 & n. 1

KENASTON: see Kinaston

KENDAL, Duke of: see Anne, Duchess of York

KENERSLY: see Kinnersley

KENNARD: see Kinward

KENSINGTON: P visits: Holland House, 1/216 & n. 2; tavern with garden and grotto, 9/166, 170, 203; other visits, 5/178, 180–1; 7/54, 95, 100; Sandwich/Lady Sandwich at, 1/210, 215; 5/174, 178; Queen at, 5/163; duel, 1/20

KENT, [John]: see Taverns etc.: Three Tuns, Crutched Friars

KENT, Earl of: see Grey, [?Henry]

KENT ST: Plague, 6/279, 297

KENTISH KNOCK, the (shoal off the mouth of the Thames): 1/254

KENTISH TOWN: 5/233

[KERKHOVEN, D.], Dutch naval commander: 6/108 & n. 3

KERNEGUY: see Carnegie

KEVET: see Kievet

KIEVET, Johan, Burgomaster of Rotterdam ('Amsterdam'):ⁿ in peace negotiations, 8/68–9 & n.

KILLIGREW, Henry, chaplain to the King: preaches at Whitehall, 4/393 & n. 2

KILLIGREW, Henry, Groom of the Bedchamber to the Duke of York: at puppet play, 7/267 & n. 1; banished from court, 7/336–7; in affray with Buckingham, 8/348 & n. 1; bawdy talk, 9/218; attacked by Lady Shrewsbury's footmen, 9/557 & n. 2, 558; also, 3/229–30, 265

KILLIGREW, Sir Peter: on Naseby, 1/132 & n. 2

KILLIGREW, Thomas, dramatist, manager of the Theatre Royal and Groom of the Bedchamber [see also Plays]:

AS MANAGER OF THEATRE ROYAL: his plans for opera, 5/230; 8/56; and for training actors, 5/230 & n. 3;

love of Italian music, 8/54–7 passim; brings Italian consort to court, 8/56, 65–6; on improvement in theatre, 8/55–6; praises Knepp's acting, 8/55, 430; employs whore for actors, 9/425; warned against putting on satirical play, 9/471

AS GROOM OF THE BEDCHAMBER: frank advice to Charles II, 7/400; repartee with, 8/368 & n. 2; appointed King's jester, 9/66–7 & n.; struck by Rochester in King's presence, 9/451–2 & n.; also, 8/497; 9/558

SOCIAL: 5/27; 8/429–30; 9/200

MISC.: his (joke) letter to Queen of Bohemia, 1/157; early passion for theatre, 3/243–4 & n.; early poverty, 9/256 & n. 4

KILLIGREW, Sir William, dramatist and courtier: at Greenwich and Deptford with King, 6/169

KINASTON (Kenaston), [Edward], merchant: P's high opinion, 8/295; Tangier business, 7/19; 8/251 & n. 1, 292, 295, 369–70, 372

KING, Col. [Edward]: 2/53

KING, Henry, Bishop of Chichester 1642–d.69: sermons, 1/195; 4/69; 6/54 & n. 3

KING, [Thomas], M.P. Harwich, Essex: lends P copy of impeachment against Clarendon, 8/523; social: 9/474

[KING, William], landlord of the Crown, Hercules Pillars Lane: wealth, 9/42 & n. 3

KING, [William], Vicar of Ashtead, Surrey ?1648–62: dull preacher, 4/247 & n. 1

KING, [?William], late of the Treasurers at War: dismissed, 1/82

KING, Dr ——, physician, of Huntingdon: 4/313

KING ST, the city: constructed after Fire, 8/562–3 & n.

KING ST, Westminster [see also Taverns etc.: Angel; Axe; Bell; Crown; Fox; Harper's; Leg; Red Lion; Rhenish winehouse; Rose; ?Ship; Sun; Swan; Trumpet; White Horse]: flood, 1/93 & n. 1; traffic block, 1/303 & n. 1; alluded to: 3/201

KINGDON, Capt. [Richard], Comptroller of the Excise Office: service under Commonwealth, 6/319–20 & n.; business with, 6/319, 332; 8/16

KING'S CHANNEL, the (off the Essex Coast): Dutch fleet in, 8/256

[KINGSDOWN], Deal, Kent: wager on height of cliff, 1/163

KING'S GATE, Holborn: 9/154, 474

KINGSLAND, Mdx: P's boyhood memories, 5/132 & n. 4; 8/211 & n. 3; P/EP at, 2/180; 5/133, 201; 7/121, 132, 220; 8/174, 211–12, 390; 9/197, 513

KINGSMILL, family of: 5/118 & n. 1

KINGSTON, Catherine, Lady Kingston, wife of John, 1st Baron: alluded to, 2/54 & n. 3

KING'S LYNN, Norf.: as port, 1/179; 2/27, 156

KINGSTON, Surrey: P visits, 3/75; 6/154, 166, 167; 7/28; Quakers to be tried, 4/271; alluded to: 2/202

KINNERSLEY, ——, of the Wardrobe: 2/121

KINWARD (Kennard), [Thomas], Master-Joiner of the King's Works, Whitehall: his work at Hinchingbrooke, 1/314, 324; 2/35; and on Penn's lodgings, 3/28, 31, 41; ~ his servant, 1/314

KIPPS, [Thomas], Seal-bearer to the Lord Chancellor: at Whitehall chapel, 1/195; Chancery business, 1/197, 204; in P's 'old clubb', 2/221; also, 1/44, 184; 2/127

KIRBY, Capt. [Robert], naval officer: killed in action, 6/122

KIRTON, [Joshua], bookseller, Paul's Churchyard [until the Fire often 'my bookseller']: P: buys books/pays bills, 3/105, 290; 4/234; 5/38, 358, 359; 6/70, 151; 7/41, 47, 64; orders books, 1/281–2; 2/239; 5/342, 343–4, 355; 6/109; collects books, 6/28; has books bound, 5/355; 6/2, 14, 28; visits shop, 2/22, 165, 238; 4/342; 5/190; 7/46, 116; lends P money, 7/101; ruined by Fire, 7/297, 309; death, 8/526 & n. 2; ~ his apprentice, 1/53–4, 307; his kinsman, 4/80; 7/309

KITE, Ellen, P's aunt: 4/131; 5/132

KITE, Margaret (Peg), P's cousin: orphaned, 2/172; left legacy, 2/173;

troublesome to P as executor, 2/179, 190, 192; marries weaver, 2/209, 231; husband demands marriage portion, 3/161

KITE, Sarah: see Giles

KITE, Mrs —— (Aunt Kite; 'my aunt the Butcher'): see Clarke, Julian

KIUPRILLI, Ahmed, Turkish Grand Vizier 1661–d.76: death reported, 5/236, 237, n. 1

KNAPP, [John]: solicits for places in navy, 4/407 & n. 1; claims to be royal physician, ib.

KNEPP, [Christopher], horse dealer, husband of Elizabeth: 9/391; jealous of P, 6/323; 7/2; social: 7/16, 369

KNEPP (Knipp), [Elizabeth], actress: CHRON. SERIES: P meets at Greenwich, 6/320 & n. 5; admires, 6/321; 7/1; she signs letter 'Bab Allen', 7/4; P replies as 'Dapper Dicky', 7/5; gives her money, 7/61; 9/309; and gloves, 7/70; his valentine, 8/86, 100; her unhappy marriage, 7/5, 7; pregnant, 7/133, 173; birth and death of son Samuel, 7/196, 198, 236; P fondles, 7/2; 8/29; 9/170, 172, 188, 189–90, 218; EP's jealousy of, 7/120, 236–8 passim; 8/25, 211, 371–2, 399, 599; 9/1, 108, 436, 469; P vows to see no more, 9/339, 368, 391; avoids in theatre, 9/381, 405

HER PERFORMANCES: T. Killigrew's opinion, 8/55, 430; P admires in *The scornful lady*, 7/422; *The custom of the country*, 8/3; *The Indian emperor*, 8/14 & n. 2; *The humourous lieutenant*, 8/27; *The Chances*, 8/46; *The troubles of Queen Elizabeth*, 8/388–9; *The northern lass*, 8/437; *The Duke of Lerma*, 9/81; *The Storm*, 9/133 & n. 1; *The sea voyage*, 9/201 & n. 1; *The silent woman*, 9/310 & n. 2; also acts in *The Goblins*, 8/28–9, 232; *Flora's Vagaries*, 8/463 & n. 5; *The Surprizal*, 9/166 & n. 2; *The Heiress*, 9/435–6; P admires her singing, 8/3, 27, 46; 9/436; and dancing, 8/388–9; alluded to, 8/196; 9/200, 282, 320

HER SINGING (at parties etc.): P enraptured by, 6/321; sings *Barbara Allen*, 7/1; Italian song, 8/57; English songs, 8/599; with P, 7/44, 69, 92–3, 95, 237, 362; he teaches her *Beauty Retire*, 7/53,

54; and *It is decreed*, 7/369; teaches P *The Lark*, 9/299; also, 6/323–4; 7/341, 343–4; 8/65, 86; 9/128, 131, 189
SOCIAL: dances, 7/73; 9/12–13, 134, 289; introduces P to Nell Gwyn, 8/27; at theatre, 7/347; 8/137–8, 156, 383, 395, 463; 9/12; theatre gossip from, 8/168–9; 9/19–20, 155–6; at Vauxhall, 9/219; also, 7/18, 84, 103–4, 257; 8/598; 9/276
ALLUDED TO: 6/342; 7/3, 15–16; 8/242 ~ her daughter, 8/57; her pretty maid Betty: 9/156; P kisses, 9/201, 320–1

KNIGHT, [John], Surgeon to the King: 3/299; ~ his wife, ib.

KNIGHT, [Mary], singer: P admires her voice, 8/453 & n. 4; 9/299

KNIGHT, Sir John, navy agent, Bristol: 9/235 & n. 2

KNIGHTLEY, [Richard], Rector of Charwelton, Northants., 1663–95: proposed as husband for Lady Jemima Mountagu, 3/84 & n. 1

KNIGHTLY, [Robert], merchant, of Seething Lane: wants churchyard limed during Plague, 7/31; social: 2/239–40; 7/31–2, 278, 280; alluded to: 6/142; ~ Mary, ?his daughter, 9/221 & n. 1

KNIGHTSBRIDGE [*see also* Taverns etc.: World's End]: P visits, 5/181; 6/89

KNIPP: *see* Knepp

KÖNIGSBERG (Quinsborough), East Prussia: stories of, 4/412

KRAG (Kragh), Otte, Danish ambassador-extraordinary to the United Provinces 1659–60: 1/153–4

KUFFELER, Johannes Siberius, inventor: his explosive mine, 3/45–6 & n.

KYNASTON, [Edward], actor: in *The loyal subject*, 1/224 & n. 3; *The silent woman*, 2/7 & n. 4; *The island princess*, 9/441 & n. 4; assaulted for mimicking Sedley in *The Heiress*, 9/435 & n. 3, 435–6

LACEY, [John], actor and dramatist [*see also* Plays]: imprisoned for part in *The change of crowns*, 8/168 & n. 1, 172–3; said to be dying, 8/334 & n. 3; imitated in puppet play, 9/445 & n. 2; P admires in *The French dancing*

master, 3/87–8 & nn.; *Love in a maze*, 3/88 & nn.; 4/179 & n. 3; 8/195–6; 9/177–8; *The Committee*, 4/181 & n. 1; 8/384 & n. 3; *The faithful shepherdess*, 4/182; *The change of crowns*, 8/167–8 & n.; also acts in *The humourous lieutenant*, 4/128 & n. 4; in own adaptation of *The taming of the shrew*, 8/158 & n. 2; dances in *The jovial crew*, 9/411–12 & n.; and in *Horace*, 9/420 & n. 2; alluded to: 7/77

[LAFRERI, Antonio, d. 1577]: print by, 7/102–3 & n.

LAM, Mother: *see* Taverns etc.

LAMB, [James], Canon of Westminster: sermon, 1/261

LAMBART (Lambert), [Rose], Viscountess Lambart (d. 1649), first wife of Richard Lambart, succ. 1660 as 2nd Earl of Cavan: 9/215 & n. 3

LAMBERT, [David], naval officer: lieutenant on *Naseby*, 1/105; P tells of diary, 1/107; his gittern, 1/169; instructs P on naval matters, 1/259; 2/13, 115; married, 2/23; house, 2/116, 123; transferred to 4th-rate, 2/90; captain of *Norwich*, 2/115, 203–4; stories of Lisbon, 2/196–7; sails for Mediterranean, 2/214, 219; and Tangier, 3/67; 4/100–1; social: 1/75, 102, 106, 107, 120, 162, 164, 166, 258–9; 2/23, 25, 49, 101, 196–7, 207; alluded to: 1/27; ~ his wife, 2/123; father-in-law, 2/197

LAMBERT, [James], naval officer: captain of *Anne* yacht, 3/63; killed in action, 6/225

LAMBERT, Maj.-Gen. John, republican (d. 1683): opposes Rump, 1/1 & n. 4; rumoured advance on London, 1/4 & n. 5; support in army, 1/7; indemnity offered to, 1/6, 7; submits to Rump, 1/8; defies Rump, 1/51 & n. 2; to appear before Council of State, 1/74 & n. 3; imprisoned in Tower, 1/81; escapes, 1/108 & n. 1; captured, 1/114–15, 117; sent to Guernsey, 2/204 & n. 1; old lodgings in Whitehall, 5/164; alluded to: 2/92

LAMBERT, ——, servant to Coventry: 4/258

LAMBETH, Surrey [For Lambeth ale, *see* Drink. See *also* Taverns etc.:

Three Mariners]: P visits, 2/25, 120; 4/213–14, 317; 7/103; 8/346; yacht building, 3/164; Plague, 6/289; bonfire, 9/172; gipsies, 9/278 & n. 2

LAMBETH MARSH etc.: 4/317; 5/219

LAMBETH PALACE: P admires, 9/554; new hall, 6/164 & n. 2; other visits, 4/217; also, 9/550

LAMBTON, [Margaret] (d. 1730): marriage, 9/512 & n. 2

LANDGUARD FORT, Harwich: Dutch attack, 8/317

LANE, Betty: see Martin

LANE, Doll: see Powell

LANE, Sir George, cr. Viscount Lanesborough 1676; secretary to Ormond (d. 1683): profits and corruption, 4/331–2 & n.; 5/73 & n. 6; lawsuit concerning Irish land, 5/324 & n. 1; also, 2/140; 3/52

LANEY, Benjamin, Bishop of Peterborough 1660–3, Lincoln 1663–7, Ely 1667–d. 75: 4/98–9 & n.

LANGFORD, [William], tailor: P's good opinion 5/106; leases Tom P's house, 5/106; 9/399; recommends cook-maid, 5/158; complains about P's father, 5/244, 251–2; in country during Plague, 7/13; as P's tailor, 5/142, 144, 240, 308; 6/62, 104, 124, 125; ~ his wife, 5/244, 252

LANGLEY, ——, government (?Exchequer) clerk: 2/31, 40; 5/30

LANGUAGES [No attempt is made to index the occasional foreign phrases, mottoes and inscriptions in the text. Asterisks denote books read.]:

GENERAL: sign language, 2/160; 7/363; 'universal characters', 5/12 & n. 4; Wilkins's book, 7/12 & n. 6; 8/554 & n. 2; dialect, 9/232; hunting jargon, 8/475; de Cordemoy's book, 9/385–6 & n.

FRENCH [see also Pepys, Elizabeth; her reading]: spoken in The Hague, 1/139; proverb quoted by Tom P, 5/86–7; Coventry requires of clerks, 8/207; (P): speaks, 1/99, 260–1; comments on spoken French, 1/139; 4/58; 9/197; hears sermons/services in, 3/207, 270, 296; 5/17, 18, 342; writes, 1/153–4; argues about word, 6/223;

reads/buys books/songs in; anon., 2/35; 4/411–12 & n.; 5/58; 9/428, 431–2* & n.; Psalms, 1/140 & n. 3; by [Besongne], 9/428 & n. 2; [de Bussy], 7/114 & n. 3; Fournier, 9/17 & n. 5; [Furetière], 6/302* & n. 2; [Gomberville], 1/35 & n. 2; [La Calprenède], 9/365 & n. 1, 545* & n. 1, Marnix, 9/428 & n. 3; Mersenne, 9/148 & n. 3, 216*; [Millot et l'Ange], 9/21–2* & n., 57–8*, 59*; [Parival], 4/410–11* & n.; Sorbière, 5/297 & n. 2; 9/206*; also, 1/90; 2/35*

GREEK: schoolboys examined in, 4/33; neglected in Colet's time, 5/38 & n. 2; (P): corrects brother's speech, 1/18; quotes Epictetus, 3/194, 231; 4/16; objects to false Greek, 4/259; examines brother, 4/269; uses in polyglot, 6/202; examines Mountagu twins, 8/472; buys lexicon, 5/198 & n. 3

HEBREW: schoolboys examined in, 4/33 & n. 4; (P): buys grammar, 1/28 & n. 5; hears in synagogue, 4/335

ITALIAN: (P): sings, 1/63; 2/126; listens to songs, 8/56; fails to understand, 8/54, 55, 599; misquotes, 3/7–8 & n.; quotes proverb, 4/137; reads translations, 7/206* & n. 4; 9/535* & n. 3, 542*; alludes to La puttana errante, 9/22 & n. 1

LATIN: spoken in The Hague, 1/139; by woman, 2/68; extemporary, 2/21; schoolboys examined, 4/33; restored in legal proceedings, 7/114 & n. 2; English pronunciation, 9/544 & n. 5; Seneca alluded to, 8/507; (P): speaks, 1/99, 142; 4/386; sings, 1/63 & n. 3; 9/194; receives letters, 1/137; 7/50; teaches young Edward Mountagu, 1/165; and Mountagu twins, 8/472; examines Sandwich's page, 1/312; objects to 'false Latin', 4/190; shocked at Carteret's ignorance, 4/217; takes sermon notes in, 4/268, 278; hears speech at Royal Society, 8/554; reads/acquires books: Alsted, 1/275 & n. 4; Bacon, Faber Fortunae, 2/102* & n. 1, 5/39*; 7/72*, 129*, 242*, 346; Bacon, Organum, 1/140 & n. 4; Barclay, 1/231 & n. 1; 4/369*; Bartholinus, 1/243 & n. 2; [Bate], 1/67 & n. 3; 4/42 & n. 1; Bible, 4/189, 190, 193, 204, 236, 269;

theatre, 8/172-3 & n.; affray at prize-
fight, 8/239; assault in King's presence,
9/451-2 & n.; by hired bullies,
9/435-6 & n., 441, 471, 557 & n. 2,
558; P fears for EP's safety, 9/549;
also, 1/215, 303; 2/30, 228-9; 3/34
& n. 2, 35-6 & n., 196, 212; 5/32 &
n. 3; 6/306-7; 7/369 & n. 3, 380;
8/90 & n. 3, 206, 208-9, 319, 321 &
n. 3, 348-9 & n.; 9/111 & n. 1, 166,
412 & n. 2, 470 & n. 1
DUELS:
　　GENERAL: P disapproves, 3/171;
proclamations against, ib. & n. 2; bill
against, 9/53 & n. 1; serving officers
arrested to prevent, 8/140-1; 9/273
　　PARTICULAR: Chesterfield and
Wolley, 1/20 & n. 1; Sandwich and
Buckingham (challenge), 2/32-3;
Cholmley and Ned Mountagu, 3/157
& n. 2; 4/47; Jermyn and Rawlins,
3/170-1 & nn.; P fears challenge from
Holmes, 4/83-4; Seymour and Commissioner Pett (challenge), 7/212 &
n. 1; Spragge and Commissioner Pett
(challenge), ib.; Ossory and Buckingham (challenge), 7/343 & n. 3, 350;
Holmes and Smith, 7/348; Porter and
Belasyse, 8/363-4 & n., 377, 384;
Buckingham and Shrewsbury, 9/26-7
& nn.; Halifax or Coventry and
Buckingham (rumoured challenge),
9/462; Leijonbergh and P (challenge,
1670), 8/22, n. 1; also, 3/53; 4/47;
7/376; 8/173
HIGHWAY ROBBERY: 3/34 & n. 2
RIOTS AND DISORDERS [for seamen's
mutinies, *see* Navy: seamen]: by
apprentices, 1/39 & n. 1, 54; 5/99-100
& n.; in churches, 3/178 & n. 2;
9/96 & n. 1; by seamen, 4/292 & n. 2,
294; 6/255, 288 & n. 5, 303; 7/330 &
n. 3, 415-16; 8/60 & n. 1, 62-3, 272;
fanatics, 6/184 & n. 3; in inns of
court, 8/223 & n. 3; 9/465-6 & n.; by
mob: for recall of parliament, 8/268;
against Clarendon, 8/269 & n. 2; for
'Reformation and Reducement', 9/
129-34 passim & nn., 152; ～ in
Paris, 8/299-300 & nn.
LAWES, Henry, composer (d. 1662)
[*see also* Musical Compositions]: ill,
1/324

LAWES, William, composer, brother
of Henry (d. 1645): *see* Musical
Compositions
LAWRENCE, Goody, P's nurse:
house at Kingsland, 5/132
LAWRENCE, [Henry], merchant: to
go to Algiers, 1/321 & n. 2
LAWRENCE, Sir John, Lord Mayor
1664-5: gives dinner, 6/126; ～ his
father [Abraham], ib.
LAWRENCE, [Samuel]: 4/265; ～ his
wife, ib.
LAWSON, [Abigail], daughter of Sir
John: her funeral, 2/131-2 & n.
LAWSON, [Isabella], wife of Sir
John: at Penn's, 4/23; 5/6, 7; also,
7/264
LAWSON, [Isabella], daughter of Sir
John: *see* Norton
LAWSON, Sir John, kted 1660, naval
commander (in 1660 'the Vice-
Admiral') and member of the Tangier Committee:
CHARACTER: 1/106, 159; 4/12, 24, 376;
6/138; 7/195; ～ cartoon, 1/45
NAVAL CAREER: under Commonwealth,
1/1, 62, 79 & n. 1; 4/375; 8/125;
relations with Sandwich, 1/95, 98,
107; 3/121-2 & n.; agrees to serve
King, 1/100, 130; commissioned,
1/110; knighted, 1/254; voyages to
N. Africa, 3/79 & n. 2, 89, 121, 263 &
n. 4, 271; 4/3-4 & n., 6, 73, 369 & n. 2,
415 & n. 1; 5/141 & n. 4, 295, 299;
accounts etc., 4/12, 104, 325, 414-15;
his ship blown up, 6/52 & n. 1;
wounded in action, 6/122, 129; death,
6/131, 132, 138; funeral, 6/145;
family impoverished, 6/150-1; alleged
plundering, 6/276; also, 1/249; 4/73;
5/15, 17; 6/10, 11; 7/227 & n. 2
TANGIER BUSINESS: proposals for construction of mole, 4/13, 26-7, 31, 35-
6; contract signed, 4/88 & n. 3; new
proposals opposed, 5/303, 343; profits, 6/71, 101, 103; 8/593; attends
meetings, 4/23; 5/11; 6/61; also, 6/39
SOCIAL: 1/114, 115, 167, 317; 2/66;
4/23, 53; 5/6
ALLUDED TO: 1/134, 153, 159
～ his daughters, 6/150
LAWSON, [?Samuel, son of Sir
John]: 6/100-1 & n., 185

[LAWSON, Miss ——]: 5/58 & n. 2
LAXTON, —— [?error for Layton],
Sandwich's apothecary: 1/73; 5/178;
~ his wife and daughters, 5/178
LAYTON: see Leighton
LEA (Leigh), [Matthias and Thomas],
under-clerks of Council of State: 1/23
LEA BAILEY, Forest of Dean: 3/114 &
n. 5
LEAD, Mr ——: makes vizard for P,
9/533(2), 547
LEADENHALL MARKET: see Fairs
and Markets
LEADENHALL ST [see also Taverns
etc.: Sun; Swan]: mum-house, 3/94;
5/191; morris-dancing, 4/120; execu-
tion, 5/23; conventicle, 9/385
LEATHERHEAD, Surrey: P at, 2/91
LE BLANC, Mlle ——, governess in
Sandwich's household: at Bartholo-
mew Fair, 2/166; at theatre, 2/214;
5/138-9; social: 2/198; 3/68; alluded
to: 2/232; 4/29
LE BRUN, [?Christian, of St Olave's
parish]: 7/246
LECHMERE (Leechmore), [Nicholas],
lawyer, kted 1689, Judge of Exchequer
Bench 1689-1700 (d. 1701): in Field's
case, 3/231
LECTURER, our: see St Olave's
Church, Hart St
LEE, Sir Thomas, M.P. Aylesbury,
Bucks.: critic of Navy Board, 9/103-4
LEE, ——, lawyer: to prosecute Vane,
3/88
LEE, Essex: see Leigh
LEESON, [Robert], barber-surgeon:
extracts EP's tooth, 9/557
LEGGE, George, son of Col. William;
cr. Baron Dartmouth 1682: his early
promotion, 9/40 & n. 1
LEGGE, Col. William, Lieutenant-
General and Treasurer of the Ordnance: to supply Tangier garrison,
5/279 & n. 3; allowance reduced,
8/178 & n. 3; at gun trial, 9/528; lends
money to Carteret, 8/180; reputedly
Catholic, 8/265 & n. 1; Duke of York's
affection, 9/39; his part in Charles I's
escape from Hampton Court (1648),
6/316-17 & n.
LEGHORN: quarantine, 4/417-18 &
n.; also, 4/201

LE HAVRE: Sandwich at, 2/32
LEICESTER HOUSE: 9/333
LEIGH: see Lea
LEIGH (Lee), [Robert]: in search for
Barkstead's treasure, 3/240-1 & n.,
246, 250-1, 284, 285, 286; stories
of Spain (alluded to), 3/251
LEIGH (Lee) ROAD, off Leigh-on-
Sea: ships in, 1/103; 6/54
LEIGH-ON-SEA (Lee), Essex: 8/136,
343, 344, 354
LEIGHTON, Sir Ellis, secretary of the
Prize Commission: his wit, 5/300 &
n. 5; counsel to Navy Board, 8/27,
131, 133; news from, 7/160; social:
5/11
LEIJONBERGH, Baron: see Barck-
mann
LEITH: 7/224; 8/425
LELY, Sir Peter: proud, 8/129; successful, 3/230; 7/209; compared with
J. M. Wright, 3/113; Huysmans,
5/254; and Hayls, 8/129; portraits:
Sandwich, 1/262 & n. 2, 271 & n. 1;
Duchess of York, 3/112-13 & n.; 7/82
& n. 1; Charles II, 3/113 & n. 2;
Lady Castlemaine, 3/113 & n. 3;
7/359 & n. 3; Lady Carteret, 5/104 &
n. 4; flag-officers, 7/102 & n. 3, 209;
maids of honour, 9/284 & n. 4; his
table book, 7/209; social: 6/166
LEMING (Lemon), Mary (b. Batten):
?1/317; ?2/19, 22, 23; 2/57, 59,
61, 78, 82; 4/218; ~ her old nurse,
3/205
LEMING, ——, of Colchester, husband of the foregoing: fatally ill,
3/169-70
LE NEVE, [Richard], naval officer:
drunken quarrel, 7/380
LEN(N)OX, Duke of: see Stuart,
Charles, Duke of Richmond and
Duke of Lennox
LENTHALL, [Sir] John, brother of
William: arrests Quakers, 4/271 &
n. 2
LENTHALL, (Sir) John, son of William; M.P. Abingdon, Berks.: censured by Commons, 1/151 & n. 3
LENTHALL, William, Speaker of the
House of Commons: resumes chair,
1/25 & n. 5; refuses to sign warrants
for elections, 1/61 & n. 2

LINCOLN'S INN FIELDS THEATRE [see also Theatres]: Davenant buried from, 9/158 & n. 2
LION QUAY: 4/273
LIPHOOK, Hants.: 9/274
LISBON: dirt and poverty, 2/197 & n. 1; Sandwich's prints, 4/286 & n. 1; Sandwich at, 2/186, 209; 3/51; Spanish fleet off, 3/110; Stayner's death, 3/249 & n. 1; also, 8/374-5 & n.
[LISLE, Thomas], Master of the Barber-Surgeons' Company: at anatomy lecture, 4/59 & n. 1
LISOLA, Franz Paul de, Imperial Resident 1666-7, 1667-8 [see also Books]: at theatre, 8/383-4 & n.; ~ his wife and pretty daughter [Eleanora], ib.
LISSON GREEN, Mdx: P visits, 1/210; 7/204-5, 240
LITTLECOTE HOUSE, Wilts.: P admires, 9/241-2 & n.
LITTLE SAXHAM, Suff.: King at, 9/336 & n. 4
LITTLETON, [James], merchant: victualling contract, 9/287 & n. 1; appointed cashier to Navy Treasurer, 9/357 & n. 2
LITTLETON, Sir Thomas, M.P. Much Wenlock, Salop 1661-79; Joint-Treasurer of the Navy 1668-71: his conversation, 7/210 & n. 1; on commission of accounts, 8/194, 252; opposes standing army, 8/353; to undertake parliamentary management, 9/71 & n. 2; criticises Navy Board, 9/103-4; appointed Joint-Treasurer, 9/341, 346, 351; claims precedence at office table, 9/365; overbearing, 9/412; critical of Board's constitution, 9/550; Duke of York distrusts, 9/408, 410, 507; at dockyard pay, 9/412, 419; navy estimates and debts, 9/444-5, 447, 493-4, 525; supports Child as Penn's successor, 9/549-50; attends meetings, 9/357, 369, 383, 393
LITTLE TOWER HILL: 4/55
LITTLE TURNSTILE (off Holborn): 9/435
LLEWELLYN, [Peter], clerk to E. Dering, timber merchant: dismissed

from underclerkship to Council, 1/23; on Naseby, 1/111, 114; returns from Ireland, 4/295 & n. 2; Irish news from, ib.; Dering's business, 4/422, 436; 5/1, 2, 5; 6/185, 242, 245; dies in Plague, 6/304; social: in mock marriage, 1/175; drunk and amorous, 1/244; bawdy story, 2/43, 50; at Bartholomew Fair, 2/166; in Hyde Park, 3/78; at taverns/cookshops etc., 1/25, 27, 31, 37, 38, 87, 92, 174, 195, 208, 212, 232, 233, 248, 257, 311; 2/193; 5/330; visits/dines with P, 2/39, 201; 3/48; 4/326, 415, 421; 5/7, 26, 78, 106, 270, 281, 294, 308, 351; 6/38, 65, 98; also, 1/26, 59, 86; 2/42, 125, 208; alluded to: 1/116; ~ his brother to go to Constantinople, 1/250
LLOYD, Sir Godfrey, military engineer: on fortifications, 8/126 & n. 2
LLOYD, [Philip], clerk to Sir W. Coventry, kted 1674: dances, 7/362; ?9/128; dismissed for idleness, 8/206
LLOYD (Floyd), Sir Richard, M.P. Radnorshire: 4/77
LLOYD, [Thomas], secretary to the Prize Commissioners: 8/58
LLOYD (Floyd), [William], chaplain to the King 1666, Bishop of St Asaph 1680; Lichfield and Coventry 1692; Worcester 1700 (d. 1717) [see also Books]: sermons, 7/382-3; 8/587 & n. 3; also, 8/541 & n. 1
LLOYD (Floyd), ——, captain of merchantman: 5/30
LOCK(E), Matthew, composer (d. 1677) [see also Music; Musical Compositions]: sings with P, 1/63
LOCK, [Matthew], secretary to Albemarle: political news from, 1/50-1; exorbitant fees, 6/260; 7/323-4 & n.
[LOCKETT, Adam]: see Taverns etc.
[LOCKHART, Sir William], Governor of Dunkirk 1658-60 (d. 1676): 5/62 & n. 2
LODUM, Mrs ——: B. St Michel's landlady, 3/286; niece to be EP's companion, 4/19, 21; social: 4/45
LOGGIN(G)S, [John], chorister Chapel Royal: 8/393-4 & n.
LOMBARD (Lumber) ST [see also

9/531–2 & n.; Parish Clerks': P dines with, 1/19; Skinners': entertains Monck, 1/106; liverymen, 4/21; Watermen's: 3/196 & n. 4; Woodmongers': surrenders charter, 8/520 & n. 4

LONDON BRIDGE: piles for, 5/188; P falls into hole, 5/307; pavers at work, 6/312; pales blown off, 7/22; difficulty of passage through: anecdote of Frenchman's fear, 3/160; tides, 3/52; 6/143, 327; 8/202; also, 1/323; 2/59, 101; 3/68, 198, 260; P shoots at night, 6/143, 156

LONDON GAZETTE, the: see Newspapers

LONDON WALL: Plague, 6/150; P drives by to avoid ruins after Fire, 7/358, 364, 395; 8/448, 451, 458, 459; 9/55, 134, 172; ruins in, 8/6

LONG, [?Israel], attorney: in Field's case, 4/201

LONG, Sir Robert, Auditor of the Receipt at the Exchequer: financial business, 4/81; 6/95, 96; 7/76, 79, 137; 8/102, 205, 576; 9/302, 387; defends Additional Aid, 6/311, 312; submits poll tax accounts, 9/82; story of battue, 7/79; house at Westminster, 4/272; and in Surrey, 6/312 & n. 2; ~ his niece, 4/272; kinswomen, 6/312

LONG ACRE: brothels, 5/50

LONG LANE: Plague, 6/150

LONGRACK, [John], purveyor of timber to the navy: wedding reception, 7/262–3

LONG REACH (in the Thames): 1/95; 7/149

LOOKER, Mr ——, gardener to the Earl of Salisbury: bawdy story, 1/59; shows P Hatfield House and garden, 2/139

LOOSDUINEN, Holland: described, 1/149; monument to 365 children, 1/148–9 & n.

LOOTEN, Jan, landscape-painter (d. ?1681): 9/514 & n. 2

LORIMERS' HALL: funeral, 9/200 & n. 2

LOTTERIES: at court, 5/214–15 & n.; management by Fishery Corporation, 5/269 & n., 276, 279, 294, 299–300 & n., 323; 6/53; Virginia lottery

alluded to, 5/323; P wins books, 7/48 & n. 1

LOUD, ——, page to Sandwich: examined by P in Latin, 1/312; also, 1/300; 2/15, 17; ~ his mother, 1/312

LOUIS XIV, King of France 1643–1715 [for his public policy, see France]: admiration for Mazarin, 4/26 & n. 2; love of work, ib.; illness, 4/156–7 & n., 159, 162, 163, 166, 169, 189; reviews guards, 4/189; rumoured assassination, 6/257, 259; shoots partridges, 7/79; his attitude to mistresses, 8/183 & n. 2; gift to Frances Stuart, 8/184 & n. 1; association with Elizabeth Berkeley, 8/338 & n. 1; prints of, 9/427 & n. 1, 451 & n. 1

LOVE, Ald. William: elected M.P. for London, 2/57 & n. 1

LOVELACE, Col. [Francis], of Cannon Row: P consults on tax assessment, 3/285 & n. 1

LOVELL (Loven), [?Charles], lawyer: P consults, 4/22, 33

LOVETT, ——, varnisher: pleasant, 7/124; lazy rogue, 7/258; 8/124, 206; new varnish, 6/97; varnishes paper for P, 6/97; 7/119–20, 124, 130, 184, 198–9, 211, 232, 353; P dissatisfied, 7/151, 258; imitation tortoise-shell, 7/184–5; varnishes prints, 7/185, 409; 8/23, 171, 204, 206; of crucifixion, 7/211, 218, 353; and of St Clara, 7/409; P godfather at son's (Catholic) christening, 7/329; to go to Spain, 8/23; social: 7/134

LOVETT, ——, wife of the varnisher: P admires, 6/97; 7/120, 134, 329; works with husband, 7/130, 198; 8/124; plays lute, 7/134, 199

LOWDER: *see* Lowther

[LOWE, Timothy], of Greenwich: 4/283; 6/242 & n. 1

LOWER (Lowre), [Richard], physician: at dissection of eyes, 9/254–5

LOWESTOFT (Lastoffe): 6/130

LOWESTOFT, BATTLE OF: *see* War, the Second Dutch: naval movements and actions (1665)

[LOWMAN, John], keeper of the White Lion prison: 8/81 & n. 5

LOWTHER (Lowder), Anthony:

MATTHEWS, Capt. Richard: 1/33 &
n. 3, 88, 163
MATTHEWS, ——, prize fighter:
4/167
MAULEVERER, Sir R[ichard]: joins
King at Breda, 1/117 & n. 1
MAWES: see Maes
MAY, Adrian, Groom of the Privy
Chamber to the King: 6/265
MAY, Baptist (Bab), Keeper of the
Privy Purse to the King: news from,
6/121; defeated in parliamentary
election, 7/337 & n. 2; profits, 8/324 &
n. 4; on country gentlemen, ib.,
8/361; supports H. Brouncker, 8/416;
plays tennis, 8/418–19; enemy of
Clarendon, 8/525; alluded to: 8/366,
412; 9/336–7
MAY, Hugh, Paymaster of the King's
Works: P's regard for, 6/200; 9/269;
on garden design, 7/213; on rebuilding of city, 7/384–5; 8/33; his new
buildings at Whitehall, 8/417 & n. 2;
9/251 & n. 4, 269 & n. 3; to examine
P's office papers, 9/417–18, 436; relations with Buckingham, 9/491 & n. 2;
pension, 9/491–2 & n.; social: 9/518,
527–8, 557–8
MAY, ——, landlady of Rochester
tavern: a bawdy jade, 8/312
MAY DAY: maypoles: 1/121, n. 1; at
Deal, ib. (2); The Hague, 1/139 &
n. 3; in Strand, ?8/206; coach parade
in Hyde Park, 1/121 & n. 1; 2/91;
4/119–20; 5/139; 8/196–7; 9/182, 537,
540–1; morris-dancing, 4/120; milkmaids dance, 8/193 & n. 2
MAY-DEW, as face lotion: 8/240;
9/549, 551
MAYER(S), [Robert], purveyor of
timber to the Navy, Woolwich:
4/103 & n. 4, 381
MAYLARD, Maylord: see Mallard
MAYNARD, Sir John, King's Serjeant: unpopularity, 2/88 & n. 1;
arbiter in dispute, 4/203; asks Backwell for loan, 8/528–9; ~ his wife
[Jane] dies, 9/141
[MAYNE, Jasper], Canon of Christ
Church, Oxford [see also Plays]:
preaches before King on adultery,
3/60 & n. 2
MAZARIN, Jules, Cardinal, French

minister: death, 2/48 & n. 5; influence
on Louis XIV, 4/26 & n. 2; Bristol's
falsity to, 4/212–13 & nn.; will,
4/411–12 & n.
MEADE, ——: 1/219
MEDALS [see also Coinage]: of Charles
X of Sweden, 1/238 & n. 1; 2/49;
Breda medal, 8/83 & n. 1
MEDICI, Cosimo de', Grand Duke of
Tuscany (Cosimo III) 1670–1723:
visits London, 9/509 & n. 2, 526, 534;
appearance, 9/509, 515; in mourning,
9/515 & n. 3, 563; firework display
for, 9/563
MEDICINE: see Health (illness etc.);
Health (remedies etc.)
MEDITERRANEAN, the (the Straits):
(royal) ships for/from, 1/119 & n. 3,
234; 2/214, 219; 6/192, 286; 7/143;
9/473 & n. 4, 513, 552; piracy, 3/13;
5/41–2 & n., 49; 6/10, 111; 9/724;
Dutch fleet, 6/8, 11; rumours of de
Ruyter in, 5/121, 309, 354; French
enforce salute, 6/278 & n. 3; 9/560 & n. 2
MEDOWS, Mr ——, servant to Lady
Wright: 6/161
MEDWAY, the, Kent: P and colleagues sail up, 6/194; P enjoys views,
9/495; 'land-admiral' in, 8/149; defences: installed, 8/84, 125, 126;
broken by Dutch, 8/260–2 passim,
268–9, 310; examined by P, 8/308,
309, 314; alluded to, 8/278, 327; new
defences, 9/57
MEGGOT (Maggett), [Richard], Rector of St Olave, Southwark: his
preaching, 5/356 & n. 2
[MEGGS, Mary], 'Orange Mall' of the
Theatre Royal: theatre news from,
7/264 & n. 3; 8/402; carries messages,
8/395, 598–9; saves theatre-goer from
choking, 8/517
[MELLO, Francesco, Marquez de
Sande de], Portuguese ambassador:
returns to Portugal, 2/128–9 & n.;
ambassador to Holland, 8/251 & n. 3
[MELLO DE CASTRO, D. Antonio
de], Governor of Bombay: refuses to
surrender, 4/139 & n. 2
MEMORY, the, faculty of: Tom
Fuller's remarkable gift, 2/21 & n. 2;
also, 5/12
MENDICANCY: beggars near Roth-

Trinity House, 3/93; 4/185; dines at, 3/190; 4/209; 7/381–2; on Chatham Chest Commission, 3/257; 6/68; Tangier Committee, 3/272; 4/319; 6/139; 9/316; and Royal Fishery, 5/199

HEALTH: lame, 4/314; 8/4; seriously ill, 7/253, 255(2), 261, 289; 8/296, 298, 314, 315, 324; also, 4/120; 5/268; 6/21, 23; 7/405; 9/276

HOUSE/HOUSEHOLD: official lodgings at Seething Lane: upper room used by P, 3/38; to exchange lodgings with Turner, 3/111; affected by P's alterations, 3/193, 194, 195, 197, 199, 205, 216, 231, 244, 252, 255, 261; 5/356; P admires, 3/262; new entry, 3/247, 249, 250; complains of accommodation, 5/278 & n. 3; lodgings at Greenwich: 6/190; leaves Turner's lodgings, 7/296; also, 3/259; 4/51, 278; 6/210; 8/552, 555; ~ his servant George, 6/200; coachman, 9/527

INTELLECTUAL INTERESTS ETC.: visits Mint, 4/143–8; quotes Chaucer, 4/184; his pictures, 4/187, 191, 319; views royal collection, 8/403; recites verse, 4/200 & n. 4; interest in chemistry, 4/218; and anatomy, 4/334; prescribes medicines for P, 4/39, 40, 329; medical attendant at court in exile, 5/242 & n. 2; claims to have translated from Dutch, 5/235

POLITICS: opposes test bill, 4/125; friend of Clarendon, 4/196

SOCIAL: his mirth and mimicry, 6/220; 7/1–2; stories: of sanitation in Portugal, 3/205; longevity, 6/237 & n. 3; ancestor's murder, 8/141; and Sir L. Dyve and others, 8/566–7 & nn.; tells bawdy story, 3/243; his stories entered in P's book of anecdotes, 4/346; 8/95; at christenings, 4/165; 8/540; gives dinner for Clarendon, 4/173; at dinners given by Lord Mayor, 4/341; Carteret, 5/15; Coventry, 5/102, 166; Lieutenant of Tower, 6/56; Sir G. Smith, 6/187; Brouncker, 6/204; 7/1–2; Cocke, 6/220; Hickes, 6/222; Sandwich, 6/273; Penn, 8/3, 77; 9/283, 505; and Gauden, 9/214; gives dinners for colleagues and associates, 5/227, 357;

6/191, 237, 333; lends coach to EP, 6/45; his tiff with Battens, 6/233, 234; dines with P, 7/353; at parish dinners, 8/218; 9/179, 559; theatre, 9/269–70; Bartholomew Fair, 9/301; and taverns, 3/279; 5/308; 6/119; 8/220; 9/115, 222, 359; visits/dines with etc. Batten, 3/189; 4/171, 230, 237; 5/216; 6/220–1; 7/226, 8/376; P visits/dines with etc., 4/28; 5/335; 6/206, 210, 212; also, 4/155, 212, 225; 5/176, 217; 6/141; 7/76; 8/389

MISC.: almost drowned near Portsmouth, 3/283–4; praises beauty of Suffolk women, 4/186; on homosexuality, 4/210; on Spanish stamp tax, 7/332; inspects new Exchange Alley, 4/214; King's bawdy joke against, 5/12; Denham's verses on, 8/380 & n. 2; news from Holland, 7/228; 8/88; assessed for poll-tax, 8/120; foundling on doorstep, 9/304

ALLUDED TO: 3/198

~ his sister, 4/74; 6/233; 8/4; niece, 4/74; 8/4; 9/505

MERCER, Anne, Mary's sister: at dances at P's house, 7/230; 8/28, 493, 511; 9/42; runs for wagers, 8/167; also, 7/200, 246; 8/11, 19; 9/12, 96, 111, 197

MERCER, Mary, companion to EP:

CHRON. SERIES: pretty, 5/360; 8/375; growing fat, 8/508; proposed as companion, 5/229 & n. 2, 256 & n. 1; engaged, 5/257, 265, 267; with EP to Woolwich in Plague, 6/143, 183, 340; returns, 7/7; dress, 6/238; helps rule Navy Office books, 7/63, 100; washes P's ears, combs/cuts his hair, 6/21; 7/95; 8/280; quarrels with EP, 6/205, 206; 7/60, 175, 176; EP's jealousy of, 5/274; 7/228, 238; P fondles, 7/104, 172; dismissed by EP, 7/273; P misses her, 7/294; unwilling to return, 7/298–303 passim; visits EP, 7/360; P fondles/kisses again, 7/364; 8/37, 150; 9/55; EP displeased with, 8/79, 118; P's valentine, 9/67; visits Cambridge with EP and others, 9/306; also, 6/25, 66, 85; 7/138; 9/19, 98

MUSICAL: plays harpsichord/viol, 5/266, 282; sings with P/EP/others, 5/266; 6/138; 7/44, 53, 110, 111, 117, 172,

183, 195, 199, 205, 212, 216, 227, 228, 230, 267; 8/37, 165, 174, 223, 283, 289, 328, 375; 9/14, 85, 120, 179, 196, 197, 199, 201, 202, 204, 216, 217, 221, 249; her talent, 7/228; 8/29; P teaches *It is decreed*, 8/35; 9/14, 16; *Canite Jehovae*, 9/194; and the Lark's song, 9/304; her style of singing, 8/165–6
SOCIAL: at theatre, 5/267, 289, 335; 6/73; 7/412; 8/27, 157, 439–40, 508; 9/14, 19, 54, 85, 100, 189, 195, 198–9, 249, 269, 278, 280–1, 296, 304, 326; visits/shopping etc., 5/301; 6/40, 48–9, 87, 89, 102, 104, 121, 128, 223, 250, 251, 270, 282, 320–1; 7/18, 72, 78, 81, 84, 128, 131, 137, 152, 169, 172, 220; 8/431–2; river trips to Gravesend, Woolwich, etc., 5/305; 6/106, 111, 119; 7/142, 233, 235; 8/346; jaunts to Islington, Bow, Hackney, etc., 6/74, 112; 7/54–5, 108, 113, 126, 129, 133, 167, 170, 181–2, 240, 267; 8/150, 174–5, 296; 9/197, 208, 221, 271–2; at Vauxhall, 7/198; 9/195–6, 198–9, 203–4, 216; and Bartholomew Fair, 9/293, 296, 299; dances, 6/262, 279; 7/43–4, 246, 362; 8/29, 493, 511; 9/12, 42, 289; toasted at Bear garden, 7/245–6; visits P's house after leaving household, 7/200, 374, 403, 419, 421; 8/11, 13, 19, 157, 166, 282, 289, 594; 9/111, 213, 244, 250; also, 7/257, 267; 8/165, 167; 9/278
ALLUDED TO: 7/15; 9/454, 519
~ her sisters, 7/230
MERCER, [Nicola], Mary's mother: ends quarrel between EP and Mary, 7/176; annoyed at Mary's dismissal, 7/273, 300, 301; social: gives parties for naval victories, 7/152, 246; also, 5/257; 6/340; 7/43, 101, 200; 9/110, 111, 197, 276; alluded to: 7/175
MERCER, William, Mary's brother: ?provides fireworks for party, 7/152; makes valentine for EP, 8/62
MERCER, [William], Mary's father: 5/265
MERCER, P's: *see* Finch
MERCERS' CHAPEL, Cheapside: P visits, 2/20; in Fire, 7/277
MERCERS' COMPANY: *see* London: livery companies
MERCERS' HALL, Cheapside: P as

schoolboy at, 2/20; Council of Trade meets, ib.
MERCHANT STRANGERS' COMPANY: *see* London: livery companies
MERCHANT TAYLORS' HALL, Threadneedle St: 7/235
MERES, Sir Thomas, M.P. Lincoln: eloquent, 8/2; supports Buckingham, 8/342
MERITON, [John], Rector of St Michael, Cornhill: his high reputation, 7/365 & n. 3; also, 6/152
MERITON, [Thomas], Rector of St Nicholas Cole Abbey: an 'old dunce', 7/365 & n. 3; preaches well, 7/365; 8/222
MERRETT, Christopher, physician: on anatomy, 3/228 & n. 2; at Dr Wilkins's, 7/12; drunk at Royal Society club, 7/21
MERSTON, Messum: *see* Mossom
MERTON PRIORY, Surrey: bought by Thomas P of Hatcham, 9/207 & n. 2
MERVIN, [John], merchant: 6/164
MESSIAH, the false: *see* Sabbatai Zevi
METEORS: *see* Science and Mathematics: astronomy
MEXICO: coinage, 4/146
MEYNELL (Maynall), Ald. Francis, goldsmith-banker; Sheriff 1661–2: entertains P and colleagues, 3/200; income, 4/17; refuses to lend to Navy, 6/121; advances money to victualler, 6/254; death, 7/315; also, 5/33
MICHELANGELO: paintings copied, 3/80 & n. 1
MICO, [Edward], merchant: Dutch compensation to, 5/52 & n. 1
MIDDLEBURG, Holland: 1/137
MIDDLEBURGH, ——, merchant: 4/396
MIDDLEGROUND, the (shoal at mouth of Thames estuary): Dutch fleet in, 8/150
MIDDLESEX, Lord: *see* Sackville, Charles, 1st Earl of Middlesex
MIDDLESEX, Lady: *see* Cranfield
MIDDLE TEMPLE: Readers' Feast, 6/28 & n. 2, 49 & n. 2; gaming in Hall, 9/3 & n. 1; riot, 9/465–6 & n., 511–12
MIDDLETON, Elizabeth/Jane: *see* Myddelton

MILLET, Capt. [Henry]: book of ships' rates, 6/217 & n. 2; evidence against Commissioner Pett, 8/502

MILLICENT, Sir John, of Barham, Cambs: anecdote of, 3/159 & nn.

MINCING (Minchen) Lane: fire, 9/245

MINNES, Mince: *see* Mennes, Sir John; Myngs, Christopher

MINORIES, the: 4/84, 434; 7/423; 8/224; 9/204

MINORS, Capt. [Richard], naval officer: E. India Company business, 4/299 & n. 2, 396; 9/37

MITCHELL, Mrs [Ann], bookseller in Westminster Hall:
GENERAL: her illegitimate daughter, 5/9; leaves town in Plague, 6/162; kinswoman as maid to EP, 7/108, 109; asks P to help son, 8/341; also, 7/394; 8/72, 202, 479, 583; 9/99
AS BOOKSELLER: P pays, 1/26, 87; buys newspapers from, 6/162; and book, 8/10; reads pamphlets at, 7/393–4; P/EP visit(s), 1/30, 31, 66, 204, 222, 279; 2/31, 139; 3/296; 4/242, 251; 7/61, 123, 186, 295; 8/47, 68, 177, 440; 9/81, 486
~ her daughter, 9/265

MITCHELL, Betty, (b. Howlett), wife of Michael:
CHRON. SERIES: betrothed to Michael's brother, 5/9; 7/75; marries Michael, 7/75, 81; moves to Thames St, 7/98, 108, 114; to Shadwell after Fire, 7/351; unhappily married, 7/284; 8/479; keeps shop for mother, 8/121
P'S FONDNESS FOR: calls her 'wife', 4/234, 242; 7/75, 89; admires, 5/9, 41; 6/330–1; 7/61, 157, 175, 235, 365; 8/20, 21, 47, 51, 91, 121, 138, 159, 224, 236, 273; 9/548–9; mistakes another woman for, 7/303; 8/400; gifts to, 8/46, 53; kisses/fondles, 7/123, 197, 207, 230, 234, 338–9, 395, 419; 8/32, 46, 53, 110, 511; 9/564; she avoids/is cold to, 7/245, 418–19; 8/34, 68, 70, 440; 9/173
SOCIAL: with husband dines at/visits P's house, 7/206–7, 243, 311, 344, 418; 8/5–6, 166, 289, 412–13, 524; 9/255, 276; P visits, 7/255; 8/37, 58, 146, 151; 9/114, 198, 297, 328; at christen-

ing, 7/394; wedding anniversary, 8/72; also, 7/142, 161, 186, 337; 8/45, 66, 255
ALLUDED TO: 8/52, 504, 514; 9/124, 168
~ her first daughter (Betty) born, 8/53, 177, 186, 199-200, 202, 224; baptised, 8/202; dies, 8/273, 277, 289; her second daughter (Betty) born, 9/260, 264; her maid, 8/54

MITCHELL, [John], flagmaker: supplies, 4/73 & n. 2; gift to P, 4/220

MITCHELL, [Michael], keeper of strong-water house:
CHRON. SERIES: marries Betty Howlett, 7/75, 81; succeeds to brother's trade and house, 7/81, 114; P calls there, 7/157, 234–5; 8/20, 32, 34, 37, 58, 66, 94, 102, 120, 151, 175, 186, 199, 224, 504; 9/198, 249, 297; cashes pay tickets, 7/174–5 & n., 319, 338; employed on cork business, 7/206; house burnt in Fire, 7/268; moves to Shadwell, 7/284, 338; new shop, 7/339; house rebuilt, 8/20; 9/75, 114, 124; relations with wife, 7/284; 8/479, 511; prevents P from seeing her, 8/316; out of town, 9/564
SOCIAL: on river, 7/161; 8/34, 66, 68; to Hackney, 7/207; at christenings, 7/394; 8/202; wedding anniversary party, 8/72; at P's house, 7/206, 243, 311, 344, 365–6, 418; 8/5–6, 21, 51, 91, 138, 166, 236, 289, 413, 524; 9/255; also, 7/123; 8/493
ALLUDED TO: 9/99, 161

MITCHELL, [Miles], bookseller in Westminster Hall: at coronation banquet, 2/86; leaves town in Plague, 6/162; garden, 7/123; social: 1/204, 222; 8/68, 72, 202; alluded to: 7/308;
~ his (unnamed) son: betrothed to Betty Howlett, 5/9; 7/75; dies of plague, 7/75; ?alluded to, 6/186; another (unnamed) son: 8/341

[MODERS, Mary], 'the German princess'; imposter [*see also* Plays: *The German princess*]: in prison, 4/163 & n. 4; tried and acquitted, 4/177 & n. 2

MOFFETT (Muffett), [Thomas], physician and author (d. 1604): story of Dr Caius, 8/543 & n. 2

MOHUN (Moone), [Michael], actor: high reputation, 1/297; his part in

Lacy's quarrel with King, 8/168 &
n. 6; quarrels with Hart, 8/569; P
admires in *The beggar's bush*, 1/297 &
n. 3; in *The Traitor*, 1/300 & n. 1;
criticises in *The Moor of Venice*, 9/438
MOHUN (Moone), Capt. [Robert],
naval officer: ship wrecked off Cadiz,
6/19 & n. 3; reputation for ill-luck,
ib. & n. 4, 6/20
[MOLINA, Antonio Francesca Mesia,
de Tobar y Paz, Conde de], Spanish
ambassador 1665–9: 8/107; 9/544
& n.4
MOLINS (Mullins), Edward, surgeon:
leg amputated, 4/340 & n.1; death,
4/345
MOLINS, [James], surgeon: operates
on Rupert, 8/41 & n.2
MONCK, Anne, Duchess of Albemarle:
LOOKS AND CHARACTER (critical comments): 2/51; 6/324; 7/10, 56 & n. 2,
57, 354; 8/147
CHRON. SERIES: trades in appointments,
1/181 & n. 4, 184; 3/43 & n. 3; 8/219–
20; book fulsomely dedicated to,
1/275 & n. 2; speaks well of P, 4/231;
8/490; slanders Sandwich, 6/324;
7/10; and Penn, 9/138–9; dislikes
Coventry, 7/196; comments on du
Teil's incompetent gunnery, 8/147 &
n. 3; and on division of fleet (1666),
8/148; also, 1/53
SOCIAL: 2/51; 3/79; 6/268
ALLUDED TO: 8/228
MONCK, Christopher, styled Earl of
Torrington, succ. as 2nd Duke of
Albemarle 1670 (d. 1688): said to be
illegitimate, 8/536 & n. 2; also, 7/240
MONCK, George, cr. Duke of
Albemarle 1660, ('the General');
Captain-General of the Kingdom:
CHARACTER: P's low opinion, 1/87;
4/435; 6/68, 298; 7/11, 12, 204, 354;
8/499, 536, 586–7, 591; Sandwich's,
1/125; Blackborne's, 4/372–3; Coventry's, 7/203, 204; satire on, 8/21 &
n. 3; popularity, 7/203, 281; 9/205;
trusted by bankers, 7/178; ballad in
praise of, 8/99 & n. 2; bravery, 8/499
CHRON. SERIES: in Scotland, 1/1; ordered
to London, 1/8 & n. 5, 13; political
intentions, 1/16 & n. 3, 22 & n. 4, 30 &

n. 1, 33, 58, 75 & n. 5, 79, 102, 111;
5/297; arrives, 1/39, 40 & n. 2; attends
on Rump, 1/43 & n. 2; his power,
1/45, 74(2); action against city, 1/46–
51 passim & nn.; requires Rump to fill
vacancies, 1/50 & n. 1, 51 & n. 1, 54 &
n. 2; in city, 1/52, 53, 71; allies with
city, 1/54–5 & n.; addresses to, 1/55
& n.4, 73 & n. 1; allies with secluded
M.P.s, 1/60, 62 & nn.; made general,
1/62; entertained by livery companies, 1/71 & n. 2, 79, 106; made joint
general-at-sea, 1/71 & n. 4, 75; actions
against republicans, 1/81, 84, 109;
elected M.P., 1/109 & n. 1; relations
with Presbyterians, 1/117, 118–19;
granted money, 1/118; welcomes
King at Dover, 1/158; invested with
Garter, 1/161; appointed Treasury
Commissioner, 1/170 & n. 3; patent
of nobility, 1/188 & n. 1; appointed
Lord Lieutenant of Ireland, 1/227–8 &
n., 228–9; in trial of regicides, 1/263;
Overton's plot against, 1/318–19 &
n.; attends coronation, 2/82, 85, 86;
exempted from place bill, 4/136 &
n. 1; at Oxford in Plague, 6/310, 320;
appointed to Treasury Commission,
8/223, 229–30; rumoured appointment as Lord High Constable, 8/269 &
n. 3, 270; sharp practice in Moyer
case, 8/325; godfather to Duke of
Cambridge, 8/438; misunderstanding
with King about Buckingham,
9/27
AS CAPTAIN-GENERAL OF THE KINGDOM:
severity against plotters, 3/237, 252;
quells brawl, 4/136; sends soldiers to
guard pressed men, 6/99; victuals
Guernsey garrison, 6/142–3; discusses
apportionment of money for army,
6/154, 155; 8/591; resents proposal to
make Duke of York general, 6/277 &
n. 2, 321 & n. 1; sent for in Fire,
7/279–80, 281; dismisses Catholic
officers, 7/354; quells seamen's riot,
7/416; sends soldiers to man ships,
8/83, 147; confident of peace, 8/128;
his measures to defend Medway,
8/257–8, 260–1 & n.; blames Lord
Brouncker for disaster, 8/271, 315; is
himself blamed by Coventry, 8/490,
492 & n. 2, 497, 505, 515, 524, 536;

orders removal of *Royal Charles*,
8/495, 502
AS ADMIRAL OF THE KINGDOM, 1665: to
act in Duke of York's absence, 6/58 &
n. 2; high opinion of P, 4/231; 6/68,
88–9, 197, 239, 258, 298, 305, 310,
310-11, 324; 7/17, 37, 69, 107; 8/370;
offers him victualling post, 6/266,
279; gives P/Navy Board news of
naval campaign, 6/81–2, 99, 103, 121,
135, 195–6, 214, 223, 243, 255–6;
financial business with Board, 6/74,
75, 78, 322; victualling business, 6/91,
103, 109, 239, 269; ordnance business,
6/131; examines captains charged with
cowardice, 6/104; receives report on
dockyard strike, 6/144; orders fleet to
be made ready, 6/192, 195–6, 196,
233, 257; in Dutch prize-goods affair,
6/258, 260, 262, 263, 273–3, 280, 291,
298; arranges convoy, 6/296; ships'
insurance, 6/328; requires Board to
meet over Christmas, 6/337; receives
P's memorandum on pursers, 7/5, 10,
14; favours recall of tickets, 7/11; also,
6/169, 264; unspecified business: 6/68,
73, 94, 98, 107, 111, 125, 145, 162, 163,
165, 168–9, 186, 199, 233, 243, 305,
334, 341; 7/2, 12, 18, 23, 24, 32, 37, 79,
97
AS NAVAL COMMANDER: appointed joint
general-at-sea, 1/71 & n. 4, 75, 109;
discusses paying off ships, 2/19; to
command battle fleet (rumour),
5/183; 6/258, 259, 310, 323, 324, 342;
goes to sea, 7/107, 108, 109, 139, 140;
in Four Days Fight, 7/143, 146–50
passim & nn.; wounded, 7/147 &
n. 1; blames officers, 7/154 & n. 2,
163, 177, 222; 8/147–8; 9/5; tactics
criticised, 7/158 (2), 160, 168, 179;
8/125, 359; 9/70; his defence, 7/177–
8; 8/147–8; loses reputation at court,
7/196, 213–14, 248, 317–18, 334,
350, 354; quarrels with Duke of York
over appointments, 7/163, 314–15;
8/147; 9/39, 76; sails again, 7/210;
poor discipline, 7/212; in St James's
Day Fight, 7/225, 227–30 & nn.;
blames Board for lack of victuals,
7/259, 260, 263, 264, 265; 8/512, 513;
quarrels with Rupert, 7/315, 323, 333,
340; his landlubber's language, 8/148

& n. 2; hopes for peace, 8/347;
thanked by Commons, 8/499 & n. 2;
his 'Narrative', 8/511–12 & n., 514–15,
518, 519, 571; also, 9/25–6, 138
PERSONAL: lodgings in Whitehall, 1/8 &
n. 5; in Broad St, 1/53, 58; at Cockpit,
Whitehall, 1/179, pictures, 3/198; his
nasty food and household, 7/84;
9/294; land grants confirmed 4/156;
granted Clarendon Park, 5/61 & n. 1,
203, 218; bank account, 8/276; ill,
2/155, 157; 8/181; portrait by Lely,
7/102 & n. 3; miniature by Cooper,
9/139 & n. 2; plaster cast, 9/487–8
AS PRIVY COUNCILLOR ETC.: his power,
3/291; 4/138; 7/55; 8/585; careless,
7/10; sleeps in meeting, 8/317; relations with Sandwich, 6/313; 7/31;
8/117; with Coventry, 7/172, 174,
231; 9/478; tries to reconcile King and
Clarendon, 8/401, 402; naval business,
7/48, 312; 8/278; also, 6/104–5, 209;
7/28
TANGIER: appointed to committee,
3/238; offends Teviot, 4/102; advises
on garrison, 5/310 & n. 1; financial
business, 5/337; 6/214; 7/20; 8/521;
victualling business, 6/252–3, 254(2);
also, 5/174; unspecified business,
3/272; 5/11, 51, 114–15, 204, 321;
6/22, 58, 61, 153, 166; 7/321; 8/60, 347
SOCIAL: entertains Sandwich, 1/179;
4/187; royal family, 1/297; P, 6/272–3,
279; P and Carteret, 6/310–11; entertained by Trinity House, 2/4; Archbishop Sheldon, 6/164; and Sir J.
Robinson, 6/268–9
MISC.: patronage of T. Turner, 7/31;
9/328
~ his chaplain, 6/289
MONMOUTH, Duke and Duchess
of: *see* Scott, Anne; Scott, James
[MONSON, Sir William], naval
commander: naval tracts, 9/447, 524
& n. 2
[MONSON, William, 1st Viscount
Monson, regicide (d.?1672)]: his
sentence, 3/19 & n. 1
MONTACUTE, family of ['Mountagus,' in error]: tombs, 9/230 & n. 3
MONTAGU(E): *see* Mountagu
MONTGOMERIE, Alexander, 6th
Earl of Eglintoun: 9/554 & n. 5

MONTOUTH (?Monteith), [?Patrick]: 9/217

MOONE: *see* Mohun

MOONE, Mr——, secretary to Lord
Belasyse: on Tangier business, 7/18,
66, 403, 417; dines with P, 7/270;
political news from, 8/30

MOORCOCK, [John], timber merchant, Chatham: gives cakes to Navy
Board, 3/82 & n. 4; 5/259 & n. 1;
timber deal, 8/231 & n. 1

MOORE, Frank, EP's cousin: letter to
EP, 6/216

MOORE, Frank, Maj.-Gen. Lambert's
man: 3/118

MOORE, Henry, lawyer, Sandwich's
man of business:

P'S REGARD FOR: 1/261, 291; 2/167;
3/196

CHRON. SERIES: P's deputy in Exchequer,
1/83, 107-8, 238; draws up P's will,
1/90; instructs P in law, 1/283; assists
him in disputes over Robert P's affairs,
2/28 & n. 2, 137, 141, 176, 196, 198,
209, 211, 217, 226, 230; 3/7, 16, 31,
33-4, 83, 196, 211, 215, 248; 4/384;
other financial/legal business with,
1/103, 316; 2/190-1, 215; 4/90;
5/101; to be appointed to Wardrobe,
3/102 & n. 3; visits Brampton, 4/307,
338; returns to town after Plague,
7/13; clears prize goods with customs,
7/31-2; criticises Lord Keeper Coventry, 7/261; also, 2/74, 157 & n. 2,
217 & n. 4; 3/84; 6/83, 84

PERSONAL: house, 1/17; chamber in
Whitehall, 2/120; and in Gray's Inn,
2/217; in love with Jemima Mountagu,
1/20; attends Mossom's congregation,
1/183; on nature of tragedy, 1/236,
239; ill, 3/215, 216, 227, 228, 232,
239, 248, 252, 294, 304; 4/3, 23, 45, 66;
grown rich, 5/80; dislikes Creed,
5/302; admires Dr Spencer, 7/133
& n. 3

AS CLERK IN PRIVY SEAL: Sandwich's
deputy, 1/173, 205, 225, 238, 247;
3/168; fees, 2/2-3; 4/378; accounts
with P, 2/25, 98, 106: at sealing day,
2/149-50; attends on Lord Privy Seal,
2/158, 187, 199, 234, 237; also, 1/245,
307, 318; 2/64

AS SANDWICH'S MAN OF BUSINESS:

Sandwich's kindness, 2/101 & n. 1;
arranges investments/loans, 1/294,
297; 6/333; 7/31, 32; 8/579, 580, 581-
2; in charge of household, 2/75;
accounts [some may refer to Privy
Seal business], 3/138, 266, 277; 4/288,
416; 7/45, 199; Sandwich's debts,
5/132, 186, 187, 238-9; 6/33-4; 7/13,
45; sea-fee, 8/405; finances (general),
8/187-8, 199, 516; 9/331, 440; hopes
for profits, 4/422; advises P in Becke
affair, 4/278, 280-1, 281, 281-2, 381,
382, 383, 385, 389-90, 395, 422; 5/42;
sends newspaper story of Sandwich's
bravery, 6/123, 128 & n. 3; prize-
goods affair, 7/260; 8/499; 9/51, 111;
hopes for another command for
Sandwich, 8/54; unspecified business,
2/47, 62, 104, 109, 229; 3/40, 69, 92,
99, 102, 103, 114, 115, 132, 207, 272;
4/22, 58, 70, 87, 94, 102, 188, 199-
200, 281, 304; 5/202; 7/199; 9/313,
474-5; also, 1/171-3 passim, 322;
3/12, 18; 7/168, 406

POLITICAL NEWS ETC.: expects return of
Commonwealth, 8/390-1; fears for
nation, 8/530-1; also, 1/45, 60, 71, 113,
171, 263, 273, 278, 303; 4/134, 213,
304; 6/277; 8/125-6, 219, 324-5, 433-
4, 436; 9/51-2, 99-100; other news,
2/159, 209; 3/76, 101, 143; 8/377

SOCIAL: EP's valentine, 1/55; watches
footrace, 1/218; at theatre for first
time, 2/6; demonstrates French method of drinking toasts, 4/189; celebrates end of dispute with Trices,
4/364; at taverns/coffee-houses with
P, 1/5, 23, 49, 173, 210, 217-18, 227,
231, 295, 310; 2/49, 50, 79, 89, 105,
158, 167, 191, 199, 211, 235; 3/35, 152,
282; 4/257; 5/246; at P's house, 1/82,
246, 261, 267, 294, 318; 2/5, 40, 173,
177, 217, 226, 231; 3/37, 200, 263, 264;
4/362, 377-8, 379; 5/321; 6/52, 112,
137; 8/325; at Sandwich's houses/
lodgings, 1/6, 32, 74; 2/48, 124, 149;
3/62, 83, 89, 117, 139, 285; walks
with P, 2/145; 3/57, 162; at theatre,
2/141, 221; 6/4; also, 1/49, 89, 181;
2/35, 66, 97; 3/43, 134; 6/159; 8/259

ALLUDED TO: 1/17, 95; 2/110

~ his kinsman, 3/199

MOORE, Jonas, mathematician, kted

calculating machine, 9/116–17 & n.; also, 1/190; 5/342; 8/420; ~ his man Herbert, 5/88

MORLAND, [Suzanne], Lady Morland, wife of Sir Samuel: visits France, 4/274 & n. 2; reproaches King for failure to reward husband, 4/275; her appearance, 5/342; 8/440

MORLEY, George, Bishop of Worcester 1660–2, Winchester 1662–d.84: consecrated, 1/276 & n. 2; preaches at Whitehall against Christmas revels, 3/292–3; alleged lack of charity, 3/293 & n. 2; rumoured suspension, 8/587 & n. 2; dismissed from court office, 9/53 & n. 2

MORLEY, Col. [Herbert], republican (d. 1667): 1/16 & n. 1

MORRICE, Mr ——: at P's stone feast, 2/60; also, 4/272; ~ his wife, 1/3, 10; 4/65, 272, 273; his sister-in-law, 4/272;? his niece, ib.

MORRICE, ——: 1/19

MORRIS (Morrice), [John], landlord of Ship Tavern, Billiter Lane: 9/284, 485–6; ~ his pretty wife, 9/284, 486

MORRIS (Morrice), Capt. [Robert], court upholsterer: supplies furniture for Sandwich, 1/181; in militia against Venner, 2/11; shows P King's Privy Kitchen, 2/175

MORRIS (Morrice), [Roger], wine cooper, of St Olave's, Hart St: business with Navy Board, 3/14; 8/135, 159

MORTALITY, BILLS OF [see also Plague, the]: 3/292 & n. 1; cited, 6/180, 191, 207–8, 208, 214, 234, 243, 284, 305, 314, 340; 7/2, 21, 32, 52, 63, 71, 91, 95

MORTLAKE (Moreclack(e)), Surrey: P at, 3/81; 6/154, 156; 7/235

MORTON, Sir John, Bt, M.P. Poole, Dorset (d. 1699): quarrel with H. Brouncker, 9/470 & n. 1

MORTON, Sir William, Judge, King's Bench 1665–d.72: 9/470 & n. 1

MORTON, bookseller: see Morden

MORTON, Lord: see Douglas

MOSCOW: described, 5/272 & nn.

[MOSELEY HALL, Staffs.]: Charles II hides at (1651), 1/156 & n. 5

MOSSOM (Masham, Massam, Merston, Messum, Mossum), [Robert], Dean of Christ Church, Dublin 1661–6, Bishop of Derry 1666–d.79: his congregation at Cary House, Strand, 1/11 & n. 3, 76, 173, 183; sermons, 1/25, 60, 91, 176; reputation, 1/25; also, 8/553 & n. 3

MOTHAM (Mootham), Capt. [Peter], naval officer: reminiscences as slave in Algiers, 2/33–4 & n.; killed in action, 7/154

MOUNT, [Jeremiah], Gentleman-Usher to the Duchess of Albemarle: 2/51; social: 1/26, 95, 232, 233, 244, 311; 4/101, 421, 436; 5/7, 136

MOUNTAGU, family of: stories of longevity, 6/237–8 & n.

MOUNTAGU, Anne, Lady Mountagu, widow of Sir Sidney; step-mother of Sandwich: at christening, 2/171; alluded to: 2/98

MOUNTAGU, Lady Anne, daughter of Sandwich [see also Mountagu, Edward, 1st Earl of Sandwich: his children]: 3/68; 8/470

MOUNTAGU, Anne, (b. Boyle), Viscountess Hinchingbrooke (d. 1671): marriage, 8/190–1 & nn., 208, 216, 252, 469; 9/28, 51; P admires, 8/498; 9/115, 117; dines with P, 9/109, 116–17; also, 9/211, 321, 322

MOUNTAGU, Lady Catherine, daughter of Sandwich (d. 1757): birth, 2/159 & n. 1; christening, 2/171; ailments, 5/189–90; 9/218 & n. 2; alluded to: 2/195

MOUNTAGU, Sir Edward, Lord Chief Justice (d. 1557): descendants, 6/238 & nn.

MOUNTAGU, Sir Edward (d. 1602): 6/238 & n. 1

MOUNTAGU, Edward, 2nd Earl of Manchester, Lord Chamberlain:

PUBLIC AFFAIRS: Presbyterian peers meet at his house, 1/111 & n. 1; chosen Speaker of Lords, 1/115; at Portsmouth, 3/70, 71; unpopular at court, 3/291; closes New Exchange after attack on King's coachman, 4/431 & n. 5; intervenes to prevent duels, 7/414; 9/467; orders M.P.s out of theatres etc. to vote, 7/399–400;

rumoured appointment to Treasury commission, 8/367–8 & n.; imprisons Doll Common, 9/415 & n. 1; also, 1/106, 266; 2/96, 97; 4/229; 8/176, 278

PRIVATE AFFAIRS: quarrels with Ned Mountagu, 4/47; dines with Sandwich, 1/75, 220

ALLUDED TO: 8/544; 9/139, 471

MOUNTAGU, Edward, (often referred to as 'my Lord'), cr. Earl of Sandwich July 1660, politician and naval commander; ambassador to Spain 1665–8; P's patron:

CHARACTER: 'a perfect Courtier', 1/269; secretive, 1/285; brave, 3/149; noble, 4/115; grown 'very high and stately', 5/42; neglectful of business, 4/28; 5/155; 9/374; Teddeman's high opinion, 7/345

PHYSICAL APPEARANCE AND PORTRAITS: moustache, 7/26; Spanish beard, 8/452–3; portrait by Lely, 1/262, 271 & n. 1, 296; copies of, 1/270–3 passim, 284, 286, 290, 292, 296, 301–2; miniature by Salusbury, 2/23; second portrait by Lely, 7/102 & n. 3

AS NAVAL COMMANDER:

UNDER COMMONWEALTH: voyage to Mediterranean (1656), 1/238; to Baltic (1659), 1/23 & n. 2, 80; his Swedish medal, 1/238 & n. 1

VOYAGE TO HOLLAND, March–Apr. 1660, to bring over King: joint general-at-sea, 1/71 & n. 4, 75; prepares to sail, 1/78, 82, 83, 84, 90; embarks, 1/95; civil to Cavaliers, 1/99, 112, 117; opposed by Lawson's captains, 1/100; shifts flag from *Swiftsure* to *Naseby*, 1/101; dismisses Anabaptist, 1/101, 109 & n. 2; Declaration of Breda etc. read to fleet, 1/123 & n. 2, 124 & n. 1, 125, 126–7, 129 & n. 2; Commonwealth flags etc. replaced, 1/130, 133–4, 136–7; sets sail from Downs, 1/133–5 passim; surrenders command to Duke of York, 1/152; accompanies King ashore at Dover, 1/158; invested with Garter, 1/160–1 & nn.; distributes royal bounty, 1/162, 164; returns to London, 1/171; pay, 1/174, 192; 2/49, 55; voted thanks by Commons,

1/176, 177 & nn.; also, 1/96, 98, 115, 167

VOYAGE TO HOLLAND, Sept. 1660, to bring over Dowager Princess Mary: his orders, 1/234 & n. 4, 239; preparations, 1/236, 241; sets sail, 1/238, 241; returns, 1/254, 258; alluded to: 1/247, 251

VOYAGE TO THE MEDITERRANEAN AND PORTUGAL, 1661–2, to bring over Queen Catherine: preparations, 2/45–7 passim, 62 & n. 3, 77, 79, 95, 99, 103, 104/(2), 108, 112(2), 114, 118, 120, 121, 127; his instructions, 2/118 & n. 3; gift of cloth to Algerines, 2/120, 122, 123, 126; expenses granted, 2/150–1 & n., 163; illness at Alicante, 2/152–4 passim, 163; action at Algiers, 2/184 & n. 2, 185, 189; in Lisbon, 2/185–6; provisions sent, 2/186; sees bull-fight, 2/209 & n. 2; action at Tangier, 2/221 & n. 3; asks for astronomical information, 3/7; ambassador-extraordinary to Portugal, 3/12 & n. 3; puts troops into Tangier, 3/18, 33; news from, 3/21 & n. 2; gifts to wife, 3/25; sends map of Tangier to Duke of York, 3/37 & n. 2; returns, 3/84, 89, 97, 120; report on Queen etc., 3/89, 90–1 & n.; gift from Queen, 3/90; his part in treaty with Algiers, 3/121–2 & nn.; determines fleet's rate of pay, 3/128 & n. 1, 129; his cash/pay/allowances/accounts, 3/93, 99 & n. 2, 115, 121; 4/101, 104, 113, 114, 116–17 & n., 135, 136, 156, 204; also, 2/167, 242; 3/18, 105

VOYAGE TO FRANCE, July 1662, to bring over Queen Mother: 3/128; in storm, 3/143, 144 & n. 1, 145, 146; bravery, 3/149; returns, 3/148, 149

1664 COMMAND: rumours of, 5/160–3 passim & n., 183; visits fleet, 5/187, 196, 197; made admiral, 5/206, 207 & n. 4; departs, 5/208–9, 211–12; at sea, 5/225, 256 & n. 3; in river, 5/265; returns, 5/299; at sea again, 5/360; also, 5/303–4

1665 CAMPAIGN: at sea, 6/13, 29 & n.1, 35, 39, 41, 50; repute, 6/50; at Nore, 6/64–5; death rumoured, 6/120; in Battle of Lowestoft, 6/121 & nn., 123 & n. 2, 127, 129, 137; his account of,

6/134-5 & n.; newspaper account, 6/128 & n. 3; unfair official account, 6/135 & nn., 149, 276; failure to pursue enemy, 8/494, 550; conduct defended by King, 8/573; returns, 6/134; at sea, 6/141; given sole command, 6/147 & n. 4; proposed joint command with Rupert, 6/148 & n. 2; jealousy of Penn, 6/148-9, 151, 230; fails to intercept Dutch E. Indiamen, 6/165, 178, 184 & n. 2; action in Bergen harbour, 6/193, 195-6 & n., 198; his defence of, 6/229; criticised for failure to capture E. Indiamen, 6/218 & n. 2, 231, 277; 8/494, 515, 538, 550; 9/68 & n. 1; puts out again, 6/205, 208; captures *Phoenix* and *Slothany* etc., 6/219 & n. 1, 223 [*see also* below, The prize-goods affair]; captures warships, 6/223-4 & n.; at Nore, 6/226, 228; lack of provisions, 6/228-9, 229, 230, 239; ability as commander, 6/230; at sea again, 6/275, 278, 287; leaves fleet to go to court, 6/307; 9/70 & n. 1, 87; criticised for failure to engage Dutch in October, 6/291 & n. 1; parliamentary motion against, ib.; criticism dies down, 7/148-9, 168, 376, 406; 8/2; also, 6/247, 300-1

THE PRIZE-GOODS AFFAIR: breaks bulk in *Phoenix* and *Slothany*, 6/219, 223, 226, 230-1 & n., 238-9; his profit, 6/238-9, 240, 241, 297-8, 334, 342; navy's allocation, 6/239; 7/27, 45, 54; distribution of goods authorised by King and Duke of York, 6/247 & n. 3, 264, 269 & n. 2, 318; 9/50; goods declared prize, 6/263-4; his action criticised by Myngs, 6/261, 266; in Commons, 6/262, ?291; in Lords, 7/309, 325; at court, 6/262, 263, 268, 276, 287, 301, 302, 311, 323; 7/6, 8; by Colvill, 6/268; Albemarle, 6/273, 313; 7/31; Coventry, 6/276, 301; 9/165; Penn, 9/165; and Duke of York, 6/287, 291, 302; Cuttance's influence, 8/549; 9/402; bill against breaking bulk, 6/274 & n. 4, 277; recovers King's favour, 6/276, 291, 301, 311, 318, 321; 7/8, 52, 54, 55; 9/67; Rupert's, 6/276; and Duke of York's, 6/311; 7/55-6; pardoned by King,

7/13, 17, 27, 55, 260, 262; exculpated by Prize Commissioners, 7/10, 52; attacked in *Second advice*, 7/407-8; affair investigated by Committee on Miscarriages, 8/485, 486, 494, 499, 521, 527, 572, 576; 9/51, 64 & n. 3, 70; and by Brooke House Committee, 9/87, 91, 92, 96, 111, 135, 165, 204, 363-4; discussed by Commons, 9/?174 & n. 5, 176 & n. 2, 177; alluded to: 7/203, 219, 260-1; 8/517, 530; 9/180

AS VICE-ADMIRAL OF THE KINGDOM: appointed, 1/221 & n. 1, 222, 225, 229, 236; subordinate appointments, 1/188; 5/162-3 & n.; with King on yacht, 1/222; provides ships, 1/249, 300; new barge, 2/110; quarrels with Mennes over flags, 3/122-3; fee, 8/405-6 & n.; attends Navy Board, 1/197, 211; 3/265, 272, 282; 4/12, 31, 418

AS ARMY OFFICER: pay, 1/7 & n. 1; regimental dinner, 1/185; regiment disbanded, 1/242, 295; also, 1/13, 14

AS CLERK TO PRIVY SEAL [*see also* Privy Seal]: takes office, 1/128 & n. 1, 176; sworn in, 1/206, 207; fees, 1/237, 238; appoints P his deputy, 1/205 & n. 3; and Moore, 3/168; also, 1/212

AS MASTER OF THE WARDROBE: appointed, 1/170, 175; visits building, 1/180; attendance, 1/303; P his deputy, 2/113 & n. 2, 116; profits, 3/287; 4/251; poundage, 8/418; is owed £7000, 5/206; accounts, 4/257, 390; 5/208; 8/253; 9/52; advised to surrender place, 8/195; also, 1/258; 5/32

TANGIER: appointed to committee, 3/238; nominates P as member, 3/170, 171, 172; rumoured appointment as Governor, 5/313; 9/387; receives money from contractors, 8/592-3 & n.; visits and reports on, 9/135 & n. 3, 355-6 & n.; other business: victualling, 4/30; mole, 4/35; 5/343; mercantile court, 4/102; Peterborough's accounts, 5/74-5, 140; local paymaster, 9/418, 419, 422; also, 9/326; unspecified, 3/232, 272; 4/97, 123, 269, 408; 5/173; 6/58, 61, 134; 9/340, 364

AS AMBASSADOR TO SPAIN: appointed,

6/320–3 passim & n.; departure, 6/342; 7/6, 52, 57; untrue rumour of recall, 7/354, 406; 8/52; and of quarrel with French ambassador, 8/36 & n. 2, 37, 42; negotiates treaty, 8/45, 107; anecdotes of his embassy, 8/451–2; overspends, 8/461–2; accounts, 8/462; 9/387, 440; return expected, 8/189, 190, 207–8, 476; recalled, 8/511; mediates in Spanish-Portuguese peace negotiations, 8/578 & n. 3; 9/59–60, 80, 222; high repute in Spain, 8/578–9; returns, 9/320

OTHER APPOINTMENTS: Deputy-Lieutenant for Huntingdonshire, 1/310 & n. 5; Master of Trinity House, 2/119; 3/29; 4/185; 5/172; work for Royal Fishery, 3/268–70 passim; 4/365–6

FINANCES [for fees etc. *see* under offices]: state of summarised, 5/206 & n. 1; makes will, 1/94, 95; King's grant to [*see also* Fox, Sir S.], 1/271–2, 285 & n. 4, 288, 290–4 passim, 297; 2/3, 47; 3/121; 4/87–8 & n., 156; 8/530 & n. 3; acquires Brampton manor, 3/102, 176 & nn.; debts, 3/55, 118; 5/186, 187(2), 192, 238–9; 7/56, 370; extravagance/insolvency, 4/37; 7/45; 8/187–8 & n., 444, 463, 470, 480, 516, 517; 9/331; lends money to Calthorpe, 1/4, 6 & n. 3, 24, 36; to Sir R. Parkhurst, 1/310 & n. 2, 311; 2/48; 4/94; Worcester money, 1/56 & n. 5, 57, 80, 91–2; borrows £1000 from T. Pepys, 2/43, 61, 62–3 & n.; 3/17 & n. 1; 5/186, 187; 6/331, 333; 7/13, 14–15, 31–2; from P, 2/61 & n. 5; 4/199–200, 286, 288, 290, 438; 5/42, 131, 211; 6/33–4; again from P, 8/579, 580, 582; P refuses to lend, 7/260; 8/187, 199; his borrowings amount to £7000, 3/92; over £9000, 5/132; £10, 000, 5/206; needs loan of £1000, 4/43, 45–6, 57; and of £2000, 9/321–2

RELATIONS WITH COVENTRY [*see* Coventry, Sir W.]

RELATIONS WITH P:

HIS REGARD FOR: 1/141, 206, 303, 323; 2/49, 113; 3/102, 133–4, 139, 187, 232, 248, 304; 5/74; 6/237, 239(2), 248, 287, 302

AS P'S PATRON: 1/129, 167; P as secretary to regiment, 1/7, 14, 25, 257, 304; and to fleet, 1/77(2); 5/65; deputy in Privy Seal, 1/169–70, 205 & n. 3; and in Wardrobe, 2/113 & n. 2, 116; promises P Clerkship of Acts, 1/184, 185, 222–3; thanked by Duke of York for introducing him, 3/215–16; advises him about Clarendon's timber, 5/202, 203, 206, 207, 208; secures his appointment to Tangier committee, 3/170, 171, 172; and to Royal Fishery, 4/366; 5/76, 79; also, 1/202; 2/121, 192; 4/196

AS P'S EMPLOYER [In the diary period P was primarily Sandwich's man of business; his domestic duties were light after his appointment as Clerk of the Acts, and varied with circumstances.]:

P as domestic steward/man of business [*see also* Andrews, J.; Creed, J.; Moore, H.; Shipley, E.; and above: The prize-goods affair; Finances]: appointment: vol. i, pp. xxii–iii; hopes for profits, 3/133; 4/422; his 'little chamber'/'turret' in Whitehall lodgings, 1/59, 186, 222; 4/22; 8/82; moves from, 2/126; overnight at, 3/187, 199, 301; 5/142; domestic duties: in charge of Whitehall lodgings, 1/24, 64; 3/146; and of servants, 3/288, 293; financial business: accounts, 1/24, 32, 104, 297, 305, 306, 307; 2/37, 56, 57, 67, 97, 106; 3/92–3, 99, 116, 120–3 passim, 124, 126, 133, 136, 138, 139, 266; 4/281, 285, 286, 416; 7/7, 41, 42; supervises Wardrobe finances during Sandwich's absence, 2/112; 3/132, 133–4, 147; 4/58; 8/253, 418; advises him on land purchase, 3/176 & n. 2; negotiates Lady Jemima's marriage settlement, 6/29, 135–6, 137; business with bankers, 6/334; misc.: sends deals to Hinchingbrooke, 1/313–14, 324; 2/8, 27, 35, 48–9, 79; advises him on garden design, 4/313; also, 1/29, 40, 78, 310–11, 312; 2/49; 4/343; unspecified business, 2/3; 3/94, 212, 215, 260, 281, 288; 4/23; 9/211

the Becke affair: P disapproves of Sandwich's liaison, 4/238, 270–1, 278, 281, 282, 286, 292, 301, 303, 313, 379; writes 'great letter of reproof', 4/382,

385–8 passim, its effects on Sandwich and on relations between them, 4/390–3 passim, 395, 396, 397, 402, 407, 408, 421, 422, 427, 428, 429, 437; 5/4, 9, 10, 18, 21–2, 26, 42, 43, 65, 70, 80, 83, 108, 110, 120, 185, 189, 192, 200; relations re-established, 5/76, 161, 203, 211, 225

misc.: gives New Year present, 1/4; advises about Robert P's estate, 1/170; 3/220, 226; 4/42; designs alterations to Brampton house, 3/206, 210; urges P to provide for Pall, 4/366; advises about W. Joyce's arrest, 5/110; and about sale of land, 5/211; concerned for during Plague, 6/231; confides in about his political standing, 7/54–6; P fails to write to in Spain, 9/321; and to pay visit of condolence, 9/474; P distrusts his associates, 9/372, 374 & n. 2; P dines/talks with, 2/54, 56, 79, 115; 3/126, 134; 4/82; 6/54–5, 60; P gives dinner for, 9/420, 423–4; also, 4/313

RELATIONS WITH EP: his regard for, 1/293, 294; 3/206, 210; admires her beauty, 4/186; makes advances to, 9/356

POLITICS [*see also* below, Court]:

HIS VIEWS: on restoration of monarchy, 1/77, 79, 107, 110, 285 & n. 2; Presbyterian discontent, 3/176; state of court and kingdom, 6/248, 277; likely effects of war, 7/55; a 'politique', 3/122

HIS POLITICAL CAREER: under Commonwealth, vol. i, pp. xxii, xxiii–vi; corresponds with King (1659), 1/125 & n. 1, 285; 4/69 & n. 2; takes out pardon, 3/121 & n. 1; returns to London, 1/44, 60, 62; elected to Council of State, 1/65; resumes seat in parliament, 1/72; dines with Presbyterian leaders, 1/75; and Lord Mayor, 1/92; elected M.P. for Weymouth, 1/108(3) & n. 2; and Dover, 1/110–11; resigns on becoming peer, 1/179; electoral influence at Harwich, 1/98 & n. 3; Cinque Ports, 1/93 & n. 2, 94, 96, 97; Weymouth, 1/103 & n. 4, 179; Dover, 1/167, 179 & n. 1; Huntingdon, 1/86–7 & n., 99 & n. 2; supports candidate at Huntingdon (1661), 2/3 & n. 5; opposes Sir R. Bernard's

influence there, 3/281–2 & n.; sworn Privy Councillor, 1/179; raised to peerage, 1/184–5 & n., 187–8 & n., 196 & n. 5; attends Lords, 1/208; 2/107; gifts of plate to Secretary and King, 1/185, 192, 193; 2/5; as judge at regicides' trial, 1/263, 266; exempted from place bill, 4/136 & n. 1; member of King's 'private council', 5/207; fears may be blamed for sale of Dunkirk, 7/55 & n. 4; rumoured appointment to Treasury, 8/195, 217; alliance with Clarendon, 1/173; 2/209–10, 221; 3/33, 122; 4/115, 366; 5/207, 208; 6/148, 291, 311; 7/5, 55; 8/418; relations cool, 6/276–7; with Duke of York and his party, 4/115; relations cool, 5/133; with Arlington, 4/115; 5/208; 6/276 & n. 5; with Albemarle, 6/313; and with Carteret, 6/148; also, 1/66, 68; 2/75; 7/28

POLITICAL NEWS FROM: 1/271; 3/237; 4/24, 57, 115–17, 366–7

COURT: attends coronation, 2/82, 86; advised to avoid court, 3/291; standing at court, 3/304; 5/207; 6/273, 276, 287, 291, 301, 302, 311, 318, 323; 7/5, 26–7, 132; 8/149, 207–8; 9/331, 339, 342; absence from court remarked on, 4/370, 379, 387–8; allies with Lady Castlemaine, 4/13, 115; also, 3/94, 157; 4/115, 239, 255; 5/161

RESIDENCES:

AT MRS BECKE'S, Chelsea: 4/97, 101, 112, 114, 117, 123–4, 160, 278, 281, 286, 402, 419; 5/173

AT LORD CREW'S, Lincoln's Inn Fields: 1/77, 87, 89, 94

HINCHINGBROOKE, Hunts. [for the house, *see* under name]: to entertain King, 4/324; visits, 1/221–3 passim, 234, 310, 312, 320; 2/47, 48, 49, 52; 3/116, ?160, 187, 287, 288, 304; 4/12, 251, 292, 313, 348; 5/32, 36, 64, 185; 7/34; 9/541; also, 1/66; 2/108

AT DEAN HODGES'S, Kensington: 5/184, 192

LINCOLN'S INN FIELDS: takes lease, 5/19–20, 43; P visits, 5/65, 74, 75, 79, 132, 202; admires house and garden, 5/74; christening in dining-room, 7/49; let to Carteret, 8/450

LODGINGS AT THE WARDROBE [P's

numerous visits – mostly social – are not indexed. His first mention of them is at 1/277; his last at 5/316.]: roomy but ugly, 1/291; 'pretty pleasant', 2/97; kitchen, 2/106; dining-room, 3/89; parlour, ib.; Capt. Ferrers's chamber, 3/81

LODGINGS IN WHITEHALL [He had lodgings in the palace from c. 1654 onwards and throughout the diary period – whether the same set is not known. P's numerous visits are not indexed. His first mention of them is at 1/17; his last at 9/553.]: next door to Lady Castlemaine's, 3/215; claimed by A. A. Cooper, 1/17, 22, 23; repaired and decorated, 3/49, 146; King's tennis court in garden, 3/147; damaged by collapse of tennis court, 4/197; Hinchingbrooke's chamber, 8/516; Sandwich's study, 1/22, ?251; stair door, 1/71; ? garden, 1/77, 220; nursery, 1/186, 203; house of office, 1/250; buttery, 2/90; drawing-room, 2/102; little new room, 2/103; great dining-room, 1/287; 3/266; also, 2/121

HOUSEHOLD [see also Lady Sandwich: household; Burfett, ——; Carleton, ——; Creed, J.; Crisp, L.; Ferrers, R.; Loud, ——; [Luffe, E.]; Turner, John]: to have French cook and master of horse, 1/269, 311; angry at servants' improvidence, 2/64; new liveries for coronation, 2/79; footboy (Tom), 1/14, 58; black footman, (Jasper), 1/82, 92, 166; other footmen, 3/196, 212; 4/348; porter, 5/202; Spanish dancer, 9/440; great coach, 1/181; 5/200

PERSONAL:

INTEREST IN ARTS AND SCIENCES: on engravings, 6/50; paints miniature of Charles II, 2/59; plans alterations to P's Brampton house, 3/206, 210; his drawings of Lisbon, 4/286 & n. 1; and of Portsmouth harbour, 6/38, 46, 50; admires Danckerts's view of Tangier, 9/541 & n. 2; musical tastes, 1/298; 4/160; composes three-part anthem, 4/418–19, 428; borrows lute, 1/218; plays and commends guitar, 6/301; plays viol, 1/114 (bass), 285; 2/39, 57;

organ, 1/287, 292, 297; his virginals, 2/121–2; sings, 1/114, 115, 118, 129, 133, 169, 285; 2/57; musical parties, 2/66, 103; 3/255, 287; takes dancing-master on voyage, 2/117; sceptical about ghost, 4/185–6; given loadstone, 4/397; astronomical observations, 5/346 & n. 3, 352; also, 3/7; 4/283

RELIGIOUS VIEWS: a 'sceptic' and favours uniformity, 1/141, 201; 'indifferent', 1/261; prefers homilies to sermons, 1/271 & n. 2

HEALTH: heavy cold, 1/202; bruised foot, 1/254; unwell, 1/262; ill (? malaria) at Alicante, 2/152–3, 154, 163; ill (? recurrent malaria), 4/17, 21, 22, 24, 25, 28, 30, 55, 58, 62, 63, 66, 68, 69, 89; 5/207; takes physic, 1/164, 166; 2/42; 3/92; 9/338

DRESS ETC.: rich new clothes, 1/141; garter dress and insignia, 1/160; 2/49; comb-case, 1/239; toilet cap, ib.; French coronation suit, 2/83; gold-buttoned suit, 4/187; watch, 1/120

LIAISONS: affair with Betty Becke, 4/97, 101, 112, 174, 238 & n. 3, 270–1, 281, 286, 292, 301, 303, 305; neglects attendance at court, 4/370, 379; P's letter of reproof, 4/383, 387–8 (see also Relations with P, above); leaves Chelsea, 4/399–400, 402, 419; still visits her, 5/173–4; affair alluded to, 9/455; liaison with Lady Castlemaine, 5/21; his portrait of, 5/200

CHILDREN [The following references are to children/daughters whose names are not given in the text. See also Mountagu, Anne, Catherine; Edward (Hinchingbrooke); James; John; Oliver; Paulina and Sidney.]: in London for coronation, 2/75; P/EP take to theatre, 2/151–2, 173–4; Tower, 3/76; Hampton Court, 3/81–2; Greenwich, 3/111; to see ship, 6/56, 57; also, 2/165, 170, 206; 3/47, 79, 94, 223

CHILDREN'S MARRIAGES: agrees terms for Lady Jemima's marriage, 6/138, 145, 148, 173; his pleasure at, 6/202; refers Hinchingbrooke's marriage negotiations to advisers, 8/190–1 & n. SOCIAL: plays ninepins on board ship,

1/131, 142, 162, 164, 169; goes fishing with Vice-Admiral, 1/169; dines with Lord Campden, 1/210; with King, 1/214, 297–8; Manchester, 1/220; Albemarle, 4/187; Peterborough, 4/270; and Povey, 9/345; entertains Ormond, 2/100; officers of Wardrobe, 2/104; and Coventry, 3/138–9; at theatre, 3/211, 216; at Lady Castlemaine's, 3/214–15; 4/238; plays at dice, 4/28; loses £100 at cards, 4/134; at Boughton, 4/307; at Whitehall chapel, 4/401; visits Lady Pulteney, 5/163; and Archbishop Sheldon, 6/239 MISC.: challenges Buckingham to duel, 2/32–3; in search for treasure in Tower, 3/240–4 passim

MOUNTAGU, Edward, styled Viscount Hinchingbrooke, eldest son of Lord Sandwich [often referred to as 'Mr Edward' before July 1660]:
CHARACTER: 'a noble and hopeful gentleman', 6/13; 'a most sweet youth', 6/188; his sobriety, 7/235–6, 358; 8/516
CHRON. SERIES: at school at Twickenham, 1/18 & n. 3, 19, 20; on *Naseby*, 1/133; has audience with King, 1/143–4; visits The Hague, Delft and Scheveningen, 1/143–4, 145, 147–50 passim; at Deal, 1/163; Latin lesson from P, 1/165; returns to London, 1/173; continues education, 2/114 & n. 1, 142, 163; 4/25, 121, 187; suspected smallpox, 2/152, 153, 154(2), 157; false report of death, 3/11 & n. 2; kills page in shooting accident, 4/138; visits Rome, 6/13; returns to England, 6/169 & n. 3, 178, 183; has smallpox, 6/191, 193; P's impression of, 7/47 & n. 2; proposed match with Elizabeth Malet, 6/110 & n. 4, 119, 193 & n. 2; 7/56, 260, 385; marriage with Lady Anne Boyle, 8/190–1 and nn., 208, 216, 252, 377, 418, 469, 498, 598; 9/28, 51; short of money, 8/276, 333; assistance in father's financial difficulties, 8/199, 463, 516, 573 & n. 2, 579, 580; dishonourable advances to EP, 9/356; also, 2/107; 3/291; 6/190; 7/46, 54, 94, 234, 356, 368; 9/318, 321
SOCIAL: plays shuttlecock, 1/15; at theatre, 2/8; sees Lord Mayor's Show,

1/276 & n. 3, 277; at christening, 7/49; visits city ruins after Fire, 7/357–8; dines with P, 7/387, 388–9; 9/109, 115, 116–17, 423–4, 553; also, 9/211, 345
ALLUDED TO: 1/151

MOUNTAGU, Edward, 1st Baron Mountagu of Boughton (d. 1644): ?6/238 & n. 2

MOUNTAGU, Edward, 2nd Lord Mountagu of Boughton (d. 1684): dines with Sandwich, 4/136; ill, 5/154; quarrels with son Edward, 5/244; alluded to: 6/155

MOUNTAGU, Edward (Ned), son of the 2nd Baron Mountagu of Boughton; Master of the Horse to the Queen Mother:
CHRON. SERIES: parliamentary candidate, 1/102 & n. 2, 167; carries letters between Sandwich and King, 1/110 & n. 2, 112, 113; on Dutch voyage, 1/135, 171, 173; manages Sandwich's business during absence abroad (1661–2), 2/118, 121, 163, 185, 186, 195, 197, 206, 229; distrusted by Lady Sandwich and P, 2/163; visits Tangier, 2/186; 3/12 & n. 1., 78; low repute at court, 3/15, 43, 289; 4/47 & n. 1; 5/207, 208; mismanagement of Sandwich's business, 3/29, 55–6; duel with Cholmley, 3/157 & n. 2; 4/47; borrows money from Sandwich, 3/157; dispute with Chesterfield, 3/289–90 & n.; 4/25; quarrel with Sandwich, 4/46–7 & nn., 114–15, 366; 5/207, 208; with father and uncle, 4/47, 187–8; 5/244; to procure Frances Stuart for King, 4/366; tries to make mischief between Sandwich and Clarendon, 4/366–7; rusticated for affront to Queen, 5/153 & n. 2, 155, 244; owes Sandwich £2000, 5/206; killed in action, 6/196
SOCIAL: 1/187; 3/139
ALLUDED TO: 2/142, 191, 193

MOUNTAGU, George, son of the 1st Earl of Manchester (d. 1681): with Sandwich on Baltic voyage, 1/44 & n. 3; custos rotulorum for Westminster, 1/79–80 & n.; M.P. for Dover, 1/167, 179 & n. 2, 183, 228; parliamentary candidate for Huntingdon, 2/3 & n. 6, 4; political news from, 1/228; 2/142; 3/15 & n. 2; 9/302; death of son in France, 3/11, 15; concern for Sandwich in prize-goods affair, 8/2, 521; 9/64, 162, 165; praises P's parliamentary speech, 9/105, 153, 302; advises him on dealing with parliament, 9/178; social: 1/30 & n. 3; 4/82–3; 9/116; alluded to: 3/92, 224; ~ his wife [Elizabeth], 3/16, 224; 9/153; his sons and daughter, 9/153

MOUNTAGU, James, Bishop of Bath and Wells 1608–16, Winchester 1616–d.18 (d. 1618): tomb in Bath Abbey, 9/238 & n. 1

MOUNTAGU, James, son of Lord Sandwich: birth and christening, 5/209 & n. 1, 211

MOUNTAGU, James, of Lackham, Wilts., 3rd son of the 1st Earl of Manchester: 8/316, n. 2

MOUNTAGU, Jemima, Countess of Sandwich (often referred to as 'my Lady'), wife of the 1st Earl of Sandwich:

CHARACTER: 'so good and discreet a woman I know not in the world', 5/257; P's esteem for, 2/49; 6/119; 8/469

HER FRIENDSHIP/KINDNESS TO P/EP: 1/264, 266; 2/117, 140, 214, 221, 235, 240; 3/54, 103, 206; 4/199; 5/65, 76; sends younger sons to P's house to avoid infection, 2/153, 157, 158; urges P to spend money on EP, 2/210, 211, 212; scolds for failure to visit, 3/143; recalls P's service in 1650s, 5/192; invites him to Hinchingbrooke, 6/176; grateful for his help as matchmaker, 6/178, 180; looks on P as one of family, 8/472

CHRON. SERIES: comes to London from Hinchingbrooke, 1/264; audience of Queen Mother, 1/282; takes up residence at Wardrobe, 2/95, 97; hears of husband's illness, 2/154; birth of daughter Catherine, 2/159, 166, 171, 178; meets Queen Catherine, 3/96, 100; at Hinchingbrooke, 3/143, 144; returns to London, 5/32, 64; has measles, 5/132, 135–8 passim, 142, 144–5, 155, 257; at Kensington, 5/174 & n. 1, 178; meets Sandwich's

mistress, 5/179, 184; birth of son, James, 5/209; dislikes Creed's proposed match, 5/286; 6/15, 88, 90; hopes for daughter's marriage to P. Carteret, 6/29, 55, 66, 71; visits Carterets, 6/148, 149, 151, 152, 153, 155, 156, 157, 161; attends wedding, 6/163, 176; ill from drinking waters, 6/151, 152; at Hinchingbrooke, 7/376; 8/49; pleased with son's marriage, 8/216, 469; forced to sell plate etc., 8/470; borrows £100 from P, 9/194, 211; also, 2/27, 32, 131, 152–3, 163, 186; 3/11–12, 55, 89, 105; 4/237, 262; 6/110–11

COURT NEWS FROM: 1/319, 320; 2/230; 3/80–1; 5/129, 232; 6/41

HOUSEHOLD: Sarah, housekeeper at Whitehall: re-employed, 1/175 & n. 6; marries and takes to drink, 3/288, 293; husband a cook, 3/251; 4/334, 342; her 'old services' to P, 3/251 & n. 2; court news from, 3/146; 4/1, 315, 342; P's amorous encounter with, 3/191; social: 1/194; 2/271, 234, 236; 3/12, 49, 87, 255; 4/5; also, 1/241, 325; 3/288, 299; 4/155, 197; other servants: new French maid, 1/293; page, 2/15, 16; 3/126; maids: Mary, 2/16; Susan, 2/106; Susan's sister, ib.; Betty, 2/236; butler Archibald dies, 2/211; new housekeeper at Wardrobe, 2/232; keeps poor house in Sandwich's absence, 2/122; 5/316

SOCIAL: at Whitehall chapel, 1/276; Lord Mayor's show, 1/277; investiture of peers, 2/79–80; talks of beauty, 1/314; and theology, 2/221; visits ships at Chatham, 2/15, 16; at Hampton Court, 2/25; 3/81–2; P's house, 2/143; gives New Year dinner, 3/1–2; criticises EP's portrait, 3/17; in Hyde Park, 3/78; at Greenwich, 3/126; shows P alterations at Hinchingbrooke, 4/308; with P/EP: at Hinchingbrooke, 3/219, 223; 8/471; Sandwich's London lodgings, the Wardrobe etc., 1/269, 272, 295, 300, 301, 312; 2/6, 8, 10, 30. 54, 64, 89, 116, 123, 126, 127, 132, 139, 145, 149, 151, 160, 162, 165, 176, 180, 184, 198, 201, 206, 217, 219, 226, 232; 3/6, 16, 21, 25, 33, 47, 49, 51, 57, 60, 64, 76, 92, 94, 102,

108; 5/119, 120, 185, 200, 238, 244–5, 333, 339, 347, 358; 6/5, 13, 17, 115; also, 1/309; 3/83
ALLUDED TO: 1/46; 2/101; 4/176; 7/154
MOUNTAGU, Lady Jemima, ('Mrs'/ 'Lady Jem'): see Carteret, Jemima
MOUNTAGU, John and Oliver, twin sons of Lord Sandwich: stay with P and EP to avoid smallpox, 2/153, 155, 157, 158; P examines in Greek and Latin, 8/472 & n. 1; alluded to: 9/335
MOUNTAGU, [Mary], (b. Aubrey) wife of (Sir) William (d. 1700): 3/1; 5/19; 8/598
MOUNTAGU, [Mary], ('Lady Mountagu'): 8/319
MOUNTAGU, Oliver: see Mountagu, John
MOUNTAGU, Lady Paulina, daughter of Lord Sandwich:
CHRON. SERIES: given page by Sandwich, 3/95; and parrot, 3/105; sent to Brampton to avoid smallpox, 4/439; 5/74 & n. 1, 95; returns to London, 5/32, 53; resents father's liaison, 5/173–4; frightened at shooting London Bridge, 5/180; 'a proper lady', 8/470; fatally ill, 9/455; death, 9/462 & n. 1; piety, 9/520
SOCIAL: on river trip, 2/142–3; at Bartholomew Fair, 2/166; at theatre, 3/57; also, 3/59, 89; 5/64, 65, 132, 184, 358; 9/211
ALLUDED TO: 5/153; 9/474
MOUNTAGU (Montagu), Ralph, son of the 2nd Lord Mountagu of Boughton, succ. as 3rd baron 1683, cr. Duke of Montagu 1705; Gentleman of the Horse to the Duchess of York (d. 1709): anecdote of, 3/43; alluded to: 3/12, 139
MOUNTAGU, Robert, styled Lord Mandeville, succ. as 3rd Earl of Manchester 1671 (d. 1683): on Naseby, 1/157; a gallant, 3/15; visits Louis XIV as ambassador extraordinary, 4/156 & n. 2; at Hampton Court, 7/27; valentine gift to Frances Stuart, 8/184; at Harwich in Medway crisis, 8/255; alluded to: 1/86
MOUNTAGU, Sir Sidney, father of Lord Sandwich (d. 1644): coarse

anecdote about, 1/261; his rise, 1/285 & n. 2; alluded to: 6/238 & n. 1
MOUNTAGU, Sidney, second son of Lord Sandwich (d. 1727):
CHRON. SERIES: stays with P and EP to avoid smallpox, 2/153, 155, 157, 158; education in Paris, 2/114 & n. 1, 142, 163 & n. 4; 4/25, 187; returns, 5/185 & n. 1; ill, 6/225; at Cranbourne, 7/54; returns from Spain, 9/321–2 & n.; welcomed at court, 9/323; to visit Flanders and Italy, 9/552; also, 3/291; 5/200
SOCIAL: sees Lord Mayor's Show, 1/276 & n. 3, 277; at theatre, 2/8; 9/419; dines with P, 9/423–4, 553; also, 9/345, 420, 541
MOUNTAGU, Abbot Walter (d. 1677): prevents duel between Sandwich and Buckingham, 2/33 & n. 1; to take charge of Sandwich's sons in Paris, 2/114 & n. 1; alluded to: 4/211 & n. 2
MOUNTAGU, Sir William, lawyer: given charge of Sandwich's will, 1/94 & n. 2, 95; his legal adviser, 1/271, 294, 310; 2/3; 4/45; loyalty to, 7/54; helps arrange Hinchingbrooke's marriage, 8/190 & n. 4; social: 3/1; 4/136; 8/598; alluded to: 8/22; 9/28
MOUNTAGU, ――, grandson of 1st Earl of Manchester: tried for arson and robbery, 8/316 & n. 2, 319; ~ his mother [Mary], 8/319
MOUNTNEY, [Richard], of the Customs House: 7/12
MOUNT'S BAY, Cornwall: 3/79; 9/320, 321
MOXON, [Joseph], type-founder and instrument maker, Cornhill: his shop, 4/302; P buys globes, 4/302 & n. 3; 5/83, 136; also, 4/350
MOYER, [Laurence], merchant, brother of Samuel (d. 1685): secures brother's release, 8/219–20 & n.
MOYER, Samuel, republican (d. 1683): imprisoned, 2/225 & n. 1; dispute over release, 8/219–20 & n., 325
MOYSE(S), Capt. [Richard], army officer: 1/57 & n. 3
MUDDIMAN, [Henry], journalist: his newsbooks, 1/12 & n. 3; 4/297, n. 2; 6/305, n. 3; at Rota Club, 1/13

9/233–4; Marlborough, 9/241; Reading, 9/243; Thetford, 9/336

MISC.: tavern/eating house music: harp, 1/15; gittern, 2/17; fiddler, 2/61, 175; harp and violin, 2/89; bagpipes and whistling, 2/101; mechanical organ, 2/115–16; dulcimer, 3/118; barber's music: 1/169; 4/237; dinner party music: 3/187; 8/4; street music: blind fiddler, 6/72; wedding music: 7/263; 8/66; also, 1/25, 59; 2/218, 233; 6/250, 251; 9/172, 313

UNDEFINED MUSIC (?instrumental, ?vocal, ?both): by P: 3/94, 184; 4/212, 213, 219, 220, 221, 266; 7/408, 412; by P with others: 3/108, 287; 5/266, 270, 310, 320; by others: 3/187

MUSICAL COMPOSITIONS:

COLLECTIONS [see also below, Lawes, Henry; Playford, John]: P's new song book, 1/161 & n. 4; his MS. song book, 1/302; French psalms in four parts, 1/140 & n. 3; three-part (?viol) music, 8/24–5; printed books of French songs, 9/428

SONGS AND OTHER COMPOSITIONS:

ANON.: ballads: 'The Blacksmith', 1/114 & n. 2; 'Chevy Chase', 8/56 & n. 3; 'St George' ['George, Duke of Albemarle'], 8/99 & n. 2; 'Joan's placket', 8/283 & n. 1; 'Mardyke', 1/41 & n. 2; 'Shackerley Hay', 6/2 & n. 1; others: 'All night I weep', 8/46 & n. 2; 'Barbara Allen', 7/1, 4, 5; 'La cruda la bella', 2/126 & n. 3; 'D'un air tout interdict', 6/223; 'Go and be hanged', 2/72 & n. 1, 78; 'Full forty times over', 8/466 & n. 3; 'The new droll', 8/5; ['I prithee sweet heart'], 2/72 & n. 1, 78; 'The Queen's old courtier', 9/242 & n. 3; 'S'io Moro', 8/174 & n. 2; 'This cursed jealousy', 3/36 & n. 2

[BANISTER, JOHN], ['Ah, Chloris now that I could sit'], 9/189 & n. 4; ['Go thy way'], 8/522 & n. 1; 9/189

[BREWER, THOMAS], 'Turn Amaryllis', 1/115 & n. 2

CARISSIMI, GIOVANNI, songs by, 5/217

DERING, RICHARD, Cantica Sacra, 3/263 & n. 2; 9/194 & n. 2; 'Canite Jehovae', 9/194 & n. 2

DRAGHI, GIOVANNI BATTISTA, opera

by, 8/54 & n. 4, 56

[HILTON, JOHN], 'Come follow, follow me', 7/383 & n. 2

HUMFREY, PELHAM: anthems by, 8/515; 9/563; also, 8/532, 534

[IVES, SIMON], 'Fly boy, fly', 1/59 & n. 1

[?KING, WILLIAM, Poems of Mr Cowley . . . composed into songs . . .], 9/208 & n. 1

[?LANIER, NICHOLAS], 'Hermit poor', 8/56 & n. 2

LAWES, HENRY, ['Ariadne'], 6/303 & n. 1; 'At dead low ebb', 8/165 & n. 2; Ayres and dialogues, 6/27 & n. 3; 'Help, help, O help, divinity of love', 1/169 & n. 3, 302; 7/205; ['The Kisse. A Dialogue'] ('What is a kiss?'), 1/164 & n. 2; ['O king of heaven and hell'] ('Orpheus Hymne'), 1/76 & n. 2; from The siege of Rhodes, 6/284 & nn.; 8/25 & n. 1, 59 & n. 1

LAWES, HENRY AND WILLIAM, [Choice Psalmes], 1/285 & n. 5; 3/281 & n. 3; 5/120, 128, 236

LULLY, JEAN-BAPTISTE, music alluded to, 7/171

LOCK, MATTHEW, 'Domine salvum' (canon), 1/63 & n. 3; Little consort of three parts, 1/114 & n. 1; 3/184; Modern church musick, 8/413 & n. 1; duo music for flageolets, 9/279 & n. 2

PEPYS, SAMUEL: see above, Music

PLAYFORD, JOHN, Catch that catch can (1667), 7/381 & n. 4; 8/168 & n. 4, 171 & n. 2, 174 & n. 2; Dancing Master, ?3/263 & n. 1, 278; English dancing-master, ? ib.; Musicks Handmaide, 4/76 & n. 1; Musicks Recreation, 4/152 & n. 2; Select ayres and dialogues, ? 1/54 & n. 6, 115 & n. 2; ?4/110

PORTER, WALTER, Mottets of two voyces, 5/261 & n. 2

RAVENSCROFT, THOMAS, The whole booke of psalmes, 5/332 & n. 1, 342

[?WILSON, JOHN], 'Great, good and just', 1/32–3 & n.; 'The lark now leaves his watery nest', 9/299 & n. 3, 303, 304

MUSKERRY, Lord: see MacCarty

MUSSEL BANK, in the Medway: 8/310

MYDDELTON, Elizabeth, wife of Richard: P admires 4/200; 7/283

NAVY, P'S SERVICE IN [i.e. as
secretary to fleet, 1660: for his work
as naval administrator, see Clerk of
the Acts; for his projected history of
the navy, see Writings (P)]:

NAVY BOARD, the [Unspecified
business is not indexed. For the
Board's building, see Navy Office.
See also Clerk of the Acts; and under
names of Principal Officers.]:

MEETINGS: to meet Duke of York weekly, 3/192 & n. 1; rules about morning/afternoon sessions, 2/143, 217; 3/31, 181; 4/49, 253; 5/88, 330; 7/95; time of the clock noted, 8/213; 9/47, 395; meets on Sunday, 5/349; at Christmas, 6/337; on Thursdays only during Plague, 6/188; interrupted by Fire, 7/281, 301, 316; by Dutch raid on Medway, 8/314; extraordinary meetings, 5/167; 7/13, 31, 82, 129, 419; 8/104, 385, 522; 9/125; meeting places (other than at Navy Office): Admiralty, 1/229, 241; Deptford and Greenwich in Plague, 6/173, 195 & n. 1, 200, 203; 7/7; Ruckholts, Essex, 6/222; Coventry's chamber, St James's Palace, 7/281; Brouncker's house, 7/284; Penn's parlour, 8/481; also, 4/322

RECORDS ETC.: books of precedents, 4/88; 'seabooks', 4/97; muster books, 7/100, 326; J. Humphrey's collection, 7/50 & n. 3; warrant book of First Dutch War, 9/300; office seal, 7/82–3; P buys books for, 4/395 & nn.; and globes, 5/117, 136; office furniture, 4/409, 436; 7/388

CHRON. SERIES [select]: given control of fleet in Duke of York's absence, 2/200; prepares for war, 5/111, 131, 262, 267, 273, 285, 293; preparations held up for lack of money, 7/210, 221, 233, 234–5, 239–40, 241, 248, 249, 255–6, 281, 284, 289, 307, 315, 339, 341, 349, 353, 383, 413; accused of negligence in supplying victuals, 7/172, 259 & n. 1, 260, 263, 264, 265; 8/513, 514, 517–18; 9/98; discusses fortification of Medway, 8/126 & n. 2; 9/56–7; provides fireships for Medway, 8/256(2) & n. 2, 259, 260 & n. 2; unpopularity in Medway crisis, 8/297–8, 302, 315, 337, 579; rumours of purge, 8/575; 9/100, 285, 290–1, 337, 380, 385, 504, 506–7, 509; attends Council enquiry into Medway raid, 8/460, 460–1; attends Commons to answer charges of Committee on Miscarriages, 8/494–6, 501, 502, 509–10, 512; its defence against charge concerning tickets, 9/97, 101, 103–4; answers enquiries

of Brooke House Committee, 9/34 & n. 4, 39, 42 & n. 1, 335, 394

BUSINESS

CONTRACTS [see also below, Business: victualling]: canvas, 5/136 & n. 3, 157 & n. 3, 238; deals, 4/232 & n. 4; fireships, 7/233; flags, 3/164; 5/178 & n. 4, 313; hemp, 3/114 & n. 1, 116, 129–30; 6/327 & n. 1; 7/150, 183–4, 358–9 & n., 385 & n. 2; lanterns, 5/117 & n. 1; masts, 3/268; 4/303–4 & n.; 5/6 & n. 4, 52, 108, 123, 215–16 & n., 239 & n. 1, 333; 7/2–3 & n.; Norway goods, 5/333 & n. 1; 6/330 & n. 2; provisions, 3/193; 5/73; tallow, 6/327 & n. 1; tar, 5/136 & n. 3, 352; timber, 4/326, 421; 5/299 & n. 3, 300–1, 303, 304; 6/77 & n. 3; timber and iron, 3/112 & n. 2, 114; yarn, 3/130; with E. India Company, 2/227–8 & n.; Board fails to scrutinise, 4/303

DOCKYARDS [indexed principally under Chatham; Deptford; Harwich; Portsmouth; Woolwich]: guard for, 2/11; accounts, 2/29 & n. 1; Admiral's Instructions to, 3/129 & n. 1; letter of 'reprehension and direction' to, 3/164 & n. 5; new mast-docks, 5/202, 231 & n. 1, 353; 6/95–6 & n.; strike, 6/216; difficulty of paying, 9/130, 419; reform of storekeepers' accounts, 9/444

SALES: (ships), 1/284, 305; 3/185–6; 8/484 & n. 3, 485; (stores), 2/45 & n. 3, 50 & n. 2, 68–9, 93 & n. 1; 4/319; Board criticised for, 9/562

FINANCIAL [general]: draws up estimates of debts, 1/231 & n. 4, 312; 2/240 & n. 1; of salaries, 2/50 & n. 1; and of ordinary charge, 4/152; is asked for estimates, 3/179 & n. 4; writes to/ consults Duke of York about insolvency, 2/119, 120, 154 & n. 1, 213 & n. 2; 3/47; 7/35(2), 36–7, 43, 123, 205–6 & n.; 8/41, 58, 62–3, 69, 70, 73, 78, 138, 140, 141, 142, 241, 274, 346, 392; 9/49, 94, 101, 115, 125, 126; applies to Lord Treasurer, Cabinet etc. for supply, 4/121 & n. 2; 6/77, 78; 7/48, 311 & n. 3; 9/122 & n. 1, 147–8, 152, 154, 171, 174, 444–5, 525, 530; presents accounts to Treasury, 3/6 &

n. 2, 280 & n. 1; 4/302 & n. 1; 5/325, 326, 330 & n. 2; 6/72; 7/294 & n. 1 (totals given); 8/57–8, 372 & n. 1, 373; and to Parliament, 7/64, 78, 93, 294, 295, 298, 305, 306, 308, 314, 356; 8/71 & n. 1, 303, 351, 448, 449; orders pursers' accounts etc. 2/29 & n. 1; examines/passes Navy Treasurer's accounts, 3/14, 240; 4/96–7, 99; 5/104 & n. 2, 105, 318, 329; 6/119(2), 203; 7/289; 8/141, 169–70, 448, 449, 458, 460; 9/222, 250; examines Comptroller's accounts, 7/76; 8/50; discusses paying off fleet, 3/252–3, 265; 6/149; hopes for money from sale of Dunkirk, 3/265, 271; assigned £200,000 p.a. by Exchequer, 3/297 & n. 1, 302; 4/81; discusses exchange rate of pieces-of-eight, 4/132, 133; draws up instructions for paying bills, 6/336 & n. 2; 'libel' against Board's failure to pay bills, 7/388; allotted £35,000 from poll tax, 8/57–8 & n., 89, 90; and £500,000 from Eleven Months Tax, 8/111–12, 205 & n. 1; bills sold at 35–40% discount, 8/201; receives £10,000 from Treasury, 8/252; discusses allocation from Treasury, 8/334; discusses pay tickets, 9/80, 263, 266; and cost of new fleet, 9/220 & n. 2; discusses expenses with Treasury, 9/444–5, 525–6, 530; credit good, 4/405 & n. 1; insolvency alluded to: 2/168; 3/210; 6/208, 211, 266, 273, 291–2, 293, 307, 322, 323, 324, 341; 7/256, 312, 313, 327, 331, 383; 8/66–7, 72, 96–7, 122 & n. 1, 206, 277 & n. 2, 315, 430–1; 9/18, 155, 180; also, 7/64, 78, 93, 383; 9/303

JUDICIAL AND DISCIPLINARY [*see also* Field, [E.]; Carkesse, [J.]]: Officers appointed J.P.s, 1/240, 252–3 & n.; 3/231; 4/78, 81–2 & n.; 8/31; commits alleged forger, 3/43–4 & n.; charges alleged thief, 3/137 & n. 2; adjudicates in dispute between captain and purser, 3/284 & n. 1; commits naval officers to trial for cowardice, 6/104 & n. 4; adjudicates between captain and master, 4/84; between captain and lieutenant, 7/380; between commander and Waith of Treasury, 7/93–4 & n.; investigates

loss of ships, 8/12 & n. 1, 28; investigates charges against dockyard officers 9/258–9 & n., 267 & n. 2

SEAMEN AND OFFICERS: chooses ship's masters etc., 2/103; 4/72; discusses establishments, 4/290; 6/339 & n. 1; (peacetime), 8/448 & n. 2; the press, 5/168 & n. 2; 6/45; 7/188; 8/394; discharges men etc., 7/327; discusses riot, 8/62–3

SHIPS AND SHIPBUILDING: hires ships, 1/242; 5/349, 350; (fireships), 7/161; (for Portugal), 3/63, 72, 85, 196; pays off ships, 1/245 & n. 1, 246, 247, 249, 283, 288, 308–9; 2/18, 19, 28, 30, 33; 8/396–7; appoints winter guard, 1/257, 266: 8/485–6; sets out ships, 2/127; 3/30–1, 125 & n. 2; 5/287 & n. 2; 6/233; 9/101, 121–2, 123, 125, 126, 130, 155, 180, 216–17, 220 & n. 2, 223(2); (for Guinea), 5/246 & n. 3, 248, 265; (fireships), 8/256(2) & n. 2, 259, 260 & n. 2; (merchantmen), 8/314–15, 316; (for Mediterranean), 9/424, 425–6, 510, 513 ~ to build ten ships, 7/193 & n. 5, 201; discusses design of masts, 9/5 & n. 1; and Heemskerck's project, 9/198 & n. 1, 206; values ships, 9/96 & n. 1; also, 5/111, 131

SICK AND WOUNDED: orders money for, 6/239 & n. 1, 243 & n. 2; approves proposal for infirmary, 7/49 & n. 2; discusses relief of prisoners, 7/201

VICTUALLING: examines/passes accounts, 3/41–2 & n., 52, 55, 62, 103, 106; 4/337; 7/74(2), 373, 403, 405; 8/47, 49, 50, 77, 208, 322; 9/250; inspects victualling office, 3/135 & n. 3; 4/84; obtains cash by sale of prize-goods, 6/239 & n. 1; discusses P's report, 7/219–20 & n.; examined by Council about complaints of Rupert and Albemarle, 7/259 & n. 1, 260; concludes new contract with Gauden, 9/252, 253, 261, 263, 287(2) & n. 1, 288 & n. 2, 301, 303(2) & n. 1, 428 & n. 4, 429; decides against direct management, 9/315–18 passim & nn.; prepares supplies for Mediterranean fleet, 9/508 & n. 2; also, 1/212–13; 4/36, 282; 7/13, 129, 135; 8/245; 9/24–5, 142

OTHER BUSINESS: petitions, 2/32; 4/50; Tangier, 2/145, 189; salutes, 2/222 & n. 3; 3/6; expedition to Bombay, 3/40 & n. 2, 41, 47, 51; Kuffeler's mine, 3/45–6 & n.; Jamaica, 3/52, 63; disputes with E. India Company, 5/26, 76 & n. 3, 232; 6/291; calculation of tonnage, 5/357–8 & n.; ordnance, 6/131; 7/43, 104; plague, 6/206; pursers: 7/10, 13, 14, 28, 106; (accounts), 2/29; want of discipline in navy, 9/39; acts of war in presence of British ships, 9/87–8; flag-officers' pensions, 9/257 & n. 2; supernumeraries, 9/290 & n. 3, 291; Board's responsibility for Ticket Office, 9/383; instructions to commanders, 9/548, 549, 563, 564

SOCIAL: Officers invited to Lord Mayor's banquet, 2/201, 203; watch Vane's execution, 3/108; meet Ordnance officers, 3/130, 187; 6/132; entertained by colleagues, 3/272; 6/119, 193, 217; 7/11; 9/250; by others, 6/208, 335–6; at theatre, 9/329; at parish dinner, 9/559; also, 6/193–4

MISC: mutual jealousy of Officers, 2/14; they lay wagers on war news, 7/250; invited to lend to government, 8/398, 399; office gallery in church, 1/225, 230 & n. 2, 233, 254, 289; office barge, 3/60, 129, 193; 4/219, 225, 228

NAVY OFFICE, the [i.e. the building. For P's office, see Clerk of the Acts; for his house, see Seething Lane; for the houses and offices of his colleagues, see under names.]:

GENERAL: P inspects, 1/192 & n. 2; Principal Officers take possession, 1/194; houses allocated, 1/198; buildings saved in Fire, 7/276, 277, 278; parties held in, 8/28–9; 9/12, 464; garden-door altered, 8/502; office cleaned, 3/126; 8/240, 525, 526

GARDEN: alterations to, 3/17, 27, 55; office records etc. buried in during Fire, 7/274; gardener, 3/17; garden (?Merchants') gate, 4/55 & n. 1, 70; broom shed, 9/46

OTHER FEATURES: inner room, 1/306; backdoor, 3/182; 9/188; grate, 4/409; stove, 4/436; table, 7/388; gates,

1/213; courtyard, 1/215; backyard, 4/433

NAVY TREASURER, the: see Carteret, Sir G.

NAVY TREASURY, the (until Sept. 1664 in Leadenhall St; afterwards in Broad St): Navy Board acquires Broad St building, 5/278 & n. 2, 282; P visits, 3/278; 7/83, 133; 8/140, 162, 355, 524; pays at, 1/310; 2/227, 237, 238; 3/44, 225, 234; 4/2, 391; 7/132–3; seamen threaten disorders, 7/137, 196, 330 & n. 3, 332; 8/524; 9/137; clerks criticised, 8/441; Navy Board's order to Pay Office, 8/531; Nonconformist services in Leadenhall St building, 9/385

NAYLOR, [Oliver], Prebendary of Exeter: eloquent sermon, 3/44 & n. 2

NAYLOR, [William], of Offord, Hunts.: 8/158

NEALE, Sir P.: see Neile

NEALE, [Thomas], projector: marriage, 5/184 & n. 2; also, 6/126

NEAT HOUSES: see Chelsea

NEGROES: colour when drowned, 3/63 & n.; mummified body, 6/215; servants: 2/36, 61, 69; 4/51; 6/244, 283, 285, 288; 8/123; 9/464, 510

NEILE (Neale), Sir Paul, courtier and astronomer: business with Robert P, 2/47; consulted by Sandwich on astronomy, 3/7; social: 6/36; 7/410; 9/163

NELLSON, ——, merchant: supplies flags, 5/305, 308(2), 312

[NES, Aert Janszoon van], naval commander: 8/359 & n. 2

NETHERLANDS, the: see United Provinces of the Netherlands

NEVILL, [Thomas], draper: 1/277

NEVILLE, [Mary], Lady Abergavenny (Aberguemy), wife of George, 11th Baron (d. 1699): 5/53 & n. 2

NEWARK, Notts.: anecdote of siege (1646), 6/30 & n. 1; mutiny (Oct. 1645), 6/30–1 & n.

NEWBERY, [Capt. Richard], naval officer: 1/110

NEWBORNE, Tom, navy solicitor: dies from eating cucumbers, 4/285 & n. 1; nickname, ib.; shared bribes with Batten, 5/141; social: 2/44, 58

NEW BRIDEWELL, Clerkenwell: P visits, 5/250 & n. 4, 289; 6/65–6, & n. 3

NEWBURY, Berks.: P at, 9/242

NEWCASTLE, Duke and Duchess of: see Cavendish

NEWCASTLE UPON TYNE, Northumberland: parliamentary election, 2/76 & n. 1; dispute between city and Gerard, 9/359 & nn.; shipping from/ to, 4/395, 397; 8/263, 285, 602; coals from, 8/426, 435, 576

NEW CHAPEL, Orchard St, Westminster: plague burials, 6/162

NEWELL, ——, clergyman: 3/199

NEW ENGLAND: masts/mastships from, 5/123, 127, 239, 321; 7/395, 397; alluded to: 4/71

NEW EXCHANGE, Strand (the Exchange): shut by King's order, 4/431 & n. 5; P spreads news at, 7/151; makes assignation, 7/385; drafts memorandum, 9/84(2); P/EP shop(s) at: for pendants, 4/100; mercers' and drapers' goods, 4/100; 7/70, 344; 8/104, 322, 424; 9/84, 188, 206–7, 400; dressing-boxes, 8/53; 9/91(2); books, 7/103, 104, 117; 8/380, 383, 387, 439, 508; 9/29, 216, 411, 449; baubles, 7/386; knives, 8/433; also visit(s) (to pay bills, or for unspecified purposes): 1/85, 251; 3/52, 65, 215; 4/58, 100, 124, 164, 286, 290, 324, 332, 336, 341, 357, 363; 5/9, 48, 55, 118, 134, 144, 155, 186, 238, 269; 6/17, 52, 100; 7/124, 131, 208, 256, 367, 369, 425; 8/27, 30, 46, 86, 99, 100, 110, 121, 151, 213, 334, 341, 353, 393, 403, 431, 460, 463; 9/6, 28, 39, 46, 89, 113, 120, 124, 158, 178, 179, 182, 215, 218, 247, 264, 269, 295, 304, 313, 333, 393, 397, 412, 419, 422, 437, 465, 449, 474, 511, 532

NEW EXCHANGE STAIRS: 7/233, 284; 8/517; 9/128

NEWGATE: 9/258

NEWGATE MARKET: P shops in: for grate, 4/409; poultry, 5/264; also, 3/294; 9/268; shambles, 3/283; Fire, 7/277

NEWGATE PRISON: prisoners escape, 8/371; malpractices of keeper, 8/562 & n. 2; alluded to: 4/5; 9/111

NEW HALL, Essex: timber at, 4/435 & n. 3

NEWINGTON, Surrey: P's father married, 5/360; alluded to: 2/91

NEWINGTON GREEN, Mdx: 5/132, ?360

NEWMAN, Col. [George]: 4/260

NEWMAN, Samuel, Puritan divine [see also Books]: foretells his death, 9/31 & n. 3

NEWMAN, ——, barber: 1/15

NEWMARKET, Suff.: King/Duke of York visit(s) races at, 4/324 & n. 2; 9/209 & n. 2, 264, 341, 343, 473 & n. 5, 535 & n. 2

NEW NETHERLAND (N. America): surrender of, 5/283 & n. 2

NEW PALACE YARD, [New York] Westminster [see also Taverns etc.: Crown; Leg; Swan]: soldiers in, 1/40, 43; Quaker meeting, 1/44 & n. 2; also, 3/177; 4/234

NEWPORT, Andrew, Comptroller of the Great Wardrobe: appointed, 9/41 & n. 3; at Exchequer, 9/477; social: 9/112

NEWPORT [Richard]: at Vauxhall, 9/218 & n. 4, 220

NEWPORT, Essex: 8/467

NEWPORT (I. of Wight), TREATY OF (1648): 4/473 & n. 2

NEWPORT PAGNELL, Bucks.: P visits, 9/224, 225 & nn.

NEWPORT ST, Westminster: 9/431

NEWSPAPERS: Muddiman's parliamentary newsbooks, 1/12 & n. 3; P's letters quoted in, 1/126, n. 2; Buckhurst's defence in, 3/35–6 & n.; Scottish news, 4/138 & n. 3; 7/387 & n. 2; Portuguese news, 4/203 & n. 1; P reads first number of The Intelligencer, 4/297 & n. 2; asked to contribute news to, 5/348 & n. 1; Moore's account of Battle of Lowestoft in, 6/128 & n. 3; P pays for newsbooks, 6/162; Oxford Gazette: P reads first number, 6/305 & n. 3; Chatham Chest business in 7/116 & n. 2; Great Fire foretold, 7/405 & n. 3, 406; report on Carkesse case, 8/216 & n. 1; French news, 9/38 & n. 1; P reads newsbooks at Brouncker's, 9/161; Lisbon gazette, 4/215 & n. 1; Dutch gazette, 8/126–7 & n. 1; also, 7/242

9/434 & n. 2; P defends Cambridge against, 9/545; the colleges: purge of fellows, 1/227 & n. 1; All Souls, 9/226 & n. 2; Brasenose, ib. & n. 3; Christ Church, 8/379; 9/226; New College, 9/544 & n. 4

OXFORD KATE'S: *see* Taverns etc.: Cock, Bow St

[OXMAN, William], rebel: executed, 2/18 & n. 2

PACKER (Parke), [John], merchant: dispute about Portuguese customs-dues, 5/43 & n. 2

PACKER, [Philip], Deputy-Paymaster of the King's Works: advises Sandwich on alterations at Hinchingbrooke, 2/48–9 & n.; social: 9/527, 559; ~ his ?wife/mother, 1/272

PADDINGTON: P at, 7/204

PAGE, Damaris: her brothel destroyed in riot, 9/132

PAGE, Capt. [Thomas], naval officer: account of Four Days Fight, 7/153

PAGE, [William], of Ashtead, Surrey: P and Creed stay with overnight, 4/245 & n. 3

PAGET, [Justinian], lawyer, of Gray's Inn: makes music, 3/184, 281, 287; 5/119; also, 1/234; 4/367; ~ his son [Justinian, of Gray's Inn], 8/365

PAGET'S: *see* Taverns etc.: Mitre, Mitre Court

PAINTER-STAINERS' Company: *see* London: livery companies

PALACE YARD: *see* New Palace Yard

PALL MALL (the alley for the game): *see* St James's Park

PALL MALL (the street) [*see also* Taverns etc.: Wood's]: Plague in, 6/147–8; Lady Castlemaine's lodgings, 7/159; Sir H. Cholmley's house, 9/122; also, 9/540

PALMER, Barbara, (b. Villiers), wife of Roger, 1st Earl of Castlemaine, cr. Duchess of Cleveland 1670:

PERSONAL: P admires her beauty, 2/174; 3/24, 82, 139, 175–6; 4/63; 5/161, 214; 7/347, 409; 8/33; her clothes on washing line, 3/87; her graciousness to child, 3/175; her dancing, 3/301; and her dress, 4/57;

dreams about, 6/191; plain dress unbecoming to, 7/306; her patches, 9/186; her beauty decays, 4/182; 5/294–5; 7/106

CHRON. SERIES: King associates/ dallies with, 1/199 & n. 4; 2/80; 3/87, 302; 4/1, 13, 30, 342; 5/164; flirts with Duke of York, 1/265; relations with Queen, 3/87, 97, 191, 202, 289; 4/68; appointment to Queen's Household, 3/147 & n. 2; leaves husband to live at Richmond, 3/139 & n. 2; moves into Whitehall Palace, 4/112, 132, 134; at Oxford with King, 4/315; ill, 3/24; pregnancy rumoured, 3/248 & n. 1; 4/1; 7/324; 8/355, 366, 368; and abortion, 5/245; 6/71 & n. 3; quarrels with King, 4/213, 216, 222, 272, 342; 8/331, 333, 334, 355; their reconciliations, 4/238; 5/20, 21; 8/366; to leave court, 8/412, 422 & n. 3, 424; at court but out of favour, 8/431–2, 590; 9/24, 219; friendly to Frances Stuart, 8/288; to Nell Gwyn, 8/402; libel against, 9/154 & n. 1; association with/power over King alluded to, 3/132, 147, 227, 282; 4/136, 137, 174, 206, 238, 256; 6/115–16; 7/8, 159, 404, 409; 8/184, 368, 377; 9/27, 417; debts paid by King, 7/404 & n. 2; 8/324–5; pension, 8/424; grant for children stopped, 8/434 & n. 3; affair with Sir C. Berkeley, 4/38; H. Jermyn, 8/366 & n. 2, 368; and Hart, 9/156 & n. 4; alleged lechery as child, 7/336–7; turns catholic, 4/431 & n. 4; attends Queen's chapel, 8/589

POLITICAL INFLUENCE [*see also* chron. series]: friend of Monmouth, 3/191; distracts King from business, 7/57; supports standing army, 8/361; makes a bishop, 8/364–5 & n.; supports H. Brouncker, 8/416; welcomes Clarendon's fall, 8/404 & n. 1, 415, 427; her part in Nicholas's fall, 8/534; alliance with Buckingham, 8/331, 342; 9/27; and enmity to, 9/336, 342; makes peace between King and Duke of York, 9/153; supports French treaty, 9/536

AT COURT: causes factions, 3/15, 245; envied by court ladies, 3/64; power, 3/237; mocks at maids of honour,

232, 234 & n. 1; abortive motion to reward Sandwich, 1/178 & n. 2; allocates excise to King, 1/303 & n. 4; orders exhumation of regicides' corpses, 1/309 & n. 4; Committee for disbandment of armed forces: appointment and proceedings, 1/245 & n. 1, 246 & n. 3, 247, 249, 283, 288 & n. 1, 308–9; 2/18 & n. 3, 19 & n. 2, 28 & n. 3, 30, 33 & n. 3, 45 & n. 1, 50; parties: Presbyterians to impose terms on King, 1/117, 118; Cavaliers and Presbyterians, 1/118 & n. 4; Episcopalians and Presbyterians, 1/229; 'factions', 2/1

PARLIAMENT (the Cavalier):
ELECTIONS: Cambridge borough, 2/56 & n. 2; London, 2/57 & n. 1; Newcastle-upon-Tyne, 2/76 & n. 1; bye-elections: court candidates defeated, 7/337 & n. 2; Quakers' candidate, 9/150 & n. 2; expenses, 8/454–5 & n.

FIRST SESSION, 8 May 1661–19 May 1662:
  HOUSE OF LORDS: examines Hutchinson's accounts, 2/100; dispute with Commons over licensing bill, 2/144 & n. 3; bishops resume seats, 2/216 & n. 4; debates Clarendon's proviso to bill of uniformity, 3/49 & n. 1; prayers, 3/61

  HOUSE OF COMMONS: receives communion, 2/107 & n. 1; orders Commonwealth legislation to be burnt, 2/108 & n. 4; bill restoring bishops to Lords, 2/111 & n. 2; benevolences, ib. & n. 4; grants supply, 2/217–18 & n.; lack of government control, 2/141 & n. 3; examines regicides, 2/224 & n. 1; orders fast, 3/10 & n. 2; militia bill, 3/15 & n. 2; hearth tax bill, 3/41 & n. 2, 43, 78; uniformity bill, 3/49; hastens business, 3/85

SECOND SESSION, 18 Feb.–27 July 1663:
  GENERAL: reassembles, 4/49; King's speech, 4/50 & n. 2; King calls on to hasten business, 4/159 & n. 3; prorogation, 4/239, 240, 249–51 & nn.; forms of royal assent to bills, 4/249–50 & nn.

  HOUSE OF LORDS: Bristol's attempted impeachment of Clarendon, 4/222–5 passim & nn., 229 & n. 3, 231 & n. 2;

defeats conventicle bill, 4/249; debates bill on popery, ib.; 'mislays' bill for sabbath observance, ib. & n. 2

  HOUSE OF COMMONS: opposes King's declaration of indulgence, 4/44 & n. 2, 57 & n. 4, 58 & n. 1, 62, 63, 82; to disqualify members refusing to abjure Covenant, 4/53 & n. 1; bill encouraging wearing of English cloth, ib. & n. 2; bill and address against popery, 4/67–8, 90 & n. 1, 92, 95 & n. 2, 249; resumption of crown lands, 4/87–8; to enquire into navy expenses, 4/103; and Queen's, 4/127 & n. 1; bill to disqualify ex-rebels from office, 3/291; 4/125 & n. 1, 126, 136 & n. 1; bill to suppress abuses in sale of offices, 4/156 & n. 4, 166, 169 & n. 2, 190; enquiries into revenue, 4/166, 193 & n. 2; bill to suppress conventicles, 4/159–60, 161, 243 & n. 3, 249; votes supply, 4/183, 187, 191, 205–6 & n., 249–50; votes £200,000 p.a. to navy from customs, 4/206 & n. 3; votes on Temple's attempt to manage House, 4/191–2 & n., 200, 207, 208, 211; Bristol's speech on, 4/207–8 & nn.; fast day for weather, 4/237 & n. 3; bill to enforce sabbath observance, 4/249 & n. 2; parties: court party, 4/57, 58

THIRD SESSION, 16 March–17 May 1664:
  GENERAL: reassembles, 5/88; adjourned and reassembles, 5/93; King's speech on triennial bill, 5/112 & n. 4; act about writs of error, 5/112; joint address against Dutch, 5/131, 135, 137; King's reply, 5/137; conference on conventicle bill, 5/147–8 & nn.; (untrue) rumour of prorogation, 5/151; prorogued, 5/247 & n. 4

  HOUSE OF LORDS: Lady Petre's case, 5/109–12 passim & nn., 126, 128–9; joint address with Commons against Dutch, 5/131

  HOUSE OF COMMONS: triennial bill, 5/93–4, 99 & nn., 102–3; Navy Board enabling bill, 5/99 & n. 1, 104, 105; merchants' petitions against Dutch, 5/107–9 passim, 113, 127, 129 & n. 2; grants £2½m. for war, 5/331 & n. 1; parties: Bristol's faction, 5/89; Presbyterian faction, 5/103, 327–8; King's party, 5/331

Commons over Carr, 8/583, 587; 9/57, 85; bill establishing Brooke House Committee, 9/8, 9; Penn's impeachment, 9/173–4 & n., 175–6, 178; dispute with Commons over Skinner v. E. India Company, 9/182–96 passim & nn.; parties: Duke of York's friends, 8/482

HOUSE OF COMMONS: supply business: backward in granting, 8/324, 331, 395, 534, 568, 591; 9/82–3, 140, 141, 163, 171–2, 173, 180, 184; demands accounts of expenditure, 9/82–3 & n.; votes £300,000 from wine and poll tax, 9/92–3 & n., 120, 123, 141, 192; clergy excused from poll, 9/120–1 & n.; also, 9/114, 115, 167; Clarendon's impeachment: thanks King for dismissal, 8/476, 479, 480; impeachment process, 8/478, 499 & n. 1, 502 & nn., 509, 522, 523 & n. 2, 526, 532–3, 533 & n. 1, 539 & n. 3; replies to Lords' objections, 8/534, 557–8 & n., 559, 561; condemns Clarendon's petition, 8/563; bill of banishment, 8/578 & n. 1; also, 8/532, 555–6; Committee on Miscarriages: appointed, 8/484–5 & n.; revived, 9/135 & n. 2, 138; terms of reference, 8/485, 494; enquires into division of fleet (1666), 8/489 & n. 1, 502; voted a miscarriage, 9/70, 74, 75; enquires into prize-goods scandal (1665), 8/486, 494, 499, 549, 576; 9/64, 80, 96; into failure to pursue Dutch fleet (1665), 8/489–90 & n., 491–2; 9/142, 166–7 & n.; voted a miscarriage, 9/80 & n. 3; into issue of tickets and failure to defend Medway (1667), 8/493–8 passim & nn., 501, 502, 504, 508–11 passim, 526–7, 538 & n. 1, 540, 545–6; 9/11, 62, 69, 70, 76, 77, 79, 84, 85; Board defended by P before committee, 8/494–6 & nn.; voted a miscarriage, 9/76, 86–7, 95, 97, 98; enquires into sale of places by Coventry, 8/504, 505; into Bergen affair, 8/538; orders to Navy Board, 8/489, 493, 501, 537–8 & n.; examines P, 8/493; and Navy Board, 8/494–6 passim & nn., 501–2, 510; criticises victualling, 9/98, 107, 142; Board defended by P before House, 9/102–6 & nn.; Committee attends Privy

Council, 9/122; Brooke House Committee (the Commissioners of Accounts): appointed, 8/559–60 & n.; 9/8–9, 63; membership, 8/559–60 & n., 569–70, 571–2, 576–7, 586; 9/30, 44; powers, 8/601; 9/50 & n. 1, 179–80 & n.; efficiency, 8/586; 9/43–4 & n., 292; enquiries into pay tickets, 9/43–4, 56, 97; prize-goods scandal (1665), 9/49–50, 63, 64, 66, 68, 92, 162, 363–4; Warren's gifts, 9/73 & n. 2, 92, 220, 254 & n. 1, 277; Navy Treasury, 9/82, 179, 214 & n. 5; allegations against Coventry, 9/258; Hewer, 9/283; Waith, 9/358 & n. 1; and P, 9/562 & n. 1; into contracts, 9/394; interim report, 9/117; also, 8/599, 602; 9/34, 162(2), 335, 394; other business: opposes standing army, 8/324 & n. 3, 332 & n. 1, 352–3, 355, 361; resents adjournment, 8/352 & n. 1, 361, & n. 1; condemns Kelyng, 8/483–4 & n., 577, 578, 579; receives petitions against Mordaunt, 8/501–2 & n.; thanks Rupert and Albemarle, 8/515; condemns Woodmongers' charter, 8/520 & n. 4; proceedings against Commissioner Pett, 8/526–7; resolution on freedom of speech, 8/547 & n. 3; proceedings against Gerard of Brandon, 8/573–4 & n., 581, 583, 587; 9/57; hostile to bill for comprehension and toleration, 9/31 & n. 4, 35, 45–6 & n., 51–2, 60 & n. 2, 104, 111, 112; vehement against nonconformists, 9/96 & n. 1, 181; debates conventicle bill, 9/177 & n. 3, 192; bill prohibiting duelling, 9/53 & n. 1; libel distributed, 9/65 & n. 2; debates King's speech, 9/70; secretary of state's intelligence service, 9/70–1 & n., 74 & nn.; Temple's 'undertakers', 9/71 & n. 2; King's evil counsellors, 9/74; Temple's triennial bill, 9/77 & n. 2; petition against Ormond, 9/119, 169; impeachment of Penn, 9/162, 163, 165, 170; expulsion and impeachment of H. Brouncker, 9/170; dispute with Lords over Skinner v. E. India Company, 9/182–3 & n., 184, 191, 192, 196; second bill for rebuilding London, 9/187–8 & n.; parties: power of 'discontented party', 8/324, 352; Duke

pp. xix–xx; 3/26–7 & n.; 8/261 & nn., 274 & n. 2; decay of, 5/134; P's immediate family listed with birth-dates, 5/360–1 & nn.; lack of hand-some women, 8/365

PEPYS, [Anne], wife of Robert, of Brampton, Hunts., P's aunt: ill of the stone, 1/320–1 & n.; 2/5, 17, 27, 52, 133, 134; sends for P's father in hus-band's last illness, 2/126, 127; trouble-some, 2/134 & n. 1, 137; provisions of husband's will, 2/134 & n. 1, 138, 148; dispute over bond, 2/164; 4/384; 5/353

PEPYS, Anne (Nan), of Worcs.: *see* Fisher, ——; Hall, ——

PEPYS, Bab and Betty, Roger's daughters, P's cousins: visit London with father, 9/446, 450; comely, 9/453; stay at P's house, 9/453–4, 455, 460; at theatre, 9/453, 454, 456, 458, 459, 476; visit Bedlam, 9/454; Westminster Abbey, 9/456–7; and glasshouse, 9/457; at P's dance, 9/463–5 passim; return to Impington, 9/477; also, 9/475; ~ their maid Martha, 9/454

PEPYS, Charles ('the joiner'), son of Thomas Pepys of London: at reading of Robert P's will, 2/153; his legacy, 4/20, 42–3, 102, 345, 346; 5/157; social: 2/172

PEPYS, Edith, P's aunt: *see* Bell

PEPYS, Edward, of Broomsthorpe, Norf., P's cousin: dies, 4/421 & n. 2, 425; funeral scutcheons and hatch-ments, 4/424–5 & n., 427; buried, 4/426; 5/10; funeral procession, 4/432; social: 1/54, 60; alluded to: 1/72; 5/76; 8/365

PEPYS, Elizabeth, (b. St Michel), wife of the diarist [*see also* entries under Dress etc.; Health: Household Goods etc.; Servants. For her relations with the Pepyses, Mountagus, St Michels and others, *see* under names.]:

PERSONAL: her beauty admired at wedding, 1/196; at theatre, 9/398; by Sandwich, 4/186; by Duke of York, 9/515; pretty wearing black patch, 1/283; in black laced gown, 2/117; in flowered tabby, 9/134; better looking than Princess Henrietta Maria, 1/299;

the only pretty woman in theatre, 9/450; her 'comely person', 6/31; washes before going to court, 1/298 & n. 3; visits bath house, 6/40 & n. 1, 41, 45; spends day getting clean, 9/372; snores, 1/266–7; rides well, 2/180; her watch, 8/51, 146

PORTRAITS: by Savill: 2/218 & n. 4, 227, 233, 234, 235; her dog added, 2/241; altered because unlike, 3/17, 19, 21; hung in dining room, 3/25, 34, 106; P wishes Huysmans to paint, 5/276 & & n. 3; 6/113; by Hayls: 7/43, 44 & n. 2, 48, 52, 53–4, 61, 65, 69, 72; a good likeness, 7/73, 74, 78, 82; improved, 9/292, 297, 299; alluded to, 7/98, 108, 117, 120; 9/138; by Cooper: 9/138 & n. 3, 139, 140, 253, 256, 258–61 passim, 263, 264, 267, 268, 276–7; not such a good likeness, 9/264, 267

CHRON. SERIES:

MAIN BIOGRAPHICAL EVENTS: mar-riage, vol. i, p. xxii & n. 13; early differences and separation, 2/153 & n. 3; 4/277 & n. 1; 5/196 & n. 2; believes herself pregnant, 1/1; 4/365; Uncle Wight's unusual attentions to, 5/14, 16, 24, 55, 65; her child to be his heir, 5/61; he proposes they have child, 5/145–6, 151; death, vol. i, p. xxxv

MOVEMENTS/VISITS TO BRAMPTON ETC: with Bowyers during P's Dutch voyage, 1/84, 85, 88, 89–90; returns to London, 1/131, 166, 177, 178; re-united with P, 1/173; moves from Axe Yard to Seething Lane, 1/199–203 passim; stays with P's father during alterations to house, 2/64–7 passim, 88, 90, 94, 96; with P visits Portsmouth, 2/90–4; rides to Bramp-ton and back, 2/180–4; at Brampton while house altered, 3/134, 140, 141, 144, 145, 148, 151, 182; returns, 3/199, 200, 206, 208, 209; with Tom P while house cleaned, 3/251; with P at Sandwich's lodgings, 3/299, 301; 4/1–6 passim; visits Brampton with Ashwell, 4/174, 176, 178, 179, 180, 183, 184, 199, 210, 212, 262; returns following quarrels, 4/271, 273, 276; visits Brampton with P, 4/306–14; without him, 5/200, 201, 224, 233–4; to stay at home till after Easter, 5/358;

to stay at Woolwich in Plague, 6/128 & n. 2, 134, 140, 143, 147; settles in with two maids, 6/149; P's visits to, 6/151–2, 153, 162, 170, 174, 183, 185, 190, 200, 205–6; joined by P, 6/207–10 passim, 212, 214, 216, 219, 221, 223, 226, 228; he visits from Greenwich lodgings, 6/242, 246, 249–50, 262, 263, 273, 303; she visits him, 6/250–3 passim, 270, 279, 280, 282, 284, 286, 295, 296; P rents rooms for at Greenwich, 6/261 & n. 3, 271; she moves to, 6/309, 313, 314; returns to London, 6/313–16 passim, 318, 341; visits P at Greenwich, 6/320, 321, 324, 326, 327, 338; 7/2, 3, 5, 6; P visits in London, 6/329(2), 332, 340; they return to house in Seething Lane, 7/7; with P visits Cranbourne and Windsor, 7/54, 56–9 passim; visits Brampton to advise on Pall's marriage, 7/86, 91(2), 92, 93, 104; with P camps in Navy Office during Fire, 7/273, 274, 275; sent to Woolwich with his gold, 7/275, 280, 283, 284, 285, 286, 289; takes gold to Brampton in Medway crisis, 8/262, 263, 264, 273; returns to London with account of burying it, 8/279, 280, 281; visits Brampton with P and Deb Willet, 8/453, 465–75 passim; at Audley End, 8/467–8; Cambridge, 8/468–9; at Brampton with Deb and others, 9/98, 125, 143, 144, 180; P visits her there, 9/210–12; and calls for at start of West Country tour, 9/224; visits Oxford, 9/226; Salisbury, 9/229; Stonehenge, 9/229–30; Chitterne, 9/231; Bath, 9/232–4, 236, 238–9; Bristol, 8/234–5; Avebury, 9/240; Marlborough, 9/241; visits Petersfield with P and Deb Willet, 9/273–4; with Deb and Hewer visits Roger P to see Sturbridge Fair, 9/301, 306, 310, 315

PUBLIC EVENTS/LONDON SIGHTS: sees burning of the Rump, 1/53; Queen-Mother and princesses dine in public, 1/297, 299; Queen in presence chamber, 3/299; hanging of regicides' corpses, 2/26–7; pre-coronation procession, 2/83; coronation banquet, 2/85; drinks King's health at bonfire, 2/87; sees alterations in St James's Park, 2/171; rides in Hyde Park coach parades on May Day etc., 3/78; 5/126, 130, 163; 6/89; 8/193, 197; 9/142–3, 260, 269, 270, 487, 515–16, 530, 533–4, 540–1, 541–2, 549, 556, 563, 564; sees wrestling at Moorfields, 3/93; visits Bartholomew Fair, 4/298; 5/259–60; 8/405, 421, 423; 9/290, 293, 296, 299; synagogue, 4/335; at Col. Turner's execution, 5/23; service in Whitehall chapel, 6/86, 87; visits Clarendon House, 7/220; sees Fire of London, 7/272; and city ruins, 7/291; watches bull baiting 7/245–6; puppet plays, 3/254–5; 7/257, 265, 267; 8/121, 157, 421; 9/296; at court ball, 7/371, 372, 373; meets Nell Gwyn, 8/27; sees block ships in river, 8/293; giant children, 8/326, 500; prize fights, 8/429, 430; 9/516; bearded woman, 9/398; giantess, 9/440; royal tombs in Westminster Abbey, 9/456–7

MISC.: receives gifts from P's business associates, 1/222; 2/225; 4/293, 295, 298–9, 391, 415; 5/45, 47, 316; interprets French for Lady Sandwich, 1/293; attends women friends in labour, 2/150, 151; 8/177(2); 9/260; on bad terms with Lady Batten, 2/161; 3/146, 249–50, 302; 4/71, 426; 5/356; ends estrangement from, 6/46, 95; helps wounded acquaintance after fight, 2/229; importuned by drunk, 4/342; fortune told by gipsies, 9/278; first rides in P's new coach, 9/379; and with his new horses, 9/399–400

RELATIONS WITH P [for the Deb affair, *see* Willet]:

HER LOVE: troubled at his going to sea, 1/84; rejoices at his becoming Clerk of the Acts, 1/199; frightened at his injured thumb, 7/37; devotion in early hardships, 8/82; comforts him before parliamentary speech, 9/102; rejoices in its success, 9/104; rejects advances from Sandwich and Hinchingbrooke, 9/356, 404 & n. 2; and from others, 9/369; also, 1/131; 2/75; 7/398

HIS LOVE: concerned at leaving her for Dutch voyage, 1/89, 92, 102, 106; happy in wife and estate, 1/166; 3/234; troubled at her absence, 1/317;

9/304; teases P over handsome maids, 6/40; 9/479; comments on his high colour after clandestine dalliance, 8/233; P prevents her meeting Martin and Burroughs, 8/375–6; mistrusts his roving eye in theatre, 9/375, 390, 395–6, 405, 421, 436; and at church, 9/482; jealous of E. Turner and daughter, 9/380; makes jealous scene over J. Birch, 9/439, 440–1; distrusts his being out late, 9/494; also, 1/16–17

HIS GUILTY FEELINGS TOWARDS: at going to theatre without, 2/177; 3/294; 6/9; 8/3, 123; at deceiving her with Betty Lane, 4/317; self-reproach for his jealousy, 4/140; for criticising her painting, 6/303; and her singing, 7/348; 8/89; dines twice to prevent her dining alone, 4/318; keeps theatre visits secret from, 8/169, 384, 395; 9/78

THEIR QUARRELS / P'S ANNOYANCE WITH:

over servants/household management: her dog's fouling house, 1/54, 284–5; badly served/cooked meals, 1/308; 2/237, 238; 4/13, 29; maid's dismissal, 3/258, 263, 264, 273; her negligence, 4/121, 287; call each other 'beggar' and 'prick louse', 4/121 & n. 1; her neglecting household business for dancing, 4/183; and for painting, 7/115–16; her complaints of: maid's lying, 4/361, 417; badly kept household accounts, 5/283; 6/46–7; 7/125, 243, 397; exchange blows over badly served food, 5/291; he gives her black eye, 5/349, 350, 356; further quarrels over dismissal of servants, 6/4(2), 26–31 passim, 295, 296; she brings him 'only trouble and discontent', 6/31; P throws trenchers about, 7/398; her failure to prepare for party, 8/104; dirty table linen, 9/402; also, 1/311; 3/7; 4/177–8, 337; 6/340; 9/411

over her extravagance: expenditure on dress, 1/247; 5/84, 100, 310; 8/392–3, 413; 9/427, 450–1; earrings, 5/196; dancing lessons, 4/133(2); 'snappish' at his refusing her money, 7/256

over her dress/appearance: ill-matched ribbons, 2/235; P calls her 'whore', ib.; unsuitable dress in church, 3/110; false

hair, 6/55; 7/346–7; 8/210–11; low décolletage, 7/379; unsuitable mourning, 8/242, 250–1; also, 2/11; 8/124, 202

over her complaints of dull life/love of pleasure etc.: her 'letter of discontent', 3/257–8; P burns it with her love letters, 4/9–10; fears losing command over, 4/150; accuses him of keeping house dirty to occupy her, 4/289; his wish 'to keep her head down', 4/262, 276; refuses to let her attend christening, 5/176; his 'gadding abroad to look after beauties', 5/286; her bad temper from too much liberty, 7/284; 9/243; he pulls her nose in quarrel over his dining out, 8/333; her want of money and liberty, 9/20–1, 245–6; his going to plays in her absence, 9/244; also, 3/85; 4/347; 8/189

misc. quarrels: P kicks her china basket, 1/265; annoyed with for leaving parcel in coach, 4/6; for being robbed of waistcoat, 4/28; for bad spelling, 4/29; pulls her nose, 5/113; for failing to keep count of singing lessons, 7/397; his silence prevents quarrels, 9/136, 304; also, 1/225; 2/94, 189; 4/133; 6/83; 8/488

SEXUAL RELATIONS: 1/217, 279; ?2/75; 3/234; 4/274, 291, 336, 347; 5/94, 200; 8/588; 9/184, 439; have not lain together for six months, 8/372–3; make love after three-month interval, 8/382; after her being unwell, 8/594; 9/90; after Deb affair, 9/363

MISC.: he dictates her letter to Lady Sandwich, 4/176; troubled at her quarrels at Brampton, 4/210, 212, 271, 273, 274, 276, 293; and at her visiting her father in poor area, 5/50; will not permit her to accept diamond locket from Hewer, 9/7

AS HOUSEWIFE:

COOKING ETC.: makes Christmas pies etc., 1/29, 291; 2/170; 3/293, 295; 4/433; kills turkey, 1/41; and pigeons, 1/189; makes marmalade, 4/361, 363; also, 1/3, 321; 4/62; 7/420; 8/82

LAUNDERING: helps with/supervises, 1/19, 301; 4/65; 5/62; calls maids early for, 1/296; 5/11, 55; promises them a holiday after, 4/348; takes washing to be bleached, 8/383–6 passim, 401; 9/283

RELATIONS WITH UNNAMED SERVANTS [for relations with named servants, *see* Servants in main series]: annoyed with for complaining of Suffolk cheese, 2/191; forgets to buy food for, 2/198; servants spoiled by her familiarity, 4/9; with P hears them read Bible, 4/383; scolds for failing to search beds for fleas, 5/260; buys presents for, ib.; permits to attend Lord Mayor's Show, 5/309; joins in Christmas games, 5/357, 358; 6/4–5; dances, 6/252; cards, 7/358

MISC.: makes caps for P, 1/85; worsted cushions, 4/180; tears up flags for bed linen, 5/48; makes shirts and smocks, 8/187; settles household accounts with P, 3/132, 289; 5/283; 6/46–7; 7/125, 243, 397; 8/444; sets up closet, 4/317, 318, 322, 324, 328, 329; works 'like a horse', 7/14; and a drudge, 7/24; helps clean house, 9/365; to learn to fold napkins, 9/423

HER ACCOMPLISHMENTS:

MUSIC: *singing*: to learn from Goodgroome, 2/190; P teaches song to, 7/111; neglects to teach, 7/228; will learn in return for dancing lessons, 7/300; lessons with Goodgroome, 7/348 & n. 1, 397; sings out of tune, 7/348; 8/89; P teaches her 'It is decreed', 7/420; learning to trill, 8/49, 108, 109; P pleased with progress, 8/119, 171, 203, 204, 209; Goodgroome's neglect, 8/109, 378, 411; sings with P/Mercer/others, 8/90, 166, 198, 206, 209, 238, 244, 250, 253, 325, 327, 344, 351, 380, 390, 458; in garden, 5/266; 7/117, 172, 183, 195, 212, 228, 230; 8/37, 165, 322, 328; on roof, 3/86; 7/110, 174; in coach, 7/267; 9/513; on river, 8/325, 346; 9/552, 555, 563; in cellars at Audley End, 8/468; *flageolet*: lessons from Greeting, 8/87 & n. 2, 89, 110, 400; fails to practise, 8/146, 205–6, 221(2); P pleased with her progress, 8/96, 232, 291, 295, 396, 430, 433, 434, 435; has lessons to encourage her, 8/205–6; she 'pipes' with him, 8/224, 235(2), 250, 253, 305, 327, 367, 369, 370, 380, 384, 436, 437, 443; resumes

lessons, 9/25, 94, 279; plays to P, 9/280; *misc.*: is taught 'some skill in' by P, 1/232, 233, 239; repeats words of French song 'D'un air tout interdit', 6/223; to learn viol, 7/377

DANCING: wishes to learn, 3/213–14; 4/106, 109; 7/300; lessons from Pembleton, 4/111, 113, 114, 122, 126, 129, 132, 133, 134, 140, 148, 149, 150, 155, 156, 161; at dances/dancing parties, 6/279, 315, 323–4; 7/18, 43–4, 73, 362–4, 422; 8/29, 104, 493, 511; 9/1, 4, 42, 128, 134

DRAWING AND PAINTING: lessons from Browne, 6/98(2) and n.; P's pride in her progress, 6/143, 162, 170, 174, 183, 200, 242; 7/232; 9/25; her talent superior to Peg Penn's, 6/185, 210; her picture of Christ, 6/242; and the Virgin, 7/241, 242, 251, 262; resumes lessons, 7/115; also, 6/303; 7/359; 9/424, 534

OTHER INTERESTS: reading: reads *Polixandre*, 1/35; *Le grand Cyrus*, 1/312; 7/122; *Imposture*, 3/247; with P reads Ovid (trans.), 3/289; *Iter Boreale*, 4/285; Fuller's *Worthies*, 5/118; he reads to her *Life of Henrietta Maria*, 1/275; *The siege of Rhodes*, 5/278; and Chaucer, 7/378; her books separated from P's, 1/268; *misc.*: P teaches her astronomy, 4/43; use of globes/geography, 4/302, 343, 344, 433–4; 5/6, 8, 16, 25–6, 49; arithmetic, 4/357, 360, 363, 364, 378, 402, 404, 406; with P experiments with microscope, 5/241

HER RELIGIOUS OPINIONS: enjoys reading missal, 1/282 & n. 1; P fears her becoming catholic, 5/39 & n. 4, 92, 103, 250; 9/378; she claims to be one, 5/92 & n. 2; 9/338, 385; attributes juggler's tricks to the Devil, 8/234; fasts on Good Friday, 6/66

SOCIAL:

ON RIVER TRIPS: sees wreck of *Assurance*, 1/315, 316–17; dines on *Rosebush*, 2/36; sees royal yachts, 2/179; fleet in the Hope, 5/197; at launch of *Royal Catherine*, 5/305, 307; and *Greenwich*, 7/153; visits the *Prince*, 6/56, 57, 59; on river trips to Hampton Court, 3/81–2; Gravesend,

3/95; 6/119, 120; Greenwich, 3/111; 4/99; 5/138, 180, 190; 6/106; 7/134; Woolwich, 4/149; 5/155; 6/111; 7/142, 233; Wapping, 5/30; Deptford, 5/72; Mortlake, 7/235; Erith, 7/402–3; Barn Elms, 8/202, 346; Putney, 9/552; Fulham, 9/555; Chelsea, 9/563; also, 2/178; 6/132

ATTENDS/GODMOTHER AT CHRISTEN-INGS, 1/234, 303; 2/146, 171, 216, 235, 236–7; 4/82; 5/265; 6/102; 7/128, 129, 329, 394; 8/164, 180, 202, 405, 540, 548; 9/84, 260

ATTENDS FUNERALS: 1/244; 2/131–2, 159, 179; 4/432; 5/38, 134, 158, 322

VALENTINES, CHOICE OF: chosen by Batten, 2/36; D. Penn, 6/35; W. Mercer, 8/62; J. Pearse, 8/65–6; and Roger P, 9/67; herself chooses H. Moore, 1/55; W. Bowyer, 3/29; T. Hill, 7/42

AT THEATRE [for her visits, *see* Plays in main series]: sees King and Lady Castlemaine at, 2/164; Frances Stuart, 8/44; to see no plays till after Whitsun, 3/58; grows more critical, 7/398; sees changing rooms at King's playhouse, 8/463; vexed that play hissed in King's presence, 8/488; sees puppet plays, 2/254–5; 7/257, 265, 267; 8/121, 157, 421; 9/296

VISITS TO PLEASURE GARDENS: Vauxhall, 3/95; 7/135–6, 198, 294; 9/249, 257, 264, 268; Mulberry Garden, 9/509–10

DRIVES IN HACKNEY COACHES ETC. [*see* under Bethnal Green, Bow, Hackney, Islington, Kingsland, Mile End, Shoreditch]

WALKS IN COUNTRY: to/at Halfway House, 3/86, 108, 115; 4/79, 112; 5/111, 124, 138, 155–6; 8/325; collects May-dew at Woolwich, 8/240, 241; also, 6/217; 8/165, 167; 9/273

MISC.: races with Theophila Turner, 1/40; dines for first time with Sandwich, 1/293; his respectful manner to, ib.; 'Queen' at Twelfth Night party, 2/7; on day out with P and others to Dartford, 2/57; Epsom, 8/335, 336–40; Barnet and Hatfield, 8/380–2; learns gleek, 3/9, 14; sees dancing at girls' schools, 4/45, 58–9; 8/396; at

Sheriff Waterman's dinner, 6/79; visits Lady Carteret at Deptford, 6/152, 156, 157; wears periwig at party celebrating naval victory, 7/246; 'housewarms' Betty Mitchell, 7/351

PEPYS, [Elizabeth], (b. Walpole), wife of Edward of Broomsthorpe, Norf.: her good looks, 4/175, 421; 8/365; at St Bride's church, 2/89; P sends her venison, 4/187; husband's death, 4/425; property in Norfolk, 8/517

PEPYS, Esther, P's sister: birthdate and death, 5/361 & n. 1

PEPYS, Esther (Widow Dickenson), fourth wife of Roger P: fat and good humoured, 9/407; P's regard for, 9/407, 450, 477; marriage, 9/431 & n. 2, 441; goes to Impington, 9/477; social: 9/409, 429, 446, 455, 460, 461, 463–4, 465, 475

PEPYS, Jacob, P's brother: birthdate and death, 5/361 & n. 1

PEPYS, John, of Cottenham and Impington, Cambs. (d. 1589); P's great grandfather: 8/261 & n. 3

PEPYS, John; P's father (d. 1680) [*see also* Correspondence (P)]:

CHARACTER: melancholy, 4/96; 5/110; 'one of the most careful and innocent men in the world', 7/164

CHRON. SERIES: birthdate, 5/360; journey to Holland, 7/22 & n. 4; EP stays with 1/131; 2/64–7 passim, 77, 79, 88, 90, 94, 96; expectations from Robert P's estate, 1/81; at Brampton in Robert's last illness, 2/126, 127, 129, 130, 132, 138, 141, 143, 148; inherits Brampton estate, 2/133 & n. 1, 134–5, 136–7, 151, 153; in disputes arising from will, 2/156, 160, 162, 181, 182; 3/100, 221; settles at Brampton, 2/157, 165, 167; admitted to Brampton lands, 3/222, 223; at manorial court, 4/308–9; 5/298; on bad terms with EP, 4/210, 211, 212, 271, 274, 276, 280, 402; 8/372, 470; 9/20–1, 98, 224, 246; informed of Tom P's last illness, 5/85, 87, 90, 91–2; in troubles arising from, 5/93, 95, 97, 101, 102, 106 & n. 2, 110, 115, 122, 142, 149–50, 154, 157, 158, 164, 225 & n. 2, 244, 251–2, 253, 258, 259, 351, 360; 7/80; 9/477; Mountagu children stay with, 5/74, 76, 95, 110,

1631): his birthdate and death, 5/361 & n. 1

PEPYS, John, P's brother (d. 1677):

EDUCATION: gives speeches at St Paul's School, 1/11–12 & n., 18, 44; gains exhibition, 1/42 & n. 4, 46; enters Christ's College, Cambridge, 1/26, 60, 61, 64–9 passim; transfers from Magdalene, 1/68 & n. 2; P gives him books/money/advice, 1/61, 69, 90, 222, 243; 2/95; 3/33; a good scholar, 2/25; elected a scholar of Christ's, 2/44; P dissuades from becoming moderator, 3/160–1 & n.; takes his B.A., 4/27 & n. 1; has studied Descartes, 4/263; and Aristotle's physics, 4/267; P complains of his idleness, 4/291, 292, 316–17, 439; is ordained and takes his M.A., 7/50 & n. 2, 112, 170

CHRON. SERIES: his birthdate recorded, 5/361 & n. 1; at Brampton, 3/219, 220, 223; with P in London, 4/261–3 passim, 266, 269, 273, 282, 300, 317; complains of EP's unkindness, 4/293; comes to London on Tom P's death, 5/91, 122; P angry with over his 'roguish' letters to Tom P, 5/91, 92, 93, 135, 137, 298; 6/134; his allowance, 5/142 & n. 3; 6/49; P makes up quarrel, 7/111–12, 170; stays with P, 7/281–3 passim, 293, 306, 316, 318, 344, 349, 362, 420, 426; 8/14, 31; wears clerical dress, 7/299, 310, 313; his lack of scholarship, 7/327, 346; helps P store his money and plate, 7/367; and to catalogue his books, 7/419, 421; 8/8, 40(2); 9/559–60; has fainting fit, 8/48–9; returns to Brampton, 8/49; 'melancholy and harmless', ib.; his prospects, 8/471 & n. 2; stays with P, 8/474, 477, 478; 9/553, 555, 563; also, 4/27; 5/157, 261; 8/122, 134, 207, 469; 9/144, 210, 212

SOCIAL: at Twelfth Night party, 1/10; P visits at Cambridge, 2/135, 181; visits Westminster Abbey, 7/322, 323, 345; plays lyra viol, 7/327; and bass viol, 8/40; at theatre, 7/398; 8/481; 9/556; dines at Hinchingbrooke, 8/471–2; also, 1/9; 7/317, 351, 366

ALLUDED TO: 1/81; 8/473

PEPYS, John, P's cousin, of Ashtead, Surrey, lawyer (d. 1652): house, 3/152 & n. 1; 4/247; 8/338; servants, 4/247; 8/338; marshal to Chief Justice Coke, 9/42 & n. 4; alluded to: 9/383

PEPYS, Dr John, lawyer, Fellow of Trinity Hall, Cambridge, P's cousin (d. 1692): P's opinion, 4/211, 389; advises on Robert P's will, 2/136; arbitrator in dispute, 3/265; recovers from illness, 4/211; also, 2/146, 147; 3/218; 4/389

PEPYS, [Margaret], (b. Kite), P's mother:

CHRON. SERIES: washmaid, 2/31 & n. 2; marriage date, 5/360; children's birthdates, 5/361 & n. 1; argues about religion, 1/76 & n. 3; unwell, 1/230, 233, 244, 245; suffers from stone, 1/283, 302, 310, 314; at Brampton, 2/5, 26, 27; quarrels with husband, 2/64, 81, 89–90, 111, 160, 183; has become simple, 2/111, 153, 160, 171; extravagance, 2/144; moves to Brampton, 2/151, 162, 165, 171, 172; ill, 3/103, 106; quarrels with EP, 3/206; 4/274; unquiet life with husband, 3/207; 4/90, 96; 5/234; quarrels with servants, 5/154; P's gifts to, 4/7; 5/268; begs him to forgive brother, 5/298; 6/134; stays with P, 6/90, 95, 99, 132, 133–4; 'impatient and troublesome', 7/104; P's bequest, 7/134; ill, 8/88, 119, 122, 123, 129, 131; dies, 8/134, 135; P's grief, 8/134; also, 1/54, 75, 93, 203; 5/85

SOCIAL: at Twelfth Night party, 1/10; P's stone feast, 2/60; christening, 6/102; visits Woolwich, 6/111; Islington, 6/112; Gravesend, 6/119; P visits at Salisbury Court, 1/9, 28, 71, 72, 205, 215, 324; 2/65, 67, 139, 141, 169; at Brampton, 3/219, 223; visits/dines with P, 1/29; 2/28, 165; also, 1/252; 2/164; 5/266; 6/107–8, 121, 128, 130

ALLUDED TO: 1/60, 81; 3/167; 9/134

PEPYS, Mary, P's aunt: birthdate, 5/360 & n. 1

PEPYS, Mary, P's sister: birthdate and death, 5/361 & n. 1

PEPYS, Mary, P's cousin; daughter of Thomas P of London: see Santhune, de

PEPYS, Paulina, P's older sister:
birthdate and death, 5/361 & n. 1
PEPYS, Paulina, P's younger sister:
see Jackson, J.
PEPYS, Richard, of Ashen, Essex, P's
cousin: 1/252 & n. 3
PEPYS, Richard, draper, of Great St
Bartholomew's, P's relative: to supply
flags for navy, 5/181–2 & n.
PEPYS, Robert, P's brother: birthdate
and death, 5/361 & n. 1
PEPYS, Robert, of Brampton, Hunts.,
P's uncle:
CHRON. SERIES: lease of Hetley's land,
2/28; business with Sir P. Neile, 2/47;
surety for loan to Sandwich, 2/62–3;
proposes P buy land at Brampton,
2/117; illness and death, 1/81, 321;
2/5, 27, 126, 129, 130, 132, 133 & n. 2;
mourning for, 3/7; also, 1/46, 72, 218;
2/3, 96
HIS WILL: P's expectations, 1/73, 77, 81,
170, 264; its terms, 2/133 & n. 1, 134
& n. 2, 135 & n. 1; estate, 2/134–5,
144; 3/275 & n. 3; P exaggerates its
value, 2/140; will discussed, 2/153;
proved, 2/160 & n. 1, 162; copied,
3/269; legacies: to P and his father,
2/133 & n. 1; 5/143; Pall, 7/15; the
Wights, 4/86; the Perkinses, 8/90, 91;
debt to Thomas P 'the Executor', 3/17;
6/100; P's papers concerning estate,
2/140; 3/48, 274, 275 & n. 2; 4/121,
122; land sold to meet debts etc.,
4/119 & n. 2; 5/211 & n. 2: 6/100;
accounts as tax-receiver (1647), 5/31,
39, 135; 6/65
DISPUTES OVER WILL [*see also* Brampton;
Godfrey, [R.]; Goldsborough, Mrs
——; Graveley; Moore, H.; Offord;
Pepys, Anne; Pepys, Charles; Pepys,
Dr John; Pepys, Roger; Pepys,
Talbot; Pepys, Thomas of London;
Pepys, Thomas, the turner; Prior,
[W.]; Trice, J.; Trice, T.; Stirtloe;
Turner, Dr John; Williams, Dr John];
copyhold lands at Brampton etc.,
2/135; 4/42–3 & nn.; annuities to
Thomas P of London and sons, 3/275
& n. 3; 4/42–3 & nn.; debt to Trices,
2/134 & n. 2; 3/265, 274; 4/384; 5/353;
also, 2/134–5, 177, 194–5; 3/7, 27, 34,
48, 80, 83, 96, 100, 219–23 passim,

232, 240, 244, 253, 256, 265, 269, 271,
274, 275, 281, 302; 4/15, 20, 28, 34,
63, 119, 126, 132, 153, 203, 344–5 &
n., 351–2, 379; 5/36, 157, 225
PEPYS, Roger, son of Talbot, and P's
cousin; lawyer; M.P. and Recorder,
Cambridge borough:
CHARACTER: simple and well-meaning,
4/389, 402; 5/351; honest, 9/377
CHRON. SERIES: at Cambridge assizes,
2/146; bound over by Kelyng at
assizes, 8/484 & n. 2, 578; advises on
dispute over Robert P's will, 2/145,
147; 3/113, 218, 253, 263; 4/28, 34, 35,
41; arbitrator between P and Uncle
Thomas, 3/256, 261, 265, 267; 4/42;
advises on Robert P's Exchequer
business, 5/135; Tom P's debts, 5/149,
250, 351; and land purchase, 8/517;
9/95; advises P's father on Robert P's
estate, 5/44, 45; intercedes for Pall,
5/44; and for John, 5/135; offers
match for Pall, 8/261 & n. 2; arranges
her marriage settlement, 9/18–19, 55,
56, 61 & n. 1, 64–5; P's gifts to, 4/232;
8/393; on committee of Canary
Company, 7/314; stories of family
history, 8/261 & n. 4, 274; reports
slander about Archbishop Sheldon,
8/364 & n. 1; also, 1/195; 8/522;
9/83–4
AS M.P.: election, 2/56 & n. 2; critical of
Cavalier M.P.s, 2/147–8; and court,
4/193, 197; 8/33, 274; finds politics
distasteful, 4/159–60; his independ-
ence, 8/33, 85–6 & n., 512; 9/114–15;
helps P in defence before Committee
on Miscarriages, 8/493, 496; 9/162;
congratulates him on parliamentary
speech, 9/113; attends debates on
ecclesiastical bills, 4/95; 4/159; journeys to and from London for sessions,
4/66, 242, 402; 8/47, 261, 365, 575;
9/113, 477; also, 9/65
NEWS FROM (mostly parliamentary):
4/65, 90, 159, 200, 229; 8/32–3, 274,
361, 510, 512, 527, 558–9, 579; 9/70,
95, 121, 171, 174, 186–7, 463
PERSONAL: marries third wife, 1/39 &
n. 3, 45, 46; enquires for rich widow,
4/159; 7/387; woos E. Wyld, 8/365;
marries E. Dickenson, 9/431 & n. 2,
441; health, 5/36–7; 9/450; income,

4/159; borrows £1000 from P, 9/357-8, 369, 375, 377; house at Impington, 3/219; London lodgings, 9/348, 353, 473

SOCIAL: at Trinity House, 4/185; funeral, 5/347; visits court, 8/33, 70; EP's valentine, 9/67; at theatre, 9/429; entertains P/EP, 2/147; 3/219; 9/222, 301, 306, 310, 315, 379, 450, 474; attends P's stone-feast, 6/124; dines with/visits P, 4/94-5; 5/337; 7/391-2; 8/362, 577, 578; 9/57, 116, 167-8, 253, 343, 430, 455, 463-4, 553, 559; at tavern, 9/163; also, 1/54; 2/130; 4/235; 9/68, 461, 475, 552

~ his maid Martha, 9/454; his man Arthur, 9/460

PEPYS, Samuel, of Ireland, clergyman; P's cousin: godfather to J. Scott's child, 2/216 & n. 2; also,3/123 & n. 2

PEPYS, Samuel, the diarist, recollections of early life of [i.e. his life before the start of the diary. The dating implied in the organisation of this section is in some cases tentative. The principal entries in the Index dealing with his life during the diary period are listed above, p. xiii.]:

CHILDHOOD AND YOUTH: put out to nurse in Kingsland, 5/132; carried to see Christmas revels in Temple, 9/3; taken to church, 3/167; plays bows and arrows in Islington fields, 5/101; plays games, 4/433; beats parish bounds, 2/106; carries clothes to father's customers, 9/113

SCHOOLDAYS AND ADOLESCENCE: witnesses execution of King, 1/280; eats oysters at Bardsey, 1/104; his 'first sentiments of love', 4/247; writes anagram on Elizabeth Whittle's name, 1/290; at Ashtead, 3/152 & n. 1; at Durdans, 4/246; cast in female part in play, 9/218; his 'boyish' papers, 5/31, 360; examined for leaving exhibition at St Paul's, 2/20; 5/221-2

UNIVERSITY: at Magdalene College, vol. i, p. xxi; 1/67; 2/220; 3/54 & & n. 1; 5/31, 203, 361; 9/212

MARRIAGE AND EARLY MANHOOD: love letters exchanged with EP, 4/9-10; 5/360; wedding ring, 1/238; marriage

ceremonies (1655), 2/194, n. 3; wedding dinner, 7/237; their temporary separation, ?2/153 & n. 3; 4/277 & n. 1; and early privations, 8/82-3; efficiency as Mountagu's servant, 5/192; member of 'club' of government clerks, 1/208 & n. 4; 2/127; 4/10; 5/30; 6/147-8; 7/375; attends Scott's divorce proceedings, 4/254 & n. 2; operated on for stone (1658), 1/1 & n. 1, 97 & n. 3; 3/153; speaks 'privately' of King during Rump, 1/204; visits Baltic fleet as messenger, 1/140, 285; 2/185 & n. 5; pawns lute, 1/91; makes notes on family history and writes out medical charms, 5/360-2

PEPYS, Sarah, P's sister: birthdate and death, 5/361 & n. 1

PEPYS, Talbot, of Impington, Cambs.; lawyer; P's great-uncle: advises on disputes over Robert P's will, 2/136 & n. 1, 181; 3/218; P overnight with, 2/147-8; Clarendon acquainted with, 2/209; 7/71 & n. 1; debts, 9/357; alluded to: 8/85

PEPYS, Talbot, Roger's son and P's cousin: law student at Middle Temple, 8/273-4 & n.; brideman to Jane Birch, 9/500; social: visits/dines with P, 9/167, 343, 519, 559; at theatre, 9/398, 414, 453, 456; Mulberry Garden, 9/510; and Hyde Park, 9/530; also, 9/511, 512

PEPYS, Thomas, of St Alphage's parish, P's uncle:

CHARACTER: P's low opinion, 2/178; 4/305

DISPUTE WITH P OVER BRAMPTON ESTATE: claims copyhold land, 2/135, 137; 139, 151, 153; denied possession by manorial court, 2/182; 3/222-3; disputes over rents, 3/219, 221; 4/15, 20, 28; arbitration attempted, 3/42, 256, 261, 265, 270, 302; enters complaint in Court of Arches, 4/33; out-of-court settlement, 4/34, 35, 36, 42-3 & nn., 72, 86, 119, 206; 6/100; surrenders mortgaged lands, 4/133, 308-9; enquires into J. Day's estate, 4/300, 310, 312; P objects to bargain with daughter, 4/344-5 & n., 346, 351; 5/303; reversionary right, 5/225 &

n. 1; 8/237, 471; annuity, 2/205; 3/17, 24, ?240; 4/43, 86, 237, 351; 5/16, 301; 7/8(2); 8/8; 9/142; also, 4/231, 305, 307, 308; disputes alluded to: 2/163, 169, 178, 184; 3/28, 39, 48, 96, 113, 218, 220, 221, 259, 263, 267, 276, 281; 4/2, 15, 20, 25, 28, 62, 179; 5/119, 225
MISC.: anxious for place, 1/78 & n. 1; stories against Carteret, 4/305–6; birth-date, 5/360 & n. 1; in mourning for daughter, 8/601
SOCIAL: visits/dines with P, 1/65; 4/40, 272, 326; 5/14, 301; 7/316
PEPYS, Thomas, ('the turner'), P's cousin, son of Thomas P of St Alphage's parish:
CHARACTER: 3/48, 266
CHRON. SERIES: P visits shop, 1/27, 43–4, 266; 2/19; 4/336; gifts to P, 1/274, 298; child's christening, 6/102; asks for employment, 7/286; shop moved to Smithfield, 8/8; stall in Bartholomew Fair, 8/409
DISPUTE WITH P OVER BRAMPTON ESTATE: at reading of will, 2/153; reversionary rights, 2/182, 193; 3/48; agrees to arbitration, 3/256; lawsuit against P's tenants, 4/15, 20; out-of-court agreement, 4/34, 35, 42–3 & n.; legacy, 4/179; 5/157; enquires into J. Day's estate, 4/307, 308, 310, 312; reversionary rights under new agreement, 4/345, 346; also, 2/163; 4/133; dispute referred to, 3/42; 4/300, 307; 5/225; 8/237, 471
SOCIAL: 1/259; 3/221; 4/308
ALLUDED TO: 2/83
PEPYS, Thomas ('the Executor', 'Hatcham Pepys'), of Westminster, P's cousin:
CHARACTER: P's low opinion, 6/331, 333
CHRON. SERIES: loan to Sandwich, 2/43, 61, 62–3 & n., 66; 3/17; 5/42, 186, 187; interest, 6/100; repaid, 6/331, 333; 7/13, 15, 31, 32; advises P on Robert P's estate, 2/140, 169–70, 184; 3/17, 28; loan to Robert P, 4/379; 6/100; asks for employment, 6/333; unwilling to become J.P., 7/112 & n. 1, 114 & nn.; despairs of nation, 8/305; favours union of Presbyterians and Anglicans, ib.; troubled by Conven-

icle Act, 9/182; also, 5/36
HIS HOUSES: in St Martin's-in-the-Fields, 2/140 & n. 1; Newport St, Covent Garden, 9/431; Hatcham, 4/235; 6/173; Merton Priory, 9/207 & n. 2
SOCIAL: 1/9, 53; 2/2, 164 & n. 1
~ his partner, 1/53
PEPYS, Dr Thomas, physician, of Impington, Cambs., P's cousin:
CHARACTER: P's low opinion, 1/230; 2/145; 3/138, 233; 5/87, 249, 351; 6/16
CHRON. SERIES: asks for place, 1/230 & n. 4; to find bride for Tom P, 3/166, 176, 233; Tom P's debt, 5/85, 225 & n. 2, 249–50, 252–3; dies, 6/16; also, 1/289; 4/211
SOCIAL: dines with P, 1/274; 2/52, 146, 157, 194, 196, 237; 3/102; also, 2/2, 7, 40, 81; 3/137–8, 161
PEPYS, Thomas (Tom), P's brother, tailor, of Salisbury Court:
CHRON. SERIES: birthdate, 5/361; at Kingsland as child, 5/132; turned out of house by father, 1/256, 257; disrespectful to parents, 2/103; P's attempts at matchmaking for, 2/158–9 & n., 163, 165, 225, 242; 3/3, 69; 4/19, 21; to benefit from sale of Stirtloe lands, 3/27, 103, 117, 226; 4/119; proposed match with Mrs Hobell, 3/166 & n. 3, 176, 177–8, 183, 185, 187, 192, 194, 195, 201, 202, 203, 207, 208, 226, 227, 228, 231; negotiations broken off, 3/232–3, 235, 244, 287; 4/12, 64, 253; at Brampton, 3/219, 223; unwell, 4/410; 5/9–10; in a consumption, 5/20, 22, 29, 79; delirious, 5/81–2, 84; (wrongly) suspected of pox, 5/85–6; deathbed described, 5/86–7; P's grief, 5/87, 88, 91; funeral and burial, 5/87–91 passim; P alters his will, 5/192; also, 1/184; 2/176; 3/29, 40, 41; 4/22, 211, 300, 410 & n. 2; 5/47, 54
AS TAILOR: supplies/makes/alters clothes etc. for P/EP, 1/186, 193; 2/39; 3/47, 82, 84; 4/112, 122, 124, 343, 357; carries on father's business, 2/144, 167; P's hopes and fears for, 2/167, 230; 3/2, 52, 55, 194; 4/15, 109, 126, 183, 271, 342–3, 356, 439; 5/81–2; P refuses loan to, 4/291, 292, 296; neglects

business, 5/82, 97; also, 1/205, 267; 2/126; 3/290; 4/417

DEBTS AND CHILDREN: P learns of debts, 5/82, 84–5, 97; examines papers, 5/87, 91, 92; makes inventory of goods, 5/88 & n. 2; arranges administration of his estate, 5/101, 102, 122 & n. 3, 142, 149–50, 157; debt to Dr Thomas P, 5/225, 249–50, 351; and to others, 6/252, 253, 258, 259; 7/80; his two illegitimate daughters, 5/113–14; demands made on P, 5/115, 142, 154, 158, 252, 253; also, 5/164, 360; 8/264

HOUSE/HOUSEHOLD: rebuilt, 4/236, 274, 291, 292, 341; cutting house, 5/81; alluded to (usually as rendezvous): 2/205, 207, 210, 235, 238; 3/61, 77, 85, 93, 96, 99, 105, 108, 206, 212, 214, 215, 230, 285; 4/18, 32, 58, 100, 111, 114, 130; Honywoods lodge at, 3/7 & n. 4; 4/167; 5/91; apprentices, 3/184, 194; 4/421; maid (Margaret), ?4/80; 5/113–14

SOCIAL: visits Cambridge, 3/224, 225; gives dinner, 4/167; brideman, 4/345; P visits/dines with, 1/15–16 & n., 32; 3/161, 275; 4/6, 25, 164; EP stays with while P's house altered, 3/230, 251, 252, 254, 255; visits/dines with P, 1/29, 75, 225, 243, 322; 2/2, 28, 146, 174, 194, 196, 208, 231, 237, 240; 3/10, 110, 132, 138, 140, 259, 296; 4/106, 202, 338, 427; 5/10, 54; at theatre, 2/7; at taverns, 2/114; 3/224; also, 1/10; 2/196; 3/7, 148

MISC.: P gives him old suit, 2/60; and bass viol, 3/131; speech impediment, 4/21; sends P maid, 4/279, 283; silver tankard, 5/90

ALLUDED TO: 1/81, 289; 2/180; 4/237, 308; 9/477

PEPYS, [Ursula], (b. Stapelton), wife of Thomas Pepys 'the Executor': 2/2, 43

PEPYS, Mrs —— (unidentified): 2/193–4 & n.

PERCY, Sir Algernon, 10th Earl of Northumberland, Lord High Admiral 1638–42 (d. 1668): gift of classical busts to Charles I, 1/188 & n. 3; instructions to Navy Board (1640), 2/23 & n. 1; at coronation banquet, 2/85; alluded to: 9/447, 524; ~ his

wife [Elizabeth], 8/138

PERCY, Sir Henry, 9th Earl of Northumberland (d. 1632): his Walk in Tower of London, 9/479 & n. 2

PERCY (Piercy), Lady Joscelin: P admires, 8/139 & n. 1

PEREPOINT, Pierpoint: see Pierrepont

PERKIN, Frank, P's cousin: a miller, 2/96; P's meeting with, 4/310; ~ his wife and children, ib.

PERKIN, Jane, sen. (b. Pepys), of Parson Drove, Cambs., P's aunt: annuity from Robert P's estate, 4/119 & n. 2; evidence about John Day's estate, 4/300, 310; P visits, 4/310; death, 8/90; ~ her children's legacy, 8/90, 91

PERKIN, Jane, jun., of Parson Drove, Cambs., P's cousin: 2/137; 4/310

PERKIN, [John], of Parson Drove, Cambs., P's uncle: P visits, 4/310; ~ his daughters, ib.

PERKINS, [?George]: witness in Carkesse case, 8/109, 200

PERRIMAN, Capt. [John], river agent to the Navy Board: complains of abuses, 8/124; news from, 8/251, 601; 9/147; advice about *Maybolt*, 8/601; navy business, 9/29; social: 8/188–9

PERSIA, envoy from: see [?Cisii, Pietro]

PETER(S), Hugh, Independent divine (d. 1660): arrested and tried, 1/240 & n. 4, 263; style of preaching, 3/42; 4/93 & n. 3; abused, 4/93; also, 4/418

PETERSEN, ——: spreads rumours of Dutch atrocities, 6/42 & n. 1, 43–4

PETERSFIELD, Hants.: P at, 2/92, 93; 3/69, 75; 9/274; King at, 2/92; plague, 8/148; Red Lion, 2/93

PETIT, Kate ('Catau'), (b. Sterpin): marriage, 1/217 & n. 2; bequests from Lady Pye, 1/272 & n. 4; lodgings, ib.; social: 1/16 & n. 6, 54, 78, 94; 2/11

PETIT, Monsieur [Henri]: marriage, 1/217, 272; educational projects, 1/272; visits P, 2/11

PETITION OF RIGHT (1628): 9/196 & n. 2

PETRE (Peters), [Elizabeth], Lady Petre (b. Savage), wife of the 4th Baron (d. 1665): 'a drunken jade',

Deptford, 2/77; Chatham, 3/153, 154; 6/182, 232; and Woolwich, 3/289; dines with/visits P, 2/209; 3/120; 4/21, 45; 5/307; 6/205–6; at taverns, 3/165; 5/329; 6/77; 7/223; also, 2/218
MISC.: ill, 4/168; barber, 6/227
~ daughter [?Agnes Crisp], 4/168 & n. 1; 6/262; daughters, 2/12; step-daughter, 2/12; kinsman, 6/262
PETT [Peter], lawyer, son of Peter: 3/113
PETT, [Phineas], Master-Shipwright, Chatham 1605–29: 8/84 & n. 3
PETT, Phineas, (Capt. Pett), Assistant-Shipwright, Chatham 1660, Master-Shipwright, 1661–80; kted 1680: to be suspended, 1/229 & n. 4, 239, 240; house, 2/69; consulted on masts, 4/287; to join in P's timber deal, 7/298 & n. 3, 300, 301; accused of selling boats, 9/499 & n. 2; dismissed but reinstated, 9/267 & n. 2; social: 2/71
PETT, Phineas, shipwright, son of John: 5/109 & n. 1
PETTUS, Sir John, of Chediston, Suff. (d. 1685): on *Naseby*, 1/103 & n. 3
PETTY, William, kted 1661, scientist and economist [*see also* Books]: P's regard, 5/12, 27; 6/38; at Rota Club, 1/14; as T. Barlow's agent, 1/191, 305; 6/33; double-keeled ships: [*Invention* II], 4/256 & n. 3, 263 & n. 1, 334, 437; 5/24–5 & n., 28, 30, 32, 47; [*Experiment*], 5/353 & n. 3; 6/35, 38, 63 & n. 1; views on public taste, 5/27–8; and dreams, 5/108; proposed bequests for scientific research, 6/63 & n. 2
PHELPS, Mr —— [?John, Auditor of the revenue at the Exchequer]: 1/47; 2/163; 9/465–6 & n.
PHILIP IV, King of Spain 1621–65: prepares for Portuguese war, 4/349 & n. 5; death, 6/257 & n. 5; mourning for, 7/39; also, 7/55
PHILIPPE, Duc d' Anjou, later Duc d'Orleans (d. 1701): marriage, 1/240 & n. 3; 2/56; anecdote, 2/29
PHILIPS, [?John], cook: 9/116
PHILIPS, —— [?Robert, Groom of the Bedchamber to the King]: 5/279

& n. 1
PHILLIPS, [Henry], Council messenger: 1/123, 126
PHILLIPS, Lewis, lawyer, of Brampton and Huntingdon: character, 9/211; consulted in disputes about Robert P's estate, 2/135, 138, 148, 183, 223, 227; 3/27, 31, 33, 221; 4/34, 45, 221; 5/40; as arbiter, 3/261, 265; consulted about land purchase, 8/282–3; political news from, 4/155; leaves Brampton, 8/220; estate, 8/585; social: 2/137, 210, 213; 9/559; ~ his wife [Judith] dies, 9/211
PHILLIPS, [?Philip]: drawing of yacht, 4/301 & n. 2
PHILPOT LANE: 7/262
PHIPPS, [?Thomas], of Rochester: 7/177
PHYSICIANS, ROYAL COLLEGE OF: 4/156
PICKERING, Dorothy, (b. Weld, Wilde), wife of Edward: social: 5/34; 9/431, 487, 504
PICKERING, Edward (Ned):
CHARACTER: a fool but well informed, 2/170; a coxcomb, 1/101; 4/239, 255; 7/295
CHRON. SERIES: on *Naseby*, 1/101, 105, 133; carries letters for Sandwich, 1/105, 137, 142, 156; in Holland, 1/144, 145, 150; disappointed of place in Queen's Household, 4/239 & n. 2; dismissed from place at court, 4/255–6 & n.; involvement in Sandwich's love affair, 4/270, 301, 303, 371 & n. 4, 392; 5/22, 184; advises P on coach horses, 9/384, 391(2), 431; house in Lincoln's Inn Fields, 7/423; also, 1/251; 3/72, 212; 6/13; 7/295
COURT/POLITICAL NEWS FROM: 1/101–2; 2/152, 156, 170, 216–17; 3/64; 4/48–9; 5/34
SOCIAL: dines/plays cards etc. with Sandwich, 2/64, 115; 3/7; 4/28, 46; at Bartholomew Fair, 2/166; 4/301; theatre, 5/34; also, 8/181; 9/431, 487
PICKERING, Elizabeth, Lady Pickering (b. Mountagu), wife of Sir Gilbert: solicits Sandwich's help for husband, 1/174, 178 & n. 4; poor lodging in Blackfriars, 1/277; visits P, 9/261–2 & n.; also, 1/179

PICKERING, Sir Gilbert, Lord Chamberlain to Oliver Cromwell: pardoned by Parliament, 1/178 & n. 4; death, 9/334 & n. 1

PICKERING, Gilbert, son of Sir Gilbert: marries heiress, 7/358 & n. 2; rogue, 8/181 & n. 4

PICKERING, John, son of Sir Gilbert: fool, 1/116, 161, 295; on *Naseby*, 1/112, 153, 161; annoys Sandwich, 1/142 & n. 5; proposed match, 1/220–1, 295; also, 2/35

PICKERING, Oliver, son of Sir Gilbert: dies of smallpox, 9/487 & n. 2

PICKERING, Sidney, son of Sir Gilbert: 9/335

PICTURES:

COLLECTIONS [*see* under owners or houses: i.e. Charles II; Clarendon; Crew, Sir T.; Evelyn, J.; Graunt, J.; James, Duke of York; Mary, Princess Dowager of Holland; Povey, T.; Audley End House]

PORTRAITS [*see* under subjects: Albemarle, by Cooper; Allin, Sir T., by Lely; Anne Duchess of York, by Lely; Arlington, by Cooper; Ascue, Sir G., by Lely; Ashley, by Cooper; Berkeley, Sir W., by Lely; Lady Castlemaine, by Lely; Catherine of Braganza, by Huysmans; Charles I, by Van Dyke; by Marshall; Charles II, by Luttichuys; by Lely; Archbishop Chichele, by S. Strong; Cleopatra, artist unknown; Colbert, engr. by Nanteuil: Lord Coventry, ?by S. Stone; Crew, Sir T., ?by Lely; Harman, by Lely; Henrietta-Maria, by Huysmans; by Van Dyck; Henry VIII, by Holbein; anon.; Hill, T., by Hayls: Jordan, Sir J., by Lely; Louis XIV, engr. by Nanteuil; Mary, Princess Dowager, by van Honthorst; Myngs, Sir C., by Lely; Ormond, ?by Loggan; Pearse, Mrs J., by Hayls; Pearse, James jun., by Hayls; Penn, Sir W., by Lely; Sarah Robartes, artist unknown; Prince Rupert, by Lely; Sandwich, by Lely; by Salisbury; Smith, Sir J., by Lely; Stuart, Frances, by Cooper; by Huysmans; Swynfen, ——, by Cooper; Teddeman, Sir T., by Lely;

Van Dyck, self-portrait]; ~ the fashion for portraits *en déshabillé*, 6/335 & n. 1

OTHER PICTURES: cartoons, 1/45; 4/400 & n. 2; *The Four Evangelists* (artist unknown), 1/70 & n. 2; *trompe-l'œuil*, 1/148, 257–8 & n.; 4/18 & n. 1, 26 (by Hoogstraten); 9/119, 352; *The Embarkation of Henry VIII* (artist unknown), 3/292 & n. 4; *Henry VIII and the Barber-Surgeons' Company* (by Holbein), 4/59 & n. 3; 9/293; Dutch drawing, 4/109; etchings of Lisbon and the Tagus (by Sandwich), 4/286 & n. 1; Venetian scene (by Fialetti), 7/60 & n. 2; landscape and still life (artist unknown), 7/81; landscape (by Looten), 9/514 & n. 2; flower-piece (by Verelst), 9/515, 516

MEDIA: on cloth, 1/148; 'paper pictures', 4/320; Evelyn explains mezzotints, 6/289 & n. 3; pastels, 7/359; chalk, ib. & n. 3; ink, 8/181; tempera, 9/434–5 & n., 465

PICTURES (P) [including those acquired for the office. It is not always possible to distinguish prints from other pictures. *See also* Prices.]:

HIS COLLECTION:

GENERAL: hangs/rehangs pictures, 3/3; 5/235–6; 7/122, 258, 409, 417; 9/271, 331(2); also, 8/455; buys pictures at The Hague, 1/148; in London, 1/298; 9/373; buys prints, 1/296; 3/2; 4/434; 5/41; 7/173, 208–9, 409; shown to guests, 9/424; also, 3/1; 7/102

ITEMS: portraits in oil [*see* under artists: P by Savill; by Hayls; EP by Hayls; by Cooper; John P, sen., by Hayls; T. Hill by Bosse after Hayls; H. Harris by Hayls]; other pictures: Dutch landscape, 7/208–9; marine scenes, 7/290, 292; Santa Clara, 7/409; royal palaces by Danckerts, 9/423 & n. 1; Rome by Danckerts, 9/504; drawings: *Resolution* by A. Deane, 9/262 & n. 4; also, 8/142 & n. 2; prints etc.: by Ragot after Rubens, 1/194; *Royal Sovereign*, 4/29 & n. 4, 43; by Lafreri, 7/102–3 & n.; the Thames, 7/290; Lady Castlemaine by Faithorne after Lely, 7/359 & n. 3,

393; crucifixion, 7/211 & n. 2, 218, 232, 353; Ormond ?by Loggan, 8/10 & n. 3; cities, 8/383 & n. 4; Thames dockyards, 9/266, 268; Louis XIV, Colbert and others by Nanteuil, 9/427 & n. 1, 451; frames etc.: vellum covers, 3/10; mock-tortoise-shell frame, 7/184–5; gilt frames, 7/290, 292; album, 9/266; 'paper pictures' (? water-colours), 4/320

HIS TASTE: admires *trompe l'œuil*, 1/148, 257–8; 4/18; 9/119, 352; and still life, 7/81; love of verisimilitude, 9/515, 516; comments on likenesses in portraits, 7/171; prefers oil to tempera, 9/434–5, 465; admires pictures in royal collection, 1/257; 3/82; compares them with Hayls's, 7/97; admires Duke of York's collection, 7/102; and Clarendon's, 8/175; criticises Povey's, 9/521; admires portraits by Huysmans, 5/254, 276; 6/43; Van Dyck, 6/222; ?S. Stone, 7/183; Cooper, 9/139

PIERCE: see Pearse

PIERCE, [Thomas], President of Magdalen College, Oxford 1661–72; Dean of Salisbury 1675–d.91: sermons before King on temptation, and against papists, 4/98 & n. 1

[PIERCE, (Peirs) William], Bishop of Bath and Wells 1632–d.70; 1/259 & n. 3

PIERCE, Serjeant ——: news from, 3/29, 43; 4/187; ? also, 2/149

PIERCE, Mr —— , formerly a soldier [? identical with the foregoing]: 1/311; ? 2/149

PIERREPONT, [Henry], 1st Marquess of Dorchester (d. 1680): quarrels with Buckingham, 7/414–15 & n.; alluded to: 7/366

PIERREPONT (Perepoint, Pierpoint), [William], politician, brother of the foregoing (d. 1678): elected to Council of State, 1/65; rumoured appointment to Privy Council, 8/265 & n. 3; appointed to commission of accounts, 8/577 & n. 3

PIERSON: see Pearson

PIGGOT, [Francis], musician: 8/437 & n. 4, 557

PIGOTT, [Richard], of Brampton,

Hunts.: dispute over mortgage, 2/137 & n. 4, 138, 182; 3/219–20, 222, 223 & n. 1, 261; to sell land in order to pay, 4/133, 179, 237 & n. 4, 309; 5/149, 281, 282; dispute alluded to, 4/308, 352; debt, 4/309; ~ his wife's interest, 4/309

PIGOTT, Sir Richard, Clerk of the Patents: 9/372, n. 2, 492 & n. 4

PILLAU (the Pillow), E. Prussia: 6/305

PINCHBECK (Pinchbacke), [John]: swallows toad with drink, 7/290 & n. 2

PINKNEY, [Charles]: 1/132; ? also, 1/19

PINKNEY, [George], King's embroiderer: anecdote of loyalty, 1/77; petitions for place, 1/132–3 & n.; in Holland, 1/148, 149; also, 1/184; social: entertains P at Parish Clerks' Hall, 1/16, 19; also, 1/21, 76–7, 229, 304; 2/99; alluded to: 2/57; ~ his sons, 1/148

PINKNEY, [? Henry], goldsmith, Fleet St: 1/307

[PIOSSASCO, Filiberto, Conte di], Savoyard envoy, June–July 1666: 7/202 & n. 2

PITT(S), [John], Secretary and Deputy-Treasurer to Lawson's fleet: irregular accounts, 4/104, 132; alluded to: 4/133

PITTS, ——, landlord of the King's Head, Islington: 5/101, 133; 7/149; death, 7/317

PLAGUE, the:

IN HOLLAND: 4/340 & n. 2, 399; 5/142, 186, 220; Dutch fleet, 5/231, 279; quarantine on ships from Holland etc., 4/340, 399 & n. 2

IN ENGLAND: 6/93, n. 2

P'S REACTION [for the movements of his household and office during the outbreak, see Pepys, Elizabeth; Navy Office]: fear, 6/120, 121, 136, 164, 173–4, 187, 192, 199, 200, 208, 217, 232, 265, 288; 7/50, 166; fears infection from periwig, 6/210; from hackney coaches, 6/311; from graveyard, 7/30, 31, 35; calmness in face of, 6/145, 192, 225, 240, 246; makes will etc., 6/125, 188(2), 189(3), 190, 192; hardened to sight of corpses, 6/256;

POSTAL SERVICES: management, 7/375 & n. 2; express, 4/306; 6/257, 260, 271(2); 7/2; 8/263–4, 429; 9/74; carrier, 1/15, 36, 46, 57; delayed by floods, 7/328–9; post-boy, 1/32; post-houses: Southwark, 2/15, 231; Charing Cross, 6/197

POST OFFICE, Threadneedle St: P rides post from, 2/133; music-meetings at, 5/238 & n. 2, 290; destroyed in Fire, 7/275; also, 1/53

POTTLE, ——, shopkeeper in New Exchange: 8/53

POULTNY: see Pulteney

POULTRY, the: 1/246; 8/180

POUNDY, [?James], waterman: witness against P in prize-goods affair, 8/531; also, 7/202, 275

POVEY (Puvy), [Thomas], Treasurer for Tangier:

CHARACTER: vain, 4/17–18; 'most excellent in anything but business', 6/215; also, 3/300; 4/297–8; 5/139, 339; 6/13, 24, 63, 87; 7/191

AS TREASURER FOR TANGIER: appointed, 3/177 & n. 1, 238; incompetence, 5/97–8, 102, 106, 123, 124, 127, 135, 139, 154; 6/18, 37, 69–70, 84–5; 7/191, 330; neglects to provide boats, 3/291; loses his papers, 6/65; victualling business, 4/30; 5/212–13, 223; Gauden's gift, 8/37, 44; drafts civil constitution, 4/88–9; freightage business, 5/23, 26, 276, 332, 336–8 passim, 340, 348; accounts criticised, 5/105; 6/13–18 passim, 33, 38, 58–60 passim, 71, 77, 77–8; 8/75; examined, 9/244, 247, 371, 449; part in examining Peterborough's accounts, 5/123, 124, 135, 154, 187, 199, 201–2; 6/68–9; other financial business, 6/100–1, 144, 157, 185, 214–15; 9/416; cheated by Vernatty, 7/342; 8/52; resigns office to P on terms, 6/58–63 passim, 79, 84, 89, 91, 94, 108, 109, 121, 130, 139; accounts with P, 7/19, 51, 71, 74, 83, 321, 335(2), 338; 8/593; 9/341–2; at committee meetings, 3/300; 4/21, 23, 269, 341; 5/11, 97, 139, 204; 7/228; unspecified business, 3/232; 4/21, 31, 394; 6/76, 103, 131, 136, 137, 151, 163; 7/156, 245, 265; 8/286–7; 9/437, 543; also, 6/22, 65–6

AS TREASURER FOR THE MANAGEMENT OF THE HOUSEHOLD OF THE DUKE OF YORK: Duke's debts, 7/191–2; 8/287; dismissed, 8/592 & n. 1; 9/38

POLITICAL/COURT NEWS FROM: criticises court, 6/266, 267; 7/228–9; pessimism, 8/286–7; also, 6/215–16; 8/295, 297, 366–7, 431–2; 9/341–2, 373, 414, 416

HOUSES, WEALTH ETC.: house in Lincoln's Inn Fields: cellar, bathroom etc., 4/18 & n. 2, 272 & n. 3, 298; 5/161 & n. 2, 199, 277; 6/139; 8/128–9; 9/345; aviary, 4/272; grotto, 4/298; 5/161; pictures, 4/18 & n. 1, 26; 5/161 & n. 3, 161–2, 212, 277 & n. 2; house at Hounslow, 6/153 & n. 3, 198, 266, 267; chariot, 6/153, 266; horses, 6/266; forced to economise, 6/267; also, 9/443

PERSONAL: bold dalliance with Mary Mercer, 6/85; unwell, 6/97; leaves London in Plague, 6/154; 7/4

SOCIAL: at court ball, 3/300; Hinchingbrooke, 5/65; at funeral, 6/114; at theatre, 4/435; at his house, 4/17–18, 26, 31, 35, 297; 5/161–2, 276; 6/13, 17, 18, 22, 76, 87, 99; 9/345, 521; elsewhere, 4/242; 5/265, 270, 330, 338; 9/434–5

MISC.: gifts to P, 4/306; 5/269, 274; nominates P to Royal Society, 6/36; attends its meetings, 6/84; 9/379; advises P to enter parliament, 9/376–7; helps choose coach, 9/342, 344, 352; introduces to Danckerts, 9/421; warns against ostentation in dress, 9/551; relations with Creed, 5/338–9 & n.; 6/89–90; 9/244, 247; advises Arlington not to buy Euston, 8/288–9 & n.; also, 5/74

~ his wife [Mary], 4/297 & n. 4; 6/199; his man Dutton's wife, 6/266, 267; his man, 7/229

POWELL, Doll, (b. Lane), of Westminster: P's valentine, 9/121, 126; has baby, 9/486; claims to be Rowland Powell's widow, 9/486, 514; amorous encounters with P: 7/337, 342, 345, 359, 386, 406; 8/3, 39–40, 393, 422; 9/78, 121, 527; misses assignations, 8/111, 113–14; 9/317; fails to find privacy for, 8/193; false modesty,

7/112; chest of drawers, 2/130; dressing-box, 8/53; looking glass, 5/347; 9/423; table, 4/6; tapestry, 5/215; 9/329, 330

HORSES: 6/180

HOUSEHOLD GOODS: bakepan, 3/294; lock, 8/226

JEWELRY ETC.: locket (with diamonds), 9/7; necklace (pearl), 6/201; 7/111, 113; also, 8/433; pendants, 5/196; precious stones: pearls, 3/200; diamonds, 6/300; rubies, ib.; rings, 6/190–1; 9/24, 67, 78, 384; watch, 6/83 & n. 2; 8/51

MUSICAL INSTRUMENTS: flageolet, 8/344; 9/30 & n. 2; harpsichord, 2/44; lute, 1/91; spinet, 9/262; theorbo, 2/203; viol, 4/284

NAVAL SUPPLIES: hemp, 6/75 & n. 2; 7/132 & n. 3, 385 & n. 2; tar, 3/137 & n. 3; timber, 4/326

PICTURES AND PICTURE FRAMES: by Hayls: 7/73, 74, 112, 125; Cooper, 9/138, 139–40, 277; Holbein: 9/293; Verelst, 9/515, 516; also, 3/10, 80, 106; 7/208–9; copies, 1/301–2; prints, 6/111, n. 5; 9/268, 313

PLATE: bowl (christening), 8/548; cistern (copper), 8/424; cups, 4/39–40; 5/45, 47(2); 6/63; (gold), 4/115; dish/standish, 4/39–40; 8/35; salt, 6/132; silver and silver-plate (per oz.), 5/301; tankards, 1/296; 2/5; 5/47

RENTS: for P's and EP's lodgings during Plague, 6/261 & n. 3, 271, 315; for other lodgings, 7/296; rise in after Fire, 7/280

SCIENTIFIC AND MATHEMATICAL INSTRUMENTS: globes, 4/302; magnifying glasses, 1/95; 2/35; microscope, 5/240; pantograph, 9/444; ruler (engraving of), 5/238; telescope, 7/241 & n. 1

SHIP: 5/75 & n. 5

TRANSPORT: horses by ferry, 6/181–2; furniture by lighters, 7/293

MISC.: barber, 9/225, 234; blackbird, 4/150; cat-call, 1/80; fortune-teller, 4/284; glass (for lamp), 5/291–2; (for coach), 9/403; guns (French pistols etc.), 5/75; knife, 1/298; leather case, 5/247, 255; musicians, 2/218; 9/13;

office-paper, 7/101; prostitute, 5/225–6; 9/297; tweezers, 3/115

[PRIDE, Col. Thomas], regicide (d. 1658): corpse exhumed and hanged, 1/309 & n. 3

PRIDGEON: see Prujean

PRIMATE, ——, leatherseller, Fleet St: project to increase royal revenue, 4/425–6 & n.

[?PRIMEROSE, David], minister, French church, Threadneedle St: sermon, 3/270 & n. 4; ∼ his sisters, 5/342

PRIN, Monsieur, musician: 8/500 & n. 2

PRINTS: see Pictures

PRIOR, [William], of Brampton: buys houses at Brampton, 2/204–5 & n., 236, 237–8; 3/28, 31, 221, 223, 286–7; 4/309; 5/279; 'a poor painful man', 5/279

PRIOR'S: see Taverns etc: Rhenish winehouse, Cannon Row

PRISONS: see Clerkenwell; Counter; Gatehouse, Westminster; Newgate; Southwark; Whitehall: guardhouse

PRI(T)CHARD, [William], ropemaker: 9/37

PRIVATEERS: see Prizes and privateers

PRIVY COUNCIL, the:

GENERAL: P's evidence, vol. i, p. cxxx; councillors' fee, 1/179; sworn in, 3/75; stationery, 8/182–3

MEETINGS: to sit every day, 8/291; 9/316; in mornings, 9/8; full extraordinary meetings, 9/152–3, 154; committees disorderly in King's absence, 6/45 & n. 6; places of [usually Whitehall or St James's but exceptionally]: Hampton Court, 3/157; 7/26; Worcester House, 5/114; 6/11, 76; 7/107; Clarendon House, 8/21, 67; Southampton House, 8/149; also, 8/151; 9/141

COUNCIL BUSINESS [for the Cabinet and Council of Trade see below. References here are to business in full council and in its other committees, both ad hoc and standing]:

NAVAL: financial (general), 1/231 & n. 4; 7/377, 383–4; grant, 8/112 &

PRIVY SEAL OFFICE:
GENERAL: warrants issued, 1/197; 3/83; 4/62, 65; 5/61 & n. 1, 79; 6/3, 8; P examines records, 4/188–9 & n.; 9/474, 477, 478; lack of method, 9/478; also, 1/295
P'S SERVICE IN: appointed Sandwich's deputy, 1/205 & n. 3, 206, 207; begins work, 1/208, 212; attends by the month, 1/218–19, 235, 303; 2/226; busy, 1/213, 218–19, 232; 2/235; 3/61; idle in King's absence from town, 1/227, 229, 230; alleged error, 1/245 & n. 2; issues free pardons, 1/310, 312, 316, 317, 320; attends sealing-day, 2/149, 150, 156, 159, 186, 187, 229, 232; misses Navy Board meeting, 2/177; fees: amounts, 1/213 & n. 1, 219, 225, 233, 320; 2/2, 3; divided between Sandwich, P and Moore, 1/237, 238 & n. 4; 2/63, 64; 4/378; decrease, 1/262; 3/80; table of, 2/209, 214; unspecified business, 1/214, 216, 217, 220, 221, 223, 224, 228, 231, 307, 318, 320; 2/64, 66, 79, 149, 150, 153, 157, 171, 175, 177, 199–200, 226, 228, 236; 3/66, 83; official stall in Whitehall Chapel, 3/67; ?5/96; resigns, 3/168; also, 1/173; 2/234; 3/66
PRIZE OFFICE, Whitehall: commissioners appointed, 5/322, 327 & n. 2, 328, 333; T. Hill assistant secretary, 6/21; officers dismissed, 7/78 & n. 1; sale of goods at, 8/14, 16; new office in Aldersgate St, 8/16; case before special commissioners, 8/231 & n. 2
PRIZES and privateers:
PRIZES:
GENERAL: act against breaking bulk, 3/118 & n. 2; revenue from, 7/130, 317; 8/446 & n. 3; dividends, 8/23–4 & n.
PRIZE-GOODS TAKEN BY SANDWICH 1665 [see also Cocke, G.; Cuttance, R.; Howe, W.; Sandwich; Penn]: capture of Dutch E. Indiamen, 6/223, 226; cargoes rifled, 6/230–1 & n. 1; goods stored, 6/236; navy's share of proceeds, 6/239 & n. 1; sold by E. India Company, 6/273 & n. 3, 280–1; P joins with Cocke to buy goods, 6/230, 238–42 passim, 244; P's profit,

6/231 & n. 1, 243, 245; advice from broker, 6/250, 254; 7/140; clears customs, 6/247, 256, 258; sells out to Cocke, 6/314, 327, 328, 341; enquiries by Brooke House Committee (and P's defence), 9/48–53 passim, 57, 61, 72, 118, 163; his narrative, 9/64 & n. 2, 68; also, 6/271–2; 7/6, 65, 80, 305; 8/531
OTHER PRIZES: Dutch ships, 5/341 & n. 1; 7/224, 249, 250, 251 & n. 3, 296–7 & n.; French, 7/350 & n. 1, 352; 9/160; Ostender, 9/96, 97 & n. 1; goods sold contrary to order, 8/14, 15–16 & nn., 20 & n. 2, 58, 144; Rupert's licence for discovery of stolen goods, 8/52; ships sold, 8/484 & n. 3, 485
PRIVATEERS [see also Algiers; Ostend; Tangier; Tunis]:
The Flying Greyhound: lent to P, Batten and Penn, 7/299, 300–1 & n.; to trade with Madeira, 7/316; prizes: at Plymouth, 8/115–16 & n.; Hull, 8/341 & n. 3, 344, 345, 349, 351–2, 369, 385 & n. 2; Newcastle, 8/435; in Holland, 9/117; *St John Baptist,* 9/147; other ships: 7/418, 424; 8/1, 7, 8; dispute with Swedish resident, 8/17, 21–4 passim & nn., 27, 123 & n. 1, 130 & n. 2, 133–6 passim, 169, 180, 181, 231; P calculates dividends, 8/232; 9/147; sells out to Batten, 8/341, 385; settles with Batten's widow, 8/462, 477, 483, 561, 569, 579, 582, 584; and with Duke of York, 9/290, 298; asked to lend to government from profits, 8/392, 393; accused of favouring ship's seamen in pays, 9/99; also, 7/360; 8/135, 159, 579; alluded to: 9/168
OTHERS: French caper, 8/162; Scottish, 8/200; Rupert's *Panther* and *Fanfan,* 8/341
PROBY, [Peter], son [-in-law] of Sir R. Ford: 4/354
PROCTOR, [William], landlord of the Mitre, Wood St [see also Taverns etc.]: with son dies of plague, 6/175–6 & n.
PROGER, [Edward], Groom of the Bedchamber to the King: influence, 5/56; news from, 8/429–30 & n.;

9/125–6; praises P's parliamentary speech, 9/105; also, 4/351; 8/435; 9/563

PROGER, [?Harry], courtier: Spanish mistress, 8/67 & n. 1

PROPHECIES: *see* Popular beliefs etc.

PROSTITUTES [*see also* Aynsworth, E.]: in Fleet Alley/Lane, 4/164, 301; 5/219, 219–20, 220–1, 224, 225–6; south of the river, 4/261–2; Long Acre, 5/50, 55; Drury Lane, 6/63; 7/72–3; P revolted by sight, 4/164, 301; tempted, 5/219–20, 220–1, 224; 6/63; visits, 5/225–6; in coach with, 9/297; brothels: M.P's summoned from, 7/399; destroyed in riots, 9/129, 130, 132; in Moorfields, 7/100; 8/319, 320, 321

PROWD, Capt. [John], Elder Brother of Trinity House: naval news, 8/349 & n. 2; 6/183 & n. 3

PRUJEAN (Pridgeon, Prugean), Sir Francis, physician: attends Queen, 4/347; examines drawing of Siamese twins, 5/319; death, 7/177 & n. 2; his judgement, ib.; also, 4/349; ~ his wife, [Margaret], 7/177 & n. 2

PRYNNE, William, M.P. Bath, Som. 1660, 1661–d.69

CHARACTER AND REPUTATION: 1/262; 7/192

CHRON. SERIES: re-admitted to Rump, 1/62 & n. 3; on writs of summons, 1/75 & n. 1; pays off ships, 1/262, 286; refuses sacrament, 2/107 & n. 4; bitter against bishops, 2/111; refuses to drink healths, 5/172 & n. 4; opposes mixed communion, 5/172–3 & n.; accuses Coventry of corruption, 3/108; as commissioner of Chatham Chest, 3/257; 5/75–6; speech against triennial bill, 5/99 & n. 4; rebuked for altering bill, 5/148 & n. 3; alleged neglect as Clerk of Records, 5/149 & n. 1; on parliamentary privilege, 7/50–1 & n.; law reform, 7/109–10 & n.; medieval parliaments, 9/15 & nn.; anecdotes by, 3/93; 4/185; also, 1/66, 69

PUCKERIDGE, Herts.: P at, 3/217; bad roads near, 2/180; the Falcon, 3/217

PUDDING LANE: Fire starts in, 7/268 & n. 1; 8/5

PUDDLE DOCK/WHARF: 1/185; 3/186

PULFORD, [?John]: news from, 1/34

PULLEYN, [Benjamin], P's schoolfellow and Fellow of Trinity College, Cambridge (d. 1690): 5/37 & n. 4

PULO RUN (Polleroon), E. Indies: dispute about, 5/160 & n. 1; rumoured loss, 8/176 & n. 1; ceded to Dutch, 8/426

PULTENEY (Poultny), [Sir William]: at Rota Club, 1/14 & n. 3; ~ his wife [Grace], 5/163

PUMPFIELD, [Edward], ropemaker, Deptford: 5/253

PUNCH: as nickname, 9/538

PUNNETT, [Augustine], river pilot 8/310

PUNT, ——: 3/261

PURCELL, [?Thomas, ?Henry sen.], musician: sings with P, 1/63 & n. 1

PUTNEY, Surrey: P visits church 8/188, 400; 9/271; river trips to 8/247; 9/552; girls' schools, 8/188 & n. 3, 400; 9/526; horse racing, 8/204

[PYE, Elizabeth], of Westminster, sister of the following: death and bequests 1/272 & n. 4; also, 1/217

PYE, Sir Robert, jun., M.P. Berkshire 1660: in Tower, 1/47 & n. 2; at coronation, 2/86

PYE CORNER: Fire in, 7/275

PYM, [William], tailor: provides clothes/ hats etc. for P, 1/92, 116, 194 221, 227, 232; 7/353, 362; out of London in Plague, 7/13; social: 1/88 223; 2/195; alluded to: ?1/143

PYNE, Capt. [Valentine], master gunner: in Medway raid, 8/308 & n. 2

QUARTERMAIN, [William], physician in ordinary to the King: 1/154 157

QUEEN ('Queen's') ST, Cheapside 9/387

QUEENBOROUGH (Quinbrough), Kent: Batten at, 4/299; P visits fleet 6/300; alluded to: 6/194

QUEENHITHE (Queenhive), Surrey P at, 2/45; 6/167, 199; 7/271; King and Duke of York at, 7/271; alluded to: 5/217

QUINSBOROUGH: *see* Königsberg

RABY, Monsieur ——: French news, 4/25–6 & n.

RADCLIFFE [Jonathan], P's schoolfellow; ?Vicar of Walthamstow 1660–2: sermon, 2/109 & n. 2

RAGOT, [François], engraver: 1/194 & n. 5

RAGUSA, Duchy of: 3/8

RAINBOWE, Edward, Master of Magdalene College, Cambridge 1642–50, 1660–4; Bishop of Carlisle, 1664–d.84: Vice-Chancellor, 4/99; bishop, 5/135 & n. 4; high reputation, 8/365; alluded to: 8/51

[RAINSFORD, Sir Richard], Baron of the Exchequer and President of the Court of Claims, Dublin 1663; Judge in King's Bench 1669–78 (d. 1680): 5/324 & n. 2

RALEIGH (Rawly), Sir Walter (d. 1618): 'sacrificed', 6/6 & n. 2

RAM ALLEY: 9/256

RAMSEY, Mrs ——, of St Bride's parish, Fleet St: bequest, 4/410 & n. 2

RAMSEY, Mrs ——: social: 1/9; 2/141, 143; ~ her grandchild, 1/9

[RAND, Capt. William], Master-Attendant, Chatham: evidence against Pett, 8/461 & n. 3; to be dismissed, 9/258 & n. 3

RANDALL, —— [?identical with the following]: 5/253

RANDELL: see Rundell(s)

RAPHAEL, painter: picture, 3/80 & n. 1

[al-RASHĪD, Mawlāy], Sultan of Morocco 1666–72: 7/214 & n. 2

RATCLIFF, Mdx: P at, 1/287; 3/111; 6/50; 8/248; 9/101; Ratcliff highway, 6/46

RATUIT, Louis, Comte de Souche (General Souche): victory over Turks, 5/228 & n. 2

[RAVEN, John], clerk of Dover castle: 1/97

RAWLINS, Col. Giles, Gentleman of the Privy Purse to the Duke of York: killed in duel, 3/170 & n. 3; also, 3/149

RAWLINSON, Daniel, landlord of the Mitre, Fenchurch St [see also Taverns etc.]: takes charge of cash for Sandwich, 1/84, 221; advises P on investment, 2/117; in country, 7/236

& n. 2; provides wine-bottles, 4/346; closes Mitre in Plague, 7/236, 241; death of servants in, 7/236, 242; political news from, 8/427; social: P visits/dines with, 1/187; 2/109, 207, 219; 3/61, 183, 298; 4/257, 318; 5/47, 235; 6/168, 298; also, 1/245; 2/220; 3/178; 4/335; 5/162; alluded to: 2/170

RAWLINSON, [Margaret], wife of Daniel: death in Plague, 7/236, 241; social: 1/187; 2/170; 3/276

RAWLINSON, Richard, antiquary (d. 1755): vol. i, p. lxxi

RAWLY: see Raleigh

RAWORTH, [Francis], barrister, Gray's Inn: in dispute over Robert P's will, 4/203

[RAY, John], scrivener, of Fleet St: legacy, 3/264 & n. 2

RAYNER, [Edmond], boatmaker at Deptford and Woolwich: P refuses gift, 6/185; his ship, 9/160 & n. 2

RAYNOLDS: see Reynolds

READE, Dr [Thomas], lawyer: loan to government, 8/397 & n. 4

'READER, our': see St Olave's Church, Hart St

READING, Berks.: P visits, 9/242–3 & nn.: Broad Face inn, 9/242 & n. 5

REAMES, Reemes: see Reymes

RED BULL, the: see Theatres

RED CROSS ST: 9/543

REDRIFFE: see Rotherhithe

REEVE(S), [Richard], optical instrument maker, Long Acre: sells/demonstrates magnifying glasses, 2/35; 7/219, 226, 243, 254, 257; 9/261; microscopes, 5/223, 240; 7/226; anchor and loadstone, 5/245; picture-box, 7/254 & n. 3, 257; frame with shutters, 7/254; telescope, 7/238–41 passim, 254, 257; camera obscura, 9/261; reading glass, 9/284; P visits shop, 5/48, 221; gives P scotoscope, 5/240 & n. 1; attempts to borrow from, 5/245; lack of theoretical knowledge, 7/254; social: 9/265; ~ his wife, 9/265; his son [John], 1/95; 2/35

REEVE(S), Ald. [Samuel], upholsterer, Long Lane: 9/329

[REGGIO, Piero], (Pedro), musician: 5/217, 226, 239

against Rupert (1648), 5/169 & n. 1; 8/306

RICHARDS, ——, tailor: 9/218

RICHARDSON, [Sir Thomas], Chief Justice, King's Bench (d. 1635): anecdote of, 8/428–9 & n.

RICHARDSON, [William], book-binder: work for P, 7/243, 303–4, 307; 8/237, 551; 9/24, 32, 46, 547–8; also, 8/71; 9/43

RICHMOND, Duke/Dowager Duchess/Duchess of: see Stuart, Charles/Mary/Frances Teresa

RICHMOND, Surrey: P visits, 3/81; 6/154; Lady Castlemaine at, 3/139; 4/238

RIDER, Sir William, hemp merchant, kted 1661:

NAVY BOARD BUSINESS: consulted about provisioning ships, 2/62; hemp contract, 3/114 & n. 1, 116, 129–30; to insure ship, 4/394, 395, 398; quarrels with Cocke, 5/51; contract for tar and canvas, 5/136 & n. 3, 352; hemp business, 6/77; payments to Carteret, 6/191; also, 4/343; 6/256

TANGIER: appointed to committee, 3/238; helps draft civil constitution, 4/89 & n. 1; and examine Peterborough's accounts, 5/48, 105, 123, 132; at meetings, 3/272; 4/83, 320, 335; 5/11, 97, 124, 135, 139; also, 5/212; 7/65

TRINITY HOUSE: Deputy-Master for Sandwich, 3/18, 29; Batten's attempt to make him Master, 6/107; blamed for sinking ships, 8/270–1; dinners, 5/15, 94, 186; also, 2/4, 26

HIS HOUSE AT BETHNAL GREEN: P admires, 4/200 & n. 5; sends valuables in Fire, 7/272, 282, 283

SOCIAL: dines with P, 1/14; 5/62; gives dinner, 4/200; at taverns, 5/341; 6/25, 83, 145; also, 5/255

MISC.: stories of Genoa, 3/7–8 & nn.; 4/201; Chatham Chest, 3/257; 7/110; arbitrates in dispute, 4/426; 5/15, 19, 36; his rise alluded to, 5/52; diary, 5/98; ill, 5/159; fears issue of war, ib.; Fishery business, 5/336; opposes building of New London, 6/170

ALLUDED TO: 2/193

~ his wife [Priscilla], 4/200

RIDER, Mr ——, merchant: 4/247

RIGA, Latvia (Sweden): yarn/cordage from, 3/101 & n. 3, 5/182; hemp, 4/49, 259 & n. 4

RIGGS, ——, servant to Albemarle: 7/203

RINGSTEAD'S: see Taverns etc.: Star, Cheapside

RIOTS: see Law and Order, offences against

ROBARTES, Sir John, 2nd Baron Robartes, cr. Earl of Radnor 1679; Lord Privy Seal 1661–73 (d. 1685):

CHARACTER: 2/149, 150; 5/73; 8/450

AS LORD PRIVY SEAL: introduces register of fees, 2/214; refuses P a deputy, 3/61; refuses to seal royal pardon, 9/52 & nn.; affixes seal, 2/150, 158, 187, 232–3, 234, 237; 6/83, 84; at Chelsea house, 2/158, 187, 201, 234, 237; unspecified business, 2/228; out of town, 2/170, 171, 175, 236; also, 2/214; 3/66, 168

OTHER APPOINTMENTS ETC.: Treasury Commissioner, 1/170 & n. 3; Lord Deputy of Ireland, 1/227–8 & n.; to be Lord-Lieutenant, 9/452 & n. 2; in cabal, 8/585; 9/427

HOUSES ETC.: Whitehall chamber, 2/150; in Chelsea: P admires, 2/187–8 & n.; visits on Privy Seal business, 2/158, 187, 199, 201, 234, 237; pictures, 2/187; 6/84

SOCIAL: 8/450

ALLUDED TO: 3/66, 168

~ his wife [Laetitia], 9/176, 177 & n. 1; his daughter [Laetitia Isabella], 9/176 & n. 4

ROBARTES, Robert, son of the foregoing: case in Chancery, 5/140 & n. 1; ~ his wife [Sara]: her inheritance, 5/140 & n. 1; P admires, 6/84; 9/176–7; portrait, 6/84

ROBERT, Prince: see Rupert

[ROBERT, Anthony], dancing master: 9/507

[ROBERTS, William], Bishop of Bangor 1637–d. 65: 1/259 & n. 3

ROBERTS, [William], merchant, of St Olave's parish: ship, 8/293 & n. 2

ROBERTS'S: see Taverns etc.: Harp and Ball

ROBINS, [?Judy]: 6/187, 202

ROBINS, Tony, of Westminster: 1/92
ROBINS, Monsieur ——, periwig-maker and proprietor of ordinary, Covent Garden: 8/211
ROBINSON, [Anne], Lady Robinson, wife of Sir John: admired by P, 5/67; 6/290; 7/415; by Cocke, 6/290; wanton speech, 6/290; 7/415; social: 6/268
ROBINSON, [Henry], merchant and author (d. ?1673): claims manage-ment of Post Office, 7/375 & n. 2
ROBINSON, Ald. Sir John, Lieuten-ant of the Tower 1660–79; M.P. London 1660, Rye, Sussex 1661–79; Lord Mayor 1662–3:
CHARACTER: P's low opinion, 4/77–8 & n.; 5/12, 307; 6/299; 8/201; love of food and wine, 7/38
AS LIEUTENANT OF TOWER: account of Vane's trial and execution, 3/103–4 & n., 116; allows search for treasure, 3/241 & n. 1, 242, 286; consulted on exemptions from militia service, 6/24 & n. 3; and on pressed men, 7/200; arranges coal supplies for poor, 6/264 & n. 3, 265(2); shirks duties in Dutch raid, 8/266; also, 4/294; 8/278, 299, 394
AS ALDERMAN AND LORD MAYOR: boasts of influence, 4/77; 5/307 & n. 2; plans new street, 4/77; 8/201; precept about coachmen, 4/77–8 & n.; disapproves of Principal Officers of Navy as city magistrates, 4/78; revives ceremonial at Bartholomew Fair, 4/288 & n. 2
SOCIAL: as Lieutenant of Tower: enter-tains King, 1/214 & n. 3; Navy Board, 2/51; 5/316; Holmes (on his release), 6/56; Albemarle, 6/268; as Lord Mayor: at Trinity House, 3/103, 187; entertains customs farmers, 4/341; other occasions: P dines with, 4/70, 294–5; 5/67; enjoyment of hunting, 6/295; and singing, 6/311–12; dines with P, 9/410–11; also, 7/11–12, 38, 226, 299; 9/108, 543
MISC.: house in Mincing Lane, 3/241; news from, 5/333; 7/268; quarrels with Capt. J. Taylor, 6/56 & n. 3, 295; as M.P., 9/92–3, 193
ALLUDED TO: 8/394
~ his son [John], 7/268

ROBINSON, Luke, M.P. Scarbor-ough, Yorks. 1645–8, 1660: delegate to Monck, 1/51–2 & n.; royalist speech, 1/122 & n. 2
ROBINSON, Capt. [Robert], kted 1675, naval officer: action against Dutch, 7/424 & n. 3
[ROBINSON, Robert, painter]: see Rogerson
ROBINSON, ——, cook: 2/102 & n. 3
ROBSON [Robinson], [Thomas], clerk to Sir W. Coventry: 7/244; 9/87, 169
ROCHE, DE LA [Peter], dentist: 2/53 & n. 1; 4/97
ROCHESTER, Kent: P visits/passes through, 1/172; 2/68, 70, 72; 3/156; 6/182, 241–2, 249; 8/311; burning of figurehead, 4/420; bridge, 1/172 & n. 5; 8/306; 9/11; cathedral, 2/70 & nn.; 8/311; castle, 6/249 & nn.; 8/311; Salutation tavern, 2/70; Crown inn, 3/153 & n. 1; 6/241–2, 249; 8/307; White Hart inn, 8/311, 312; cherry gardens, 8/312; alluded to: 2/15, 55, 57, 67; 6/256; 7/162; 9/50
RODER: see Rothe
ROETTIER(S) (Rotyr), [John], en-graver to the Mint: bust of King on coins, 4/70 & n. 3; his dies, 4/147 & n. 2; engraves Navy Board seal, 7/82–3; Breda medal, 8/83 & n. 1; P admires his work, 4/147; 8/83
ROGERS, [?Matthew], of St Margaret's parish, Westminster: 1/47
ROGERS, ——: 9/58–9
ROGERSON [?Robinson, Robert], painter: 9/420 & n. 1
ROLLS CHAPEL: see Chancery
ROLT, Capt. [Edward], Gentleman of the Bedchamber to Oliver Cromwell: his former greatness, 2/108 & n. 1; P's admiration, 8/29; cornet, 8/323 & n. 1; building works in Whitehall, 9/302 & n. 1; social: sings with Mrs Knepp, 6/320–1, 323; 9/166; and Harris, 9/175; at dance at Navy Office, 8/28, 29; at taverns, 2/119, 120; 9/186, 220; also, 2/121; 7/2, 100; 8/51, 172–3, 575; 9/203, 218–19
ROMAN CATHOLICISM [see also Religion (P)]:
STATUS OF/OFFICIAL POLICY TOWARDS:

for Council, 7/96 & n. 2; 8/553; Councillor, vol. i, p. xxxix; 7/96, n. 2; President (1684–6), ib.; subscribes to new building, 9/146; pays dues, 9/165 & n. 4

MEETINGS: visitors at, 8/11; Duchess of Newcastle, 8/243 & nn.; meeting day changed, 8/242–3; vacation, 9/334; club meetings, 6/36; 7/148

SUBJECTS OF MEETINGS/DEMONSTRA-TIONS: P lacks 'philosophy' to understand, 6/48; effects of heat on glass, 5/123 & n. 3; viol with keyboard, 5/290 & n. 3; French bread, 6/48 & n. 3; comets, ib. & n. 1; effects of poison on dog, 6/57 & n. 1; of vacuum on kitten, 6/64 & n. 1; of poison on hen, dog and cat, 6/84 & n. 4, 95–6; design of coaches, 6/94 & n. 2; human foetus, 6/96 & n. 1; felt making, 7/51 & n. 3; blood transfusion, 7/370–1 & n., 373, 389; 8/543 & n. 1, 554 & n. 4; gunpowder, 8/11 & n. 1; lodestones, microscopes etc., 8/243 & n. 3; refraction of light, 8/555; 9/113 & n. 5; otacousticon, 9/146 & n. 3; circulation of blood, 9/263 & n. 1; elections, 7/96; 8/553; 9/379; unspecified subjects, 6/41, 52, 112; 7/21, 43, 79, 147; 8/17, 528, 540–1; 9/334

OFFICERS: the operator, 9/337

ROYSTON, HERTS.: 3/224; 8/268

RUBENS: engravings after, 1/194 & n. 5; work at Nonsuch House (attrib. to), 6/235 & n. 3

RUDDIARD (Ruddyer), [Thomas], of the Excise Office: 1/33, 192; 2/50

RUMBOLD (Rumball), [Henry, jun.]: ?7/23

RUMBOLD (Rumball), [William], Clerk of the Great Wardrobe: his claret, 1/277; son's christening, 2/230 & n. 2; also, 1/301; 3/2; 4/69; ?7/23; ~ his wife, 3/2; 8/369–70 & n.

RUNDELL(S), [Edward], house carpenter at Deptford and Woolwich yards: sends P blackbird, 4/150; overcharges for wharf, 4/284 & n. 2

RUPERT, Prince ('the Prince', Prince Robert), Privy Councillor and naval commander:

CHARACTER: 1/255; 5/169–70, 304; 6/12, 139; 7/332

CHRON. SERIES: defence of Bristol (1645), 5/169–70 & n.; leads mutiny at Newark (1645), 6/30–1 & n.; at court for first time, 1/255 & n. 2; made Privy Councillor, 3/75; at Council committee for navy, 9/152; at Cabinet, 9/525; rumoured to have pox, 6/12; portrait by Lely, 7/102 & n. 3; ill of head wound, 8/15, 16, 38; operated on, 8/34–5, 40, 41 & n. 4, 45, 46–7, 52, 58, 145–6; granted licence for stolen prize-goods, 8/52, 531; privateers, 8/341, 342, 344, 349, 385

AS NAVAL COMMANDER: jealous of Batten (1648), 5/169 & n. 1; given command, 5/183, 258; in *Henrietta*, 5/262; refuses to command whole fleet, ib.; sails to Downs, 5/264, 291, 295; returns to Portsmouth, 5/301; fears attack by Dutch, 5/304; in Battle of Lowestoft, 6/121, 122, 127, 135, 137, 146; refuses joint command with Sandwich, 6/148; parliamentary grant proposed, 6/291; relations with Sandwich, 6/276, 291; 8/117; new command, 6/323, 342; 7/108, 109; responsibility for dividing fleet before Four Days Fight, 7/139 & n. 3, 141, 143–4 & n., 149; 8/489; 9/70; conduct in, 7/147, 148, 158, 160; sails again, 7/210, 210–11; reputation declines, 7/212, 213–14, 231, 299, 340, 349–50, 354; conduct in St James's Day Fight, 7/225, 344–5; blames Navy Board for victualling deficiencies, 7/172, 259 & n. 1, 260, 263, 264, 312–13; 8/315, 511–12, 513; 9/107; differences with Albemarle, 7/315, 323; his 'narrative' in self-defence, 8/511–12 & n., 513, 514–15, 518, 571; thanked by Commons for services, 8/499 & n. 2; appointments to fleet, 9/5–6, 39, 75–6; favours small fleet, 9/121–2, 216; hopes of command frustrated, 9/126, 140, 148, 216; offended by Penn's appointment, 9/125, 126, 131, 140; supports Heemskerck's ship-design, 9/206; also, 8/496

TANGIER: appointed to committee, 3/238; attends meetings, 3/272; 5/167; 7/321; frivolous behaviour, 5/167

SOCIAL: at court ball, 7/372; at theatre, 8/196

SALISBURY COURT [see also Taverns etc.: Standing's; Theatre]: Fire in, 7/386; also, 3/99; 4/427

SALISBURY, Wilts.: P visits, 9/228–31; Siamese twins, 5/319; court at during Plague, 6/189, 221, 243; assizes, 8/428; George Inn, 9/228 & n. 6, 229, 230; Cathedral and close, 9/229, 230 & n.; Bishop's Palace, 9/229 & n. 3; alluded to: 9/529

SALISBURY PLAIN, Wilts.: 9/229, 231, 497

SALLI, (Sally), N. Africa: English interest in, 4/336 & n. 1

SALMON: see Soulemont

SALSBURY, ——, painter: P admires his work, 2/59, 145; miniature of Sandwich, 2/23 & n. 2; shows P portraits, 2/59; also, 1/195, 264; 3/80

SALTONSTALL ('Sanderson'), Lady Saltonstall: killed in storm, 3/32 & n. 4

[SALVIATI, Marchese Giovanni Vincenzo], Tuscan ambassador March –Sept. 1661: state entry, 2/55 & n. 3; first audience, 2/57 & n. 3

SALWEY (Salloway), [Maj. Richard], M.P. Appleby, Westmorland (d. 1685): suspended and imprisoned by Rump, 1/21 & n. 2

SAMFORD, Mr —— [? Samuel Sandford, Commonwealth official]: 1/244, 248

SANDERS: see Saunders

SANDERSON, Bridget, Lady Sanderson, (b. Tyrrell), wife of Sir William, Mother of the Maids of Honour to the Queen c. 1662–d. 82: 3/83 & n. 6

[SANDERSON, Robert], Bishop of Lincoln 1660–d.63: consecrated, 1/276 & n. 2

SANDERSON, [Sir William], historian, relative of P: book on Charles I, 1/132 & n. 4; travels to Charles II in Holland, 1/132, 133

'SANDERSON', Lady: see Saltonstall

[SANDFORD]: see Samford

SAN DOMINGO, Hispaniola: 9/556 & n. 3

SANDWICH, Earl and Countess of: see Mountagu, Edward and Jemima

SANDYS (Sands), Col. [Samuel],

M.P. Worcestershire (d. 1685): 8/583

SANDYS (Sands), [William], M.P. Evesham, Worcs. (d. 1669): congratulates P on parliamentary speech, 9/105

SANDYS, [William], 6th Baron Sandys (d. 1669): 8/381 & n. 4; ~ his wife [Mary], (b. Cecil, d. 1667), ib.

SANKEY (Zanchy), [Clement], Fellow of Magdalene College, 1660–?9; Rector of St Clement Eastcheap 1666–1707; drinks King's health, 1/67, 68; marriage, 2/220 & n. 4; appointed to living, 8/17 & n. 5; high repute, 8/151; social: in Cambridge, 1/69; 2/136, 146; at theatre, 2/219, 226; 3/58; also, 2/225; 5/135; 8/167

SANSUM, Rear-Adm. [Robert], naval commander: killed in action, 6/122, 129

SANTHUNE, Mary de (b. Pepys), wife of Samuel: legacy, 4/344–5 & n., 346 & n. 3, 351; marriage portion, 4/344–5, 346; death, 8/590 & n. 4, 601

[SANTHUNE, Samuel de], P's relative: repays debt, 5/342 & n. 4; also, 4/307; 5/303

SANTIAGO (St Jago), Cuba: captured, 4/41 & n. 5, 54, 94

SAUNDERS, Capt. [Francis], naval officer: bravery in Four Days Fight, 7/148

[SAUNDERS, Capt. Joseph], naval officer: killed in action, 7/231, n. 4

SAUNDERS, ——, musician, of Cambridge: dies in Plague, 8/468 & n. 4

SAUNDERS (Sanders), ——, porter: 7/185; 8/264, 272

SAUNDERS, Capt. [? Gabriel], naval officer: on pursers, 5/202

SAUNDERSON, Mary, ('Ianthe'): see Betterton

SAVAGE, Sir Edward, Gentleman of the Privy Chamber to the King: 8/220; 9/280 & n. 2

SAVILE, Sir George, Viscount Halifax, cr. Marquess of Halifax 1682, politician (d. 1695): created baron and viscount, 9/2 & n. 5; on Brooke House Committee, 9/254, 255; rumoured duel with Buckingham, 9/462; visits Coventry in Tower, 9/468 & n. 3

SAVILE, Henry, Groom of the Bed-chamber to the Duke of York: alleged affair with Duchess of York, 6/302 & n. 1; his part in Coventry's attempted duel with Buckingham, 9/462, 467; imprisoned, 9/466, 469; forbidden to attend Duke of York, 9/493; also, 9/491

SAVILL, ——, painter: P commissions portraits, 2/218 & n. 4; P/EP sit for, 2/221, 226, 227, 233, 235; 3/4; her dog added, 2/241; her portrait amended, 3/19; pictures paid for, 3/10; hung, 3/34; varnished, 3/106; miniature of P, 3/33, 35, 37, 39, 41, 49–50, 65, 76, 106; also, 2/234

SAVOY, Dowager-Duchess of: *see* Christina

SAVOY, Duchy of, envoy from: *see* [Piossasco]

SAVOY, the, Strand [*see also* French Church]: House of Lords Committee at hospital, 2/100 & n. 2; sermon at chapel, 2/29, 98; also, 1/214, 227; 3/160

[SAWYER, John], landlord of the Pope's Head tavern, Lombard St: 7/329 & n. 1

SAWYER, [Robert], lawyer, kted 1677; P's contemporary at Magdalene: as counsel, 7/386 & n. 3; 9/214; prospers, 8/567 & n. 4; ~ his wife [Mary] and child [Margaret], 8/567

SAXONY, Elector of: *see* John George II

SAYER(S), [John], Master-Cook, King's privy kitchen: 2/175

SCARBURGH, [Charles], physician; kted 1669 (d. 1694): on children's eye-sight, 1/157; on stone, 4/59–60

SCAWEN (Scowen), [Robert], M.P. Cockermouth, Cumb. 1662–d. 70: P asks favour of, 1/257 & n. 2; also, 4/18; 8/248, 294, 480

SCHELLING: *see* Terschelling

SCHEVENINGEN (Scheveling), Holland: P at, 1/140, 143, 145, 148, 150; King's embarkation, 1/127, 135; house of entertainment, 1/140; church, 1/150 & n. 2

SCHOOLS [*see also* Eton College; Huntingdon; St Paul's School]: for boys: Twickenham, Mdx, 1/18, 20,

276; 7/209; Bromley, Kent, 6/223; Royal Latin school, Buckingham, 9/225 & n. 1; for girls: Bow, 8/448, 451; Chelsea, 4/45, 59, 82; Clerkenwell, 2/232; 4/132; Hackney, 8/174 & n. 4; 9/512; Putney, 8/188, 210; 9/526

SCHRAM, [Volkert], naval commander: commands squadron, 6/108 & n. 3

SCIENCE AND MATHEMATICS, P's interest in [For P as Fellow of the Royal Society, *see* Royal Society. *See also* Books; Clerk of the Acts: learns his trade; Scientific and Mathematical Instruments.]:

GENERAL: limited understanding, 3/131 & n.; 6/48; 8/247; 9/416

ARITHMETIC: learns multiplication table, 3/131 & n. 1, 134, 135; his arithmetic books, 4/406; discusses duodecimal system, 4/178 & n. 2; P teaches EP, 4/343, 344, 357, 360, 363, 364, 378, 402, 403, 404, 406

ASTRONOMY: instructs EP, 4/43; studies skies, 7/238–41 passim; discusses, 7/254; reports? comet/meteor observed at Amsterdam, 5/134 & n. 1; comet of Nov. 1664–March 1665, 5/346 & n. 3, 348, 354–5, 355–6, 357; Hooke's lecture on, 6/48 & n. 1; that of April 1665, 6/75 & n. 1; of Aug. 1665, ?6/194 & n. 1; and of May 1668, 9/207–8 & n.

HIS OBSERVATIONS ETC. (MISC.): believes 'baboon' product of miscegenation, 2/160; watches demonstrations of Prince Rupert's drops, 3/9 & n. 3; of anatomy, 4/59–60 & nn.; injection of dog with opium, 5/151 & n. 1; dissection of eyes, 9/254–5; processes used at Royal Mint, 4/143–8 passim & nn.; shown *hortus hyemalis*, 6/289 & n. 6; and mechanism of watch, 6/337; observes phosphorescence in river, 6/241 & n. 3; wonders why guns heard in London not Dover, 7/145 & n. 4; comments on infant's manner of feeding at breast, 8/200

HIS CONVERSATIONS (MISC.): on inability of infants to focus eyes, 1/157; spontaneous generation, 2/105 & n. 4; authority of Scripture, ib.; levers, 2/112; snakes catching birds, 3/22 &

n. 2; tarantula stings, 3/23 & n. 1; anatomy (general), 3/72–3, 228; 4/334; mathematics (general), 4/31; 9/191; etymology, 4/185; ghosts, 4/185–6 & n.; chemistry, 4/218; 5/144; Galenical *v.* chemical medicine, 4/362 & n. 2, 378; Descartes, 4/263 & n. 2, 267; Aristotle's physics, 4/267 & nn.; explosives, 4/378 & n. 4; hibernation of swallows etc., 4/412–13 & n.; refrigeration of food, 4/412, 413; floating islands, 5/94–5; dreams, 5/108; microscopic images of wings of birds etc., 5/235; archaeology, 5/274; Siamese twins, 5/319; lactation in women, 6/63; need for symbols to describe taste, ib.; philosopher's stone, ib; botany, 6/253; respiration, 7/21 & n. 3; perspective machines, 7/51 & n. 4; man as fruit-eating animal, 7/223–4; optics, 7/224, 225, 254; sound and vibration, 7/239 & n. 1; human maturation and speech, 8/554; 'universal characters', 9/331 & n. 3; also, 9/544

SCIENTIFIC AND MATHEMATICAL INSTRUMENTS: [armillary sphere]: 1/14 & n. 2; calculating machine: 9/116–17 & n.; compasses: P buys, 4/336; 5/271; dial, double horizontal: P studies, 4/171–2, 173; globes: P buys pair, 4/302 & n. 3: [for his teaching EP their use, *see* Pepys, Elizabeth: her accomplishments]; hydrometer (Boyle's): 9/390 & n. 2; microscope: P buys, 5/48, 221, 223, 235, 240; uses, 5/241; 7/226; Napier's bones: P to buy, 8/451 & n. 1; pantograph: P buys, 9/414, 444; uses, 9/417; also, 9/340, n. 1, 389–90; 437, 531; perspectives/perspective glasses: *see* spy-glasses, below; perspective machine: Rupert's model, 7/51 & n. 4; P acquires Wren's model, 9/537–8 & n., 548; also, 9/513; picture-box: P uses, 7/254 & n. 3; buys, 7/257; protractor: alluded to, 9/437; scotoscope (spy-glass for use at night): P acquires, 5/240; uses, 9/261; slide-rules [*see also* Napier's bones]: P buys White's ruler, 4/84 & n. 2, 85 & n. 1, 103; buys pocket model, 4/124, 125, 132, 266, 267; has

tables engraved on, 4/237, 238, 239, 270, 277; also, 4/178, 180, 181, 234; 5/17; spy-glasses: P buys for Sandwich, 1/95; for himself, 2/35; 6/273; 7/257; quizzes church congregation with, 8/236; thermometer: P buys 3/203; 4/84; telescope: Sandwich's, 4/160; P buys one, 7/240, 241 & n. 1, 243, 257; uses it, 7/238–9, 240, 254, 257

SCILLY, Isles of: *Royal Oak* wrecked, 6/36 & n. 1; also, 3/78; 8/162

SCOBELL, [Henry], Clerk of the Parliament, 1649–58 [*see also* Books]: censured by Rump, 1/12–13 & n.; in Chancery case, 1/48; bequeaths lands to nephew, 1/230 & n. 1; foretells death in dream, 4/415; 5/8

SCOBELL, Richard: at parties with P, 1/175, 212, 248; 2/34; ~ his wife, 1/175, 208, 244, 248; his kinswoman, 1/208; her mock marriage, 1/175

SCOT, the; preacher (?lecturer/reader) at St Olave's, Hart St: sermons, 3/236; 4/12, 96, 106, 165, 177, 190, 235, 348, 369, 426, 435

SCOTLAND: disorders in Galloway, 4/130–1 & n., 138, 168–9 & n.; Lauderdale's power, 5/57 & nn.; Cromwellian forts slighted, 5/346 & nn.; Pentland Rising, 7/377 & n. 4, 378, 381, 382 & n. 1, 384 & nn., 387 & n. 2, 390 & n. 6, 391, 395–8 passim & n.; music, 7/224–5; timber from, 7/298 & n. 3, 300, 301; P family origins in, 8/261 & n. 4

SCOTLAND YARD, Westminster: 1/319; 7/158; 8/205

SCOTT, Anne, Countess of Buccleuch, wife of James, Duke of Monmouth (d. 1732): marries, 3/297 & n. 4; 4/107 & n. 1; at court balls, 3/301; 7/372; in court masque, 6/29; and play, 9/23; dislocates hip, 9/191 & n. 3, 201, 262, 311; also, 9/468

SCOTT, [Benjamin], pewterer, of Holborn, P's 'cousin': P godfather to son, 2/216 & n. 2; owed money by Tom P, 5/85; acts as administrator of Tom's estate, 5/102 & n. 1, 106, 122, 124–5 & n., 142, 149–50; wife's death, 5/142; his funeral, 5/347–8 & n.; social: 1/10, 179, 252; 2/2, 7, 113; 3/94; 4/18, 427

SCOTT, [?Blundell], surgeon: treats Jemima Mountagu, 1/26, 36 & n. 3, 41; 6/160; ∼ his wife, 1/36

SCOTT, [Carolina], Lady Scott (b. Carteret), wife of Thomas (d. 1722): marriage, 4/254 & n. 1; 5/15; also, 6/168

SCOTT, Lady Catherine (b. Goring), wife of Edward of Scot's Hall, Kent (d. 1686): 4/254 & n. 2

SCOTT, [Edward], of Scot's Hall, Kent: his lawsuits against wife concerning son's legitimacy, 4/254 & n. 2

SCOTT, Sir Edward: at Spanish ambassador's, 9/544

SCOTT, James, ('Mr Crofts'), cr. Duke of Monmouth 1663, illegitimate son of Charles II (d. 1685):

CHARACTER: 'a most pretty spark', 3/191; lively, 6/170; vicious and idle, 6/167; 7/411

CHRON. SERIES: King's fondness, 3/303; 4/113–14, 123; 5/21, 41, 56; Queen and Queen Mother kind to 3/191; honorary degree at Cambridge, 4/99 & n. 3; made Knight of the Garter, 4/99 & n. 2, 108; married, 4/107 & n. 1; coat of arms, ib. & n. 2; lodgings, ib.; 4/371; career in Guards, 4/371 & n. 2; 8/246, 255, 436; 9/308, 557; book dedicated to, 5/58; visits Deptford with King, 6/169; ill, 8/581; also, 3/297; 4/425–6; 5/154; 8/156; 9/474

HIS CLAIM TO SUCCESSION: rumours of/ controversy about legitimacy, 3/238 & n. 4, 303 & n. 1; 4/134, 138, 376; 7/411; 8/434, 438, 518; rumour of advancement, 8/596; of his becoming Prince of Wales, 9/373; claim resented by Duke of York, 3/290; 5/21, 58; to take precedence of dukes, 4/38; wears royal Prince's mourning, 5/21; threatens to kill anyone denying his legitimacy, 5/56

SOCIAL: at court: 3/299; at ball, 3/300; 4/113; 7/372; dances in masque, 6/29; acts in play, 9/23; in Park, 8/185, 288; at theatre, 3/260; at eating-house, 9/172

SCOTT, [Judith], P's cousin, wife of Benjamin: 'a good woman', 5/134; son dies, 1/244, 252; son christened, 2/216; her death, 5/40, 53, 134 & n. 2,

142; social: 1/10; 2/2, 7; 3/88; 4/18, 101, 427; alluded to: 9/477

SCOTT, Sir Thomas, of Scot's Hall, Kent: his legitimacy, 4/254 & n. 2; marriage, 4/254; 5/15; 6/178 & n. 3

SCOTT, [Thomas], regicide (d. 1660): opposes Lambert (Dec. 1659), 2/92 & n. 3; appointed Intelligencer, 1/14 & n. 4; emissary to Monck, 1/51–2 & n.; trial, 1/263 & nn.

SCOTT, [Thomas], son of the regicide: arrested, 4/168 & n. 3

SCOTT, Walter, novelist: review of the diary (1825), vol. i, p. lxxxii

SCOTT, Mr ——: 6/98

SCOTT, Mrs ——, shopkeeper in Westminster Hall: 7/425

SCROGGS (Scruggs), Sir William, Justice Common Pleas 1676–8; Lord Chief Justice 1678–81 (d. 1683): eloquence, 8/22 & n. 4

SCROOPE, Col. Adrian, regicide: excepted from Act of Indemnity, 1/232–3 & n.

SCULL, ——, waterman: 1/33

SCULPTURE:

STATUARY: Charles I's statue at Royal Exchange, 1/89 & n. 3, 99 & n. 3, 113; his bust at Swakeleys, 6/215 & n. 1; Northumberland's antique busts, 1/188 & n. 3; statuary at Arundel House, 2/110 & n. 2; on façade of Nonsuch, 6/235 & n. 3; carved heads on pillars, Wells Cathedral, 9/239 & n. 2

MONUMENTS: in Oude Kerk, Delft, 1/145–6 & n.; Nieuwe Kerk, Delft, 1/146 & n. 2; Canterbury Cathedral, 1/172 & n. 3; St Mary Overie, 4/214 & n. 2; Westminster Abbey, 5/268; 9/456–7 & n.; Hatfield, 8/381 & n. 5; the Temple, 8/545 & n. 2; Norton St Philip, 9/232 & n. 4; Bath Abbey, 9/238 & nn., 238–9 & n.

MISC.: alabaster St George for EP's closet, 4/409; plaster head of P, 9/442, 449

[SEABROOK, ?John], Rector of St Andrew-by-the-Wardrobe: 2/171 & n. 2

SEALE, Capt. [Thomas], naval officer: in action against Dutch, 6/20

SEAMOUR: see Seymour

SUBJECTS: Gal., iv, 4, 1/3; life of Christ, 1/11; authority of St Peter, 1/32; 1 John, iii. 1, 1/42; widowhood, 1/60; commandments, 1/68; charity, 1/76; Ezra, vi. 10, 1/91; Christian duty, 1/97; stewardship, 1/220; 'The Lord is my Shield', 1/237; 'Teach us the old way', ib.; 1 Cor., ix. 24, 1/251; war, 2/37; drunkenness, 2/42; evil imaginings, 2/48; love, 2/74; patience, 2/98; the Restoration, 2/109; Acts, iii. 21, 2/161; Grace, 2/211; 8/381; church music and behaviour in church, 2/215; 5/172; Jas., i. 17, 2/219; miraculous appearance of the Virgin and St John, 2/239 & n. 4; redemption, 3/12–13; regicide, 3/20; 'Cast thy bread upon the waters', 3/21; Micah, i. 10, 3/42; godliness, 3/60; Gal., v. 13, 3/70; John, iv. 14, 3/84; peace, 3/167; Psalms, i. 1, 3/182; uniformity, 3/190; resurrection, 3/270; frivolity at court, 3/292; David and Saul, 4/29; Josh., xxxiv. 5, 4/36–7; sowing and reaping, 4/69; nonconformity, 4/92–3, 185; temptation, 4/98; popery, 4/98 & n. 1; 8/587; brotherly love, 4/112; John, xv. 14, 4/259; Lot's wife, 4/268; Jas., iii. 17, 5/66–7 & n.; puritans, 5/96–7; duty to parents, 5/342; 1 Sam., xii. 24, 6/87; limits of science, 6/289; purgatory, 7/123; truth of Christianity, 7/206; imitation of Christ and the saints, 7/383; Eccles,. xi. 8, 8/21; the meek shall inherit the earth, 8/116; Luke, xii. 31, 8/144–5; 9/286; adultery, 8/362–3, 366; scribes and pharisees, 9/482

P's APPRECIATION: nature of his reports, vol. i, pp. cxvii–cxviii; takes notes in Latin, 4/268, 278; samples several, 1/205, 302, 324; 2/230; 3/47, 91–2, 252; 4/163; 5/190, 256, 285; reads during, 1/42; sleeps, 1/97, 322; 2/215; 4/106, 165, 177, 190, 348, 369, 435; 5/125; 8/236; dislikes excessive eloquence, 1/60; disapproves of political, 1/195; dislikes Presbyterian, 2/74–5; 3/58, 81, 99; buys *Evangelium Armatum*, 4/111 & n. 4; reads H. King's sermon on regicide, 6/54 & n. 3; borrows volume of Jeremy Taylor, 6/312 & n. 3; enjoys readings from

sermon against Rome, 8/587 & n. 3; reads A. Wright's *Five sermons in five several styles*, 9/300 & n. 5; prefers puritan style, ib.

SERVANTS (P) [Servants named below are those employed by P and referred to by their Christian names only. Those with surnames are entered in the main series, with cross-references here. Servants of other households are indexed with their employers.]:

GENERAL: numbers employed in P's household, 2/1, 241; 3/301–2; 4/438; 5/257, 359–60; 6/143; 7/426; 8/134; black servants, 2/36, 61, 69; 4/51; 6/215, 244, 283, 285, 288; 8/33, 123; 9/464, 510; man cook hired, 3/53; 4/13; 7/388, 389, 392; 9/115–16; table layer, 9/115, 423; testimonials: 4/78–9 & n., 131, 294; wages: cookmaids, 3/53; 4/86; 5/158–9; lady's companion, 7/311; 9/362

SERVANTS IN P'S HOUSEHOLD:

ALICE, COOKMAID: unpromising, 6/70; accompanies EP to Woolwich in Plague, 6/149, 313; leaves, 7/85; alluded to: 6/143

ASHWELL, MARY: *see* Ashwell

BARKER: *see* Barker

BESS, COOKMAID: good temper, 4/399, 438; 5/91, 290; recommended by Creed, 4/320–1 & n.; helps at Tom P's death and funeral, 5/88, 91; promoted to chambermaid, 5/101, 360; scolded, 5/185; at Brampton with EP, 5/224, 234; dismissed, 5/270, 290, 318; 6/49, 51; ingratitude, 6/51; also, 4/354, 362, 399; 5/111, 124, 137, 196, 249, 290, 305

BRIDGET, COOKMAID: cooks well, 9/184; leaves, 9/510; a thief, ib.; also, 9/165, 166

DOLL (DOROTHY, DOROTHÉ), CHAMBERMAID: enters service, 2/151, 174; talkative, 2/204, 221; dismissed, 2/220, 221

DOLL, COOKMAID, a 'blackmoore': good cook, 9/510

ELY, FOOTBOY: *see* Jenkins, Eliezer

GOSNELL, [Winifred]: *see* Gosnell

HANNAH, COOKMAID: engaged without references, 4/78–9 & n.; good cook, 4/86, 90, 95; stays up all night cleaning kitchen, 4/253; scolded for leaving house dirty, 4/264; dismissed for stealing, 4/279; also, 4/100, 205, 236

JACK, FOOTBOY: arrives from Impington, 9/348; livery described, 9/372; reads to P, 9/372, 373; accompanies in London, 9/453, 530, 550, 557; also, 9/424, 439–40, 464, 469, 527, 530, 552

JANE, COOKMAID: enters service, 5/158-9 & n. 1, 191, 201; P pleased with, 5/225; dismissed by EP, 6/4(2), 26, 28; EP neglects to pay wages, 6/29, 30, 31

JANE (BIRCH). *see* Edwards

JANE (GENTLEMAN): *see* Gentleman

JINNY: parish child, engaged by EP, 4/282; runs away, ib.; dismissed, 4/283–4 & n.

LUCE, COOKMAID: arrives, 7/183; 'ugly and plain', ib.; falls downstairs, 7/188; drinks, 8/126; P kicks for carelessness, 8/164; found drunk and departs, 8/221–2

MARY, COOKMAID: arrives, 2/176; and leaves, 2/196

MARY, CHAMBERMAID: to replace Jane Birch, 4/34; works well, 4/40, 41; tries to corrupt cookmaid, 4/100; dismissed, 4/113

MARY, CHAMBERMAID: engaged by EP, 6/40, 51; at Woolwich during Plague, 6/149; EP quarrels with, 6/214, 246, 250, dismissed, 6/295, 296; engaged by E. Pearse, 6/317; 7/93, 103; also, 6/119, 143

MARY, COOKMAID: arrives, 7/121; and leaves, 7/183

MARY, UNDER-COOKMAID: arrives, 8/225; and leaves, 8/328; her love of gaming, ib.

MATT, CHAMBERMAID: EP tells of her good looks, 9/479, 481, 487; arrives, 9/502, 504; dismissed, 9/559

MERCER, MARY: *see* Mercer

NELL: arrives, 2/196; unwilling to sleep in room with P and EP, 2/213; 'a simple slut', 2/233; lazy, 3/8; dismissed, 3/57; alluded to: 2/241; ~ her mother, 2/196

NELL, COOKMAID: arrives, 8/419;

cooks well, 9/184; cuts P's hair, 9/201; dismissed, 9/332

NELL (PAYNE): *see* Payne

SARAH: enters service, 2/218 & n. 3, 222; ague, 3/46, 47, 51, 53, 65; combs P's hair, 3/96; washes his feet, 3/97; P pleased with, 3/113, 135; accompanies EP to Brampton, 3/65, 141, 151, 206; EP quarrels with, 3/135, 184; her proposed dismissal, 3/213, 258, 263, 273; departure, 3/274, 278; warns P against B. St Michel, 3/285; joins Penn's household, 3/295, 302; her gossiping, 4/7; dismissed, 4/92; also, 2/241; 3/95, 108, 110, 116, 208; 4/276; 6/141; ?7/268

SUSAN, COOKMAID: recommended by B. St Michel, 3/279; her cooking, 3/301; 4/34; ill, 4/41, 85, 86; replaced by Hannah, 4/86; twice returns temporarily, 4/150, 279; dismissed for drinking, 4/154, 280, 281

SUSAN, ?COOKMAID: 'an admirable slut', 5/55; the 'little girl', 4/438; 5/307, 318, 320; arrives, 4/284; EP angry with, 4/363; beaten for negligence, 5/13; 6/39; combs P's hair, 6/185; 7/95; at Woolwich with EP during Plague, 6/209, 282, 313; sent away with suspected plague, 7/115(3), 116(2); returns, 7/122; also, 5/165, 225, 257, 323, 360; 6/49, 143; 7/100, 108; ~ her father a sexton, 7/116; her mother, 7/116

WAYNEMAN: *see* Birch

WILL, FOOTBOY: enters service, 1/189, 193; combs P's hair, 1/222; dismissed for stealing, 1/233, 234, 237, 240; also, 1/203, 206; ~ his father, 1/233, 240

WILLET, DEB: *see* Willet

ANONYMOUS SERVANTS: coachman, 9/393, 464, 527; maids, 4/297, 304; 7/109, 111; 9/332, 510

SERVINGTON: *see* Cervington

SESSIONS HOUSE, Old Bailey: trials, 1/263, 266; 3/303; 4/294; funeral, 2/159 & n. 3; also, 8/316, 319

SEVERUS, Emperor A.D. 193-211: severity cited in sermon, 5/96 & n. 4

SEVILLE: high standard of coins minted at, 4/146

SEWERS, Commissioners of: 4/45-6 & n.; 5/353

SEX LIFE, P's [*See also* Pepys, Elizabeth: relations with P; Prostitutes; and (principally) Bagwell, Mrs ——; Burrows [Elizabeth]; Crisp, Diana; Daniel, Mrs ——; Knepp [Elizabeth]; Martin, Betty; Mitchell, Betty; Powell, Doll; Udall, Frances; Udall, Sarah; Welsh, Jane; Willet, Deb]: 1/222; 2/44; 4/204, 210, 230, 232; 6/191, 331; 7/365, 419; 8/588; 9/21–2, 57–8, 59, 184

SEYMOUR (Seamour), [Edward], M.P. Hindon, Wilts.; Commissioner for Prizes: conceited, 6/288; seizes prize-goods, 6/261 & n. 4, 262, 263–4; dines with W. Coventry, 5/11 & n. 2

SEYMOUR (Seamour), Capt. [Hugh], naval officer: wears hat in presence of Navy Board, 6/339; challenges Peter Pett to duel, 7/212 & n. 1; killed in action, 7/226 & n. 2, 231

SEYMOUR, Jane: *see* Jane (Seymour)

SEYMOUR, [John], Comptroller of Customs, London: 9/514 & n. 1

SEYMOUR, [John], servant to Sandwich: 9/331 & n. 1

SEYMOUR, William, 3rd/7th Duke of Somerset (1652–71): attends meeting of Royal Society, 8/243

SHA 'BĀN (Shavan Aga), Pasha of Algiers: 4/370 & nn., 386

SHADWELL, [Thomas], clerk in the Exchequer: 2/241

SHADWELL, [Thomas], dramatist and poet (d. 1692) [*see also* Plays]: at theatre, 9/310 & n. 3; theatre news from, 9/522.

SHADWELL, Mdx: 7/284, 338

SHAFTESBURY, 1st Earl of: *see* Cooper

SHAFTO, [Robert], Recorder of Newcastle-upon-Tyne: 9/359

SHAKESPEARE [*see also* Plays]: cited by P, 6/191 & n. 3; quoted by Coventry, 7/265 & n. 1

SHALCROSS (Shelcrosse), [Thomas, draper]: 6/165–6

SHALES, Capt. [John], victualling agent, Portsmouth: business, 4/364, 371; gifts to P, 5/72, 152; recommended by P to Brouncker, 9/331 & n. 2

SHAR, Monsieur ——: *see* Esquier, d'

SHARP(E), [James], Archbishop of St Andrew's 1661–d.79: on *Naseby*, 1/128 & n. 2

SHATTERELL, [Robert], actor: 7/77

SHAVAN AGA: *see* Sha 'bān

SHAVING: *see* Dress and Personal Appearance

SHAW, Sir John, merchant and customs farmer: Clarendon's confidant, 5/219; pluralist, 8/398 & n. 3; complains about hemp, 9/214 & n. 1; also, 3/188; 6/126, 258

SHAW, Robin, clerk in the Exchequer 1660; later clerk to Ald. Backwell: political news from, 1/21; ill, 1/215, 257; death of first wife, 1/215 & n. 1; marries rich widow, 3/255–6 & n.; at Backwell's, 2/120; illness and death, 6/165, 169, 171; 7/215; social: 1/7, 8, 57, 259; 2/31

SHEERES, [Henry], military engineer, kted 1685: returns from Spain, 8/429, 443; stories of travels, 8/444, 451–2; 9/404, 509; engraving of Tangier, 9/419 & n. 2; paid for work at Tangier, 9/419, 429–30; gifts to P, 9/429–30, 536–7; teaches EP perspective, 9/534; EP fond of, 9/541; P jealous, 9/504, 522, 532, 533; his poetry, 9/504 & n. 1; leaves for Tangier, 9/541; also, 9/545 & n. 1; social: at theatre, 9/419, 435, 522; in May Day parade, 9/540; also, 9/420, 436, 437, 488, 509–10, 516–17, 539, 544

SHEERNESS, Kent: project for new yard, 6/194 & n. 2, 194–5; ships sail from, 7/189, 211, 212, 231; ship capsizes, 7/345; fortifications planned, 8/84, 98 & n. 2; King and Duke of York visit, 8/125, 126–7 & n.; capture by Dutch, 8/258, 259, 260; Dutch fleet off, 8/365; investigation into failure of defences, 8/496; 9/75

SHEFFIELD, John, 3rd Earl of Mulgrave, cr. Marquess of Normanby 1694, Duke of Normanby and Buckinghamshire 1703 (d. 1721): house, 9/317

SHELCROSSE: *see* Shalcross

Deptford 1666; wrecked 1694): her men come up from Portsmouth, 8/272 & n. 1, 275; *Catherine* (King's yacht; 8–10 guns; captured by Dutch 1673): built, 2/12 & n. 2, 14, 36, 76; beats *Mary* in race, 2/104; and *Bezan*, 6/194; victualled, 2/122; weathers storm in Channel, 3/140, 143, 146; drawing of, 4/301; returns from Flanders, 7/141–2, 145; also, 2/121, 179; 3/111 & n. 3, 126, 164; 4/99; 5/197; *Charity* (36–46 guns; prize 1653; captured by Dutch 1665): P on board, 2/121; *Charles* (yacht; 6 guns; built Woolwich 1662; given to Ordnance Office 1668): runs aground, 4/50; court-martial aboard, 9/497–8; *Charles: see Royal Charles; Charlotte* (yacht): P on board, 4/296; *Cheriton: see Speedwell; Chestnut* (8–10 guns; built Portsmouth 1656; wrecked 1665) paid off, 1/310; *Church* (20–6 guns; prize 1653; hulk at Harwich 1659): sold, 1/305 & n. 1; *Concord* (merchantman; 28 guns): arrives from Mediterranean, 5/41–2 & n., 49; *Convertine* (4th-rate; 40–50 guns; Portuguese prize 1650; captured by Dutch 1666): alluded to, 3/31; *Coventry* (5th-rate; 20–6 guns; Spanish ship taken from royalists 1658): captured, 7/390 & n. 3; 8/511; *Crown* (merchantman): P on board, 5/30

Dartmouth (5th-rate; 22–32 guns; built Portsmouth 1655; wrecked 1690): paid off, 3/193 & n. 2; court martial concerning, 9/505; [*Defiance*] (3rd-rate; 66 guns): built, 6/7 & n. 2, 169; measured, 7/69 & n. 1; enquiry into her loss by fire, 9/481 & n. 1, 488, 494, 497–8 & nn.; also, 7/119; *Diamond* (40–50 guns; built Deptford 1651; captured by French 1693): in action, 6/82; overturns during careening, 7/345 & n. 2; *Dover* (40–50 guns; built Shoreham 1654; rebuilt 1695): to sail to Constantinople, 1/224; *Drake* (6th-rate; 12–16 guns; built Deptford 1652; condemned 1690): paid off, 3/58; *Dunbar: see Henry;* [*Dunkirk*] (E. Indiaman): mustered, 4/241 & n. 1; alluded to, 7/150 *Eagle* (merchantman; 44–56 guns):

hired to carry victuals to Tangier, 5/167 & n. 3, 276, 292; *Eagle* (hulk bought 1592; sold 1683): her boat, 3/150; *Edgar* (3rd-rate; rebuilt 1700): built at Bristol, 8/270 & n. 4; 9/231, 235 & n. 1; *Elias* (frigate; 5th-rate; 26–32 guns; Dutch prize c. 1646): brings timber from Forest of Dean, 4/20; and masts from N. America, 5/127 & n. 3; founders, 5/321 & n. 3; *Elizabeth* (ketch): 9/160; *Essex* (48–60 guns; built Deptford 1653): captured by Dutch, 7/154, 157

Fanfan (privateer; 6th-rate; 4 guns; built Harwich 1665 or 1666; made a pitch boat 1693): 8/341; *Fellowship* (hulk; 28 guns; taken from royalists 1643): sold, 3/185 & n. 2; *Flying Greyhound* (privateer; 6th-rate; 24 guns; Dutch prize 1665; rebought by Navy Board 1668; sunk for foundation Sheerness 1673): *see* Prizes and Privateers (P); *Foresight* (4th-rate; 34–48 guns; built Deptford 1650; wrecked 1698): overturns during careening, 7/345 & n. 2; also, 3/153; *Fox* (14 guns; prize 1658; fireship and expended 1666): paid off, 2/93 & n. 3; *Franklin* (fly-boat; given away 1669): sunk as part of river defences, 8/270 & n. 4; *French Ruby* (3rd-rate; 66–75 guns; prize (*Rubis*) 1666; made 2nd-rate 1672; wrecked 1682): captured, 7/350 & n. 1; her guns, 7/352; to be altered, 7/352; 8/121

[*George*]: *see St George; Gift: see Great Gift; Gloucester* (3rd-rate; 50–62 guns; built Blackwall 1654; wrecked 1682): in action, 7/148; *Golden Hand* (fireship; 6 guns; Dutch prize 1665; founders 1673): to sail to Holland, 8/257 & n. 3; *Golden Phoenix* (Dutch E. Indiaman; 3rd-rate; 70 guns; sunk to block Thames 1667): captured by Sandwich, 6/219 & n. 1, 230–1 & n., 234; to be unloaded, 6/236; in river off Erith, 6/242, 249, 273; P on board, 6/300; *Grantham* (22–30 guns; built Southampton 1654; renamed *Guardland* 1660; fireship 1688; reconverted 1689; sold 1698): carries royalists to Flushing, 1/117; *Great Charity* (merchantman): captured by Dutch, 6/118

& n. 1; [*Great*] *Gift* (26–40 guns; French prize 1652; fireship and expended 1666): carries deals to King's Lynn, 2/27; paid off, 3/44; in action off W. Africa, 5/355 & n. 1; [?*Great President*]: paid off, 1/262 & n. 3; *Greenwich* (4th-rate; 54 guns; built Woolwich 1666; rebuilt 1699): launched, 7/153; overturns during careening, 7/345 & n. 2; *Greyhound* (merchantman): 5/41–2 & n., 49; [*Griffin*] (12 guns; taken from royalists 1656; wrecked 1664): paid off, 1/262 & n. 1; 2/237 & n. 2; *Guernsey* (5th-rate; 22–30 guns; built Walberswick 1654 as *Basing*; condemned 1693): paid off, 3/53–4 & n.; accidentally rams *Portland*, 7/142

Half Moon (30–6 guns; prize 1653): sold, 1/284 & n. 3; *Hampshire* (38–48 guns; built Deptford 1653; sunk in action 1697): to sail to India, 2/62; paid off, 2/45 & n. 1; ?3/58–9 & n.; returns from Mediterranean, 7/143; *Happy Return* (44–54 guns; built Yarmouth 1654 as *Winceby*; captured 1691): renamed, 1/154; mutiny in, 8/251 & n. 3; *Harp* (frigate; 8–10 guns; built Dublin 1656; sold 1671): alluded to, 1/90; *Hector* (ex-*Three Kings*; 22 guns; prize 1657): paid off, 1/262 & n. 1; lost in action, 6/219; *Henrietta* (50–62 guns; built Horsleydown 1654 as *Langport*; wrecked 1689): renamed, 1/154; paid off, 1/283, 286 & n. 2; *Henrietta* (yacht; 8–12 guns; sunk in action 1673): designed partly by King, 4/123 & n. 1, 149; carving valued, 5/24 & n. 1; Rupert to go to sea in, 5/262; court-martial in, 9/488 & n. 4; *Henry* (64–82 guns; built Deptford 1656 as *Dunbar*; accidentally burnt 1682): renamed, 1/154; Mennes to fly Vice-Admiral's flag in, 2/70; in Four Days Fight, 7/143, 154, 155; cut loose from moorings in Dutch raid, 8/310; also, 5/317; 7/11; *Hope* (4th-rate; 44 guns; Dutch prize (*Hoop*) 1665): wrecked, 7/390 & n. 3
[*Invention II*] (Petty's double-keeled vessel): wins race, 4/256–7 & n.
Jemmy (yacht; 4 guns; broken up 1722): races against *Bezan*, 3/164 &

n. 4, 188; also, 4/64; 5/317; *Jersey* (4th-rate; 40–50 guns; built Maldon 1654; captured 1691): P made her captain, 9/481 & n. 1; under repair, 9/484; [*Joseph*] (fireship; 4 guns; bought 1666; accidentally burnt 1667): alluded to, 8/39 & n. 3

Kentish ('Kent'; 4th-rate; 46–52 guns; built Deptford 1652; wrecked 1672): P's accident on board, 4/64; *Kingfisher* (merchantman): hired for voyage to Tangier, 7/27 & n. 2, 28, 32; *Kinsale* (8–10 guns; prize 1656; sold 1663): accident to, 1/316; paid off, 3/180 & n. 1; *King Solomon* (Dutch merchantman): sunk, 6/19 & n. 3

Langport ('*Lamport*'): renamed *Henrietta*, 1/154; alluded to, 1/109 & n.*a*; *Lark* (frigate; 8–10 guns; prize 1656; sold 1663): her voyage from Holland, 1/135; *Leopard* (4th-rate; 54–8 guns; built Deptford 1659; sunk for foundation Sheerness 1699): runs aground, 6/8 & n. 3; dispute over freightage charges for, 9/410 & n. 1, 494 & n. 2; also, 4/432 & n. 3; 5/160 & n. 2; [*Leopard*] (E. Indiaman): P musters, 4/241 & n. 1; *Lewes* (merchantman; 32 guns): ? to be released from hire, 8/293 & n. 2; also, 3/50; *Lily* (6th-rate; 6 guns; built Deptford 1657; sold 1667): in action, 8/357; *London* (64–76 guns; built Chatham 1656): P on board, 1/114; 4/228; to carry Queen Mother and Princess Henrietta to France, 2/11; Sandwich's flagship, 5/187 & n. 1; wrecked by explosion, 6/52 & n. 1, 54; alluded to, 6/53; 7/106; *Loyal George* (hired; 42–4 guns; captured 1666): missing after action, 7/154; *Loyal London* (2nd-rate; 90 guns): built to replace *London*, 6/53 & n. 4, 170; surveyed, 6/295 & n. 2; launched, 7/160 & n. 3; to be fitted out, 7/181; guns tried, 7/183 & n. 1; its high repute, 7/215; builder's accounts for, 8/105 & n. 3, 108, 152; burnt by Dutch in Chatham raid, 8/266, 308; alluded to, 7/106

Malaga [*Merchant*] (fireship; 4 guns; bought 1666; sold 1667): in action, 8/47 & n. 4; *Maria:* alluded to,

3rd-rate; 60 guns; hulk 1667; sold 1686): captured by Sandwich, 6/219 & n. 1, 230–1 & n., 234; to be unloaded, 6/236; in river off Erith, 6/242, 249, 273; P on board, 6/300; *Sophia* (26–34 guns; prize 1652; sold 1667): paid off, 2/237; *Speaker* (50–62 guns; built Woolwich 1650; wrecked 1703): P admires, 1/115; renamed *Mary*, 1/154; alluded to, 1/86; *Speedwell* (20–8 guns; built Deptford 1656; wrecked 1678): formerly *Cheriton*, 1/154; alluded to, 1/221; *Success: see Old Success;* [*Surprise*] (merchantman): carries King to France (1651), 1/156 & n. 2; *Swallow* (ketch; 6 guns; bought 1661; sold 1667): sermon on, 3/72; *Sweepstakes* (5th-rate; 36 guns; built Yarmouth 1666; sold 1698): in action, 7/148, 215 & n. 3; *Swiftsure* (44–6 guns; built Deptford 1621; rebuilt 1653): P and Sandwich on board, 1/95–102 passim; reported missing in action, 7/154–7 passim
Tangier-Merchant (merchantman): hired for Tangier, 4/20 & n. 2; 5/139; *Tholen* (Dutch): burnt in action, 7/229 & n. 5; *Tredagh* (50–66 guns; built Ratcliffe 1654; renamed *Resolution* 1660): carries Dowager Princess Mary and Sandwich from Holland, 1/254
Union (merchantman): hired for Tangier, 5/340; *Unity* (4th-rate; 42 guns; Dutch prize 1665): in Medway raid, 8/501; *Urania: see Orange*
Vanguard (40–60 guns; built Woolwich 1631; sold 1667): in action, 6/129; sunk in Medway raid, 8/310
Wakefield (22–6 guns; built Portsmouth 1656; fireship 1688; reconverted 1689; sold 1698): renamed *Richmond*, 1/154; *Wexford*: alluded to, 8/81, 100; *Weymouth* (12–16 guns; taken from royalists 1646): sold, 3/185 & n. 2; *White Bear* (1st-rate; built 1563; rebuilt 1600): engraving of, 8/84 & n. 3; *Wild Boar* (flyboat; 6th-rate; prize 1665): sold, 8/484 & n. 1; *William* (merchantman): on convoy duty, 5/340 & n. 2; *William and Mary* (merchantman): hired for Tangier, 4/368 & n. 4; *Winceby: see*

Happy Return; Wolf (6–16 guns; Spanish prize 1656; sold 1663): paid off, 1/290; *Worcester* (48–60 guns; built Woolwich 1651; renamed *Dunkirk* 1660; rebuilt 1704): alluded to, 1/109
Yarmouth (44–54 guns; built Yarmouth 1653; broken up 1680): in action, 6/82 & n. 1; also, 1/137; *York* (3rd-rate; 52–60 guns; built Blackwall 1654 as *Marston Moor*; wrecked 1703): in action, 7/176 & n. 3; *Young Lion* (6th-rate; 10 guns; prize 1665; sunk for foundation Sheerness 1673): sold and bought back, 9/160 & n. 2

SHIPTON, MOTHER: prophecy of Great Fire, 7/333 & n. 2

SHISH, Jonas, Assistant-Shipwright, Deptford: his yard, 4/104; ketches, ib.; builds *Charles*, 9/101 & n. 2; business, 5/75, 217; 8/188; 9/29; appointed Master-Shipwright, 9/128 & n. 1

SHOE LANE [*see also* Taverns etc.: Gridiron]: cockpit, 4/427; also, 2/156; 9/297

SHOOTER'S HILL, Kent: gibbet, 2/72–3 & n.

SHORE, Jane, mistress of Edward IV: Lady Castlemaine compared to, 3/68 & n. 4; alluded to in sermon, 5/97

SHOREDITCH: 4/432; 7/121; 8/212

SHORTGRAVE (Shotgrave), [Richard], operator to the Royal Society: 9/337

SHORTHAND: P learns Shelton's system, vol. i, p. xxi; the system, vol. i, pp. xlviii–lix & nn., lxxii, lxxvii, lxxxvii & n. 91, xc; problems of transcribing, vol. i, pp. lvii–lxvii & nn.; P records use of, 5/174; 7/374 8/448, 553; demonstrates it, 9/269 Coventry reads psalms in, 2/76 & n 3; prefers clerk with knowledge of 8/207; used by Hewer, 7/374 & n. 1 9/483

SHORT'S: *see* Taverns etc

SHOTERELL; *see* Shatterell

SHOTT, ——, woodmonger: P order firing from, 1/81; also, 1/33

SHREWSBURY, Earl and Countes of: *see* Talbot

SHREWSBURY, [William], book

SLINGSBY, [Margaret], Lady Slingsby, widow of Sir Guildford Slingsby: 2/26

SLINGSBY, Col. Robert, ('the Comptroller'), cr. bt 1661, Comptroller of the Navy 1660–1:

CHARACTER: P's regard, 2/108, 120, 202

AS COMPTROLLER: appointed, 1/240 & n. 1; visits Deptford, 2/11, 12, 76; Woolwich, 2/11; and Portsmouth, 2/89; memorandum on state of navy, 2/20 & n. 3; disbanding business, 2/39; victualling business, 2/62, 104; acquires official logdings, 2/108, 110–11, 114, 119; plans to expand Navy Office, 2/143 & n. 4, 160–1; unspecified business, 1/290; 2/38, 184–5; also, 1/242, 254

SOCIAL: 1/253, 292; 2/24, 25–6, 30, 51, 76, 111, 131, 175, 179

MISC.: news from, 1/315, 318 & n. 2; 2/39; advises P to enter parliament, 2/42; King's debt to, 1/288 & n. 2; house and bowling-alley, 1/290; 2/15, 115; recites his verses, 1/302; projected order of Knights of the Sea, 1/314 & n. 2; created baronet, 2/61; unsuccessful parliamentary candidate, 2/76 & n. 1; illness and death, 2/200, 201, 202, 204

ALLUDED TO: 2/13, 25

~ his wife [Elizabeth], 2/24, 26, 76, 179; his daughter, 2/24; his sister, 1/290

SMALLWOOD, [Matthew], Canon of St Paul's 1660–71, Dean of Lichfield 1671–d.83: examiner at Apposition Day, St Paul's School, 5/38 & n. 3

SMALLWOOD, [William], barrister, Middle Temple: advises P in dispute with Trice, 2/217 & n. 3, 230; 4/352

[SMEGERGILL, alias Caesar, William], musician: plays lute, 5/344; 7/182; 8/118, 325, 333, 529, 530, 558; treble viol, 7/338; teaches lute/theorbo to Tom Edwards, 5/344; 6/86; 7/182, 226–7, 338, 375; to Lady Crew's page, 8/333; recommends gut string as fishing line, 8/119; stays in Westminster in Plague, 7/40–1

[SMETHWICK] (Smithys), [Francis]:

burning-glass, 9/113 & n. 5

SMITH, Sir George, merchant: to leave London during Plague, 6/205; city news from, 6/251–2; 7/174; social: Lady Robinson's crony, 6/290; entertains P and others, 6/187, 192 & n. 1, 307, 311–12; 7/4; also, 6/186, 257, 299; alluded to: 6/234; ~ his wife [Martha], 6/312

SMITH, Capt. Jeremy, naval commander, kted 1665; Navy Commissioner 1669–75: reputation, 4/196; 6/129; 7/158, 333, 344; 9/123, 137; P's opinion, 6/264; 9/382; leader of Albemarle's faction, 7/158, 333; pay, 4/325; conduct at Battle of Lowestoft, 6/122, 135; with fleet, 6/278; sails for Mediterranean, 7/9 & n. 5, 39–40, 45; at Cadiz, 7/46, 71; portrait by Lely, 7/102 & n. 3; commands *Loyal London*, 7/181, 215; accused by Holmes of failure to pursue enemy, 7/339–40 & n.; their duel, 7/348; charges against, 9/107, 118; to be land admiral at Portsmouth, 8/149; to command fleet, 9/123; appointed Navy Commissioner, 9/350, 551 & n. 2; also, 8/263–4; 9/383, 466; social: 8/479; 9/468, 469

SMITH, [John], herald painter: makes hatchment, 4/424–5 & n.

SMITH, John (d. 1870), first transcriber of the diary: vol. i, pp. lxxvi–lxxix, lxxxiii, lxxxviii, xc, xcii; edition of P's Tangier Journal, vol. i, p. lxxxv

SMITH, [Richard], boatswain, Woolwich yard: tells P of malpractices, 5/117

SMITH, [Robert], Navy Office messenger: to prosecute forger of pay tickets, 2/73 & n. 3; his part in Field case, 3/231 & n. 3, 262, 280; 4/16; helps to prepare King's yacht, 3/140; dines with Navy Board, 3/14; also, 1/253; 3/19; 7/250

SMITH, Sydney, author (d. 1845): opinion of diary, vol. i, p. lxxxiii

SMITH, [?Theophilus], mercer: 7/80 & n. 3

SMITH, [Thomas], formerly secretary to the Lord High Admiral and Navy Commissioner: chamber in Navy

and Frenchmen, 1/10; English natural affection for, 2/188 & n. 4; bullfights, 3/90; revenues 5/68; shortage of bullion, 6/23; stamp tax, 7/332 & n. 2; court, 7/201; 8/452; army, 7/201; 9/6 & n. 2, 396–7 & nn.; anecdote of friar, 8/67; dress at court, 8/79; effects of Inquisition on cloth industry, 8/79–80 & n.; beards, 8/453; customs, 8/111 & n. 3, 451–2 & nn.; the Pantéon at Escorial, 9/118 & n. 5; food: *oleo*, 9/509–10, 544; sauce, 9/443; also, 3/251

CHRON. SERIES: resents loss of Tangier, 3/33; English merchants fear break with, 3/115; Spanish reaction to raid on Santiago, 4/94 & n. 3; trade treaty with England (May 1668), 8/30, 45, 69 & n. 2, 74 & n. 2, 75, 107 & n. 2, 190 & n. 1, 246, 453 & n. 2

SPANISH NETHERLANDS: French threat to Flanders, 8/74, 75, 92 & n. 3, 107–8, 175; Louis XIV's claim, 8/186 & n. 2, 254 & n. 1; French invasion, 8/186, 432; 9/38 & n. 1; English troops for, 8/246 & n. 3; Flemish ships in Thames, 8/266; wars in (1650s), 9/396 & nn.; also, 3/246; 7/229

SPARGUS (asparagus) Garden, ?Whitehall: 9/172

SPARKE(S), [Edward], clergyman: 1/60

SPARLING, Capt. [Thomas], naval officer: on voyage to Holland, 1/102, 119, 168; gift to P, 1/164; changes Dutch money for, 1/168, 178–9; social: 1/167; ~ his harper, 1/119, 124, 153

SPAS: see Banbury; Barnet; Bath; Bourbon l'Archambault; Epsom; Tunbridge Wells

SPELMAN, [Clement], Cursitor Baron of the Exchequer 1663–79 (d. 1680): 6/65 & n. 3

SPELMAN (Spillman), Lady: 5/130

SPENCER, Dr [John], Fellow of Corpus Christi College, Cambridge 1655–67; Master 1667–93; Dean of Ely 1677–d.93 [see also Books]: his learning, 7/133 & n. 3

SPENCER, Robert, 2nd Earl of Sunderland, Secretary of State 1679–81, 1683–8 (d. 1702): breaks off

engagement with Lady Anne Digby, 4/208–9 & n.

SPICER, Jack, clerk in the Exchequer: Sandwich's money deposited with, 1/290, 291, 292, 294, 312; at Nonsuch in Plague, 6/235–6; deals with P's Tangier tallies, 7/32–3; counts money for P, 7/251; also, 1/43, 44, 317; 3/296–7; 9/78; social: at P's dinner for old Exchequer colleagues, 2/241; at taverns, 1/7, 8, 33, 57, 201, 229, 270; 2/4, 6, 50, 227; 6/162; 7/398; 8/590; also, 1/41, 257, 259

SPITAL (Spittle), [Square], Spital-fields: Spital sermons at, 3/57–8 & n.; 9/517

SPITALFIELDS: 9/528

SPITTS, the (roadstead off Sheppey): 1/104

SPONG, [John], Chancery clerk and optical-instrument maker:

CHARACTER: P admires, 6/92–3; his 'plainness and ingenuity', 9/417; also 3/120; 5/235

CHRON. SERIES: engrosses P's Chancery bill, 1/197–8, 198, 204; and his agreement with Barlow, 1/205; arrested as suspected plotter, 3/237–8 & n.; experiments with microscope, 5/235; 7/226; visits glass maker, 7/218–19; demonstrates magic lantern, 7/254 & n. 3; and pantograph, 9/340 & n. 1 389–90 & nn., 417; supplies P with pantograph, 9/437, 443–4; also, 1/273

MUSICAL/SOCIAL: sings with P, 1/63, 205, 268, 272, 274; 3/99, 120; plays flageolet, 1/71; at music meeting, 5/290; dines with P, 8/105–6; 9/406, 524–5; also, 2/161

~ his mother, 1/272

SPORTS: see Games etc.

SPRAGGE, Capt. Edward, kted 1665, naval commander: at council of war, 6/230; influence in fleet, 7/158, 178, 179; protégé of Rupert, 7/178–9; responsibility for division of fleet, ib.; 8/148; enquiry into, 8/515; challenges Commissioner Pett to duel, 7/212; appointed to command in river, 8/149; squadron in action, 8/354, 359; conduct in Medway raid, 8/308, 351, 379, 501; 9/11; criticises officers of Ordnance, 8/496; enemy of

Povey, 7/51, 71, 335(2); Belasyse, 7/190, 191, 330, 338, 423; 8/22–3; 9/202; Vernatti, 7/265, 338; Middleton, 9/325, 328

OTHER FINANCIAL BUSINESS: negotiations with bankers, 6/108, 115, 193, 266, 267, 268; 7/170, 174, 242; 9/78 & n. 1, 315 & n. 1, 325, 328; his accounts with, 6/204–5, 207; enquiries into expenditure by Brooke House Committee, 9/562; also, 6/144, 146; 7/66; 8/100, 103, 123, 203, 244, 329, 341, 348, 372, 383, 390, 407, 518, 520(2); 9/152, 214, 249

SHIPPING BUSINESS: freightage, 4/52 & n. 1, 85; 5/167(2) & n. 3, 175, 186, 199, 201, 255, 276, 292, 332–3, 335, 337 & n. 1, 338, 340 & n. 2, 341; hire, 5/252; 6/27, 28, 32, 70; ships' passes, 7/20 & n. 3, 36, 38, 64, 98, 167

VICTUALLING BUSINESS: Yeabsley's accounts, 7/110, 121; 8/515; payments to Gauden, 6/322, 325; 7/402; Andrews, 6/227, 337; and Lanyon, 8/102, 146, 252; empowered to order bread, 4/21; discusses victualling with Sandwich, 4/30; inspects oats, 5/179, 187; his expenses allowed, 5/200; drafts contract with Alsop and Lanyon, 5/195, 196, 202, 204, 213, 223, 226, 229, 236; with Andrews, 6/37, 98; discusses contract with Gauden, 6/171–2, 253–4; with Andrews, 6/185, 201, 226–7; with Yeabsley, 8/438, 483, 515; also, 7/9

MISC. BUSINESS: appointment of river agent, 4/93; supply of deals, 5/277(2), 279; advised not to press enquiries into mole, 5/343; canvas, 6/65–6 & n.; lighters, 6/146 & n. 2, 172; 7/227

PERQUISITES, PROFITS AND BRIBES: general: hopes for, 4/85; 5/167, 249, 252, 258, 267, 277(2) 332–3, 337, 338, 340; 6/7, 27, 28, 32, 37, 70, 109, 146, 157, 172, 204, 208, 251, 252–3; 8/513; receives c. £250 in one month, 5/276; Tangier 'one of the best flowers in my garden', 5/280; fears discovery, 5/340 & n. 2, 348; willing to admit to, 9/99; justifies gains, 5/195, 214, 279; and retainer, 8/593; insists on paying for candlestick, 9/429–30; money: from

Lanyon and partners (victuallers), £300 p.a., 5/210, 223, 224, 226, 227, 263, 267; £36, 6/57; £222, 6/202; £64, 6/227; £210, 6/337, 340; £200, 7/162, 168; from Gauden (victualler), £500, 6/322, 325; £500, 8/35, 37, 44; from Cholmley (contractor for mole), £200 p.a., 6/306; 8/592, 593; £100, 7/19; from Houblons (ship's pass), £200, 7/64, 66, 98, 167; from other merchants (hire and freightage), £26, 5/175; £50, 5/186, 199, 201–2; £30, 5/255, 276; £117, 5/340, 341; £200, 6/286; 7/24; £100, 7/227; from Fitzgerald, £20, 7/173; also, 4/93; 6/26, 37, 242(2); 7/402; 8/372; other gifts, 7/167

TANNER, Mr ——: plays violin with P, 1/78

TAPESTRY: see Textiles etc.

TASBOROUGH, [John], clerk to Povey: 6/73, 153

TATNELL, Capt. [Valentine], naval officer: enmity to Coventry, 9/108 & n. 2, 129; also, 9/147

TAUNTON, Som.: Blake's defence (1644–5), 5/169 & n. 3

TAVERNS, inns, alehouses and eating-houses [mentioned by name and in London, Westminster and immediate environs, i.e. Bow, Chelsea, Clerkenwell, Holloway, Islington, Knightsbridge, Lambeth, Mile End, Rotherhithe and Stroud Green. Those not in this area are indexed under place-names. Those not named are indexed under streets etc. In this list where P gives sufficient information the street location is added. Asterisks denote the occasions on which he had a meal elsewhere than in an eating-house. For other houses of refreshment, see Cakehouses; Cookshops; Coffee-houses; Gardens: pleasure-gardens; Milk-house; Whey-house. See also Entertainments.]

GENERAL: closed during church services, 1/54 & n. 1, 270; 6/5; brewhouse, 1/119; dining clubs, 1/208; 7/375; bar, 1/301; 8/345; convenience of ordinaries, 4/131; French taverns compared with English, ib.; P rarely visits in mornings, 9/220

Lamb's (Mother Lam's) alehouse, Gardiner's Lane, Westminster: P visits, 1/14; Leg, King St, Westminster (Clerke's): P visits, 1/74*, 173*, 183*, 200*, 207*, 208*, 212*, 217–18*, 224*, 229*, 231*, 257*, 263*, 272*, 310*; 2/18*, 108*, 200*; 8/74; Leg tavern, New Palace Yard: P dines, 1/188*, 296*; 2/35*, 66*; Leg, Westminster (probably King St; possibly New Palace Yard): P visits, 2/4; 3/196; 5/102*, 149*; 6/106, 162*; 9/106; food supplied from, 2/219; [Lockett's] ordinary, Charing Cross: newly established, 9/317 & n. 2; P dines, ?9/206, 317

Mitre, Cheapside: P visits, 2/220; Mitre, Fenchurch St (Rawlinson's) [see also Rawlinson, D.]: P pays bill, 4/353; Sandwich's wine bought, 5/36; in ruins after Fire, 8/427; P visits, 1/174, 195, 200, 216, 220, 239, 256, 302; 2/34, 36, 45, 58, 76, 77, 79, 89, 99*, 103, 107, 109*, 132, 153, 161, 167, 170, 191, 202, 207*, 219, 231, 241*; 3/61*, 124*, 165*, 166*, 173*, 276, 294, 298*; 4/10, 364*; 5/36, 47*, 191; alluded to, 3/178; Mitre, Fleet St (Steadman's): music, 1/25 & n. 4, 59; Mitre tavern, Mitre Court, Fleet St (Paget's): alluded to, 1/25; Mitre, Wood St [see also Proctor, [W.]]: 'a house of greatest note', 1/248; P visits, 1/244, 248*; alluded to, 6/175–6; [Mother Redcap], Holloway: alluded to, 2/184 & n. 1; Mouth tavern, Bishopsgate: alluded to (in error), 5/285 & n. 2

Nag's Head tavern, ?Cheapside: P visits, 5/37; New Exchange tavern, nr Royal Exchange [see also Stanley, B.]: landlord P's old playfellow, 4/384; P visits, ib.

Old/Great James, Bishopsgate St: P visits, 5/15, 19, 23*, 136*, 341*; 6/77*, 83; 7/65*; alluded to: 2/26 'Old house, the', Islington: see King's Head; Old Swan, Thames St: P visits, 8/412; alluded to, 7/75, 114; Oxford Kate's: see Cock, Bow St

Paget's: see Mitre tavern, Mitre Court; Penell's, Fleet St: P visits,

2/56; Pope's Head tavern, Chancery Lane: P visits, 1/94; 4/352; Pope's Head tavern, Pope's Head Alley, Lombard St: painted room, 9/420; P visits, 3/41; 5/204; 6/311, 322*, 325(2)*, 328, 329*, 332*, 340*; 7/25*, 83*, 104*, 223*, 370*; 9/420; moved after Fire, 7/329 & n. 1; Price's, Old Palace Yard: P visits, 1/270, 319; Prior's: see Rhenish winehouse, Cannon Row

Quaker's, the, eating-house: P dines, 1/211 & n. 1; 9/162, 163; Queen's Head, Bow: P visits, 8/112*

Rawlinson's: see Mitre, Fenchurch St; Red Lion inn, Aldersgate St: P rides for Brampton from, 5/296; P's father to arrive at by coach, 8/231; (Red) Lion, King St, Westminster: P visits, 1/78; 2/187; Reindeer, Westminster: P visits, 1/259; Rhenish winehouse (Prior's), Cannon Row, Westminster: the further Rhenish winehouse, 4/203; new cellar, 2/170; P visits, 1/39; 2/170; 3/285; 4/203; ?9/220; Rhenish winehouse, King St, Westminster: the 'old' Rhenish winehouse, 1/221; P drinks 'Bleakard', 4/189; first visit for seven years, ?9/220; visits, 1/45, 88, 174, 210, 217, 221, 263, 301; 2/34, 105, 230; ?alluded to, 8/323; Rhenish winehouse, Steelyard: P visits, 2/40, 233; 4/58, 101, 343; 6/95; Ringstead's: see Star tavern, Cheapside; Roberts's: see Harp and Ball; Robins, Monsieur, his ordinary, Covent Garden: P dines, 8/211; Rose tavern, King St, Westminster: P visits with Doll Lane, 7/359; 8/3, 111, 193; Rose tavern, Russell St, Covent Garden: P visits, 8/589; 9/193*, 198, 203*; Rose tavern, Tower St: P sends for wine, 2/211; Rose (and Crown), Mile End: P visits, 8/389; 9/88, 255; [?Rose and Crown alehouse, Tower Stairs]: 2/229; shut during Plague, 6/225 & n. 4; Royal Oak tavern, Lombard St: P drinks Haut Brion, 4/100; entertained to dinner, 6/38

Salutation tavern, Billingsgate: P dines, 1/76–7; ?Salutation tavern, Charing Cross: see Jacob's; Sampson,

Paul's Churchyard: P visits, 2/124★, 161; Saracen's Head, nr Wardrobe: P visits, 2/211; Ship tavern, Billiter Lane, Fenchurch St [see also [Brome], ——; Morris, [John]]: P visits to admire landlord's daughter, 8/156, 345, 443; 9/51, 284, 485-6; pays his debts, 8/443; also, 4/404; Ship tavern, [?King St], Westminster: alluded to, 1/95; Ship tavern, ?Temple Bar: P visits, 2/173; Ship tavern, Threadneedle St: P dines, 3/150; Short's alehouse, Old Bailey: P visits, 3/100; Spring Garden, Vauxhall, house at: P visits, 6/164; Standing's, Fleet St: P visits, 1/250, 290, 303; 2/17, 25, 180; Star tavern, Cheapside (Ringstead's): P visits, 1/14, 52, 307; 2/109, 238; 3/91; 4/424; Star Tavern, ?Tower St: P visits, 4/424; Steadman's: see Mitre tavern, Fleet St; Sugar Loaf, Temple Bar: P visits, 1/48, 49; 9/477★; Sun tavern, Chancery Lane: P visits, 1/24; Sun tavern, Fish St Hill: P visits, 1/84★, 88★, 212★, 321★; 2/208, 210★, 213-14★; 7/91★; Sun tavern, King St, Westminster: P visits, 1/57★, 73, 75, 181★, 192, 194, 207, 209, 211, 217, 229, 231, 235, 265, 292, 296, 304; 3/192; 9/271; P's old drawer George alluded to, 1/229; Sun tavern, Threadneedle St ('behind the Exchange'): aviary, 4/85; Buckingham at, 8/299; P visits, 1/80; 2/196, 219; 4/85★, 172; 5/35, 271; 6/27★, 30★, 39★, 44★, 77★, 86★; 7/36, 38★, 299; 8/49★, 108★, 135, 516★; alluded to, 8/302; Swan tavern, Chelsea: 7/94; Swan tavern, Dowgate: 'a poor house', 1/185; Swan tavern, King St, Westminster: P visits, 2/97; 7/305; Swan tavern (Herbert's), New Palace Yard [see also Udall, Frances; Udall, Sarah]: 'my old house', 6/253; P visits, 1/7, 16, 45, 244, 294, 320; 2/219★, 3/296; 5/128; 6/1, 6, 17★, 65, 75★, 103, 111, 132, 141, 145, 253, 310; 7/32, 62, 81★, 99, 103★, 117, 201, 317, 319★, 355, 392, 396, 413; 8/34, 35★, 68, 120, 124, 133, 158-9, 224, 400, 456, 588; 9/75, 136, 161; new maid, 9/551; alluded to, 9/86; Swan tavern, Old Fish St: P dines, 3/165; juggler,

ib.; Swan tavern, Westminster [probably the Swan in New Palace Yard, in some cases possibly that in King St]: P visits, 1/43, 49, 55, 74, 91, 196; 2/49, 117; 3/43, 299; 7/39; 108, 134, 173★, 231-2★, 278, 279, 398; 8/102, 295, 323, 367, 590; 9/36, 56★, 295, 560★; his assignations with Doll Lane, 7/385-6; 8/193, 422; 9/317(2); Swan-with-two-Necks, Tothill St: W. Joyce in custody of Black Rod, 5/111; Swayne's, eating-house, New Palace Yard: P meets Doll Lane, 7/49-50

Three Cranes tavern, Old Bailey: wedding party, 3/16; Three Cranes tavern, Poultry ('at the Stocks'): farewell party, 2/163; Three Mariners, Lambeth: P visits, 2/120; noted for ale, ib.; Three Tuns tavern, Charing Cross: the old Three Tuns, 1/185; P visits, 1/185, 253; 2/206, 227; 9/359-60★; landlord [—— Darling], 2/206; his sister, ib; daughter, 2/228; Three Tuns tavern, Crutched Friars: newly established, 7/373; affray, 8/208; parish dinners, 8/218; 9/559; P visits, 7/373; 8/218★, 220★; 9/222★, 559★; landlord [John Kent], 8/208; Three Tuns tavern, Guildhall yard: P visits, 1/50; Triumph tavern, Charing Cross: Portuguese ladies at, 3/92; Trumpet, King St, Westminster (Mrs Hare's): P visits, 1/214; 5/9, 242, 340; 6/18 [White Hart], post-house, Charing Cross: 6/197 & n. 2; [?White Hind] inn, Cripplegate: coaches at, 6/95 & n. 4; White Horse, King St, Westminster: horse stabled, 1/85; White Horse tavern, Lombard St [see also Browne, Frances]: P visits, 5/330★, 338★; 7/63★, 68★; alluded to, 8/82 & n. 1; White Lion, Islington: alluded to, 9/32; Will's alehouse, Old Palace Yard [see also Griffin, W.]: P visits, 1/5, 6, 7, 14, 15, 16, 20, 21, 26, 32, 33, 34, 37, 40, 43, 45, 56(2), 57, 61, 64, 71, 78, 87, 173, 174, 257, 290, 294; 2/4(2)★, 6, 31, 40; Wood's, Pall Mall: 'our old house for clubbing', 1/208; P visits, ib.; shut in Plague, 6/147-8; World's End, Knightsbridge: P visits, 9/549, 564

TAXATION [for P's taxes, see Finances (P)]:

n. 2; Irish viscountcy (1645), 8/126 & n. 1

TITUS, Capt. [Silius]: on *Naseby*, 1/130 & n. 3; story of French attack on Jijelli, 5/295

TOBACCO: shop by Temple Bar, 2/117; remedy for consumption, 2/128 & n. 1; plague, 6/120 & n. 2; and for the staggers, 8/390 & n. 1; taken by naval commanders, 6/287; chewed by Albemarle, 7/227; grown illegally in Gloucestershire, 8/442 & n. 2

TOLHURST, Maj. [Jeremiah], customs officer, Newcastle-upon-Tyne: acquaintance of P's in 1650s, 4/10; stories of collieries, ib. & n. 1; social: 1/200

'TOM OF THE WOOD', hermit: predictions, 8/270

TOMKINS, Sir Thomas, M.P. Weobley, Heref. (d. 1674): motion about sale of places in navy, 4/170 & n. 3; speech against standing army, 8/352 & n. 2

TOMPSON, [?Richard, printseller]: 6/339; 8/383

[TOMPSON, Joseph], Vicar of St Dunstan-in-the-West: sermon, 8/389 & n. 4

TONG, [Thomas], naval official: 9/312 & n. 3

TOOKER, [Ann], housekeeper, Payhouse, Chatham 1669; at Chatham, 9/495; ~ her daughters, ib.

TOOKER, Frances: pretty looks, 6/262; 7/50; fondled by P, 6/307; 7/4–5, 153; 8/114; stays with P and EP, 7/80–1, 89; moves to London, 7/202; said to have gonorrhoea, 8/79; and the pox, 8/114; low repute, 8/157; social: 6/262, 263, 278, 279, 284, 315, 317, 333

TOOKER, [John], river agent to the Navy Board: inspects oats, 5/179; memorandum on King's revenue, 5/281 & n. 4; appointed river agent, 6/74 & n. 1; stores prize goods, 6/256, 258; candidate for victualling post, 6/272; supplies P with lighter, 7/273; name used as cover by P, 7/295; death, 8/315; also, 6/73–4, 309; 7/1, 37, 284

TOOKER, Mrs ——: good looks, 6/279; low repute, 8/79

[TOPHAM, John], City Remembrancer 1659–60: 1/183 & n. 1

TORRIANO, [?George, merchant]: 1/33

TORRINGTON, Earl of: *see* Monck, Christopher

[TORTUGA], Virgin Is., W. Indies: taken by French, 9/556 & n. 3

TOTHILL FIELDS, Westminster: Plague burials, 6/162

TOTHILL ST, Westminster: 5/111

TOUCHET, James, 3rd Earl of Castlehaven (d. 1684): to raise regiment against Turks, 4/349 & n. 2; and against French in Flanders, 8/246; kills buck in St James's Park, 5/239

TOULON: 6/278

TOWER DOCK: 7/273

TOWER HILL [*see also* Little Tower Hill; Taverns etc.: Angel]: gate in city wall, 3/111 & n. 1; Navy Office back door, 3/182; regicides paraded, 3/19 & n. 1; Sir H. Vane executed, 3/108–9 & n.; P's lodgings, 3/182–209 passim; comet allegedly seen from, 5/355; damage to buildings from Fire, 7/273, 357; market established, 7/281; seamen demonstrate, 7/415; King's speech to trainbands, 8/264 & n. 1

TOWER OF LONDON, [*see also* Ordnance, Board of; Robinson, Sir J.; Royal Mint]:

CHRON. SERIES: Spanish bullion in (1640), 7/253 & n. 1; held against Rump (1659), 1/39 & n. 2; King at, 1/214; 5/316; Dunkirk money stored in, 3/265 & n. 1; guns fired for Queen's birthday, 4/382; and Holmes's 'Bonfire', 7/249

P VISITS: to see menagerie, ?1/15 & n. 2; 3/76 & n. 2; to search for Barkstead's treasure, 3/240–2 & nn., 244, 246, 248, 250–1, 256, 284, 285, 286; to watch Fire, 7/268; to see Crown jewels, 9/172 & n. 2; to visit Coventry, 9/470, 471, 473, 475, 478, 481, 486

OFFICERS: 2/231; warders, 5/67; gentleman porter, ib.

PLACES: Brick Tower, 9/468; cellars, 3/242; chapel, 5/67; Coleharbour, 3/242; garden, 3/285; Governor's

Queen at, 4/251, 272; 7/214 & n. 3; King at, 7/228; Lady Sandwich made ill by waters, 6/152; alluded to: 7/260

TUNIS: peace with, 3/263 & n. 4, 271

TURBERVILLE, [Daubigny], eye specialist: P consults, 9/248 & n. 6; 249, 251, 255; sees eyes dissected, 9/254–5

TURENNE (Turin, Turein), Henri de la Tour d'Auvergne, Vicomte, Marshal of France (d. 1675): anecdote of, 8/127 & n. 2; to command in Flanders campaign, 8/186; Colbert his rival, 9/397 & n. 2

TURKEY/Turks: *see* Algiers; Ottoman Empire, the; Tangier; Tunis

TURKEY COMPANY: *see* Levant Company

TURLINGTON, [John], spectacle maker, Cornhill: P buys spectacles from, 8/486 & n. 2; advice to P, 8/519; ∼ daughter's advice to, 8/486

TURNER, Betty, daughter of John: her good looks, 5/337–8; 9/409, 464, 481, 512; P glad to have goodlooking kinswoman, 9/407; to go to school, 9/512, 526; social: at P's Twelfth Night party, 9/409; dances a jig, 9/464; at Mulberry Garden, 9/509–10; at her mother's house, 9/446, 482, 506; at P's house, 9/463, 478, 519; at theatre, 9/476; also, 9/510, 511, 521; alluded to: 9/540

TURNER, Betty, daughter of Thomas of the Navy Office:
CHRON. SERIES: plays badly on harpsichord, 4/120; sings worse than EP, 9/35; grown a fine lady, 8/389; in dancing display, 8/392, 396; helps P title books, 9/49; accompanies EP to Brampton, 9/144, 145, 210; and to West Country, 9/229, 231, 233, 234, 238; also, 9/123; ∼ her sparrow, 9/225
SOCIAL: dances at P's house, 8/511; 9/42; and at Twelfth Night party, 9/12; at theatre, 9/133; at P's house, 8/557; 9/28, 29, 38, 126, 244, 250, 265, 301, 325, 380; also, 2/175; 9/54–5, 245, 259, 261

'TURNER, Betty' (error): *see* Mordaunt, [Elizabeth], Lady Mordaunt

TURNER, Charles, son of Jane: 3/88; 9/446

TURNER, [Elizabeth], wife of Thomas of the Navy Office:
P'S OPINION: shares Batten's dislike, 5/293; a gossip, 7/105, 121 & n. 1
CHRON. SERIES: supports P in Field case, 4/53; loses lodgings, 7/105, 296 & n. 2, 359; which Brouncker claims, 8/24, 29, 31 & n. 4; his unkindness, 8/36, 40, 51; new lodgings, 8/51, 63, 398; 9/36, 200 & n. 8; her balsam, 7/37, 40; her strong waters, 4/221; 9/145; tends P's sprained ankle, 8/340; gives EP shells, 7/105; joins her in collecting May-dew, 8/240; and at bleacher's, 8/401; seeks employment for son (Frank), 8/155, 172, 457; 9/38–9; consults P about son (Thomas), 9/279; P's help in promoting husband, 9/334–5; P gives her gloves, 9/120; caresses, 9/312, 314; also, 6/23; 7/274; 8/490, 580; 9/115–16
GOSSIP FROM: about court, 4/177; Brouncker's ménage, 8/51, 75, 225–6; Penn's, 8/63, 141–2, 155, 226–9, 423, 595; Batten's, 8/159; also, 8/315; 9/157
SOCIAL: visits Cambridge, 2/136; Deptford, 3/198; 8/435; Epsom, 8/335–40; Barnet and Hatfield, 8/380–2; Mile End, 9/180, 208; at Greenwich, 6/212, 299; 7/1; at dances in Navy Office, 8/29; 9/13; Battens', 2/24; 4/218, 221, 230; Penns', 8/3, 371; in garden at Seething Lane, 8/391; 9/252, 261; at theatre, 8/433; 9/170, 189; P/EP visit(s)/dine(s) with, 4/278; 7/120; 8/395–6; 9/46, 222–3, 276; at P's house, 7/67; 8/4, 282, 433, 437, 441, 447; 9/28, 123–4, 138, 144, 184, 198, 213, 244, 258, 265, 278, 306, 325, 380; also, 2/38, 175; 5/303; 7/53; 8/378, 389, 581; 9/245

TURNER, Frank, naval officer, son of Thomas of the Navy Office: commission expires, 8/150, 155, 172, 228; joins E. India Company, 8/457; 9/38–9; social: 8/437, 580

TURNER, 'Col'. [James], criminal: arrested with wife for robbery, 5/10–11 & n.; trial and conviction, 5/13, 17,

VIVIAN, Mr ——, of Westminster: 1/248

VLIE ('Fly'), the, Zeeland: Dutch ships burnt in, 7/247 & n. 1

VOWS (P):

GENERAL: makes/renews/reads over/ writes out vows, 3/209, 245, 296, 301; 4/6, 16–17, 306, 338, 348, 360, 417, 438; 5/4–5, 249; 6/10, 13, 72–3, 103, 253; 7/65, 117, 118, 164; 8/3, 6, 527; reads over on Sundays, 3/141, 162, 167, 182, 296; 4/43, 74, 96, 112, 191, 202, 218, 247, 259, 268; 5/31, 54; 8/43, 70; his benefit from, 3/167, 245; 4/438; 5/74

PARTICULAR:

AGAINST DRINK: 1/84; 2/142, 242 & n. 1; 3/98, 125, 207; 4/235; 6/336; 1; 3/98, 125, 132, 207; 4/235; 6/336; 7/15; observed, 4/341–2; excuses breaches, 3/298; 4/4, 280, 284, 354; 6/226; 8/130

AGAINST THEATRE-GOING: 2/200, 242 & n. 1; 3/89, 93, 98, 125, 132, 207, 294; 4/8, 182; 5/3, 33; 8/399, 527; observed, 4/431, 433, 434; 5/2–3; 8/7, 225; 9/47; breaks and pays forfeit, 2/200; 3/230, 294; 4/56–7, 164; 7/401; 8/45; excuses breaches, 4/128–9; 5/78, 224 & n. 1, 232, 236, 240, 282; 8/122–3, 429

AGAINST IDLENESS: 4/123; 5/25, 31, 195, 250; 7/15, 25, 63, 86; 8/171–2, 175; breaks, 5/284; 7/23; excuses breaches, 5/192, 193; 8/224

AGAINST EXTRAVAGANCE: 3/40, 80, 302; observed, 5/14; breaks, 5/55; excuses breaches, 4/395; 5/128

MISC.: to rise early, 1/308; 6/55; to allow EP dancing lessons, 4/149–50; to say family prayers twice weekly, 5/14; not to be alone with Betty Lane for more than quarter of an hour, 5/113; *laisser aller les femmes* for one month, 6/20, 29; observed, 6/35, 53; breaks, 7/205; excuses breaches, 7/303, 396; to draw up will, 6/187; to refrain from visiting Deb Willet, 9/545; sums paid in forfeits: 3/230; 4/123, 149–50, 431; 5/55, 193, 284; 6/29; 7/205, 401

VRIES, Tjerk Hiddes de; naval commander: killed in action, 7/229 & n. 3, 231

VYNER, [Abigail], Lady Vyner, wife of Sir George: her beauty, 8/174, 408

VYNER (Viner), Sir George, goldsmith-banker: 8/174

VYNER (Viner), [Mary], Lady Vyner, wife of Sir Robert: wealth and good looks, 6/215 & n. 2

VYNER (Viner), Ald. Robert, goldsmith-banker, Lombard St, kted 1665 cr. bt 1666

GENERAL: character, 6/108; wealth, 6/215; profit from recoinage, 6/326; credit after Fire, 7/323; cash reserves, 8/275–6 & n.

BUSINESS WITH P:

OFFICIAL: consulted about canvas, 6/65; cashes/gives credit on tallies for navy/Tangier, 6/115, 121, 164(2), 224; 7/12, 174, 201, 205, 339; unwilling to lend to government, 6/266; 7/330–1; 8/276, n. 1; also, 6/108; 8/221

PRIVATE: supplies plate, 7/37, 405, 409, 413, 415, 420; and christening-bowl, 8/548; P deposits money with, 7/34; withdraws, 7/66, 84, 85; buys guineas from, 7/346, 348

UNSPECIFIED: 6/297, 311, 340; 7/323, 328, 366; 8/37, 38, 74, 83, 170

P's ACCOUNTS WITH: 8/87, 124, 151, 180, 203, 209, 233

OTHER BUSINESS: with Cocke, 6/334; Sandwich, 7/32; 8/581–2 & n.; J. Pearse, 8/270; Carteret, 8/598; also, 7/38; 8/196

MISC.: leaves London in Plague, 6/205; house at Ickenham, 6/214–15, 266; lodgings at African House, 7/323; concerned in rebuilding after Fire, 8/81; account of origin of Fire, 8/82; also, 6/163; ~ kinsman buried, 8/101

VYNER (Viner), Sir Thomas, goldsmith-banker, Lombard St: provides cash for fleet, 5/15; pays P freightage, 5/340; funeral, 6/114 & n. 1

WADE, [Thomas], of Axe Yard, victualling official: profits on Baltic voyage (1659), 1/83 & n. 1; attempts to discover treasure in Tower, 3/240–2, 244, 246, 248, 256, 285, 286; social: 1/16, 57

WADLOW, Capt. [John], landlord of the Devil tavern, Fleet St: in

Dutch off Harwich, 8/281 & n. 4; threaten colliers, 8/285 & n. 5; in Thames, 8/296, 298, 303; land near Harwich, 8/317 & nn., 322 & n. 2; off s. and e. coasts, 8/327 & n. 1, 345 & n. 1; invade Thames again, 8/349 & n. 1; beaten off, 8/350, 351; defeated in Second Battle of N. Foreland, 8/354 & n. 3, 357–60 & nn.; gunfire heard at Whitehall, 8/367; Dutch plans for next year, 8/568; also, 8/163, 170; other engagements: French expedition to W. Indies, 8/2 & n. 1; take Antigua, 8/38 & n. 1; defeated off Martinique, 8/430 & n. 1; English privateers in Caribbean, 8/75 & n. 1; Harman in W. Indies, 8/132 & n. 3, 147, 153, 156; English squadron in Mediterranean, 8/43; also, 8/47, 162

PUBLIC PESSIMISM: 7/395; 8/306; merchants', 7/371; P's, 6/6, 218; 7/371, 374, 376, 378, 395, 426; 8/68, 88, 113, 146, 249, 274, 289, 305, 306, 363, 366, 377, 532, 602; Lord Crew's, 6/6; 7/387; Coventry's, 6/291–2; Cocke's, 6/218; Houblon's, 7/371; Carteret's, 7/383; Evelyn's, 7/406; 8/248–9, 278, 377; 9/484; Batten's, 7/416; Ford's, ib.; Reymes's, 8/68; and Povey's, 8/289

PEACE NEGOTIATIONS: overtures to Dutch and French, 7/411; Dutch demands, 7/369–70 & n.; venue, 8/17 & n. 3, 61–2 & n., 69, 72–3, 74, 80 & n. 4, 92 & n. 2, 106 & n. 2; Breda agreed on, 8/124, 125–6; King's speech to Parliament, 8/52; appoints plenipotentiaries, 8/61 & n. 3; Arlington's part in, 8/68–9 & n.; French part in, 8/69 & n. 2, 106–7 & n., 113, 170 & n. 5, 297; negotiations with Spain, 8/74 & n. 2; Dutch terms, 8/88, 95–6 & n., 100, 113; Dutch fear French making separate treaty, 8/153; plenipotentiaries assemble, 8/138 & n. 4, 145 & n. 3, 155, 161, 189, 216, 218; rumoured terms, 8/176 & n. 1; Dutch demands high, 8/244, 249; draft treaty, 8/322, 323, 326 & n. 3, 327, 329–30; its severity, 8/335; treaty sealed, 8/352; announced to Parliament, 8/361; further Dutch demands, 8/375; peace ratified, 8/378, 396 & n.

1, 397 & n. 1; proclaimed in London, 8/399; terms concerning prisoners, 8/407–8 & nn., 425–6; and territorial disputes, 8/426; printed copies, 8/453 & n. 3

PUBLIC REACTION TO PEACE: need for recognised by court, 8/62; by P, 8/176, 323, 324, 328–9, 329; by bankers, 8/285; and by Albemarle and Council, 8/347; terms feared/disliked by merchants, 8/157–8, 354–5, 362, 398–9; by court and nation, 8/361–2, 398–9; by P, 8/396; by Downing, 8/425–6; opinion in United Provinces, 8/225, 345

PEACE ALLUDED TO: 8/63, 93, 120, 128, 139, 285, 289, 317, 326, 354, 384, 386, 388, 391

WARCUP, Edmund, magistrate, bailiff of Southwark: in prize-goods affair, 6/269 & n. 3; 7/203–4, 219; disgraced, 7/219 & n. 4; allergy to roses, 7/204; social: 7/23

WARD, [Lieut. James], naval officer: questioned by Brooke House Committee, 9/204 & n. 1

WARD, [Richard], Muster-Master: 8/15 & n. 3, 19

WARD, [Seth], Bishop of Salisbury 1667–d. 89, Fellow of the Royal Society: preaching admired by King, 8/116 & n. 5; praises Abraham Cowley, 8/383 & n. 3; P visits, 9/229 & n. 4

WARD, Mr ——, [?of the Exchequer]: 6/235

WARD, Mr ——: 2/7; ∼ his wife, ib.

WARDOUR, [William], Clerk of the Pells in the Exchequer: 6/244

WARDROBE, the KING'S GREAT, Puddle Dock [see also Mountagu, E., 1st Earl of Sandwich; Newport, A.; Reymes, Col. B; Townshend, T.]: officers dine together, 3/172; give Christmas dinner for tradesmen, 3/294; houses belonging to, 4/422; debts and shortages, 8/417–18 & nn.; economies proposed, 9/7; reorganisation, 9/41 & nn.; moves to Hatton Garden after Fire, 8/597 & n. 1; the building: an orphanage during Interregnum, 1/180 & n. 1; Jane Shore's Tower, 2/118 & n. 2; Master's

WARWICK, Sir Philip, secretary to Southampton, Lord Treasurer:
CHARACTER: P's regard, 5/70; 6/110; 7/382; 8/213
BUSINESS: advises P on marine insurance, 4/395; on presenting estimates, 5/327, 329, 330; views on revenue and trade, 5/68–70 & nn.; taxation, 5/327–8 & nn.; Additional Aid, 7/61, 130–1 & n.; state of nation, 7/61; exchanges confidences about national and naval finances, 6/46, 75; P discusses navy finances with, 4/81, 305, 317; 6/48, 83, 95, 257; 7/64, 125, 233, 313; applies to for money for Tangier, 6/91, 92, 119, 121, 123, 127; 7/116–17, 137, 233; 8/32, 46, 52, 100, 123, 203, 205; other Tangier business, 5/229; his emoluments, 5/69; unspecified business, 5/321; 6/9, 16, 70, 71; 7/38, 39; also, 6/3; 7/295; 8/198, 219
MISC.: his new house, 6/3; 7/64 & n. 1; his drawleaf table, 6/109; recalls Southampton's last words, 8/213; ~ his wife [Joan], 2/29; his clerk, 6/154
WARWICK HOUSE, Holborn: 1/75 & n. 4, 272
WARWICK LANE: 5/20
WASHING, SHAVING etc.: see Dress and Personal Appearance
WASHINGTON, Col. [Henry]: 1/264
WASHINGTON, Mrs [Henry], shopkeeper, Westminster Hall: 9/187; ~ her husband, ib.
WASHINGTON, [Richard], purser: 1/174, 190
WASHINGTON, ——, of the Exchequer: social: 1/21, 41, 79; 2/227
WATCHES and clocks:
WATCHES: P's silver, 6/83 & n. 2, 100, 101; alarm, 6/158 & n. 3; minute, 6/221 & n. 3; plain, 7/293; 'of many motions', 7/293 & n. 1; 9/4; EP's, 8/51, 146; Lady Penn's gold, 8/228; Brouncker dismantles and reassembles, 6/337; P. Carteret makes, 9/109; also, 5/272; 9/489
CLOCKS: King's bullet, 1/209 & n. 2; Queen's night, 5/188 & n. 4
WATERHOUSE, [Edward], physician: ordained, 9/215 & n. 1; his

preaching, 9/432–3 & n.
WATERHOUSE, [Nathaniel], Master of the Green Cloth 1654–9: 1/34 & n. 4
WATERMAN, [George], Sheriff 1664–5, kted June 1665, Lord Mayor 1671–2: entertains Navy Board, 6/78–9
WATERMEN: see London: livery companies; Travel (river)
WATERS, [Edmund]: see Taverns etc.: Sun, King St
WATKINS, [William], clerk in Privy Seal Office: troubled at P's appointment in Privy Seal, 1/207; dies, 3/76, 80; also, 1/173, 197
WATLING ST: Fire, 7/269
WATSON, [Francis]: patent for lacquer, 9/531–2 & n.
[WATTS, ——], father of Esther St Michel: unwilling to give jointure, 3/286
WATTS, ——, merchant: offers P £500 for Clerkship of Acts, 1/185
[WAYMOUTH, Robert], mastergunner: in court-martial, 9/498 & n. 2
WAYNEMAN: see Birch, W.
WAYTE, Wayth: see Waith
WEATHER [No attempt is made to index passing references to the daily weather or to short-term changes. This section is designed to list long-term spells, storms and P's comments.]:
GENERAL: effects of hot weather on plague, 3/10, 18 & n. 3; 6/305, 306; and theatre attendance, 8/171; damage to ships by lightning, 4/200–1; effects of thunder on beer, 4/365 & n. 2; on wine, 7/256; Fire preceded by drought, 7/269; Duke of York's method of forecasting, 9/150
CHRON. SERIES:
  1660: unusually bad spell (20 May; in Holland), 1/150–1; first rain after dry spell (16 June), 1/176
  1661: mild winter, 2/19–20 & n., 25, 39; thunderstorm (23 Apr.), 2/86; wet summer, with fear of famine, 2/112–13 & n.
  1662: unseasonably warm spell (Jan.), 3/10 & n. 3; storm (18 Feb.), 3/31–2 &

n., 35, 42; first snow and frost for three years (Nov.–Dec.), 3/267, 268, 270, 271, 274, 276, 279, 280

1663: first rain after drought (17 Feb.), 4/45; storm at Northampton (6 May), 4/139 & n. 1; wet spell of three months (Apr.–June), 4/200 & n. 1, 204, 205, 206, 220; storm at Deptford (25 Sept.), 4/317–18

1664: unusually thundery weather in England and France, 5/195–6; thunderstorm (16 Aug.), 5/243 & n. 3

1665: 'one of the coldest days . . . ever felt in England' (6 Feb.), 6/32; 'as hard a winter as any hath been these many years', 6/66–7 & n.; 'the hottest day that ever I felt in my life' (7 June), 6/120; 'very hot beyond bearing' (11 July), 6/155; 'as great a Storme as was almost ever remembered' (14 Nov.), 6/298 & n. 2

1666: the 'Great Storme' (23–4 Jan.), 7/21–2 & n.; 'all cry out for lack of rain' (18 March), 7/75 & n. 4; 'mighty hot' (29 Apr.), 7/112; 'wonderous hot' with sheet lightning (10 May), 7/121; thunderstorm (31 May), 7/138; showers after dry spell (26–7 June), 7/183, 184; 'the hottest night that ever I was in in my life' (7–8 July), 7/197; thunderstorm, ib.; drought continues (2 Sept.), 7/269; ends (9 Sept.), 7/283 & n. 2; hailstorm at Harwich (16 July), 7/207–8; storm (17–18 Sept.), 7/289 & n. 1

1667: the coldest day ever remembered (6, 7 March), 8/98 & n. 6, 102; dry spell ends (21 Apr.), 8/175 & n. 2; hot spell (May), 8/245; 'mighty hot' spell (July), 8/333; month's drought ends (27 July), 8/356

1668: heatwave (July), 9/262, 263, 264; 'summer weather' (27 Sept.– 1 Oct.), 9/319, 322, 325; the first frost (7 Dec.), 9/386

1669: 'mighty temperate' (14 March), 9/482; dry spell ends (18 Apr.), 9/526

WEAVER, [Elizabeth] (b. Farley), actress: mistress of Charles II, 9/19 & n. 4

WEAVER, [Richard], of Huntingdon: discusses Brampton business, 8/71;

death, 8/162 & n. 3; social: 2/213; ~ his wife, 9/451

WEDDINGS and MOCK-WEDDINGS: see Marriage

[WEEDON, Richard]: see Taverns etc: Dolphin, Tower St

WELD (Wilde), Dorothy: see Pickering

WELD (Wiles, Wild), [George], M.P. Much Wenlock, Salop (d. 1701): coxcomb, 3/242; 9/103; as Deputy-Governor of Tower, 3/242; at cockfight, 4/428; enemy of Navy Board, 9/103–4; also, 8/307

WELL BANK, the, North Sea: Dutch fleet near, 6/219 & n. 2

WELLING: see Welwyn

WELLS, [John]; Storekeeper to the Navy: his MS. on ship-building, 5/108 & n. 2

WELLS, [William], Vicar of Brampton, Hunts: 3/220 & n. 2

WELLS, [Winifred], Maid of Honour to the Queen: story of alleged miscarriage, 4/37 & n. 4, 56; in riding-dress, 7/162; her beauty, 9/563

WELLS, Som.: Cathedral carvings, 9/239 & n. 2

WELSH, Jane, maidservant to Jervas, the Westminster barber: P attracted by, 5/212, 224, 246; 6/20; she breaks assignations, 5/260, 267–8, 273; 6/1, 5, 18–19; cold to P, 5/275, 340; he meets briefly, 5/287, 316, 332; 6/6, 9; Jervases try to marry off, 5/260; 6/16; deceived by bigamous fiddler, 6/9, 16–17, 22, 74–5; 7/103; to go to Ireland, 6/75

WELWYN (Welling), Herts.: P at, 2/183; 5/233–4, 296; Swan Inn, 5/296

WENDY (Wendby), [Thomas]: elected M.P. Cambridgeshire, 1/112 & n. 2

WENTWORTH, Thomas, 1st Earl of Strafford (d. 1641): attainder (1641) 8/518–19 & n.

WENTWORTH, Thomas, 1st Earl of Cleveland, Captain of Gentlemen Pensioners: death, 8/154 & n. 2

WENTWORTH, 'Squire', [Thomas]: to be tried for manslaughter, 3/34 & n. 2; defence, 3/36

WERDEN, Col. Robert, Groom of the Bedchamber to the Duke of York: 8/406

WEST INDIES: Myngs's fame in, 7/166; French expedition, 8/2 & n. 1; Spaniards suffer from English privateers, 8/75 & n. 1; Harman's expedition, 8/132 & n. 3, 147, 153, 156

WESTMINSTER: P hopes for clerk-ship of city, 1/79–80 & n.; flood, 1/93 & n. 1; horseferry, 3/289; Plague in: 6/132, 141, 144, 147–8, 154, 163, 210, 268 & n. 4, 289; no doctors left and only one apothecary, 6/268; streets empty, 7/3; crowds in street demand recall of parliament, 8/268

WESTMINSTER ABBEY:

GENERAL: bishops at, 1/259; regicides' bodies exhumed, 1/309 & n. 4; coronation service, 2/83–4; funerals, 1/249 & n. 2; 6/127 & n. 3; 9/158 & n. 2; Dean and Chapter allegedly harsh landlords, 8/198–9 & n.

P ATTENDS SERVICES: comments on restored prayer-book service, 1/190, 261; thin congregation, 1/257; and music, 1/283 & n. 1, 324; 6/18; sings in choir, 2/240; also, 1/201 & n. 1, 201–2, 251–2, 259, 276; 2/48, 83–4

HENRY VII'S CHAPEL: 1/201, 259; 7/160; 9/457

OTHER PLACES ETC. IN: cloisters: P makes assignations in, 5/260, 267–8, 273; also, 9/168; tombs, 5/268; 9/456–7 & n.; churchyard, 7/160; west door: P makes assignation at, 7/240; Deanery, 9/89

ALLUDED TO: 6/5; 7/345

WESTMINSTER BRIDGE: see Westminster Stairs

WESTMINSTER HALL:

GENERAL: 1/140; regicides' heads displayed, 2/31 & n. 4; coronation banquet, 2/84–5; to be repaired, 4/232; full again after Plague, 7/38; fire near, 7/263; as storehouse in Fire, 7/278

LAW COURTS: judges' procession, 1/272 & n. 3; new location, 2/101 & n. 3; Chancery Row, 1/61; [Common Pleas], 7/391 & n. 1

SHOPS: closed on fast day, 7/359; in early evening, 8/353; P/EP at: for pictures, 1/19; books/newsbooks/pamphlets, 1/275, 301; 2/4; 3/52, 296; 4/111; 6/162; 8/40, 86, 98, 422; caps, 2/39; 7/346; gloves, 7/156; 8/121; ribbon, 9/165; also, 3/5; 4/368; 7/129, 186, 295, 368–9, 393; 8/151

P VISITS [omitting passing visits – e.g. on his way to parliament – and casual visits to meet friends or shopgirls]: in term-time, 2/31, 124; 3/22, 253; 4/25; 5/40, 184; 8/177, 193, 291, 360; 9/552; absent from, 5/331; takes EP to see and be seen, 7/89; full when parliament in session, 8/360; empty at night, 8/583; 'walks'/'talks' in, 1/4–5, 7–8, 13, 17, 46–7, 50, 56, 58, 65, 74, 75; 2/130, 139, 170, 210, 227; 3/3, 11, 43, 49, 83, 173–4, 238; 4/44, 58, 62, 66, 68, 91, 113, 126, 135, 159, 170, 173, 191, 213, 222, 232, 242, 303, 348, 370, 431; 5/33, 34, 71, 111, 128, 138, 215, 246, 249, 338; 6/13, 17, 75, 115, 141, 186; 7/61, 81, 88, 98, 108, 116, 201, 229, 256, 291, 295, 296, 308, 313, 314, 319, 323, 337, 339, 342, 360, 378, 380, 381, 392, 396, 406, 413, 415; 8/1–2, 35, 46–7, 52(2), 102, 110, 111, 113, 120, 158, 181, 199, 203, 205, 223, 224, 248, 294, 299, 317, 323, 329, 341, 348, 462, 377, 393, 440, 479, 480, 491, 493, 497–8, 510, 529, 532, 544, 555, 557, 558, 564, 574, 575, 579, 588; 9/6, 55, 56, 60, 73–4, 76–7, 83, 85, 92–3, 105–6, 112, 112–13, 113, 114, 115, 116, 119, 121, 135–6, 136, 153, 163, 165, 174, 176, 177, 178, 182, 185, 186–7, 187, 190, 193, 197, 208, 220, 277, 317, 322, 348, 369, 462(2), 486, 513, 526, 527

WESTMINSTER PALACE [see also Exchequer; Old Palace Yard; New Palace Yard; Parliament; Westminster Hall]: Court of Exchequer Chamber, 8/181, 231; Court of Wards, 1/48; 7/324; 9/107; Inner Court, 7/304, 305; gate/gatehouse, 1/208; 4/114; 6/132; Star Chamber, 1/34

WESTMINSTER STAIRS: drowned man on, 2/227; also, 2/30; 3/196; ?7/103; ?8/180

WESTON, Charles, 3rd Earl of

theatrical news from, 1/59; 3/204; 4/239, 347, 411; also, 1/24, 86; 3/94, 290; 4/426; 5/90; 8/136, 599; 9/452

WREN, Christopher, kted 1673: perspective machine, 7/51 & n. 4; 9/537–8 & n., 548; views Streeter's paintings, 9/434; appointed Surveyor of King's Works, 9/491 & n. 3; social: 8/64

WREN, Matthew, Bishop of Ely 1638–d.67: at Whitehall chapel, 1/186 & n. 5; also, 2/74

WREN, Matthew, secretary to Clarendon 1660–7; to the Duke of York 1667–72 [see also Books]:

EARLY CAREER: approves of P's memorandum on Fishery, 5/315; accused of corruption as Clarendon's secretary, 7/342 & n. 1; also, 6/79

SECRETARY TO THE DUKE OF YORK AS LORD HIGH ADMIRAL: appointment: 8/414, 419, 424; begins duties, 8/420, 431; resolved to attend Board regularly, 8/440; and not to sell offices, 8/447; business: warrant for *Maybolt*, 8/441, 479; shortage of money, 8/454; lists for parliament, 8/493; Albemarle's narrative, 9/5; bungles navy estimates in Commons, 9/93; appointment of B. St Michel as Muster-Master, 9/247; and of Navy Commissioners, 9/441; investigation of alleged embezzlement, 9/281 & n. 3, 291; P's report on faults of office, 9/287, 289–92 passim, 301, 305, 306, 308, 338, 344, 349, 360, 370, 374; appointment of storekeeper, 9/327; suspension of Anglesey, 9/340–1, 345; storekeeper's accounts, 9/474; also, 8/298; 9/382, 481; unspecified, 9/190, 406, 473, 486, 494; ~ lodgings at St James's, 9/330, 332

POLITICAL: critical of court party in Commons, 7/408; and of court, 9/319; news of Clarendon's fall, 8/24, 527, 563; attends conference on Clarendon's impeachment, 8/551; attempts to mediate between Clarendon and Buckingham, 9/361; account of Buckingham faction, 9/375, 447–8 & nn.; other news from parliament, 9/95, 416, 426; and from court, 9/140, 489, 491

SOCIAL: 7/38, 68, 404; 8/284–5, 394,

431; 9/280, 410–11, 550, 554

ALLUDED TO: 9/173, 273, 350, 518

WREN, ——, naval officer: 9/160

[WRICKLEMARSH, Kent]: T. Blount's house and vineyard, 6/94 & n. 3; alluded to: 6/213

WRIGHT, [Anne], Lady Wright, wife of Sir Henry: witty but conceited, 2/217 & n. 1; entrusted with Sandwich's letters, 1/32, 57; at investiture of peers, 2/79–80; views on fashion, 2/226, 230; social: sings to harpsichord, 2/104; plays billiards, 6/160; also, 1/26; 3/76; 4/25, 46, 47; 6/159; 7/17; 8/99; alluded to: 1/47, 176; ~ her little daughter, 6/160; her chaplain, 6/160; his death from plague, 6/174

WRIGHT, [?Anne], cousin of Sir Henry: at christening, 4/83; suggested as bride for J. Creed, 5/286

WRIGHT, Sir Henry, of Dagnams, Essex, Sandwich's brother-in-law: elected M.P. for Harwich, 1/98 & n. 3; goes to Holland, 1/135; Sandwich at his London house, 1/41, 71, 84, 87, 93, 182, 288, 323; coach, 1/95; death, 4/411 & n. 3; also, 1/36; 2/153; social: 1/177; 3/12

WRIGHT, John, of Brentwood, Essex: recommends preacher, 1/86; on board *Royal Charles*, 1/171; maid ill of suspected plague, 6/181; ~ his pretty wife, 1/71; 6/181

WRIGHT, John Michael, painter (d. ?1700): P's opinion of his work, 3/113 & n. 4

WRIGHT, [?Laurence], physician: at The Hague, 1/149

WRIGHT, Nan: see Markham

WRIOTHESLEY, Thomas, 4th Earl of Southampton, Lord Treasurer 1660–d. 67:

CHARACTER AND REPUTATION: goodness and piety, 4/138; 8/213, 219, 222; honesty and loyalty, 4/389; 8/222; inefficiency, 6/218; 7/313; 8/179, 219, 230, 537; 9/40; Coventry's high opinion, 9/448, 489–90

AT THE TREASURY: appointed Commissioner, 1/170 & n. 3; takes office as Treasurer, 2/31 & n. 3; resignation/replacement rumoured, 4/137–8 & n.;

LIST OF ILLUSTRATIONS IN VOLUMES I TO IX

BIBLIOGRAPHY

In the footnotes to the text of the diary, references to printed books are usually given in a deliberately brief form. Further details, where necessary, are therefore given here. Books listed under 'Editorial Abbreviations' in volumes i and x are not included. Titles are in some cases abbreviated. The place of publication is London unless otherwise stated.

Abbott, Wilbur C., *Conflicts with oblivion*, Cambridge, Mass. 1935
Adair, John E., *Roundhead General: Sir William Waller*, 1969
Adams, John Q., *Dramatic records of Sir Henry Herbert 1623–73*, New Haven, Conn. 1917
Addison, Sir William, *Audley End*, 1953
    English fairs and markets, 1953
Ailesbury, Earl of, *Memoirs* (ed. Buckley), 2 vols. Roxburghe Club 1890
Albion, Robert G., *Forest and sea power . . . 1652–1862*, Cambridge, Mass. 1926
Anderson, Matthew S., *Britain's discovery of Russia 1553–1815*, 1958
Anderson, Roger C., *Lists of men-of-war 1650–1700*, pt i, *English Ships 1649–1702* (Soc. Naut. Research), Cambridge 1939
Anderson, Roger C. and R., *Sailing Ships*, 1947
André, Louis, *Michel le Tellier et Louvois*, Paris 1943
Andrews, Charles M., *British committees of trade 1622–75*, Baltimore 1908
Andrews, William, *Bygone Punishments*, Hull 1890
Arber, Edward (ed.), *The Term Catalogues 1668–1709*, 3 vols., 1903–6
Arlington, Earl of, *Letters to Sir William Temple [1665–70]*, (ed. T. Bebington), 1701
Ashley, Maurice P., *Financial and commercial policy under the Protectorate*, Oxford 1934
    John Wildman, 1947
Ashton, John, *History of English lotteries*, 1893
    History of gambling in England, 1898
    Hyde Park, 1896
Atkinson, Thomas D. (intro. by J. W. Clark), *Cambridge described and illustrated*, 1897
Auerbach, Bertrand, *La France et le Saint-Empire Romain*, Paris 1912
Aylmer, Gerald E., *The King's servants: the civil service of Charles I*, 1961
Aylward, James de V., *The smallsword in England*, 1945
Bagwell, Richard, *Ireland under the Stuarts*, 3 vols, 1906–16
Baillie, Granville H., *Watches, their history, decoration and mechanism*, 1929
Bankoft, George, *The story of surgery*, 1947

Barber, Richard W., *Samuel Pepys Esquire*, 1970
Barbour, Violet, *Henry Bennet, Earl of Arlington*, Washington, D.C. 1914
   Capitalism in Amsterdam in the 17th century, Baltimore 1950
Barlow, Edward, *Journal* (ed. Lubbock), 2 vols, 1934
Barrett, Charles R. B., *The Trinity House of Deptford Strond*, 1893
Barrow, Albert S. ('Sabretache'), *Monarchy and the chase*, 1948
Barton, Margaret, *Tunbridge Wells*, 1937
Bastide, Charles, *The Anglo-French entente in the 17th century*, 1914
Baxter, Stephen B., *The development of the Treasury 1660–1702*, 1957
Beck, William and Ball, T. F., *London Friends' Meetings*, 1869
Beckett, Ronald B., *Lely*, 1951
Beloff, Max, *Public order and popular disturbances 1660–1714*, Oxford 1938
Bent, James T., *Genoa*, 1881
Bentley, Gerald E., *The Jacobean and Caroline stage*, 7 vols, Oxford 1941–68
Beresford, John J., *The Godfather of Downing St: Sir George Downing*, 1925
Beresford, William, *Lichfield*, 1883
Bernbaum, Ernest, *The Mary Carleton narratives 1663–73*, Cambridge, Mass, 1914
Bertin, Ernest, *Les mariages dans l'ancienne société française*, Paris 1879
Beveridge, Sir William (et al.), *Prices and wages in England*, vol. i, 1939
Bewes, Wyndham A., *Church Briefs*, 1896
Birch, Walter de G. (ed.), *Cartularium Saxonicum*, 3 vols, 1883–93
   (ed.), *Historical charters of London*, 1884
Black, William G., *Folk-Medicine*, 1883
Bloch, Marc, *Les rois thaumaturges*, Strasbourg 1924
Blundell, William, *Crosby Records: A Cavalier's notebook* (ed. Gibson), 1880
Boseley, Ira, *Ministers of the Abbey Independent Church 1650–60*, 1911
Bosher, Robert S., *The making of the Restoration settlement . . . 1649–62*, 1951
Boswell, Eleanore, *The Restoration court stage*, Cambridge, Mass. 1932
Bourel de la Roncière, Charles G., *Histoire de la marine française*, Paris 1899–
Brady, W. M., *The episcopal succession in England . . . 1400–1875*, 3 vols, Rome 1876–7
Braithwaite, William C., *The beginnings of Quakerism*, 1912
   The second period of Quakerism, 1919
Brand, John, *Popular Antiquities* (ed. Hazlitt), 2 vols, 1905
Brereton, Sir W., *Travels in England* etc. (ed. Hawkins), Chetham Soc., 1844
Brett-James, Norman G., *The growth of Stuart London*, 1935
Bridge, Sir Frederick, *Samuel Pepys, lover of musique*, 1903
Brittain, Frederick, *Latin in church: the history of its pronunciation*, Alcuin Club, 1955
Broodbank, Sir Joseph G., *History of the port of London*, 2 vols, 1921
Brooke, George C., *English coins from the 7th century to the present day*, 1950
Brown, Louise F., *Political activities of Baptists etc. during the Interregnum* Washington, D.C. 1912

The first Earl of Shaftesbury, N.Y. 1933

Brown, R. Allen: *see* Colvin

Browne, Sir Thomas, *Works* (ed. Keynes), 4 vols, 1964

Browning, Andrew, *Thomas Osborne, Earl of Danby 1632–1712*, 3 vols, Glasgow 1944–51

Bulstrode Papers [newsletters from the collection of Alfred Morrison], 1897

Bund, John W. Willis (ed.), *Diary of Henry Townshend*, 2 vols, Worc. Hist. Soc., 1920

Burton, Robert, *Anatomy of melancholy* (ed. Shilleto), 3 vols, 1893

Byrom, John, *Private Journal . . .* (ed. Parkinson), 4 vols, Chetham Soc., 1854–7

Callender, Sir Geoffrey, *Portrait of Peter Pett and the Sovereign of the Seas*, Newport (I. of W.) 1930

Carl, Philipp, *Repertorium der Cometen – Astronomie*, Munich 1864

Carlton, William J., *Shorthand Books (Descriptive catalogue of the library of S. Pepys*, pt iv), 1940

Carr, Cecil T. (ed.), *Select charters of trading companies 1500–1707*, Selden Soc., 1913

Carte, Thomas, *Ormond*, 3 vols, 1735–6

Cavendish, Margaret, *Life of the Duke of Newcastle* (ed. Firth), 1886

Chappell, William, *Popular music of olden time*, 2 vols, 1853–9

Chapuis, Alfred and Droz, E. (trans.), *Automata*, Neuchatel 1958

Charrington, John, *Catalogue of engraved portraits in the library of S. Pepys*, Cambridge 1936

Chatterton, E. Keble, *Ship-models*, 1923

Chavagnac, Gaspard de (i.e. G. Courtilz de Sandras), *Mémoires*, Paris 1900

Chester, Joseph L., *Marriage etc. registers of . . . the . . . abbey of St Peter, Westminster*, Harl. Soc., 1876

Chéruel, Adolphe, *Histoire de la France sous Mazarin*, 3 vols, Paris 1882

Chettle, George H., *The Queen's House, Greenwich*, 1937

Christie, William D., *Shaftesbury*, 2 vols, 1871

Clark, Alexander F. B., *Boileau and the French classical critics in England 1660–1830*, Paris 1925

Clark, Alice, *The working life of women in the 17th century*, 1919

Clark, Sir George N. (and A. M. Cooke), *History of the Royal College of Physicians*, 3 vols, Oxford 1964–72

War and society in the 17th century, Cambridge 1958

Clark, John W. and Gray, A., *Old plans . . . of Cambridge 1574–1798*, Cambridge 1921

Clarke, Martin L., *Classical education in Britain 1500–1900*, Cambridge 1959

Clarke Papers (ed. Firth), 4 vols, Camden Soc., 1891–1901

Clement, Pierre, *Lettres etc. de Colbert*, 8 vols, Paris 1861–82

Cleveland, John, *Poems* (ed. Morris and Withington), Oxford 1967

Cobbett, Richard S., *Memorials of Twickenham*, 1872

Cole, Charles W., *Colbert and a century of French mercantilism*, 2 vols, N.Y. 1939

Cole, Francis J., *Early theories of sexual generation*, Oxford 1930

Coleman, Donald C., *Sir John Banks*, Oxford 1963

Collinson, John, *History of Somerset*, 3 vols, Bath 1791

Colvin, Howard M., *Biographical dictionary of English architects 1660–1840*, 1954

   (ed.), *The King's Works* (vol. ii, ed. R. Allen Brown et al.)

Cooper, Charles H., *Annals of Cambridge*, 5 vols, Cambridge 1842–53

   Memorials of Cambridge, 3 vols, Cambridge 1860–6

Corbett, Sir Julian S., *Drake and the Tudor navy*, 2 vols, 1899

   England in the Mediterranean 1603–1713, 2 vols, 1904

   (ed.) *Fighting Instructions 1530–1816*, Navy Rec. Soc., 1905

Costello, William T., *The scholastic curriculum at early 17th-century Cambridge*, Cambridge, Mass. 1958

Cowper, Francis H., *A prospect of Gray's Inn*, 1951

Craig, Sir John, *The Mint*, Cambridge 1953

Crawfurd, Sir Raymond, *The King's Evil*, Oxford 1911

Creighton, Charles, *History of epidemics in Britain*, 2 vols, 1965

Croft-Murray, Edward F., *Decorative painting in England 1537–1837*, 2 vols, 1962–70

Cunnington, Cecil W. and P., *History of underclothes*, 1951

Curtis, Mark H., *Oxford and Cambridge in transition 1558–1642*, Oxford 1959

Cussans, John E., *History of Hertfordshire* 3 vols, 1870–81

Dale, Hylton B., *The fellowship of woodmongers*, [n.d.]

Danby, Henry C., *The draining of the fens*, Cambridge 1940

Davies, Godfrey, *The restoration of Charles II 1658–60*, San Marino, Calif. 1955

Davies, John S., *History of Southampton*, 1883

Davies, Kenneth G., *The Royal African Company*, 1957

Davies, Randall R. H., *Chelsea Old Church*, 1904

Dawson, Oliver S., *The story of Wanstead Park*, [n.d.]

Defoe, Daniel, *Tour* (ed. Cole), 2 vols, 1927

Desdevises du Dézert, Georges N., *L'Espagne de l'ancien régime*, 3 vols, Paris 1897–1904

Dews, Nathan, *History of Deptford*, 1884

Dietz, Frederick C., *English public finance 1558–1641*, 1932

Dingley, Thomas, *History from marble* (ed. Nichols), Camden Soc., 1867

Dutuit, Eugène, *Manuel de l'amateur d'estampes*, vols 1, 4, 6 only pub., Paris 1881–5

East, Robert, *Extracts from the records of Portsmouth*, Portsmouth 1891

Elder, John R., *Royal fishery companies of the 17th century*, Glasgow 1912

Esdaile, Arundell J. K., *List of English tales etc. published before 1740*, 1912
Esdaile, Katharine A., *English church monuments 1510–1840*, 1946
  English monumental sculpture since the Renaissance, 1927
  Temple Church monuments, 1933
Evans, Florence M. G., *The Principal Secretary of State 1558–1680*, Manchester 1932
Evans, Willa McC., *Henry Lawes*, N.Y. 1941
Evelyn, *Diary and Correspondence* (ed. Wheatley), 4 vols, 1879
  Miscellaneous Writings (ed. Upcott), 1825
Fagan, Louis, *Descriptive catalogue of the engraved works of William Faithorne*, 1888
Fanshawe, Herbert C., *History of the Fanshawe family*, Newcastle upon Tyne 1927
Feavearyear, Sir Albert E., *The pound sterling*, Oxford 1931
Feiling, Sir Keith, *History of the Tory Party 1640–1714*, Oxford 1924
Fellowes, Edmund H., *Charles I, his death, his funeral, his relics*, Windsor 1950
Fiennes, Celia, *Journeys* (ed. C. Morris), 1947
Firth, Sir Charles H. and Lomas, S. C., *Notes on the diplomatic relations of England and France 1603–88*, Oxford 1906
Fisher, Frederick J. (ed.), *Essays in honour of R. H. Tawney*, Cambridge 1961
Fisher, Sir Godfrey, *Barbary Legend 1415–1830*, N.Y. 1957
Foord, Alfred S., *Springs, streams and spas of London*, 1910
Forbes-Leith, William, *The Scots men-at-arms in France*, 2 vols, Edinburgh 1882
Foss, Edward, *Judges of England* [1066–1864], 9 vols, 1848–64
Foster, Joseph, *Grantees of arms* (ed. Rylands), Harl. Soc. Pub. vol. 66, 1915
Foster, Sir Michael, *Lectures on the history of physiology*, Cambridge 1901
Foster, Sir William, *English factories in India* [1618–69], 13 vols, Oxford 1906–27
  John Company, 1926
Fox, George, *Journal* (ed. Penney, rev. Nickalls), Cambridge 1952
  Short Journal (ed. Penney), Cambridge 1925
Fox, Levi (ed.), *English historical scholarship in the 16th and 17th centuries*, Dugdale Soc., 1956
Foxcroft, Helen C., *Life and letters of the 1st Marquis of Halifax*, 2 vols, 1898
Foxon, David F., *Libertine literature in England 1660–1745*, 1964
Franklin, Kenneth J., *A short history of physiology*, 1933
Fraser, Peter, *The intelligence of Secretaries of State 1660–88*, Cambridge 1956
Fraser, Sir William, *Memorials of the Montgomeries*, Edinburgh 1859
Freeman, Andrew J., *Father Smith*, 1926
Frost, Maurice, *English and Scottish psalm and hymn tunes c. 1543–1677*, Oxford 1953
Fulton, Thomas W., *The sovereignty of the sea*, 1911
Funke, Otto, *Zum Weltsprachenproblem in England im 17. Jahrhundert*, Heidelberg 1929

Gardiner, Dorothy, *The story of Lambeth Palace*, 1930

Gardiner, Samuel R., *History of the Great Civil War 1642–9*, 4 vols, 1893

Gasztowtt, Anne-Marie, *Une mission diplomatique en Pologne 1665–8*, Paris 1916

Gatty, Charles T., *Mary Davies and the manor of Ebury*, 1921

Gelder, Hendrik E. van, '*s Gravenhage in zeven eeuwen*, Amsterdam 1937

George, John N., *English pistols and revolvers*, Onslow Co., N.C. 1938

George, Mary D., *English political caricatures to 1792*, Oxford 1959

Gérin, Charles, *Louis XIV et le Saint-Siège*, 2 vols, Paris 1894

Goddard, Edward H., *Wiltshire Bibliography*, [?Trowbridge] 1929

Gras, Norman S. B., *The evolution of the English corn market*, Cambridge, Mass. 1915

Gray's Inn: Pension Book 1569–1800 (ed. Fletcher), 2 vols, 1901–10

Green, Henry and Wigram, R., *Chronicles of Blackwall Yard*, 1881

Greville, Charles C. F., *Memoirs 1814–60* (ed. Strachey and Fulford), 8 vols, 1938

Gunning, Henry, *Reminiscences of Cambridge*, 2 vols, 1854

Gunther, Robert W. T., *Oxford Gardens*, Oxford 1912

Haley, Kenneth H. D., *The first Earl of Shaftesbury*, Oxford 1968

Hall, A. Rupert and Marie (eds), *Correspondence of Henry Oldenburg*, Madison 1965–

Handover, Phyllis M., *History of the London Gazette 1665–1965*, 1965

Hardacre, Paul H., *The Royalists during the Puritan Revolution*, The Hague 1956

Haring, Clarence H., *Buccaneers in the W. Indies in the 17th century*, 1910

Hart, Cyril E., *Commoners of the Dean Forest*, Gloucester 1951

   Free Miners of Dean, Gloucester 1953

Hartmann, Cyril H., *Clifford of the Cabal*, 1937

   The King my brother, 1954

   The King's friend, 1951

   La Belle Stuart, 1924

Hasted, Edward, *History and topographical survey of Kent*, pt i (ed. Drake), 1886

Hastings, James (ed.), *Encyclopaedia of religion and ethics*, Edinburgh 1908–26

Havran, Martin J., *Caroline Courtier: the life of Lord Cottington*, 1973

Hawkins, Edward et al., *Medallic illustrations of the history of Great Britain to the death of George II*, 2 vols, 1885

Hayes, Richard F., *Old Irish links with France*, Dublin 1940

Hazlitt, William C., *Old cookery books*, 1902

Herbert, Arthur S., *Historical catalogue of printed editions of the English Bible 1525–1961*, 1968

Hervey, George F. and Hems, J., *The Goldfish*, 1948

[Hill, Frank], *Sackville College*, East Grinstead 1913

Hill, George, *An historical account of the Macdonnells of Antrim*, Belfast 1873

Hind, Arthur M., *Wenceslaus Hollar and his view of London and Westminster*, 1922

Hinton, Raymond W. K., *Eastland trade and the commonweal in the 17th century*, Cambridge 1959

Hodges, Harold W. and Hughes, E. A. (eds), *Select naval documents*, Cambridge 1936

Holdsworth, Sir William, *History of English law*, 13 vols, 1922–52

Hole, Christina, *English home-life 1500–1800*, 1949

Holles, Gervase, *Memorials of the Holles family* (ed. Wood), Camden Soc., 1937

Hollond, John, *Two discourses of the Navy* (ed. Tanner), Navy Rec. Soc., 1896

Hooke, Robert, *Diary 1672–80* (ed. Robinson and Adams), 1935

Horden, John R. R., *Francis Quarles, a bibliography*, Oxford Bibliog. Soc., Oxford 1953

Hore, John P., *History of Newmarket and annals of the turf*, 3 vols, 1886

Horsefield, John K., *British monetary experiments 1650–1710*, 1960

Hoskins, Samuel E., *Charles II in the Channel Islands*, 2 vols, 1854

Houblon, Lady A. Archer, *The Houblon family*, 2 vols, 1907

Howell, James, *Epistolae Ho-Elianae or Familiar Letters* (ed. Jacobs), 2 vols, 1892

Howell, Roger, *Newcastle upon Tyne and the Puritan revolution*, Oxford 1967

Howell, Thomas B. and Howell, T. J. (eds), *A complete collection of state trials*, 34 vols, 1816–28

Hubaud, L-J., *Dissertation littéraire . . . sur deux petits poèmes*, Marseilles 1854

Hughes, George M., *History of Windsor Forest*, 1890

Hulton, Paul H. (ed.), *Drawings of England in the 17th century*, 2 vols, Walpole Soc., 1959

Humpherus, Henry, *History of the Watermen's Company*, 3 vols, [n.d.]

Hutchinson, J. R., *The press-gang afloat and ashore*, 1913

Huygens, Christiaan, *Oeuvres Complètes*, 22 vols, The Hague 1888–1950

Ingram, Bruce S. (ed.), *Three sea journals of Stuart times*, 1936

James, Percival R., *The baths of Bath in the 16th and 17th centuries*, Bristol 1938

Jewitt, Llewellyn, *Corporation plate and insignia of the cities and towns of England and Wales* (ed. Hope), 2 vols, 1895

Johnson, Basil H., *Berkeley Square to Bond Street*, 1952

Jones, E. Alfred, *Plate of St George's Chapel, Windsor Castle*, 1939

Jones, Philip E. (ed.), *The Fire Court*, 1966–

Jonge, Johan C. de, *Geschiedenis van het nederlandsche zeewesen*, 2 vols, Haarlem 1858–9

Josselin, Ralph, *Diary 1616–83* (ed. Hockliffe), Camden Soc., 1908

Josten, Conrad H. (ed.), *Elias Ashmole, his autobiographical notes etc.*, 5 vols, Oxford 1966

Judson, J. Richard, *Gerrit van Honthorst*, The Hague 1959

Jusserand, Jean A. J., *A French Ambassador*, 1892

Kaufman, Helen A., *Conscientious Cavalier: Bullen Reymes 1613–72*, 1962

Keevil, John J. et al., *Medicine and the navy, 1200–1900*, 4 vols, Edinburgh 1957–63

Kennedy, James, *The manor and parish of Hampstead*, 1906

Keynes, Sir Geoffrey (ed.), *Blood Transfusion*, Bristol 1949

Kingsford, Charles L., *The early history of Piccadilly*, Cambridge 1925

Kingston, Alfred, *East Anglia and the Great Civil War*, 1897

Kirby, Ethyn W., *William Prynne*, Cambridge, Mass. 1931

Kitchin, George, *Sir Roger L'Estrange*, 1913
    Survey of burlesque and parody in English, Edinburgh 1931

Lafontaine, Henry C. de (ed.), *The King's Musick: records relating to music and musicians 1460–1700*, [1909]

Lambley, Kathleen, *The teaching of the French language in England in Tudor and Stuart times*, Manchester 1920

Lamont, William M., *Marginal Prynne, 1600–69*, 1963

Lane Poole, Rachel, *Catalogue of portraits in Oxford*, 3 vols, Oxford 1912–25

Lane Poole, Stanley, *The life of . . . Stratford Canning*, 2 vols, 1888

Lang, Jane, *The rebuilding of St Paul's after the Great Fire*, 1956

Latimer, John, *Annals of Bristol in the 17th century*, Bristol 1900

Laughton, Sir John K. (ed.), *State papers relating to the defeat of the Spanish Armada*, 2 vols, Navy Rec. Soc., 1894

Legrelle, Antoine, *La diplomatie française et la succession d'Espagne*, 4 vols, Paris 1888–92

Lemaire, Louis, *Le rachat de Dunkerque: documents inédits*, Dunkirk 1924

Lennard, Reginald V. (ed.), *Englishmen at rest and play 1558–1714*, Oxford 1931

Leuridant, Félicien, *Une ambassade du Prince de Ligne en Angleterre 1660*, Brussels 1923

Lewis, Michael A., *England's Sea-officers: the story of the naval profession*, 1939
    The Spanish Armada, 1960

Lewis, Lady Theresa (ed.), *Lives of friends of Clarendon*, 3 vols, 1852

Liber Albus: the White Book of the City of London (ed. Henry T. Riley), 1861

Loisel, Gustave, *Histoire des ménageries*, Paris 1912

Lowe, Robert W., *Betterton*, 1891

Lower, Sir William, *A relation of the voyage etc.* [*of Charles II*], The Hague 1660

Lubimenko, Inna, *Relations commerciales de l'Angleterre avec la Russie avant Pierre le Grand*, Paris 1934

Lufkin, Arthur W., *A history of dentistry*, 1948

Lyons, Sir Henry, *The Royal Society 1660–1940*, Cambridge 1944

McCloy, Shelby T., *French inventions of the 18th century*, Lexington, Ky 1952

McCulloch, John R. (ed.), *Select collection of early English tracts on commerce*, 1856

Macdonald, Hugh and Hargreaves, M., *Thomas Hobbes: a bibliography*, Bibliog. Soc., 1952

McDonnell, Sir Michael, *The registers of St Paul's School 1504–1748*, 1957
  The History of St Paul's School, 1909
McKisack, May, *The parliamentary representation of English boroughs during the
  Middle Ages*, 1932
McLachlan, Jean O., *Trade and peace with Old Spain 1667–1750*, Cambridge
  1940
Maclure, Millar, *Paul's Cross sermons 1534–1642*, Toronto 1958
Madan, Francis F., *A new bibliography of the Eikon Basilike*, Oxford Bibliog.
  Soc., 1950
Madge, Sidney J. *The Domesday of Crown lands*, 1938
Magne, Emile, *Images de Paris sous Louis XIV*, Paris 1939
Marburg, Clara, *Mr Pepys and Mr Evelyn*, 1935
Markham, Christopher A. and Cox, J. C., *Records of Northampton*, 2 vols, 1898
Marples, Morris, *A history of football*, 1954
Martin, John B., '*The Grasshopper' in Lombard Street*, 1892
Matthews, Arnold G., *Calamy Revised*, Oxford 1934
Maxwell-Lyte, Sir Henry C., *Historical Notes on the Great Seal*, 1926
Mercier, Ernest, *Histoire de l'Afrique septentrionale*, 2 vols, Paris 1888
Millar, Sir Oliver, *Tudor, Stuart and early Georgian pictures in the collection of
  H.M. the Queen*, 1963
Mitchell, W. Fraser, *English pulpit oratory from Andrewes to Tillotson*, 1932
Monson, Sir William, *Naval Tracts* (ed. Oppenheim), Navy Rec. Soc., 5 vols,
  1902–14
Mordaunt, John, Viscount Mordaunt, *Letter Book 1658–60* (ed. Coate), Camden
  Soc., 1945
Morison, Samuel E., *Harvard College in the 17th century*, 2 pts, Cambridge,
  Mass. 1936
Morley, Henry, *Memoirs of Bartholomew Fair*, 1859
Muddiman, Joseph G., *A history of English journalism [to 1666]*, 1908
  (ed.) *The trial of Charles I*, 1928
Mullinger, James B., *Cambridge characteristics in the 17th century*, Cambridge
  1867
Neale, Sir John, *The Elizabethan House of Commons*, 1950
Needham, Raymond and Webster, A., *Somerset House*, 1905
Nef, John U., *The rise of the British coal industry 1550–1700*, 2 vols, 1932
Nethercot, Arthur H., *Abraham Cowley*, 1931
Nettel, Reginald, *Seven centuries of popular song*, 1956
Newton, Lady Evelyn C. Legh, *Lyme Letters 1660–1760*, 1925
Newton, Samuel, *Diary* (ed. Foster), Camb. Antiq. Soc., Cambridge 1890
Nicholls, Henry G., *The Forest of Dean*, 1858
Nicolson, Marjorie H. (ed.), *The Conway Letters 1642–84*, New Haven, Conn.
  1930
  Pepys' diary and the new science, Charlottesville, Va. 1965

Notestein, Wallace (ed.), *The journal of Sir S. D'Ewes*, New Haven, Conn.
    1923

Nuttall, Geoffrey F. and Chadwick, O., *From uniformity to unity 1662–1962*,
    1962

O'Donoghue, Edward G., *Bridewell Hospital*, 1923

O'Donoghue, Freeman and Hake, H. M., *Catalogue of engraved portraits in the
    British Museum*, 6 vols, Oxford 1908–25

Ogg, David, *England in the reign of Charles II*, 2 vols, Oxford 1955

Oliver, Harold J., *Sir Robert Howard*, Durham, N.C. 1963

Ollard, Richard L., *The escape of Charles II after the battle of Worcester*, 1966
    Man of War: Sir Robert Holmes and the Restoration navy, 1969

Oman, Sir Charles, *The coinage of England*, 1931

Ornsby, George (ed.), *Correspondence of John Cosin*, 2 vols, Surtees Soc.,
    Durham 1869–72

Osborne, Mary T., *Advice-to-a-painter poems 1633–1856*, Austin, Texas 1949

Overall, William H. and H. C. (eds), *Analytical index to the Remembrancia of the
    City of London 1579–1664*, 1878

Overton, John H., *Life in the English Church [1660–1714]*, 1885

Page, Frances M., *The estates of Crowland Abbey*, Cambridge 1934

Parkes, Joan, *Travel in England in the 17th century*, Oxford 1925

Parsons, Frederick G., *History of St Thomas's Hospital*, 3 vols, 1932–6

Pastor, Ludwig (trans.), *History of the Popes*, 1891–

Pearce, Ernest H., *Annals of Christ's Hospital*, 1901

Pearsall Smith, Logan, *The life of Sir Henry Wotton*, 2 vols, Oxford 1907

Pearson, Karl and Morant, G. M., *The portraiture of Oliver Cromwell*, 1935

Penn, William, jun., *My Irish journal 1669–70* (ed. Grubb), 1952

Penney, Norman (ed.), *Extracts from state papers relating to Friends 1654–72*,
    1913

Percy, Thomas, *Reliques* (ed. Wheatley), 3 vols, 1876

Perrin, William G., *British Flags*, Cambridge 1922

Petitjean, Charles and Wickert, C., *Catalogue de l'œuvre gravé de R. Nanteuil*,
    Paris 1925

Petty, Sir William, *Economic Writings* (ed. Hull), 2 vols, Cambridge 1899

Petty-Southwell Correspondence 1676–87 (ed. Marquess of Lansdowne), 1928

Pevsner, Sir Nikolaus, *Buildings of England: Hertfordshire*, 1953
    (with Nairn, rev. Cherry), ib.: *Surrey*, 1971

Phillips, Frank T., *History of the Company of Cooks*, London, 1932

Picciotto, James, *Sketches of Anglo-Jewish history*, 1875

Pinks, William J., *The history of Clerkenwell*, 1881

Pinto, Vivian de Sola, *Sir Charles Sedley*, 1927

Playfair, Sir Robert, *The scourge of Christendom*, 1884

Plomer, Henry R. (with A. Esdaile), *Dictionary of printers and booksellers in
    England*, 2 vols, Bibliog. Soc., Oxford 1907–22

Plumb, J. H. (ed.), *Studies in social history: a tribute to G. M. Trevelyan*, 1955

Pontalis, Antonin L., *John de Witt* (trans.), 1885

Pool, Bernard, *Navy Board contracts 1660–1832*, 1966

Pooley, Charles, *Notes on the old crosses of Gloucestershire*, 1868

Porritt, Anne G. and E., *The unreformed House of Commons*, 2 vols, Cambridge 1903–9

Povah, Alfred, *Annals of St Olave, Hart St*, 1894

Powell, John R., *The navy in the English Civil War*, Hamden, Conn. 1962

Prestage, Edgar, *Diplomatic relations of Portugal 1640–68*, Watford 1925

Preston, Arthur E., *Christ's Hospital, Abingdon, almshouses, hall and portraits*, Oxford 1929

Purnell, Edward K., *Magdalene College*, Camb. Coll. Histories, 1904

Raven, Charles E., *English naturalists from Neckam to Ray*, Cambridge 1947
John Ray, Cambridge 1942

Records of Lincoln's Inn: Black Books (ed. Baildon), 4 vols, 1897–1902

Reddaway, Thomas F., *The rebuilding of London after the Great Fire*, 1951

Redgrove, Herbert S. and I. M. L., *Joseph Glanvill and psychical research in the 17th century*, 1921

Reresby, Sir John, *Memoirs* (ed. Browning), Glasgow 1936

Rex, Mildred B., *University representation in England 1604–90*, 1954

Riemer, Jacob de, *Beschryving van 's Gravenhage*, 2 vols, Delft and The Hague 1730–9

Roberts, Clayton, *The growth of responsible government in Stuart England*, Cambridge 1966

Rogers, James E. T., *History of agriculture and prices in England 1259–1793*, 7 vols, Oxford 1866–1902

Rogers, Philip G., *The Dutch in the Medway*, 1970

Rohde, Eleanour S. (ed.), *The garden book of Sir T. Hanmer*, 1933

Rollins, Hyder E. (ed.), *A Pepysian garland*, Cambridge 1922

Roncière: *see* Bourel de la Roncière

Rose-Troup, Frances, *The Western rebellion of 1549*, 1913

Roseveare, Henry, *The Treasury*, 1969

Rouse Ball, Walter W., *Notes on the history of Trinity College, Cambridge*, 1899

Roxburghe Ballads (ed. William Chappell and J. W. Ebsworth), 9 vols, Hertford 1871–99

Russell, J. M., *History of Maidstone*, Maidstone 1881

Savile Correspondence (ed. William D. Cooper), Camden Soc., 1858

Sayle, Robert T. D., *The barges of the Merchant Taylors' Company*, 1933
Lord Mayors' pageants of the Merchant Taylors' Company, Reading 1931

Scholes, Percy A., *The puritans and music in England and New England*, 1934

Scott, James R., *Memorials of the family of Scott of Scot's Hall*, 1876

Scott, Sir William R., *Joint-stock compamies to 1720*, 3 vols, Cambridge 1910–12

Selden, John, *Table Talk* (ed. Pollock), 1927

Sergison Papers (ed. Merriman), Navy Rec. Soc., 1950

Shaw, William A., *The Knights of England*, 2 vols, 1906

Shrewsbury, John F. D., *The history of bubonic plague in the British Isles*, Cambridge 1970

Simon, André L., *Bottlescrew days: wine-drinking in England during the 18th century*, 1926

   History of the wine trade in England, 3 vols, 1907–9

Simpson, Claude M., *The British broadside ballad and its music*, New Brunswick, N.J. 1966

Singer, Charles J, et al. (eds), *History of Technology*, 5 vols, Oxford 1954–8

Slothouwer, D. F., *De paleizen van Frederik Hendrik*, Leiden [1946]

Smith, Adam, *The wealth of nations* (ed. Cannan), 2 vols, 1904

Smith, Frederick F., *History of Rochester*, Rochester 1928

Smith, H. Maynard (ed.), *The early life of John Evelyn*, Oxford 1920

Smyth, Charles H. E., *Church and parish: studies in the history of St Margaret's Westminster*, 1955

Smyth, John, *The Berkeley manuscripts: the lives of the Berkeleys* (ed. Maclean), 3 vols, Gloucester 1883–5

[*Somers Tracts*], ed. Walter Scott, 13 vols, 1809–15

Speaight, George G., *The history of the English puppet theatre*, 1955

Speed, John, *History of Southampton* (ed. Aubrey), Southampton Rec. Soc., 1909

Spencer, Hazelton, *Shakespeare Improved: the Restoration versions in quarto and on the stage*, Cambridge, Mass. 1927

Steinman, George S., *A memoir of Barbara, Duchess of Cleveland* (with Addenda), Oxford 1871–8

Stern, Walter M., *The porters of London*, 1960

Straker, Ernest, *Wealden Iron*, 1931

Straus, Ralph, *Carriages and coaches*, 1912

Strode, William, *Poetical Works* (ed. Dobell), 1907

Strong, Sir Roy, *Holbein and Henry VIII*, 1967

Stuart, Dorothy M., *The English Abigail*, 1946

Summers, Montague, *The Playhouse of Pepys*, 1935

   The Restoration Theatre, 1934

Summerson, Sir John, *Architecture in Britain 1530–1830*, 1953

Symonds, Richard, *Diary of the marches of the royal army* [*1644–5*] (ed. Long), Camden Soc., 1859

Swart, Koenraad W., *Sale of offices in the 17th century*, The Hague 1949

Sykes, Norman, *From Sheldon to Secker*, Cambridge 1969

Tanner, James R., *Samuel Pepys and the Royal Navy*, Cambridge 1920

Tate, William E., *The parish chest*, Cambridge 1951

Thompson, Edward M., *Correspondence of the family of Hatton 1601–1704*, 2 vols, Camden Soc., 1878

Thomson, Gladys S., *Life in a noble household 1641–1700*, 1937
Thomson, Mark A., *Constitutional history of England 1642–1801*, 1938
Thorn-Drury, George (ed.), *A little ark of 17th century verse*, 1921
Thorndike, Lynn, *History of magic*, 8 vols, London, 1923–58
Thornton, Archibald P., *West India policy under the Restoration*, Oxford 1956
Thurloe, John, *Collection of state papers* (ed. T. Birch), 7 vols, 1742
Tibbutt, Harry G., *Life and letters of Sir Lewis Dyve 1599–1669*, Beds. Hist. Soc., Streatley 1948
Tighe, Robert R. and Davis, J. E., *Annals of Windsor*, 1858
Townshend, Henry, *Diary* (ed. J. W. Willis Bund), Worc. Hist. Soc., 1920
Turnbull, George H., *Hartlib, Dury, and Comenius*, Liverpool 1947
Turner, Edward R., *The Privy Council 1603–1784*, 2 vols, Baltimore 1927–8
Turner, Francis C., *James II*, 1948
Turner, G. Lyon, *Original records of early nonconformity*, 3 vols, 1911–14
Uffenbach, Z. C. von, *London in 1710* (ed. Quarrell and Mare), 1934
Underwood, Edgar A. (ed.), *Science, medicine and history*, 2 vols, 1953
Varley, Frederick J., *Oliver Cromwell's latter end*, 1939
Vertue, George, *Notebooks*, 7 vols, Walpole Soc., Oxford 1930–55
Villari, Luigi, *The Republic of Ragusa*, 1904
Vincent, William A. L., *The state and school education, 1640–60, in England and Wales*, 1950
Wagner, Sir Anthony R., *Historical heraldry of Britain*, 1939
  Records and collections of the College of Arms, 1952
Walford, Edward, *Greater London, its history etc.* 2 vols, [n.d.]
Walpole, Horace, *Anecdotes of painting* (ed. Wornum), 3 vols, 1849
  Correspondence (ed. Lewis et al.), New Haven, Conn. 1937–
Wardale, John R. (ed.), *Clare College letters and documents*, Cambridge 1903
Warner, Sir George F. (ed.), *The Nicholas Papers*, 4 vols, Camden Soc., 1886–1920
Warnsinck, Johan C. M., *De retourvloot van Pieter de Bitter*, The Hague 1929
Watson, Foster, *English grammar schools to 1660*, Cambridge 1908
Weiss, D. G., *Samuel Pepys, curioso*
Westergaard, W. (ed.), *The First Triple Alliance 1668–72*, New Haven, Conn. 1947
Westrup, Sir Jack A., *Henry Purcell*, 1960
Wheatley, Henry B., *Samuel Pepys and the world he lived in*, 1880
Whitaker, Wilfred B., *Sunday in Tudor and Stuart times*, 1933
White, Eric W., *The rise of English opera*, 1951
Whitelocke, Bulstrode, *Memorials of the English affairs [1625–60]*, 4 vols, Oxford 1853
Whiting, Charles E., *Studies in English puritanism 1660–88*, 1931
Wickham Legg, John and Hope, W. H. St J. (eds), *Inventories of Christchurch Canterbury*, 1902

Wickham Legg, Leopold G., *English coronation records*, 1901

Wilks, George, *The Barons of the Cinque Ports*, Folkestone 1892

Willcox, William B., *Gloucestershire 1590–1640*, New Haven, Conn. 1940

Williams, J. B. (J. G. Muddiman), *History of English journalism to* [1666], 1908

Williams, Neville J., *Powder and paint*, 1957

Williamson, J. Bruce, *History of the Temple*, 1924

Willis, Robert and Clark, J. W., *Architectural history of Cambridge*, 4 vols, Cambridge 1886

Wilson, John H., *Nell Gwyn*, New York 1952

 A rake and his times: George Villiers, 2nd Duke of Buckingham, New York 1954

Winstanley, Denys A., *Unreformed Cambridge*, Cambridge 1935

Withington, Robert, *English Pageantry*, Cambridge, Mass. 1918

Wolf, Abraham, *History of science etc, in the 16th and 17th centuries*, 1950

Wood, Alfred C., *Nottinghamshire in the Civil War*, Oxford 1937

Woodfill, Walter L., *Musicians in English society from Elizabeth to Charles I*, Princeton, N.J. 1953

Woodruff, Charles E. and Danks, W., *Memorials of Canterbury*, 1912

Woodward, John, *Tudor and Stuart drawings*, 1951

Wright, Arthur R. (ed. Lones), *British calendar customs: England*, 3 vols, Folk Lore Soc., 1936–40

Wright, Lawrence, *Clean and decent*, 1962

 Warm and snug, 1960

Yonge, James, *Journal* (ed. Poynter), 1963

Young, Sidney, *Annals of the Barber-Surgeons of London*, 1890

Zook, George F., *The Company of the Royal Adventurers trading into Africa*, Lancaster, Pa. 1919

CORRECTIONS, VOLUMES I TO IX

[Some of these corrections have been made in the reprints issued since 1971. Oblique lines are used to separate the corrigenda from the corrections. A minus sign before a line number indicates its position above the bottom line.]

VOLUME I

Preface and Introduction
p. xiii, l. −7: X/XI
p. xxi, ll. 6–7: Boughton, Northamptonshire/Kimbolton, Huntingdonshire
p. xxxvi, l. 9: depts/debts
p. l, l. 13: September/October
p. lxii, l. 21: 16 March/8 March
p. lxix, l. −2 & n. 11, l. 4: January/December
p. lxxiv, l. −7: 'Cuppe'/'Cupp'
   l. −6: 'tee'/'Tee'
p. lxxxix, l. 11: 15 May/18 May
p. xc, l. −6: than/that
p. cx, l. 16: Richard/William
p. cxliv, l. 15: *delete* 'about 3000'
   l. −3: Fot/For

Text
p. 15, l. 4: *add* '[Crew]' *after* 'Walgrave'
p. 44, l. 6: *add* asterisk *after* 'Palace'
p. 56, l. −4: *add* '[Crew]' *after* 'Walgrave'
p. 85, 12 March, l. 1: rise/ris
p. 207, l. 12: *delete* asterisk

Select Glossary
BALLET: *delete* 'broadside' (recurrent)

CAUDLE: *add* 'made with wine' (recurrent)

Notes
p. 16, n. 1, l. 4: Henry/Herbert
p. 25, n. 4, l. 2: violonist/violinist
p. 49, n. 4, l. 1: *add* '[Girolamo Franzini],' *before* '*Las*'
p. 54, n. 1, l. 5: Joseph/Joshua (recurrent)
p. 70, n. 4, l. 2: Much Munden/Great Munden
p. 80, n. 3, l. 1: n. 6/n. 5
p. 87, n. 1, l. 5: borough/county
p. 105, n. 3: *replace by* 'The 16th-century artillery forts of Walmer, Deal, and Sandown.'
p. 140, n. 4: *add* 'The *Novum Organum*;' *before* 'probably'
p. 183, n. 2, l. 4: 94/203
p. 197: *delete* note *a*
p. 267, n. 4, l. 4: it/she (recurrent)
p. 272, n. 3, l. 4: 1672/1673
p. 314, n. 1, l. 4: 14/114
p. 334, l. 6 (St Michel): Mary/Dorothea (recurrent)
   l. 22 (Trice): half/step (recurrent)

VOLUME II

Text
p. 67, 7 April, l. −1: Battnes/Battens
p. 124, l. 3: her/him (MS. 'her')
p. 197, l. 14: *delete* semi-colon
p. 203, l. 2: Therobo/Theorbo
p. 240, 28 December, l. 3: *delete* 'too' (MS. 'into to')

Notes
p. 6, n. 3, l. 5: *delete* 'well'
p. 41, n. 2, l. −1: June/January
p. 43, n. 2: p. 62; 17 December 1665/pp. 62–3 & n.; vii. 32

p. 58, n. 5: James/Benjamin
p. 110, n. 2, l. 2: 4th/2nd
p. 132, n. 1, l. 3: 72/74
p. 137, n. 2, l. 1: Kt/cr. bt 1662
p. 146, n. 1: *delete* note
p. 160, n. 3, l. 1: sailed . . . 1662/in July returned from W. Africa
p. 165, n. 1, l. 3: Chapeton/Chapoton
p. 192, n. 5: Josias/James
p. 198, n. 3: George/?Richard
   n. 4, last line: Committee/Corporation
p. 204, n. 1, l. 6: Yarrington/Yarranton

p. 217, n. 1, l. 3: Pepys/Sandwich

p. 239, n. 4: *replace by* 'This is said to be the first known instance of a record of a Marian apparition. The saint was St Gregory Thaumaturgus (c. 213–c. 270): F. L. Cross, *Oxf. Dict. Christian Church* (Oxf. 1974), p. 601.'

VOLUME III

Text

p. 3, 5 January, l. 3: beef./beef,

p. 64, l. —9: Warren/Batten (MS. 'Warren')

p. 78, l. —5: Lue[ll]in/Luein

p. 83, last line: me,/met

p. 105, l. 2: form/from

p. 120, 25 June, l. 6: ships/shops

p. 158, l. 1: *add* superior 1 after 'perticularly'

p. 171, l. 17: Sandwiches/Sandwich (MS. 'Sandwiches')

p. 174, 23 August, l. 1: words/works

p. 194, l. 2: γχ́/ουχ

p. 228, 19 October, l. 7: by/be

p. 237, l. 8: jealouses/jealousys

p. 243, l. 8: should not/should (MS. 'should not')

p. 285, l. 12: for/from (MS. 'for') 17 December, l. 4: if/it

p. 300, l. 4: *delete* comma *after* 'Gauden '

Notes

p. 9, n. 3, l. 3: *delete* 'blown'

p. 14, n. 3, l. 6: five/c. fifty

p. 15, n. 2, l. 1: Huntingdon/Dover

p. 30, n. 3, last line: 216/214

p. 44, n. 2, l. 1: Olwin/Oliver

p. 52, n. 1, l. 5: 1686/1676

p. 85, n. 1, l. 2: 1682/1681

p. 113, n. 3, l. 8: 10 July 1664/vii. 359 & n. 3

p. 142, n. 3, l. 7: below,/above, l. 8: 13 February 1665 & n./p. 137 & n. 3

p. 159, n. 2: *replace by* 'Millicent, of Barham, Cambs., was said to be "the best extemporary fool" at James's court: A. Weldon, *Court . . . of James I* (1650), p. 92. James's monopolies had been notorious'.

p. 173, n. 1, ll, 1–2: i. 222 & n. 1/ii. 179 & n. 1

p. 194, n. 1, ll. 1–4: *Replace by* 'Dr R. Luckett writes: Pepys is loosely paraphrasing, or inaccurately recalling, Epictetus (*Encheiridion* I. i): τῶν ὄντων τὰ μέν ἐστιν ἐφ' ἡμῖν, τὰ δὲ οὐκ ἐφ' 'ἡμῖν ('Of things, some are in our power, others are not'). He accidentally writes οὐχ for οὐκ (he intended τὰ ἐφ' ἡμῖν καὶ τὰ οὐκ ἐφ' ημῖν); the slip is a natural one given the extensive use of ligatures in the seventeenth century. That it was a consequence of accident rather than ignorance is demonstrated by his correct rendering of οὐκ at iv. 16.'

p. 221, n. 1: 205/204 & n. 2

p. 232, n. 1, ll. 1–2: below, 15 October 1666 & n./above, ii. 195, n. 3

p. 235, n. 3, l. 3: some/two

p. 270, n. 4, l. 2: 1708/1713

p. 303, n. 2, l. 2: 221/222

VOLUME IV

Text

p. 16, l. 3: ἐφ ηυῖῦ/'ἐφ' ἡμιῦ

p. 61, 28 February, l. 4.: Batten/Warren (MS. 'Batten')

p. 75, l. —4: *repunctuate* sees, and saith,

p. 98, l. 3: *add* '[?plain]' *after* 'most'

p. 118, l. —5: wood/woo'd

p. 133, l. 7: up,/up [to]

p. 144, l. —5: over/*over*

p. 145, l. 9: leade/gold (MS. 'leade')

p. 155, l. 3: fist/first

p. 298, 4 September, l. —5: place and/placed at (MS. 'place and')

p. 366, l. 13: Lord it/Lord in

p. 367, l. —2: *add* '[him]' *after* 'have'

p. 369, l. 7: Hear/Here

p. 380, l. —2: rooms/room

p. 386, last line: *transpose* 'I pray' *to* beginning of l. 1 p.389

p. 405, 5 December, l. 3: *repunctuate* 'Allen home to dinner,'

p. 409, l. —1: *repunctuate* 'and I,'

p. 428, l. 3: this/these (MS. 'this')
p. 436, 29 December, l. 12: not/nor (MS. 'not')

Notes

p. 17, n. 1: *delete* note
p. 20, n. 2, l. 1: 7/6
p. 25, n. 1, ll. 3–4: Sir William Berkeley/Sir Charles Berkeley, jun.
p. 37, n. 3: *add* ',1660' *after* 'borough'
p. 41, n. 5, l. 4: St Jago/Santiago
p. 73, n. 1, l. 10: Solebay/Lowestoft
p. 75, n. 3, l. 6: 68/61
p. 91, n. 1: *replace first sentence by* 'The stempiece was the main vertical timber of the bow'.
p. 95, n. 3, l. −5: during the Interregnum/in the 1620s
p. 105, n. 2, l. −1: 1663/1652
p. 119, n. 2, l. 5: Sturtlow/Stirtloe
p. 126, n. 2, l. 12: not/nor
p. 159, n. 4: Should be n. 1, p. 160 and should read 'See below, p. 243 & n. 3'
p. 164, n. 2: milk/cold milk
p. 187, n. 3, l. 1: *add* 'eldest' *before* 'sons'
p. 210, n. 1: *add* '*Recte* manslaughter.' *before* 'See'
p. 235, n. 2: *replace* last sentence *by*

'PL 1075(11).'
p. 255, n. 1, last line: *Varii Sectiones/Variæ Lectiones*
p. 304, n. 1, l. 8: 419/421
p. 308, n. 1: *replace* first sentence *by* 'Near Kettering, Northants.'
p. 312, n. 2: Huntingdon/Brampton
p. 319, n. 1: Hart St/Seething Lane
p. 320, n. 2: *delete* second sentence
p. 322, n. 1, ll. 10–11: *delete* 'and N. America'
p. 349, n. 1, ll. 5–6: *delete* 'appears . . . She'
p. 354, n. 1, l. 1: James/Benjamin
p. 363, n. 1, l. 2: 437/439
p. 372, n. 3, l. 2: excluded/extruded
p. 382, n. 3, l. 2: *replace* 'App. B, pp. 440–1' *by* 'pp. 387–8'
p. 423, n. 1: *replace by* 'Cf. B. J. Whiting, *Proverbs, sentences &c.* (Camb. Mass. 1968), item F635. The verse, in various forms, was in current use within living memory.'
p. 424, n. 2: 402/404; n. 3: 412/421
p. 435, n. 1: 393, n. 1/395, n. 2
p. 441, n. 2: *replace* 'Calabrian . . . Excelsior' *by* 'and *sal prunellæ*, with three ounces of Calabrian manna (dried sap of *Fraxinus ornus L.*)'

VOLUME V

Text

p. 7, last line: *add* '[her]' after 'commend'
p. 16, 15 January, para. 4, l. 1: with/that
p. 283, l. −6: *repunctuate* 'angry, . . . plain;'

Notes

p. 8, n. 2, ll. −3 & −2: The year date should be '1659/60'
p. 42, n. 2: *replace by* 'See above, iii. 17 & n. 1'
p. 53, n. 3, ll. 1–2: *replace by* 'At Tooting Bec (C. A. F. Meekings, ed., *Surrey Hearth Tax 1664*, 1942, p. 86).'
p. 56, n. 4: 405/407
p. 63, n. 1, l. 7: 1660/1661
p. 73, n. 5: *delete* 'trotting'
p. 116, n. 1, col. 1, l. −8: 24 May 1669/

December 1672
p. 117, n. 4, ll. 6–7: *delete* 'and . . . will'
p. 170, n. 3, l. 4: French/Spaniards
p. 184, n. 2, l. 2: *delete* 'groom-porter'
p. 189, n. 2: *replace by* 'Drawing the outline for the mould of a ship. Cf. PL2910.'
p. 190, n. 1, l. −1: hat/that
p. 237, n. 3, l. 2: *add* 'and arithmetic' *after* 'penmanship'
n. 4, l. 2: ll. 146–73/ll. 1461–3
p. 244, n. 2, l. −1: quarrel with his father/disgrace at court
p. 281, n. 1, l. 1: *delete* 'Sir'
p. 289, n. 2, ll. −5 to −2: *delete* 'Pepys . . . 162'
p. 316, n. 2: *replace by* 'Now the New Armouries'
p. 321, n. 3, l. 4: Holmes's/Nicholls's

p. 342, n. 1: Christopher Cisner/David Primerose

n. 2: *delete* queries

p. 346,   n. 3,   l. 11:   November/

December

p. 353, n. 1, l. 4: Allin's/Holmes's

p. 361, n. 1, ll. 13–14: both . . . 1680/ who died in 1680 and 1689

VOLUME VI

Text

p. 125, 12 June, l. 4: sleeve-bands/ sleeve-hands

p. 135, 23 June, l. —3: *add*, 'did give him' *after* 'Albimarle'; *delete* note *b*

p. 162, 19 July, l. 3: Falconer/Falconbridge

Notes

p. 24, n. 2, l. —1: *Office/Board*

p. 37, n. 2, l. 1: Harvey/Hervey (recurrent)

p. 41, n. 2: Charlotte/Lady Charlotte

p. 53, n. 5: v. 269 & n. 2/v. 323 & n. 2

p. 95, n. 2, l. 2: 32/34

n. 4: *delete* second sentence

p. 100, n. 5: iii. 17 & n. 2/iv. 379

n. 6: n. 1/n. 2

p. 101, n. 1, l. 5: son Samuel/cousin John

p. 102, n. 6: Wanstead/Walthamstow

p. 126, n. 1, l. 5: son/grandson

p. 149, n. 2: n. 1/n. 2

p. 152, n. 2, ll. 2–3: *delete* 'whom . . . Cambridge'

p. 160, n. 1, ll. 4–5: probably . . . Romford/St Peter's, South Weald

p. 163, n. 4: *alter to* 'were London merchants'

p. 166, n. 1: Greenwich tradesman/ Westminster draper

p. 279, n. 2, l. 3: *delete* 'iron'

p. 280, n. 1, l. 3: 255, n. 1/254, n. 2

VOLUME VII

Text

p. 44, l. 4: How/Hewer (MS. 'WH')

p. 107, l. —9: in/is (MS. 'in')

p. 150, l. —2: Ball/Bell (MS. 'Ball')

p. 183, l. 13: *repunctuate* 'work, so is'

p. 229, l. 11: him/it (MS. 'him')

Notes

p. 41, n. 2, l. 1: John/Edward, son of John

l. 2: *delete* 'son of'

l. 3: *delete* 'of the same name'

p. 54, n. 1, l. 3: lieutenants/rivals

p. 94, n. 6, l. 7: Herts./Hants.

p. 108, n. 4: p. 93, n. 1/p. 44, n. 2

p. 111, n. 2: iv./v.

p. 114, n. 3, l. 10: 1655/1665

p. 115, n. 2: n. 3/n. 4

p. 132, n. 3, l. —3: 220–1/385 & n. 2

p. 145, n. 7, l. 1: John/Samuel

p. 154, n. 3, l. 5: elder brother/cousin

p. 225, n. 2: Weilings/Wielings

p. 229, n. 3, l. 2: Koenders/Coenders

p. 243, n. 3, l. 3: possibly Edmond/ probably William

p. 245, n. 4, l. 4: 1662–6/1662–83

p. 271, n. 2: *alter to* 'Barbara Sheldon'

p. 290, n. 2, l. —1: 1641/?1652

p. 309, n. 1, last line: 4/3

p. 341, n. 2: *add* 'The Queen's birthday was in fact on 15 November: see below.'

p. 346, n. 1, l. 5: 1667/November 1666

p. 352, n. 5: *replace by* 'Clerk-Comptroller of the Green Cloth'

p. 375, n. 2, l. 6: Henry/William

p. 383, n. 3: *replace by* 'John Ashburnham, Groom of the Bedchamber'.

p. 385, n. 2, last line: 245 & n. 5/132 & n. 3

p. 386, n. 3, l. 5: 1654/1652

p. 391, n. 1, ll. 8–9: Henley, Som./ Bramshill, Hants.

p. 403, n. 3, l. —1: George/Charles

VOLUME VIII

Text

p. 27, l. −5: Ball/Hall (MS. 'Ball')

p. 29, l. −1: they ng/they not being

p. 73, 20 February, l. 14: *repunctuate* 'closet, all our business lack of money'

p. 111, l. −5: believe she/believes he

p. 215, 15 May, l. 13: Cholmely/ Chichely (MS. 'Ch.')

p. 239, l. 2: [?coach]/[water]

p. 270, l. 5: foretell/[did] foretell

p. 345, ll. 11 & 12: *add* comma *after* 'pretty'; *delete* comma *after* 'fast'

p. 495, l. 4: *add* comma *after* 'series'

p. 564, l. 12: Edwd/Richard (MS. 'Edwd')

Notes

p. 19, n. 2: Peter/John

p. 37, n. 2: John/James

p. 45, n. 1, l. 2: n. 3/n. 1

p. 56, n. 6: *replace by* 'Vicenzo Albrici'

p. 85, n. 3, l. −1: the borough/ Cambridge borough

p. 131, n. 1: *replace by* 'Sir William Turner.'

p. 144, n. 3, l. 3: n. 3/n. 4

p. 154, n. 2, l. 2: 1664/1665

p. 171, n. 5, l. 2: 15/13

p. 179, n. 2: *add* at beginning 'The New Armouries:'

p. 205, n. 2, l. 2: purchase/acquisition

p. 218, n. 3, l. 6: 1880/1884

p. 236, n. 2, l. −3: *Works/Writings*

p. 241, n. 1, ll. 1–3: had been a fellow . . . Cambridge/had presumably been a private tutor to Brookes

p. 257, n. 5: *replace by* 'The defences of Gravesend.'

p. 265, n. 1, l. 8: *delete* 'the Presbyterian'

p. 267, n. 2: *replace by* 'Thomas Wilson, newly appointed storekeeper at Chatham.'

p. 269, n. 1: n. 2/n. 1

p. 275, n. 3: *replace by* 'Cf. below, ix. 500 & n. 1.'

n. 4, l. 2: n. 4/n. 5

p. 330, n. 5, l. 2: 3rd/1st

p. 347, n. 1: n. 5/n. 7

p. 367, n. 2: a lieutenant . . . *Royal Charles*/captain of a frigate

p. 377, n. 2: [n.]4/n. 3

p. 381, n. 2: *replace by* 'In the High St.'

p. 384, n. 1, l. 2: Ferdinand III/ Leopold I

p. 418, n. 1: n. 4/n. 3

n. 3, l. −1: *delete* 'Sir'

p. 421, n. 3: *delete* note

p. 425, n. 3: who became messenger . . . 1670/Groom of the Privy Chamber from 1660

p. 446, n. 6: *preface by* '?'

p. 464, n. 1, l. 5: n. 1/n. 2

p. 469, n. 1, l. 8: 1603/1626

p. 505, n. 2, l. 1: 1553/1552

p. 511, n. 3, l. −2: 1660/1666

p. 515, n. 4: 514 & n. 1/513 & n. 2

p. 526, n. 4, l. 3: Charles I/Charles II

p. 538, n. 3: Robert/John

p. 557, n. 2: n. 2/n. 4 *add* '(E)'

p. 582, n. 2, l. 2: *delete* '(Batten's son-in-law)'

p. 585, n. 6: *replace* second sentence *by* 'Ensum had died in 1666 . . . Jackson'

VOLUME IX

Text

p. 12, l. −2: house/office (MS. 'house')

p. 78, l. −1: *add* comma *after* 'at it'

p. 148, last line: Aldersgate/Aldgate

p. 154, l. −9: House/[?Gate-]house

p. 158, l. 10: *delete* comma *after* 'coaches'

p. 180, l. −9: to anything/to [do] anything

p. 201, l. −2: bands/hands

p. 410, 8 January, ll. 13–14: no great/ great (MS. 'no great')

p. 411, 10 January, l. 1: *add* comma *after* 'Accidentally'

p. 429, 28 January, l. 1: afternoon/ morning (MS. 'afternoon')

p. 468, l. −1: Maids/Maid

p. 480, l. 15: Chancer/Chancery

p. 520, 15 April, l. 5: Aldersgate/ Aldgate

p. 531, 22 Apr. 1669, l. 6: given/give

p. 554, l. −9: the Bishop make himself/ the Bishop (MS. 'the Bishop make himself')

Notes

p. 6, n. 1: discharged/dismissed

p. 83, n. 1, ll. 2, 4: 1666/1667

p. 108, n. 2, l. 4: n. 1/n. 2

p. 117, n. 3: Eliezer/Eliezer Jenkins

p. 147, n. 2: David/Daniel

p. 157, n. 2, ll. 5–6: Sir William ... Yorks./the late Ald. Robert Lowther of London

p. 161, n. 2: *replace by* 'Mary Hammon, Sir John Mennes's sister.'

p. 163, n. 5: *replace by* 'Of prize goods.'

p. 184, n. 1: *delete* note

p. 207, n. 3: *delete* 'at Aubrey's house'

p. 215, n. 3, ll. 1–3: *replace* first sentence *by* 'Probably Viscountess Lambart (d. 1649) an Irish acquain- of Penn's. I owe this suggestion to J. Ferris.'

p. 231, n. 2: n. 2/n. 1

p. 238, n. 4: 1620/1621

p. 241, n. 1: *replace by* 'All the Avebury stones and most of those at Stonehenge were of local sarsen.'

p. 293, n. 1, l. 11: ib./id.

p. 341, n. 1, last line: 67, n. 3/64–5

p. 347, n. 1, l. 4: 1662/1661

p. 383, n. 3: 1659/?1652

p. 416, n. 1, ll. 4–5: first President/ first pre-Charter President

p. 430, n. 1, l. 1: Jennings/Jennens n. 3, l. 2: Philip/Henry

p. 441, n. 4, l. 4: n. 4/n. 3

p. 460, n. 5, l. 5: *add* 'W. Chappell and' *before* 'J. W. Ebsworth'

p. 506, n. 1, l. 11: 1633/1660

p. 507, n. 3: Charles ... London/ Thomas Foulkes, Groom of the Buckhounds

ACKNOWLEDGEMENTS, VOLUMES I TO IX

It is with deep regret that I have to record the death in 1975 of my co-editor, the late Professor William Matthews. It therefore falls to me at this point to acknowledge the debt to the large number of institutions and individuals who have assisted in the publication of the volumes of text since 1970, in addition to those whose names appear in the list of acknowledgements published in volume I:

To Magdalene College, the Trustees of the Leverhulme Foundation and the Goldsmiths' Company, for financial help without which it could not have been done.

To the late Prof. Edward Wilson of Cambridge for his translations of Pepys's Spanish; and to Esmond de Beer, Richard Ollard and MacDonald Emslie for help with the proofs.

To the archivists who have extended me every courtesy on my visits to their collections – at the Admiralty; the Berkshire County Record Office; the city of Bristol; Christ Church, Oxford; Eton College; the Goldsmiths' Company; Gray's Inn; Guildhall, London; the House of Lords; Huntingdon Borough and Huntingdonshire County Record Offices; the Mercers' Company; the Middle Temple; the National Maritime Museum; the North Yorkshire County Record Office; the University of Cambridge; the Dr Williams Library; Messrs Williams & Glyn; and the parish priests in charge of the parochial records at Brampton, Huntingdon, and St Olave's, Hart St.

To the officials I have consulted by letter – of the Victoria and Albert Museum; the Rijksmuseum, Amsterdam; the London Survey Committee of the Greater London Council; the Royal Geographical Society; the College of Heralds; the county record offices of Hertfordshire, Kent and Norfolk; the town libraries of Brentford and Chiswick, of Deal, Dover, Lambeth, Norwich, Portsmouth, Rochester, Shrewsbury, Walthamstow, Wandsworth and Woolwich; the county library of Wiltshire; the William Andrews Clark Library, Los Angeles; the Huntington Library, San Marino; St Paul's School; Westminster School and Canterbury Cathedral.

To the following for information on particular points – P. J. Adams, Dr S. O. Agrell, Lee Ash, Prof. V. Barbour, R. A. Barker, J. Berryman, M. F. Bond, Prof. W. H. Bond, Dr D. S. Brewer, Dr G. L. Broderick, Dr R. A. Brown, Prof. D. Chandaman, I. A. Crawford, Mrs P. E. Cunnington, J. Daniels, the late Prof. Alun Davies, G. Devey, Prof. G. Donaldson, Prof. K. Downes, Prof. J. D. Fage, C. Farthing, Dr P. J. Fitzpatrick, Dr D. Foxon, Miss D. Gifford, Mrs P. Glanville, the late

Prof. D. V. Glass, Dr J. Gmitro, G. H. Gollin, Sir J. Graham, Dr G. S. Graham-Smith, Rev. D. N. Griffiths, Dr R. Gwynn, Prof. J. R. Hale, Dr G. Hammersley, Miss F. Harman, C. E. Hart, Prof. R. Hatton, A. M. Hawker, Prof. H. T. Heath, R. L. Helps, P. Heselton, J. E. Hobbs, Miss C. Hole, Lord Hylton, Dr C. Imber, the late Sir G. Isham, Dr D. Johnson, Rev. M. O. W. Johnson, Dr C. H. Josten, Prof. H. A. Kaufman, Miss L. Kirk, Prof. E. H. Kossmann, Prof. W. A. Lamont, Dr P. Laslett, R. E. Latham, Prof. R. Leslie, B. Lillywhite, W. Lockwood, Sir R. Mackworth-Young, Dr G. C. R. Morris, the late Dr. A. N. L. Munby, Rev. Prof. G. F. Nuttall, J. C. T. Oates, Lt-Col. C. D. L. Pepys, R. L. Percival, J. Porteous, the late Maj.-Gen. M. W. Prynne, W. J. Rasbridge, M. Richardson-Bunbury, Dr P. Rickard, C. A. Rivington, Prof. C. Robbins, G. Roper, Dr V. A. Rowe, Dr I. Roy, the late J. Saltmarsh, Miss M. L. Savell, D. Scott, Dr A. Sharp, Maj.-Gen. H. B. Sitwell, R. S. Smailes, Prof. T. R. Smith, Sir R. Somerville, G. D. Squibb, P. Strong, Sir J. Summerson, Prof. G. H. Turnbull, Mrs S. Tyacke, Sir A. Wagner, Prof. R. R. Walcott, H. M. Walton, Rev. J. Watson, J. J. Wells, the late Prof. D. Whitelock, Dr T. D. Whittet, C. J. Whitwood, Col. F. B. Wiener, J. Wilson, Cmdr H. B. Wise, Prof. A. H. Woolrych, and Brig. P. Young.

And finally to the friends and correspondents who have commented on the volumes as they appeared and offered suggestions for their improvement – particularly John Ferris, J. J. van Herpen, Richard Luckett, Dr J. C. Mitchell, R. G. Pascoe, Dr T. D. Rogers and Capt. A. B. Sainsbury.

Robert Latham